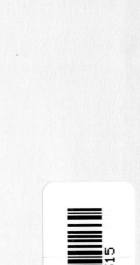

THE HOLY RULE

THE HOLY RULE

THE HOLY RULE

*Notes on St. Benedict's
Legislation for Monks*

by DOM HUBERT VAN ZELLER

SHEED AND WARD — NEW YORK

© Sheed & Ward, Inc., 1958

Library of Congress Catalog Card No. 58-10554

The Library of Congress catalog entry for this book
appears at the end of the text.

Nihil obstat:

> Dom Dunstan Pontifex, O.S.B.
> Dom A. M. Young, O.S.B.
> January 21, 1958

Imprimatur:

> H. K. Byrne, O.S.B.
> *Abbas Praes. Cong. Ang.*
> January 29, 1958

Nihil obstat:

> Thomas J. McHugh
> *Censor librorum*
> June 10, 1958

Imprimatur:

> ✠ Jerome D. Hannan
> *Bishop of Scranton*
> Scranton, June 13, 1958

Manufactured in the United States of America

To a group of men who hoped to observe the Rule exactly as St. Benedict wrote it

PREFACE

Had this book been given the title of commentary it would have had to compete with the works of Dom Martène, Dom Mège, Dom Calmet, Dom Delatte, and others of an earlier time. As a book of notes and comments it will escape the scrutiny of scholarship. Critical apparatus has been left aside in an attempt to discover a more deductive, practical, and empirical approach. Not even the whole of St. Benedict's text comes under review, the repetitions and passages of doubtful authenticity being discarded together with some of the instruments of good works which required no comment. While such a selective method would be inexcusable in one who claimed to be a scientific commentator, it should not offend the reader who looks to the writer for no more than the work presumes to offer.

Among its other shortcomings, a notebook which was designed originally for private use will, even when carefully revised and polished up for publication, be weak in its references. Though references have been given in footnotes wherever possible, many quotations have been included which have not been traced. It was thought that if people's opinions were worth giving, they would be found good enough to appear without a label.

Not altogether, but again so far as possible, questions of controversy have been side-stepped. Since the book covers a wide range, it is inevitable that the interpretation of certain points in the holy Rule will not please everyone. But what would be the use of a book of interpretation which did?

The aim of the book is simply to present a working exposition
of St. Benedict's Rule for the understanding of twentieth-century
minds bent upon the serious service of God in the monastic life.

It has not been thought necessary to give the Latin text. The
English version is more that of Dom Justin McCann, as printed in
his translation of Abbot Delatte's *Commentary*, than anyone else's,
but other translations have been used as well. Grateful acknowledgement is made here to the publishers who have given permission for material reprinted and to the many writers quoted
throughout the book, especially those, living and dead, whose
references have opened up new lines of investigation. Among the
more modern works, those most drawn upon in the present study
have been Dom Delatte's *Commentary* (New York, Benziger,
1921), Dom Butler's *Benedictine Monachism* (London, Longmans,
Green, 1919), Dom Morin's *L'Idéal Monastique*, Dom Besse's
Le Moine Bénédictin, Dom Berlière's *L'Ascèse Bénédictine*, Sister
Schroll's *Benedictine Monasticism* (New York, Columbia University Press, 1941), Dom van Houtryve's *Benedictine Peace* (Westminster, Newman, 1950), Dom de Monléon's *Les XII Degrés de
L'Humilité*, and some unpublished lecture notes most generously
supplied by Father Merton of Gethsemani Abbey. In the biograph-
ical field, which is enormous, the two works which have proved
more helpful than any are Dom Justin McCann's *St. Benedict* and
Mr. T. F. Lindsay's book of the same title (New York, The Macmillan Company, 1950). A final acknowledgement of gratitude
must be made to Miss Clare Nicholl, who has kindly corrected
the typescript and made constructive suggestions.

CONTENTS

Chapter		Page

Contents

Contents

THE HOLY RULE

PROLOGUE

St. Benedict's opening paragraphs show unmistakably three things: his purpose in writing, the public which he is addressing, and—though perhaps unintentionally—his own cast of mind. What the Prologue amounts to is this: monks aim only at seeking God, and the way they are to do so is by compunction and contemplation. Such is the postulate. All that follows in the holy Rule is an elaboration of this theme.

Hearken, O my son, to the precept of your master, and incline the ear of your heart: willingly receive and faithfully fulfil the admonition of your loving father, that you may return by the labour of obedience to Him from whom you had departed through the sloth of disobedience.

The condition for future service is to "hearken" and "willingly receive." The monk's essential act is to listen for the word of God as expressed in one form or another, and then, when it has been recognized, to "fulfil it faithfully."

There is a distinction between hearing and listening. A man may hear and pay no attention. He may even listen and decide to ignore. The proof lies in the kind of response which a man gives to what he hears.

"He that hath looked into the perfect law of liberty, and hath continued therein, not becoming a forgetful hearer, but a doer of the work; this man shall be blessed in his deed."[1] The holy Rule is designed to be a law of liberty. Not restrictive but liberative. The monk who continues in it, never forgetting what he hears and always trying to be a more perfect doer of the work, must inevitably be blessed in his deed.

[1] James 1;25.

I

But he must be ever on the alert to hear correctly. And to hear all that is spoken. Vocation is the right relation between the word uttered and the response given. Everything depends upon the right reception and interpretation of what is enunciated. Misinterpret the call, and it is better never to have heard it.

"The voice of my beloved," sings the bride in the Canticles, "behold my beloved speaketh to me: Arise, make haste, my love, my dove, my beautiful one, and come."[2] This is the summons, this is the religious vocation. Deny it, or give to it an earthly and a purely natural meaning, and it is better not to have heard it at all.

"The voice of my beloved knocking," sings the bride again, three chapters later. "Open to me . . . my love . . . my undefiled . . . I have put off my garment, how shall I put it on?"[3] It is here, as in the passage quoted from St. Benedict's Prologue, that we learn how to respond: we put off the old garment. Having "departed from Him through the sloth of disobedience" we return to Him freely and unencumbered. Freely we submit to the yoke of obedience.

The word of God is spoken by the voice of authority. It is also spoken to the monk in the *lectio divina* and in the *opus Dei*. Indeed, since every circumstance of a monk's life is covered by his vows, the word of God is being spoken to him all day long.

To wait always upon God's word is to live according to His will. It is to abide in His love. It is to walk in His presence.

If union with God is the meaning of the monastic vocation, then the soul must learn to search for God's love and abide in it. The soul must learn the mystery of God's presence, must learn to recognize the inflection of His voice. The presence of God is hidden; His voice comes from behind a cloud.

Thus when St. Benedict tells us to "incline the ear of your heart" he is telling us to listen in faith. As the religious vocation unfolds, it is seen to be nothing else but the life of faith. Observance would be useless without faith. The vows would be impos-

[2] Cant. 2;8,10.
[3] *Ibid.*, 5;2,3.

sible without faith. Faith is the secret of the whole thing, and the only guarantee of love.

Faith expresses itself in obedience. Obedience is to faith what humility is to truth and what homage is to beauty. Where faith is strong, obedience follows. Throughout the Rule, St. Benedict will be seen building up the life of faith. That is why he makes, throughout the Rule, so much of obedience. Obedience is the sign and the seal.

Where faith is weak, obedience will be inexact, inconstant, proportionately natural. "The sloth of disobedience" reveals the unfaithful man; by the "labour of obedience" he must return to God and grow in faith.

The strength of the religious life lies not in its devotion but in its constancy. That is in its faithful obedience. "Thy neck is as a tower of ivory," says the Beloved of the bride in the Canticle, "thy head is like Carmel . . . thy stature is like to a palm tree."[4] It is not only her fervour that makes the bride lovable; her beauty lies also in her strength.

Fervour is not to be despised—indeed it is one of the signs of love—but neither is it to be preferred before obedience. A monk may not always find it possible to persevere in fervour; he will always find it possible to persevere in obedience. True fervour is found in obedience. St. Benedict develops the idea of obedience in his next paragraph.

> To you, therefore, my words are addressed, whoever you are, that renouncing your own will, you do take up the strong and bright weapons of obedience in order to fight for the Lord Christ, our true King

The "return to God" can be effected only by labour, renunciation, obedience. Though made in the image of God, man is born of rebellion. He is the son of wrath, not of love.[5] Even when he has been baptized and is the child of God, man can destroy his likeness to God by following his own will instead of God's. So he

---

[4] *Ibid.*, 7;4,5,7.
[5] Eph. 2;3.

must return to the likeness of God by renouncing his own will by obedience.

For a rebellion to end, it is not enough to obtain a pardon. Rebellions end only when there is conformity with the will of authority. We, the rebels, must work our way back to favour, to our original status. We come over from the wrong side of the line to the right. "We take up the weapons of obedience, and fight for Christ."

St. Benedict strikes a personal note: "you, whoever you are." I can forget for the moment about the estrangement of mankind from God, about the destiny of the universe and the purpose of creation: what I must work out for myself is the conformity which I, individually called by God to a particular life, can bring. By obedience I can bring order where there was not order before.

By obedience I return not only to God's will but also to my destined self, to my proper self. I return to my likeness to Him who made me in His image. When my obedience is such that the mask of my self-love has been replaced by God's image, I will be what I am meant to be—which is a saint.

It is by my obedience that I shall come to be united with God and with my true self. The real and the ideal will then be one. It is my obedience, which binds me to the will of God instead of to my own will, which makes me free: it allows me to be the person whom God has planned. I can then be natural, I can then be myself.

If I am to fight for Christ, I must be free from the tyranny of self. Renunciation is not only the mark of the monk, it is the condition of the monk's response to the vocation. If the monk is to "re-establish all things in Christ,"[6] he must be ready to disestablish all things in himself. Like Christ, he must empty himself becoming obedient unto death.[7]

St. Benedict comes back to the theme later on in the seventy-first chapter: "Let the brethren know that it is by the way of obedience they shall come to God." He leads his subjects by one

[6] *Ibid.*, 1;10.
[7] Phil. 2;8.

method only—in union with Christ in His subjection. Only in this subjection is true liberation.

If liberty is the ability to be true to God's idea of me—that is, to myself and my vocation—I must first know what is wanted of me, and then I must be single-minded enough not to waste myself on other things. Thus I must listen to what God tells me of His will ("Hearken, O my son,"—and you will come to know what your life is expected to produce), and I must deny myself of whatever may stand in the way ("renouncing your own will . . . returning by the labour of obedience").

When I have learned what is my true vocation, then I am free of the things that stood in the way. Those things upon which I was tempted to expend energy are no longer the obstacle to my perfection which once they were. Either God has renounced them for me, placing them outside my range, or they have been transformed in the alchemy of His love and have become helps.

Outside interests either bring something to my spirituality and personality or they take something from it. Creatures, if they are not a means of developing the essential movement of the soul, have a delaying effect upon it.

To look for a variety of activities outside the soul is to find a weakening of activity within it. But when the soul has found itself in Christ, the outward activities become inward activities. *My* things become *God's* things.

It is a curious paradox in the spiritual life that to them that have much, more shall be given; and to them that have little, the little which they have shall be taken away from them. Poverty misunderstood is further impoverished; wealth understood rightly is further enriched.

But the religious vocation does not stop short at the combined work of renunciation and bringing the interests and activities of life into order: it is also a matter of taking up weapons and doing battle for Christ. St. Benedict would have us live creative lives, not merely ordered lives. "The fig-tree hath put forth her green figs":[8] it does not exist to fill a gap among the other trees.

It is not enough for a monk to have the general intention of

[8] Cant. 2;13.

living his life to please God: he must go on to do the work willed by God. To discover the environment in which union with God is to be achieved will be the first necessity; to strive, labouring with the means supplied within that environment, to achieve such union will be the second. "Take up . . . fight," says St. Benedict.

The environment is the condition only: it helps, but it does not of itself produce. A man, whether in religion or in the world, does not produce his life's work unless he is brought to that pitch of perfection (or fitness, or rectitude) which enables him to perform it according to the requirements of the particular excellence in view. A violinist does not play a piece of music unless he knows how to handle the bow.

"Go forth, and follow after the steps of the flocks," the Beloved urges the bride who is still unsure of herself, "and feed thy kids beside the tents of the shepherds."[9] The life of love is not the life of idle languishing. And to help in the labours of love the Beloved provides his "company of horsemen," and reminds her of the support which she has had from him in the past.

Having warned the neophyte at the outset that he will have to work, St. Benedict goes on to tell him how to set about it. If the monastery is, as our holy Father will tell us later, a school and workshop, the approaches to the craft are of the greatest importance.

> In the first place, whatever good work you begin to do, beg of Him with most earnest prayer to perfect it . . . we must always so serve Him with the good things He has given us that not only may He never, as an angry father, disinherit His children, but may never, as a dread Lord, deliver us to everlasting punishment as most wicked servants who would not follow Him to glory.

Our good works are good only when they are His. God rewards none but His own works. For whatever we do, we need grace: "Without me you can do nothing."[10] That the beginner should realize this before he goes any further in religion is St.

[9] *Ibid.*, 1;7.
[10] John 15;5.

Benedict's primary concern—so the would-be monk is urged to pray for divine support in every undertaking.

The undertaking which is of supreme importance to the beginner is the religious life itself, and if he is to launch himself along the right lines he must do so on the impulse of prayer. For this adventure, which is supernatural or it is nothing, there must be complete dependence on God. If we had first chosen Him, we might have reason to think that we could attain to Him by force of character and human effort. But He has chosen us, and if our vocations are to bear fruit we must ask the Father in Christ's name that our work may be to His honour.[11]

Not only at the initial summons but throughout the whole course of the religious life, the soul must know how the magnetic operation of grace effects its end. What we must realize is that it is not only His grace that attracts us in the first place but that it is His grace in us that enables us to respond.

Indeed it is His grace in us that *is* the attraction. Where God sees Himself reflected, He is drawn to that reflection. The perfect cannot but be attracted to the perfect. Consequently when He sees that element of Himself which He has put in our souls He attracts us closer to Himself. This is the story of every vocation. He calls us because He loves us: because He loves Himself.

Since we see so much more of our action than of His in our vocations, we think of the process too much in terms of affection reciprocated. We think of it too much in terms of time sequence —as it were God opening the relationship with a call to the soul, then the soul rousing itself to listen, then the human intellect grasping the call's significance, then the will deciding to respond. But a vocation is not what *we* do; it is what He does.

We can get nearer to the mystery of God's call to the soul if we think of Him as saying: "I know you will want to come to Me if I inspire this urge in you. You will not draw near to Me unless I do the drawing for you. I will therefore come to you and be the attraction."

God is therefore the mover and the moved, the lover and the

[11] John 15;16.

loved, the caller and the called. "My beloved to me, and I to him."[12]

St. Thomas, treating of the necessity of faith,[13] teaches that the mind is moved by God in the same way that objects which are lower in the created order are moved by those which are higher. Just as in nature the irrational creature responds to a superior created force—the tide answers to the attraction of the moon—so the rational creature answers to uncreated light.

So just as the mind knows truth because it is immediately exposed to God (the doctrine of the *Logos* as the element in which human intelligence lives was the dominant thought in the early Christian theology), the soul in the same way knows the drawing of grace, of vocation.

Without fear of illuminism, St. John can say that there is a "true light which enlightens every man coming into this world."[14] Far from being illuminism, it is on the contrary the doctrine of faith. As St. Thomas points out, it is *because* the mind is directly under God, *because* the eyes of the soul see the world by His light, that faith is necessary.

A creature may move after its own fashion, but it *is moved* (such is St. Thomas's argument) by a superior nature. In the order of grace, and we are here considering the question of vocation, the movement comes from God. Moving "after its own fashion," and at the same time moved by the divine impulse, the soul responds in faith. Faith is essentially that which combines the two requirements.

Since vocation finds its consummation and explanation in sanctity, the principle which has been applied above to the initiation is found also to apply to the fulfilment. Thus St. Thomas in the same article, proceeding from the consideration of truth and faith, rounds off his thesis with a paragraph about sanctity.

"Rational nature," says St. Thomas, "in as much as it apprehends the universal notion of good and being, is immediately related to the universal principle of being. Consequently the per-

[12] Cant. 2;16.
[13] *Summa*, IIa IIae;q.2,a,3.
[14] John 1;9.

fection of this rational creature consists not only in what belongs to it in respect of its nature, but also in that which it acquires through a supernatural participation of divine goodness. Hence it was said above [15] that man's ultimate happiness consists in a supernatural vision of God, to which vision he cannot attain unless he be taught of God, according to St. John who says that everyone who has heard of the Father and has learned comes to Me.[16] Now man acquires a share of this learning not indeed all at once, but little by little according to the mode of his nature, and everyone who learns thus must needs believe in order that he may acquire knowledge in a perfect degree."

In faith, therefore, God teaches and man learns. In the case of religious vocation, God calls and man responds. In the case of sanctity, God directs and man co-operates. But in each instance the initial illumination from God to which the human soul cannot of itself do justice becomes a relationship, a correspondence between master and disciple, which culminates in the soul's perfection.

The soul advances, St. Thomas notes, not all at once but by stages. The soul moves from stage to stage not by its own power but by faith—by the faith which is in the soul by baptism. Enlightened by the Holy Spirit, the soul is taught by the Holy Spirit how to respond. The lover and the Beloved are espoused in faith.

In such a relationship there must necessarily be absolute docility on the part of the soul: failing this, the proffered perfection is not guaranteed on the part of God.

The soul must know, moreover, that the power to sanctify and the sanctity are one—that they are God. Human light, human power, human perfection—these things will not avail. The Holy Spirit is the one Sanctifier, and He is in the midst of us.

This perfect continuity is known to the soul because the illuminating *Logos* has become Man. Thus St. John goes on from saying that "He was the true light that enlightens every man

[15] *Op. cit.*, Ia, IIae;q.3,a.8.
[16] John 6;45.

coming into the world" to explain that "He was in the world, and the world was made by Him . . . and the Word was made flesh . . . and we saw His glory, the glory of the only-begotten of the Father, full of grace and truth."[17] Faith, sight, further faith.

The continuity and harmony in God are reflected in the correspondence and progressive sanctification of man. "Draw me," the bride begs of the Beloved, "and we will run after thee to the odour of thy ointments."[18] We cannot run of ourselves: we need to be drawn, and at every step we need new strength.

St. Benedict's words have perhaps not needed the kind of amplification which they have here received. The reason for such a treatment may be found in the type of soul whom he is presumed to be addressing. If there is one truth which the applicant to the monastic life must assimilate before he even begins to follow the routine of the monastery, it is the truth that whatever he sets out to achieve must be achieved in him by grace. "Whatever good work you begin to do, beg of Him with most earnest prayer to perfect it."

"If God made you man," says de Osuna, "and you made yourself a saint, you would have done more than He; for it is greater to be holy than to be merely a man, as the one thing is added to the other." The same authority goes on to say, almost as if he had the above-quoted article from St. Thomas in front of him: "We learn that natural bodies bear within themselves the principle of their operation, and our Lord has only to arouse in them the seminal force they contain to make them work. For instance a grain of wheat has within itself the power to produce under favourable natural conditions. But this is not the case with man in respect to works of merit . . . for though we have within us our operative principle, which is our will, we have no gratuitous principle . . . we must seek and beg for it from God, for it is His doing alone that makes our faulty and trifling services acceptable and pleasing to Him."[19]

[17] John 1;10,14.
[18] Cant. 1;3.
[19] *Third Spiritual Alphabet*, Treatise 19; ch. 3.

Let us then arise, since the Scripture stirs us up saying: "It is the time now for us to rise from sleep." And our eyes being open to the deifying light, let us hear with wondering ears what the divine voice admonishes us, daily crying out: "Today if ye shall hear His voice, harden not your hearts."

The sentence about our eyes being open to the deifying light is an echo of what has been said above in connection with St. John and St. Thomas. The light of grace is "deifying"—it translates and transforms.[20]

It is not so much that we awake from sleep and see the light as that the light wakes us up. Once awake to the reality of the light, we are stirred to action. It is now that we must keep our ears open to the admonishing voice or we shall go to sleep again.

To prevent the hardening of the heart which sometimes comes instinctively to the soul who hears God's voice, there must be a readiness to silence the voices of the world which counsel every sort of alternative. The soul must be deaf to the voice of the world which speaks through self-love.

The world will suggest a greater caution in following up the impulses of grace, will cite examples of those who have come to grief from listening too closely to the voice of God, will preach the doctrine of sweet reasonableness, will talk about the virtue of not aspiring to spiritual heights. The world will never say openly: "Go on—harden your heart."

But sometimes it is not the insinuations of the world which make us harden our hearts, nor even the world's straightforward attraction. More often it is simply the weariness of well-doing. We get tired of day-to-day perseverance in good. The commonplace forms a crust, and before we realize the extent of our indifference we have hardened. That is why it has to be *today* when you shall hear His summons, respond at once.

The interior life, according to St. Gregory of Nyssa, is an indefinitely repeated beginning. So also is the monastic life—an endless series of spiritual clothings. The soul "puts on" Christ.

[20] *Deus, qui humanae substantiae dignitatem mirabiliter condidisti et mirabiliter reformasti,* as we have it in the Mass.

The specifically Benedictine vow of *conversio morum* is nothing else but a constantly renewed turning towards God. It is a turning away from the world and a "conversion" in grace. Not a conversion in the sense of a moment of enlightenment and decision, but a conversion in the sense of transformation. *Conversio morum* is, as we shall see when we come to treat of the vow as such, a tending—an unrevoked declaration of the desire to advance in the love of God.

If I am to be supple in the service of God, my response has to be today. If I wait till tomorrow I shall hear only yesterday's voice. It is not enough that my conversion to God should rest on a memory of yesterday. For the response to be effective there has to be the immediate relationship.

To rely upon the mind's reconstruction of a grace is not to rely upon grace. It is to rely upon an experience, and we can all too easily misconstrue past experiences. The grace of the present moment is the only sure foundation of our continued conversion.

We pray "Give us this day our daily bread"—neither yesterday's bread nor tomorrow's. The approach to grace must be realist, immediate, even urgent. If it is not, it will become idealized out of true proportion. To romanticize a vocation is a common error; it is possible also to romanticize the sudden impulses of grace. But the danger of mismanaging grace is always bound to be less if it is responded to without delay.

The man who cross-questions the stirrings of his conscience, who seeks chapter and verse from a hundred different authorities before he risks an answer to the call of God, who asks advice from spiritual directors in one camp and men of the world in the other—such a man may not be delaying through laziness but he is certainly delaying through an excessive desire for intellectual assurance. Such a one must guard against subtlety.

When the bride invites the Beloved to "get up early to the vineyards [to see] if the flowers be ready to bring forth fruits, if the pomegranates flourish,"[21] she is asking to escape from the multiplicity of life in the valley so that her sensibilities may be

---

[21] Cant. 7;12.

sharper for the superior delights of the hillside. The soul must rise early and mount high if the fragrance of the morning is to be enjoyed.

Quoting from the twelfth chapter of St. John, St. Benedict warns the hesitating soul that there is no time to lose: the light will not last for ever. To be caught in the night is death. It is not simply a matter of basking in the sunshine on the heights while the rest of men toil and sweat in the smoke of the cities down below; it is a question of toiling and sweating also in the clearer air.

And the Lord, seeking His own workman in the multitude of the people to whom He thus cries out, says again: "Who is the man that will have life, and desires to see good days?" And if you, hearing Him, answer: "I am he," God says to you: "If thou wilt have true and everlasting life, keep thy tongue from evil, and thy lips that they speak no guile. Turn from evil and do good: seek peace and pursue it. And when you have done these things, My eyes will be upon you and My ears will be open to your prayers. And before you call upon Me, I will say unto you: Behold, I am here."

Having issued the general invitation and given his warnings, St. Benedict now comes to speak of the conditions: he states the terms of discipleship. You are volunteering? you think you would like to be a monk? Right; read over the thirty-third psalm, and you will see what is required of you. It is nothing new that I, Benedict, am asking; I am merely making sure that you know what the Lord has always expected of His disciples.

The monk must speak no wrong, must turn from evil, must be active in good, must know where to find true peace and must make for it. The programme is simple. But it is also uncompromising. Fidelity to such a course means going clean contrary to nature, to self.

St. Benedict has chosen these verses from the psalm because they refer to the qualities which he will most want to develop later on. Self-restraint, silence, charity, positive and outgoing service, cultivation of peace: all these will receive their measure of attention: indeed they are fundamental to Benedictine spirituality and monasticism.

It is worth noting that St. Benedict concludes his and the psalmist's list of essential qualifications by saying that when we have *done* all these things we shall be granted certain favours. Allowing that what He does in the matter of our monastic lives is of far greater importance than what we do, there has to be effort: we must at least register *that*. A good intention is not enough; it must be reinforced.

The monk, throughout his life, will fail to keep his lips from occasionally speaking guile; but provided he has turned from evil and done good, provided he has seriously sought after the peace of Christ, his failures will not be marked against the record of his achievement. He has not gone back on what he has set himself: he has trained his tongue to speak good.

There is a tendency among modern spiritual writers to make little of achievement. To put the whole virtue in the desire is good enough as far as it goes, but if it leads to scorning the achievement it is bad. There is a danger of valuing the work *because* it has failed—and suspecting it if it has succeeded. Nothing could be further from St. Benedict's mind.

Unless monks are trained to be objective in outlook—in their prayer more concerned with God than with themselves, in their work more concerned with others than with their own interests —they are in danger of becoming introverts.

What St. Benedict is particularly guarding against is the idea that a man joins a monastery on a wave of golden dreams, and thereafter finds himself carried along towards God by the tide of pious intention. The monastic life is not a pageant, and there is no such thing as holy dalliance.

When the conditions have been fulfilled, the eyes of God will look favourably upon us and His ears will be open to our prayer. Then comes a significant statement. St. Benedict gives it as a promise of God that before we even call upon Him, He will tells us that He is present.

The mystery of God's presence is simply this, that all the time —before we have adverted to the fact as well as after we have

acknowledged it but have been drawn away by other interests—
He is operating within us. The doctrine of the Divine Indwelling
means no more and no less than that the Holy Trinity exists in
the human soul (supposing it to be in the state of grace), and
that the soul, dwelling already in God, is forever being drawn
to closer union with Himself.

So even before the soul calls upon God in prayer, God has
proclaimed His presence. The soul does not have to ask God to
listen; God has been listening before it entered into the head of
the soul to ask. God has indeed put it into the head of the soul
to ask.

This should considerably simplify our ideas about prayer. It
means that we can dispense with any elaborate ritual which, in
our multiplicity, we may have devised for "putting ourselves in
the presence of God." All we have to do is to acknowledge the
fact of God present. When we address ourselves to the act of
praying we are already praying.

We do not have to ask, with the bride in the Canticles, where
He dwells and whether the watchmen have seen Him.[22] We can
find Him within ourselves. Our very search is evidence of His
presence.

Search we must, but always we should know that our search
is not the cause of His presence. Our search is merely one of the
effects.

We could not come to want Him if He had not placed Himself
within us as the object of our desire. It is only in heaven that we
shall know how far our desire has been fulfilled.

There would be no desire on our part, either in this life or
in heaven, if God had not first desired us. It is God's continuous
desire that awakens the responding desire in us.

There would be no prayer, either in this world or among the
blessed, if there were not already the prayer of the Persons in
the Blessed Trinity. All that we do when we pray is to echo the
prayer of God. It is the greatest thing we can do.

Having our loins, therefore, girded with faith and the
performance of good works, let us walk in His paths by the
[22] Cant. 3;3.

guidance of the Gospel, that we may deserve to see Him who has called us to His kingdom ... [let us be as one that] has taken his bad thoughts, while they were yet young, and dashed them down upon Christ.

St. Benedict is a master in the work of dovetailing quotations from the Scripture. In the above passage there are echoes of St. Luke,[23] Ephesians,[24] I Thessalonians,[25] I Corinthians,[26] and Psalms.[27] It has been suggested that St. Benedict, like St. Teresa, quoted from memory, and therefore often got the wording wrong. It is at least as likely that he got the wording wrong because to have combined a number of texts in the way he did would have made it impossible to get the wording right.

Loins girt about with faith: we must be so wrapped up in faith that all our works may follow from virtue. It is as though our rebellious bodies—or, if you like, our sick bodies—were bandaged tight by the hand of the Good Physician. Once trained, we become capable of ordered movement.

The idea is that the bandage of faith, applied at first to outward conduct but afterwards to habits of thought, not only represses what is contrary but enhances movement: it operates in its own direction. Thus we find ourselves "walking in His paths by the guidance of the Gospel."

It is in the Gospel that we learn about His kingdom. Without the Gospel's guidance, our pilgrimage is idle. It is no good our finding a kingdom if it does not happen to be Christ's. The world can point to a variety of kingdoms which possess a show of authenticity, but it is only from the Gospel that we can come to know the true city of God.

That faith in Christ is the theme of the whole Rule, underlying St. Benedict's teaching with regard to obedience and the social life of the community, will be seen to prove itself as the course of the Rule is followed. Growth in the habit of faith and growth in Christ are taken as one thing.

[23] 22;35.
[24] 6;14,15.
[25] 2;11.
[26] 10;4.
[27] 136;9.

The man who dashes his evil impulses against the rock of Christ is safe. He is a man of faith. And since evil impulse is ever likely to spring up, such a man lives always on the alert. As he grows in watchfulness and faith, he grows in recollection. "Those who set the Lord always in the sight of their soul," says Cassiodorus, "do not give way to sin."

"I have placed the Lord ever before me; for he is at my right hand that I be not moved. Therefore my heart has been glad and my tongue has rejoiced; moreover my flesh also shall rest in hope."[28] Inevitably joy and hope must follow faith. When we know that Christ is our support, refuge, defence, we can rest at last in cheerful confidence.

The elder Tobias told his son to "have God in mind all the days of thy life,"[29] and St. Jerome, commenting on this, says that it is the memory of God that drives out all evils. Where human beings are concerned, their memory is not the same as their presence; where God is concerned, to remember Him is to recognize His presence.

When we are told that a certain prophet or judge in the Old Testament "stood before the face of the Lord" we think of the act of intercession, the single act of prayer. But surely the secret of the prophet's strength lay in the fact that he stood before God the whole time.

For Elias to inform Achab that "as the Lord liveth, the God of Israel, in whose sight I stand, there shall not be dew nor rain these years, but according to the words of my mouth"[30] was to state a condition: his was the habit of prayer and faith. For Eliseus to inform Joram that "as the Lord of hosts liveth, in whose sight I stand, if I did not reverence the face of Josaphat king of Juda, I would not have hearkened to thee"[31] was again to proclaim a stage of grace, a favour implying the habit of contemplation.

The field of contemplation is recollection, and recollection is nothing else than the exercise which summons the faculties of

[28] Ps. 15;8,9.
[29] Tob. 4;6.
[30] 3 Kings 17;1.
[31] 4 Kings 3;14.

the mind to attend upon the presence of God. When memory
and imagination have been drawn in, like the horns of a snail,
from their outward perceptions—when they have become obedient to the desire of the will for prayer—then the rebellious
impulses of nature are found to break upon the rock which is
Christ. Then is reason, enlightened by grace and "walking by the
guidance of the Gospel," preparing itself for the final vision of
"Him who has called us to His kingdom."

> Therefore are the days of our life lengthened for the
> amendment of our evil ways, as says the Apostle: "Knowest
> thou not that the patience of God is leading thee to re-
> pentance?" For the merciful Lord says: "I will not the
> death of a sinner, but that he should be converted and live."

The need for repentance is constantly before St. Benedict's
mind. Even though he may be addressing young people who
have hardly had time to get themselves tainted by the world, he
wants to develop in them the sense of their responsibility for sin.

Recognition of sin is a challenge to reparation. Trust in God's
willingness to forgive does not lessen the need to seek pardon
by penance; on the contrary it should increase the sense of compunction and the desire to amend.

The monk's penance is not a pious extra, suitable enough to
his calling but not really required in strict justice. There is nothing fictitious about the necessity for penance. Penance is the
monk's answer, admittedly inadequate but no less necessary on
that account, both to the debt incurred by original sin and to
the implications contained in being a member of Christ's suffering body.

To "respond" is to render the "responsible" answer. Morally
responsible, we must be always ready to meet the reckoning.
Without a lively awareness of the debit side to our lives we shall
be lacking in that filial remorse which preserves our love from
complacency.

St. Benedict wants nothing left out in our response to God,
and he knows that if we are deficient in compunction we shall
have only an incomplete idea of God's mercy. Once we are clear

about God's mercy, the whole position of self-denial in our lives will be assured. We shall see the point about reparation.

Preoccupation with guilt is a more generally recognized obstacle to contemplation than indifference to guilt. But if St. Benedict's emphasis on contrition, reiterated throughout the holy Rule, is anything to go by, the second of the two dangers warrants the closer attention on the part of spiritual writers.

Just as compunction without amendment would be nothing but emotion, so contemplation without compunction would be nothing but emotion. This is not to say that compunction must always be expressed; it is to say that it must always be there.

We must hasten to do now what will profit us for all eternity. We have therefore to establish a school of the Lord's service, in the institution of which we hope to order nothing that is harsh or rigorous. But if anything be somewhat strictly laid down, according to the dictates of equity, for the amendment of vices or the preservation of charity, do not therefore fly in dismay from the way of salvation whose beginning cannot but be strait.

St. Benedict has now begun to speak specifically of the monastic life. Narrowing the conception of the Christian life to a particular form, he derives from the Greek σχολή (Latin, *schola*) the idea of leisured learning. The education provided in St. Benedict's monastery has to do with the science and service of God.

Accordingly the monk is expected to consider himself always a beginner, always more or less a new-boy in a school career which lasts a lifetime. Since the study of God's love is limitless, the student is never fully qualified.

Like the bride in the Canticle, the soul looks forward to being taught by the Beloved. "There thou shalt teach me"—in the house of my profession—"and I will give thee a cup of spiced wine."[32] The cup of wine is the tribute of monastic service, spiced with suffering.

But this phrase "school of the Lord's service" must be rightly understood. The Greek connotation, or even the Roman *schola* with its suggestion of university debates, should not allow us to

[32] 8;2.

imagine that St. Benedict envisaged a strictly intellectualized approach to religion. Nor on the other hand is he providing for a course of pietistic moralism. When our holy Father talks about a school of the Lord's service he means a place of serious religious effort, a training-ground of saints, a household in which prayer, labour, study and recreation combine under a discipline and according to a routine which recall one's days at school.

Since St. Benedict knows well enough that those who are subject to school rules are liable to question the value of those rules, and even to fly in dismay from the state of subjection, he reminds the would-be monk that in the interests of charity and self-reform there is bound to be an element of severity.

Severity without the harshness that wounds is St. Benedict's aim. We have seen how he associates guilt with responsibility; he is trying now to resolve the perplexities and complications arising from the guilt by tempering the dreads which are associated with the responsibility.

In the vineyard of the Beloved, myrrh and aloes mingle with every sweet scent:[33] on the way of salvation the stones are sometimes rough. The monk must keep up his hope with the knowledge that discipline is essentially reasonable, salutary, inevitable.

If every flower smelled sweet, the result would only be sickly; if all the way were smooth, where would be the test in walking it?

You must not be put off, St. Benedict warns his readers and future subjects, by what seems to you an unendurable contradiction to your nature. It is only a necessary contradiction, and it will not turn out to be unendurable. Your pride and self-will have demanded it, and later on, when you have become moulded to the religious life, you will be glad to see the lower part of your nature coming to heel.

"The flowers have appeared in our land; the time of pruning is come."[34] Religious discipline, though appearing to run contrary to nature, is assisting its development. If the plant had faith, it would not resent the pruning-knife.

[33] Cant. 4;14.
[34] *Ibid.*, 2;12.

Still less would the pruning be resented if the plant had love. Knowing that if it were to flower more and love more it would also have to be pruned more, the plant would gladly submit to the knife.

When the soul has begun to learn the way of love it seeks instinctively the way of sacrifice. Self-giving, whether the resulting flower is ever to be enjoyed or not, is felt to be the appropriate expression of its desire.

Thus the words from the Canticle can be taken to fit two aspects of the one principle. They can mean either "now that the plant is in bloom, the moment has come to lop off its branches" or "now that the plant is growing, it cries out for the knife."

That St. Benedict has something of this kind in mind—namely the tendency on the part of the soul to fall in with the discipline of suffering as it advances in God's service—is seen from the sentence which immediately follows in the text.

> But as we go forward in our life and faith, we shall with hearts enlarged and unspeakable sweetness of love run in the way of God's commandments. So that never departing from His guidance, but persevering in His teaching in the monastery until death, we may by patience share in the sufferings of Christ.

St. Benedict assumes that in the monastic life these things will go together: progress in love will mean patient suffering with Christ, and re-living the life of Christ will mean for the monk stability in the place of profession.

Already in the Prologue, then, the characteristic element of the Benedictine way of life is declared. Whether in the individual case it is the greatest consolation or the greatest penance, stability is the specific quality of the Benedictine Rule.

If it is by "persevering in the monastery until death" that monks develop their likeness to Christ, the subject of stability must come in for a much fuller treatment than that given here. St. Benedict is content in his Prologue to touch upon what he considers to be the fundamentals: he will enlarge upon these basic ideas as the legislation follows in its sequence.

That there is to be special weight attaching to stability, and that the sequence of his Rule is carefully planned, is shown by the way in which St. Benedict continues the closing thought of his Prologue in the opening chapter of his legislative code. Though the framework of the whole is flexible, and there is no scruple about repetition, the general direction of the Rule is consistent. The dominant movements, certainly, are clear.

CHAPTER I

OF THE VARIOUS KINDS OF MONKS

As Abbot Delatte points out, the first seven chapters of the Rule give us the constitution of the monastery; all the rest are concerned with enactments. Three of the first seven deal with the monastery's organic structure—the relationship between subjects and abbot—while the other four outline the monastic and interior training which life under such a system is designed to promote.

It is plain that there are four kinds of monks. The first are the cenobites: that is, those who do their service in monasteries under a rule and an abbot.

If there is a society there has to be a common bond. The monastic society, if it is to be a true society and not an aggregation of individuals, must stand on certain agreed principles. St. Benedict, in his opening chapter, gives what he conceives to be the basic elements of social monastic life.

Cassian is St. Benedict's authority for putting cenobites first in the list of monks. The distinguishing marks of the cenobites are that they live together as a firmly constituted family, that they follow the same rule, and that they have an abbot at their head. The cenobite is a fixed member of a defined unit; stability is his foundation and his frame.

Friars, canons regular, members of religious congregations, are therefore, though they live in community, not strictly cenobites. It is not the common life that makes the cenobite; it is rather the permanency of the personnel, subjects and superior alike.

In the fifth century, monasticism had not yet taken shape in the West. It was still modelling itself on the Egyptian pattern, and though Pachomius had brought organization and rule to the religious life of his time in the East, the current idea of a monk was still that of a solitary.

The word "monk" comes from the Greek μόνος, "alone." Even after the introduction of the cenobitic character (κοίνος βίος, "to live in community"), monasticism continued in public estimation, and to a certain extent in fact, in its individualistic tradition. It was as a group of hermits united in common worship, subjection, material goods, that monasteries were thought of. It was left to St. Benedict, the Father of Western Monachism, to develop the cenobitic ideal so as to include closer community ties and responsibilities.

At the end of this first chapter St. Benedict declares his purpose of writing his Rule for one sort of monk only, the strongest sort (*"fortissimum genus"*), and that this is the cenobite. Following his arrangement of material, we shall return to the discussion of the cenobite ideal when we have noted what St. Benedict has to say of the other sorts of monk.

> The second are the anchorites: hermits, that is, who, not in the first fervour of their religious life but after long probation in the monastery, have learned by the help and experience of others to fight against the devil; and going forth well-armed from the ranks of their brethren to the single-handed combat of the desert, are now able to fight safely without the support of others, by their own strength under God's aid, against the vices of the flesh and their evil thoughts.

In St. Benedict's time it was easy enough for a man to become a hermit. All he had to do was to find a suitable master who would give him the habit and his blessing, a suitable site for his hermitage, and some means of supplying himself with food. The Church did not frown on such men. Canon Law was not there to make conditions.

St. Benedict's first experience of the monk's life was as just such a hermit. From the monk Romanus the young man had re-

ceived his *melota*, the habit of sheepskin which had been adopted
by the Egyptian monks as their distinctive dress, and at Subiaco
he had worked and prayed in solitude for three years. When St.
Benedict speaks of the trials peculiar to the eremitical life, he
speaks with inside knowledge.

But he does not look upon his own early experiment as one to
be imitated. It was what God wanted at the time, and it was a
success, but as a general rule, for a man to step straight from the
world into the desert would be folly. St. Benedict insists accordingly on a course of preliminary training which will both expose
the traps which particularly endanger such a life and at the same
time test the authenticity of so unusual a call.

"A thousand are for thee, the peaceable, and two hundred are
for them that keep the fruit thereof."[1] The cenobitic vocation
is the more normal and the more peaceable; it is also the best
preparation for the state which enjoys the fruit thereof.

St. Benedict knew that solitude could exercise an attraction
which might wholly mislead a soul. What can be more alluring
than the thought of escape from worldly care, from the company
of one's fellow men, from the drudgery of household routine,
from authority? Apart from such negative considerations there
is the glamour attaching to the idea of the silent man of God,
hidden away in his little hut and never seeing anybody.

Countless illustrations could be drawn from the lives of the
fathers of the desert to show how deceptive the call to isolation
can be. Eccentricity, delusion, heresy even, will spring up in the
desert; in a community these dangers will normally be avoided.
St. Benedict is not against the eremitical life as such—in fact he
provides for it—but he wants to make sure that it is embarked
upon in the right dispositions. What are the conditions he demands?

First, the candidate for solitude must have got over his early
enthusiasm: his bent for single-handed service must have stood
the test of time. St. Gregory says that time, not fervour, is the
true test of good desires. Decisions may not be made on the wave
of emotion, and the zeal for God's service which is experienced

[1] Cant. 8;12.

in the first flush of conversion may be no valid indication of the deep interior correspondence between God and the soul.

Second, the impulse should come from the abundance of fraternal charity and not from the lack of it. Bitterness towards the brethren would neither explain nor excuse the vocation; if the call does not emerge out of sympathy, it is not of God but of self. Clearly in the true vocation to the solitary life there will be an element of flight. But the element of flight will be secondary: the dominant element will be pursuit.

Where the primary motive is desire for God, the motive of escape will not greatly signify. The escape will be sufficiently reluctant as to be more of a renunciation than an escape. There is all the difference between turning your back on what is distracting and running away from what is disagreeable.

Next, the cenobite who aspires to the state of the anchorite must know that he is engaging himself in total war. If he imagines he will find peace in the desert, he is wrong. Up till now he has been fighting in the ranks, he has been supported and armed and trained by men of flesh and blood like himself; henceforward he is to use his own weapons and his own initiative, and the trials which he must endure will be of a more subtle order.

The solitary has still the flesh to fight against—and St. Benedict warns him that the flesh gathers power in the desert—but what he will find harder to bear will be the struggles of the spirit.

Lastly, the would-be hermit must have humility. Unless he goes to his new life "under God's aid," as St. Benedict says, and not on the strength of his own character, he is doomed to disappointment. Confidence in God is the touchstone of the eremitical vocation—as it is of any other.

Before we leave this section about hermits and the Rule, we should note that a certain Mark, a monk of Monte Cassino shortly after St. Benedict's time, claims that our holy Father used himself to withdraw at times into complete solitude while still ruling the monastery.

If the tradition mentioned by the poet-monk Mark is correct, two questions arise: Did St. Benedict, while legislating for the cenobitical life, accept the eremitical life as being the higher of the two? Did he make practical provision at Monte Cassino for those who wanted to be hermits?

There can be no certain answer to either question. As regards the first, all that can be said is that in decisively recommending the cenobitical life he nowhere claims it to be the most perfect. He puts the cenobite first in the list (and will later refer to him as the "strongest sort" of monk), but this may simply be a way of saying: "All things considered, the safest kind of monk to be is the kind I mean to write about."

Nor, as regards the second question, do we know if facilities existed at Monte Cassino for passing from the monastery to the hermitage. There is no evidence to show that there were special buildings put up for the purpose. But we do know that St. Benedict's contemporary, Cassiodorus, who was, if not a follower of the Rule at least an admirer of the legislator, arranged in the planning of his monastery for two separate establishments—the one catering for the common life, the other for the solitary.

The passages in the Rule where St. Benedict will be found to soft-pedal the superiority of the life, speaking of his Rule for example as a "little rule for beginners" and of the observance which he wants of his monks as slight when compared with the requirements of Basil and the ancient Fathers, are thus perhaps explained. Though a convinced community man himself, he is not ashamed to admire the ideal of the more withdrawn service of God—and even to benefit by it in practice when inspired to do so by the Holy Spirit.

The anchorite, then, is the man who lives apart. (The name is again from the Greek ἀναχωρέω: those who dwell in seclusion.) But it is one thing to be a recluse for life and another to withdraw into retreat. In our own time the need for intermittent periods of solitude is becoming increasingly felt. In some communities it is bravely recognized and met. Whatever the course this trend may take in the future, it would be going against both the letter and spirit of the Rule to deny the possibility of an eremitical element in the Benedictine vocation.

If St. Benedict can envisage as a development of the contemplative life the emergence of a true eremitical vocation from a cenobitical setting and training, then to quote the claims of stability or obedience or humility is to quote St. Benedict against himself.

A third and detestable kind of monks are the sarabaites, who have been tried by no rule nor by experience but, being as soft as lead, still keep faith with the world in their works, while, as their tonsure shows, they lie to God. These in twos or threes, or even singly without a shepherd, shut up not in the Lord's sheepfolds but in their own, make a law to themselves of their own pleasures and desires: whatever they think fit or please to do, that they call holy; and what they like not, that they consider unlawful.

Where there is justification for the hermit life, regularized and under certain conditions, there can be no justification for the life of the sarabaite. For a monk living in community to become an anchorite, St. Benedict supposes the permission and blessing of the abbot. No abbot would sponsor the call to become a sarabaite.

No call from God could prompt a soul to embrace the sarabaite way of life. The sarabaites were not a sect or an order; they were free-lance nomads, wandering where their fancy led them. Their name, not derived from the Greek this time but from the Aramaic *sarab*, means rebellious.

Cassian speaks of Egyptian sarabaites, "each man for himself," who shunned the common life and feared affiliation to an established monastery. The curious thing is that they should be regarded as monks at all. Their claim to monastic status appears to have rested on their conversion from the world, their habit and tonsure, and possibly also their poverty and chastity. Of obedience and stability they showed no sign.

It is not difficult to account for the existence of sarabaites. In an age when the religious state knew no regular initiation and demanded no precise allegiance to authority other than the allegiance demanded of the layman, the idea of roving about in a habit and earning the respect of the uninformed by a show of piety and a willingness to speak of holy things would have made a distinct appeal.

St. Benedict calls this interpretation of monasticism "detestable." To dress up as a monk and not to show the essential marks of the monk is to travesty the monastic ideal. It is to live a lie. Such men have evaded the hardships and have claimed the rewards; they are soft and pretend to be austere; they have renounced the world and have clung to the pleasures of the world.

So far as monasticism goes, the sarabaite genus is today extinct. But the sarabaite attitude of mind is as common now as it was in St. Benedict's time. "Whatever they please to do, they call holy; what they like not, they consider unlawful." A religious man can all too easily assume that because he is a religious man his religious impulses come from God. But self can operate through religious impulses as easily as through any other. The only way to test the religious impulse is to stand it before the bar of objective religion—to submit it to obedience.

Where the sarabaite is at fault is not so much in his wandering mind—he may not be altogether responsible for this—but in his assumption of virtue where in fact there is nothing but natural selfishness. If a man is a gypsy let him admit it; let him not parade as a monk. The last degradation is, as Socrates proclaims, to call black white and white black. When we have given up being sorry for our sins, and have begun to account for them as virtues, then we have put ourselves virtually beyond reclaim.

The modern sarabaite is the monk who, though living under an abbot and a rule, follows his own monastic whim. Now a hermit, now an advocate of the social life, now an enthusiast for the choir, now a champion of mental prayer to the exclusion of all else, now sedulous in manual labour, now pleading the cause of work among souls and recreation among souls. Nor is it only in the quality of steadfastness that the modern sarabaite is deficient: he reflects his ancestors also in his softness, his obstinacy, his hypocrisy. If the would-be anchorite is a thorn in the side of authority, the psychological sarabaite is an open sore. Both kinds of subject are likely to be importunate, but where one keeps out of the way of the brethren in order to get his way with authority, the other makes factions among the brethren in order to win a following against authority. "In twos or threes without a shepherd, they make a law to themselves of their desires."

The fourth kind of monks are those who are called gyrovagues, who spend all their lives wandering about divers provinces, staying in different cells for three or four days at a time, ever roaming, with no stability, given up to their own pleasures and to the snares of gluttony, and worse in all things than the sarabaites.

Still more debased is this fourth class of monk. The gyrovague is no better than a tramp—without even the tramp's excuses. The sarabaite at least imagined himself to be a monk, verifying the fiction as far as he could with a display of prayer and work. But in the case of the gyrovague there is not even the pretence of prayer or work: he is a man pledged to poverty only so that he may continue as a parasite.

Cassian has something to say about the sarabaites, but is evidently too contemptuous of gyrovagues to classify them as monks at all. From other sources it is known that such wandering religious scroungers as St. Benedict describes were a recognized manifestation. They would come as pilgrims, or as students wanting to consult the library, and would batten on the monastery's hospitality until either they got tired of it or were urged by the community to move on. The same business would then be tried all over again at the next monastery.

Since it has always been one of the first principles of monasticism that strangers must be received as if they were Christ Himself, communities necessarily lay themselves open to being imposed upon. They expect this, and it is as it should be. But this does not lighten the responsibility of the stranger who knocks at the monastery door.

The stray vagrant who asks for a meal is given one and goes his way. St. Benedict's blessing rests upon him. The casual labourer who has taken to the road but who is willing to work while he lodges at the monastery is accommodated in the same way. The man whom St. Benedict objects to is the one who looks like a monk and who expects to be treated as a monk, but who shies away from the work and the prayer of monks.

The force of St. Benedict's attack upon this now extinct brand of monk carries a significance for monks of today. The vagabond spirit is not entirely dead. Leaving till later the discussion of enclosure and stability, we can note briefly here that monks who for one good reason or another are visiting other Benedictine houses will avoid the charge of being gyrovagues if they are careful to attend the choir, observe the rules of silence, and bring with them work to do when not engaged in community exercises.

St. Benedict is not against monks visiting, with the approval of their superiors and for some good reason, other monasteries. He makes this clear in his sixty-first chapter, where he says that any serious-minded and devout monk-guest who shows signs of wanting to stay on, even for good, should be encouraged to do so. What our holy Father particularly wants to avoid is the unstable idler whose criticisms will either annoy or unsettle the brethren.

The lay guest who is troublesome has to be allowed for. He has not been trained in monastic usage. He does not know that the brethren are seeing Christ in him. For the gyrovague monk there is not the same excuse: he is supposed to know the principles and ideals of monastic hospitality.

> Leaving these alone therefore, let us set to work with the help of God to lay down a rule for the cenobites—that is the strongest race of monks.

In drawing up his list at the beginning, St. Benedict had said that there were four interpretations in the field. Whatever his own private view about the excellence of the life lived alone with God in solitude, he comes out firmly in favour for the conventual life: it is about this, anyway, that he will treat.

It is moreover "with the help of God" that he will lay down rules. He is merely the human legislator, the agent, the scribe. If monasticism is a matter of supernatural vocation, the work of casting the code will follow suit. This is not to say the holy Rule is on the level of the Scriptures, or anything like it; it is to say that any written word which has as its aim and inspiration the closer union of souls with God—and is justified by Catholic tradition in a way that the holy Rule has been justified—can be claimed to have the Holy Spirit at its source.

St. Benedict has no other aim but to further the life of grace within the souls of men. He is not trying to spread a system or organization; he is trying to provide for the religious, and particularly for the contemplative, life. His ambitions are not clerical, they are purely spiritual. The ecclesiastical side of monasticism—as also the missionary, the educational, the agricultural, and the scholarly—can be left to develop in the course of history. Our holy Father's sole and immediate concern is the sanctity of those who come to him as disciples and would-be subjects.

"Already," writes Dom Delatte in his commentary, "even from the exclusions that form the theme of almost the whole of this first chapter, the great main lines of Benedictine life disengage themselves; that life will be conventual, ruled by obedience, vowed to stability."[2]

[2] *The Rule of St. Benedict; Commentary by Paul Delatte;* translated by Justin McCann, p. 34.

CHAPTER 2

WHAT KIND OF MAN THE ABBOT OUGHT TO BE

If it is true, according to Aristotle, that "those who dwell in the State take after their rulers," it is true also of those who dwell in the monastery. If the monks are to re-live Christ, they must have someone at their head who will re-present Him.

The abbot's whole duty is that of reproducing Christ's attitude towards His disciples, and therefore of exercising authority in Christ's name. St. Benedict does not say that the abbot is required to be outstandingly clever, able, strong-minded, or even experienced in the direction of souls. The first requirement is a lively sense of his responsibility before God.

Insight into the characters of his monks, and gentleness in the handling of them, can be counted upon to the extent that the abbot relies upon Him whose place he takes. So long as he does not rule in his own right, but only as one who has to render an account of the power that has been entrusted to him, he can have the fullest confidence in the support of grace. St. Benedict's first degree of humility is not for subjects only.

An abbot who is worthy to rule over the monastery ought always to remember what he is called, and correspond to his name by his works. For he is believed to hold the place of Christ in the monastery, since he is called by His name, as the Apostle says: "Ye have received the spirit of the adoption of sons, in which we cry: Abba, Father."

33

"Worthy to rule" is not the same as "able to preside." Whatever the man's natural shortcomings, the one placed at the head of a Benedictine community must train himself for the office; there is more in the conception of abbacy than chairmanship. The abbatial idea was not arrived at for the purpose of conveying a title, but for the purpose of conveying an authority. Rule passes from the source of authority itself to those ruled. The title *Abba* is the reminder of this.

Though the power to govern comes as the result of election, it does not come from those who have elected. It is vested in an individual, but it does not originate in an individual. To look at an abbot's authority in terms either of a majority vote or of personal gift for rule would be to miss the essential quality of religious obedience. The essential quality is faith.

For the abbot's position to be understood, both by himself and by his subjects, there must be faith in the dependent authority of man as related to the independent authority of God. Thus the abbot must know that his acts (or as the quoted paragraph calls them, his "works") are to be referred beyond the chapter that elected him, and his monks must know that the terms of their obedience have not been dictated by themselves.

Without such a supernatural view of monastic authority you may get government by natural leadership, but you will get neither spiritual responsibility on the part of the superior nor spiritual submission on the part of the subjects.

That in his own life St. Benedict acted on this principle, and demanded its recognition from the monks whom he ruled, is seen from an incident recorded by St. Gregory in the *Dialogues*.[1] A monk who in the world had belonged to a family of rank was serving his turn in waiting upon the abbot. In the course of performing this duty, which involved holding a light while St. Benedict was eating his evening meal, he began "secretly to indulge such thoughts as these: Who is this man whom I am waiting on . . . who am I to be doing such service?" St. Benedict, supernaturally made aware of the monk's state of mind, severely warned the brother of his danger and further used the occasion

[1] Bk. 2; ch. 20.

to drive home to the community the necessity of seeing in one's abbot the vicegerent of Christ. Whatever the social status of one's family in the world, considerations of class must lose themselves in the supernatural status of one's family in religion.

Precisely because the community is a family and not merely an organization, it must be ruled by one who is a father and not merely a president. St. Benedict's quotation from St. Paul which points out that the very name of abbot derives from the word "father" is only a restatement of the opening sentence of the Prologue: obedience given to the abbot is obedience given to a "loving father."

In the course of the Rule the abbot is variously called father, shepherd, physician, teacher, master, steward. To choose such names is as much as to describe the character of the office. Certainly the idea of a dictator is eliminated. The terms "father" and "shepherd" occur more often than the rest, so if the brethren are to think of themselves as belonging primarily to a household and a flock, they are at least meant to be spared the fear inspired by an autocrat and the coldness occasioned by the figurehead.

It is as much a community's misfortune as a family's that the father should be either a martinet or a detached bystander. If parenthood is to have any real meaning, the father must not only concern himself with the affairs of the household but concern himself in a spirit of sympathy and solicitude.

From all this it is clear, and it becomes clearer still later on in the Rule, that the abbot is intended by St. Benedict to govern the community for life. The conception of fatherhood implies permanence. You may be able to change your physician, your steward, your master, and even—though with more danger to the object immediately involved—your shepherd; but you can not change your father.

The continuity of influence which the vow of stability is designed to secure can hardly be maintained where every few years one father is exchanged for another. If St. Benedict deliberately selects the natural family as the type best suited to illustrate the unity and stability of monastic life, he obviously means its implications to be studied. If the head is to be replaced at convenient intervals, a more apt simile than that of the family body could have been devised.

Experience shows that where the superior is not elected for life there is an inevitable restriction of influence—active or passive, and usually both. Either the abbot, regarding himself as a caretaker, hesitates to lay down a policy which is likely to be reversed at the next election, or else the monks, regarding themselves as bound in loyalty to their superior only for so long as his term of office lasts, envisage alterations at a determined date. Thus the abbot feels cramped, while his monks, however true their respect for him and however supernatural their obedience, lack the continuity of doctrine which monastic formation requires. Monastic formation is not as a rule something which can be picked up piecemeal from a series of temporary providers, and in regulating for life-abbots St. Benedict was trying to secure a consistent tradition of instruction as much as a stable form of government.

But though the ideal is clearly expressed in the Rule, the expediency of the temporary abbacy has, at different times and in different congregations, been found to produce good results. On this subject Abbot Butler writes as follows: "It is urged that any manner of government that has worked well is thereby to be recognized as falling within the limits of legitimate Benedictine tradition: for instance that the annual abbots of St. Justina are as Benedictine as the life-abbots of the Rule. This seems to be a kind of pragmatism, taking as a test of the true and the good the fact that it works well. Or an application of the law of thought: whatever is, is." To say that these temporary abbots are "as conformable to Benedictine tradition and as congenial to Benedictine life as the life-abbot of the Rule," concludes Abbot Butler, "would be running into monastic latitudinarianism."[2]

We have seen that the function of abbot is not the establishment of despotic mastery or aloof patronage. But nor is it simply that of efficient management. For the running of the house there are the prior, the cellarer or bursar, the deans, the guestmaster,

[2] *Benedictine Monachism*, pp. 412, 413.

and the other officials. If the abbot's time is wholly taken up with the work of administration, he will, in putting material needs before spiritual, lose touch with the most significant element in the lives of those whom he rules. A religious superior may explain his ignorance of his subjects' interior lives by saying that he is constantly having to care for their exterior lives. It is an explanation but not an excuse. St. Benedict makes it abundantly clear that an abbot's first charge before God is the care of souls. Again the principle finds support in the analogy of the family: the parent may not neglect the moral welfare of the children on the grounds that less important matters have to be settled first, and that these less important matters excuse from the obligation.

It is the responsibility of the father to secure the harmony of the household of which he is lord and master. There can be no true harmony where there is a lack of due balance. Where material concerns are given more weight than spiritual concerns there is unbalance. Disproportion between the spiritual and the material leads quicker to decay in religious life than in any other. The reason for this is obvious, since it is the spiritual in the religious life that gives meaning to the material.

Again the family-life ideal is easily lost sight of if the head of the household is more often than not away. Absentee parents weaken filial responsibility. However judicious the delegation of authority, obedience is never quite the same when given to an intermediary. It *should* be the same, because religious obedience is given to Christ, but in fact it is harder to see this when obeying delegates.

Especially must the abbot show himself a "loving father" when dealing with his more difficult subjects. Before God they are sons. In the same way he is urged to show paternal solicitude towards the sick, the aged, and the very young. Conscious that power, when vested in a single individual, leads readily towards absolutism, St. Benedict does his best to see that the government of his monasteries should be patriarchal.

Any lack of profit which the father of the household may find in his sheep, shall be imputed to the fault of the shepherd. Only then shall he be acquitted, if he shall have bestowed all pastoral diligence on his unquiet and disobedient flock, and employed all his care to amend their corrupt manner of life: then shall he be absolved in the judgment of the Lord, and may say to the Lord with the prophet: "I have not hidden Thy justice in my heart, I have declared Thy truth and Thy salvation, but they contemned and despised me."

Commenting on this passage, Dom Delatte says: "It would even seem that St. Benedict dreaded defect rather than excess in the exercise of authority." Heli, shutting his eyes to his sons' faults, is evidently more to be blamed than Roboam for all his intemperate zeal.

Certainly St. Benedict himself did not err by default in the matter of correcting refractory monks. We read in the *Dialogues* how the saint, miraculously informed of a lapse on the part of some brethren who had been absent on business from the monastery, "demanded 'Where dined you?' They answered: 'Nowhere.' To whom he said: 'Why do you lie? Did you not go into such a one's house, eat such and such meats, drink such a number of cups?'"[3] On another occasion St. Benedict "very sharply rebuked" a monk who had hidden some napkins which were apparently a personal gift from a community of nuns.[4] We read also how the disobedience of the cellarer "much displeased" St. Benedict, and how the saint "called the brothers together, rebuking the disobedient monk before them all for his pride and unfaithfulness."[5]

But in avoiding the temptation to buy peace at any price, the abbot is warned by our holy Father against small-mindedness and fault-finding. The abbot who is over-demanding in the minutiae of the religious life will create a nervous atmosphere in the house. A fussy superior, spreading furtiveness and suspicion among the brethren, is the last thing St. Benedict wants. And wherever sharp correction has been administered, complete forgiveness must fol-

[3] Bk. 2; ch. 12.
[4] *Ibid.*, ch. 19.
[5] *Ibid.*, ch. 29.

low the subject's acknowledgment of guilt. "But he straightway pardoned them, persuading himself that they would never afterwards attempt the like."[6]

Let him show by his own actions that those things ought not to be done which he has taught his disciples to be the law of God; lest, while preaching to others, he should himself become a castaway.

Communities are not moulded only by the conferences which they hear in the chapter-house. One human being responds to the person rather than to the word of another human being, and persons express their true selves by what they do rather than by what they say. The abbot forms and informs his community by his behaviour, by his example.

But example does not act *ex opere operato*: the subject has to be ready to receive it. In St. Benedict's case, the subjects at Vicovaro were not ready to receive the example which he gave them, and the experiment was a failure. Acting on the principle of take-it-or-leave-it, St. Benedict decided that the way of life which he had outlined for the monks of Vicovaro might well find response from other communities. "Did I not tell you that my ways and yours would never agree?" was the saint's reproach as he parted from the brethren at Vicovaro. It was his ways, not his words, that the monks had found insupportable. So it would be his ways, even more than his words, which would be the dominant influence in his subsequent monastic ventures.

It is not surprising that when he comes to write his Rule, then, St. Benedict counsels the abbot to preach chiefly by good example. Not only has his own experience taught him its value, but the two authorities to whom, apart from the Scriptures, he owes most, namely St. Basil and Cassian, are emphatic on this subject.

"How presumptuous should I not be," Abbot Chaeremon is recorded as saying, "to teach others what I do not practise myself. How can I exhort others to walk courageously and fervently in those exercises in which I myself have become careless and

[6] *Ibid.*, ch. 12.

lukewarm? This is the reason why I have never allowed any
young religious to dwell with me, lest the example of my degen-
eracy should cool the ardour and austerity of others. For the
words of him who instructs have no force or authority, unless
his example impresses upon the hearts of his hearers what he
teaches."[7]

The history of monasticism shows, even if nothing else were to
show it, that personal holiness in the head is the surest way to
secure personal holiness in the members. The classical instance
of this is seen in the story of Cluny, where for two centuries the
house flourished in sanctity under four successive saints and then
immediately declined under a man who was far from being a
saint. Only under the fifth of its abbot-saints, Peter the Venerable, did Cluny recover its early spirit.

"For them do I sanctify myself"[8] might well be the beacon-
text for any religious superior. Personal sanctification not only
shows the way to others but mediates on behalf of others. As
Abraham's merits interceded before God, and as Moses fought
the battles of the children of Israel by his prayers, so the holiness
of the abbot obtains graces from God for his community and
turns away the punishment to which it is liable.

> Let him make no distinction of persons in the monastery.
> Let not one be loved more than another unless he be found
> to excel in good works or in obedience. Let not one of
> noble birth be put before him who was formerly a slave
> unless some other reasonable cause exist for it . . . we are
> all one in Christ.

It is charity, not equity, that must be the rule of this impartial
attitude on the abbot's part. The abbot must rise above personal
preferences not only for the sake of fairness but much more for
the sake of charity—for the sake of Christ. St. Benedict's words
are not so much a safeguard against the sense of grievance which
a monk who has been "put upon" may feel, but rather an exhor-

[7] *Cassian's Conferences*, 11; ch. 5. See also St. Basil's *Longer Rule*,
ch. 43.
[8] John 17;19.

tation to the love which would eliminate causes of grievance.

Of all the abbot's responsibilities, impartiality in dealing with his monks is probably the hardest to handle. Evidently St. Benedict felt it to be one of the most important qualities in the government of the monastery: he comes back to the idea in several places. In winning souls to God the balance must be kept between extending too much gentleness to the sensitive and too much severity to the tough, between excessive variation in the cause of personal need and excessive uniformity in the cause of the general good.

It can be a temptation for the abbot, sheltering behind St. Benedict's injunction (later in the same chapter) "to accommodate himself to the diversity of characters," to let himself be dominated by the personalities of his monks. With the best intentions in the world, and imagining that he is acting in accordance with St. Benedict's mind, he can virtually surrender his authority in the monastery.

It is all too easy for one in office to associate almost exclusively with those whose views he shares, whose support he can count upon, or for whom he has a natural affinity. Instinctively we gravitate towards men whose interests, tastes, and backgrounds are the same as our own.

Favouritism in a religious superior is an offence not only against distributive justice but against the idea of a sovereign right held in fealty to God.

Just as the abbot will feel inclined to share his recreations, journeys, activities generally, with the more agreeable among the brethren, so he will feel inclined to put obligations that are likely to be found irksome upon the more docile. It is far less trouble to issue commands to those who will not raise objections, but if he indulges this evasion of equitable rule he will not only overburden the submissive but will find himself getting more and more out of touch with the restive.

It is possible for a superior who has experienced difficulties with a subject, or to whom the subject's very presence is a source of irritation, virtually to dismiss the man's need from his mind. For weeks, without perhaps consciously avoiding one another, the two may not meet. One of the things most to be avoided in the family life of the monastery is the estrangement of father and son.

If, in the terms of the holy Rule, the abbot cultivates an affection for all indiscriminately, he should be able to meet each of his community without strain. He may have to disguise his natural antipathies, but at least his supernatural regard for them will drive him to take an interest in their individual lives.

In the appointment of offices the abbot will have to be careful not to act on personal predilection. There can be self-deception in advancing, on the grounds of their precocious wisdom, the inexperienced. Often it is the penalty of this weakness in a superior that he should later on find himself hampered in his authority by those whom he has injudiciously promoted.

For the abbot to be under the influence of a party is as harmful to the community as to be under the influence of a person. Inevitably there will be a gulf between himself and the main body. Monks who gladly follow one man may justly resent following a number. At our profession we do not vow our obedience to an oligarchy.

It is not enough for the abbot to know what the majority want, what the minority want, what the individual monk wants: he must also know what *he* wants, and must enforce it in his own way. If he takes his ideas from others, frames his policy according to the will of others, exercises his authority through the medium of others, he has as good as sold his position to a board of directors.

> The abbot ought always to remember what he is and what he is called, and to know that to whom more is committed, from him more is required; and he must consider how difficult and arduous a task he has undertaken, of ruling souls and adapting himself to many dispositions. Let him so accommodate himself to the character and intelligence of each, winning some by kindness, others by reproof, others by persuasion, that he may not only suffer no loss in the flock committed to him but may even rejoice in their virtuous increase.

St. Benedict is saying frankly that the abbot's function is to win souls to God by any legitimate means he can devise. For one man to gain the confidence of many, different approaches have to be tried and different manners adopted. There is nothing hypocritical about this: it is only following out St. Paul's recommendation to be all things to all men.

Leaving aside the question of personal charm, which is almost a charisma of its own and not to be legislated for, there is the question of confidence. The abbot will have to show confidence if he is to receive a return of it. He will have to expect much from his subjects if he is to extract much. This will mean the exercise of understanding. It will mean taking an interest in the interests of the brethren. It will mean not being shocked, disappointed, disillusioned, or despairing. A man does not have to be a born leader in order to practise these things; he has merely to be patient and to possess an invincible belief in humanity.

By the superior no less than by the subject the fact must be faced that the grace of state does not assume miraculous insight, inspired direction, an illumined practical judgment in decisions to be made. The grace of state is like any other grace: it guides and strengthens, but does not compel or guarantee (except in the case of the Papal prerogative) supernatural intervention. A monk is a man, the same man, before and after his abbatial election. What the abbot has to do is to look with greater faith at those who lately were his fellow subjects; what the subject has to do is to look with greater faith at him who now represents divine authority.

From the abbot downwards each monk in the community has to discover his true identity as it exists in the mind of God. In helping others to make this discovery of themselves, the abbot will himself find his own true identity. In deepening his contemplation of the Father of Light, he will come to see both himself and his community in truth. His subjects will be his sons in Christ. *His* sons, because sons of the Father whom he represents.

Having ensured in his abbot a sense of duty towards those entrusted to him, St. Benedict goes on to ensure that, while making himself accessible to his monks, the abbot does not neglect his

own spiritual life. Abbots must be spared from becoming overwhelmed with the cares of their office; St. Benedict now sees to
it that the material pressures inescapable in the running of a
Benedictine house do not smother the abbot's spiritual vitality
but rather stimulate it.

> Let him not be more solicitous for fleeting, earthly, and
> perishable things; but let him ever bear in mind that he has
> undertaken the government of souls of which he shall have
> to give an account. And that he may not complain for want
> of worldly substance, let him remember what is written:
> "Seek first the kingdom of God and His justice, and all
> these things shall be added unto you." And again: "Nothing
> is wanting to them that fear Him." . . . And thus, while he
> is careful on other men's accounts, he will be solicitous also
> on his own. So, while correcting others by his admonitions,
> he will be himself cured of his own defects.

St. Benedict, in the grand tradition of faith, is confident that
if you make sure of the eternal, the temporal makes sure of itself.
So far as the monastery is concerned, this applies not only to
economic security but also to the matter of recruitment. Vocations will not be lacking to the community which puts spiritual
things first. To the community which puts material things first,
the lack of vocations is a signal of warning as well as a punishment.

Granted that the religious life is supernatural or it is nothing,
confidence in divine Providence follows as a necessary consequence. God either wants the monastery to continue or He does
not. If He does, He will provide what is necessary in the way of
substance and subjects; if He does not, He will bring to nothing
the efforts of those who labour to prolong its existence. So, provided the brethren do what in them lies, why worry?

Temporal necessity is, for St. Benedict, an occasion for the
exercise of faith. We read how, when Campania was suffering a
famine, and the supply of wheat in the monastery had been exhausted ("so that but five loaves remained for the brethren's refection"), the saint "endeavoured by a mild and gentle reproach
to reprehend their pusillanimity, and with fair promises to com-

fort them, said, 'Why are your souls sad for want of bread? Today you are in want, but tomorrow you shall have plenty.' "[9] On another occasion "the man of God gave all he had in his monastery to those in want, insomuch as there was almost nothing left in the cellar save only a little oil in a glass vessel"—and even this he ordered to be given away. So great was the increase of oil, granted miraculously in answer to St. Benedict's prayer, that the barrel in which oil was normally kept, but which lately had stood empty, was filled to overflowing.[10]

This trust in the Providence of God is easier to practise when the occasion is not so much one of physical sustenance as continuance of existence as a religious body. The test, however, is still one of discerning between the temporal and the eternal, between the immediate and the remote.

It is much easier, because it appears so much more altruistic, to justify attachment to the monastery and its future than to justify attachment to creature comforts and even physical necessities. But unless the scope of faith extends to place and to the general good, it is merely something private and personal.

A monk's supernatural view of life should show him that the monastery's existence, its prestige in the eyes of the world, its work and prosperity are relative and not absolute goods. He should not love the monastery for its own sake but for God's sake, and if God has other ideas about it, His will is to be recognized as absolute.

This should not discourage the monk from praying for vocations, for the success of the monastery's undertakings, for the intentions of the brethren—indeed he is urged to do so—but it does prevent his making the monastery's temporal advancement an end in itself. Under cover of love for our monastery, we can rival in partisan zeal advertisers, company promoters, political propagandists. We are not salesmen, and such a monastic loyalty is misconceived, worldly, profane.

That our holy Father felt keenly a love for his foundation, prayed earnestly for its furtherance in good, was dismayed at the

[9] *Dialogues*, Bk. 2; ch. 21.
[10] *Ibid.*, ch. 29.

threat of dissolution, but at the same time bowed to the permissive will of God, is seen from one of the most revealing passages in the *Dialogues*. This seventeenth chapter shows us a St. Benedict of flesh and blood, torn by human dreads and loyalties, whom other chapters are inclined to leave hidden.

"Theoprobus, converted by his admonition, was very intimate with the Father Benedict. He one day entered into the cell of the man of God, and found him weeping bitterly. When he had waited a while and saw that he did not cease (though it was the saint's custom in prayer mildly to weep), he boldly asked him the cause of so great grief. To whom the man of God presently replied: 'All this monastery which I have built, with whatsoever I have prepared for my brethren, are, by the judgment of God, to be delivered to the heathen. I could scarce obtain to spare even the lives of those in this place.' His words Theoprobus heard, and we see them verified in the destruction of the monastery by the Lombards." The moral is that we may not put our trust in human and temporal enterprises, however holy, but must so understand earthly circumstances as to treat them solely in relation to the Divine plan. The abbot may never think, for example, that the true welfare of the community has been promoted when the temporalities have been conscientiously attended to. He cannot satisfy his essential obligation towards his brethren unless he thinks in terms of faith.

Preoccupation with material concerns has secularized many monasteries, has spoiled the spirituality of many abbots. "The keepers of the walls took away my veil from me," complains the bride in the Canticles, "they struck and wounded me."[11] The masonry is not the most important part of the city of God.

[11] Cant. 5;7.

CHAPTER 3

OF CALLING THE BRETHREN
TO COUNCIL

In this chapter we see the two forces in St. Benedict's characteristically Roman nature combining to make a single principle of action and order. In his patriarchal character he arrogates to himself, and therefore to his conception of the abbacy, the power of making final decisions; as a true republican, but with the Gospel as his frame of reference, he allows on the part of subordinates free expression of opinion.

The society which St. Benedict is forming is essentially cenobitical, reflecting the Roman *familia*. Only to lend greater spiritual stature to the position of the abbot does the legislator introduce an element of democracy. The function of counsellor is not designed to act as a brake upon the abbatial will: it is designed to give confirmation where the abbatial will is found to hesitate.

Though the life of any organism derives its immediate direction from the head, the head is able to direct more surely where the state of the members is known. It is again the difference between an organization and an organism: a monastery is an organism in which each separate organ plays a part, and for the healthy life of which each organ's needs are consulted. A Benedictine council and chapter are the ordinary and public occasions at which these needs are expressed and listened to. There is no guarantee that the opinions ventilated will be acted upon, but at least the opportunity is given to the abbot of benefiting from what he hears.

In the sequence of these earlier chapters can be seen the orderliness of St. Benedict's mind. Having neatly catalogued the different kinds of monks to be found in religion, having based the
cenobitical society upon the authority of the abbot, he now
defines the practical structure of the monastic society.

As often as any important matters have to be transacted
in the monastery, let the abbot call together the whole community, and himself declare what is the question to be settled. And, having heard the counsel of the brethren, let him
weigh it within himself, and then do what he shall judge
most expedient. We have said that all should be called to
council, because it is often to the younger that the Lord
reveals what is expedient.

So it is clear that the abbot may not act, even if they appear
to come straight from God, upon his private impulses. Because
his rule is to be sovereign it does not mean it may be arbitrary.
His measures are not, any more than are the acts of his subjects,
unanswerable. The abbot who is dictated to by his whims is as
badly placed as the community that is at their mercy. Precisely so
as to obtain the benefit of right reason, the abbot is enabled to
judge matters of importance in the common light of many minds.
Where you have a community of souls who are seriously
walking in the ways of grace, you have reserves of supernatural
wisdom from which to draw. A superior, however clear his own
light upon a given issue, should feel glad of the chance to put his
projects before the brethren assembled in chapter. The opinions
which he will hear should strengthen his faith in the Holy Spirit's
guidance of the community.
In laying down these regulations St. Benedict is not calling for
anything new. He is simply formulating the early monastic tradition of government. Even the secular government of his day
was run on the same kind of system and recognized the same
kinds of power: one man in charge and a senate to help him. Like
the secular, the monastic system was hierarchic: officials appointed by the head, each one enjoying a delegated and defined
authority. These officials, removable at the abbot's will, were to

take no important step without consultation with the abbot. Where matters of general moment were in question, it was for the abbot to summon the whole community for open discussion.

It would seem that the more important the issue, the wider the forum of consultation. St. Benedict distinguishes beween *praecipua* and *minora*. On minor points, as we shall see, the abbot was to consult a body of selected seniors. From the wording of the Rule it seems clear that St. Benedict's intention was to leave his abbot free to ignore, even in weightier matters, the majority opinion. Rome has since overridden this intention, and today less is left to the abbot's discretion. While there are still a whole number of questions which he may determine himself, there are others for which he needs the consent of the *familia*.

It is interesting, and perhaps contrary to expectation, to find that St. Benedict sets store by the opinions of the young. One might imagine that in taking the *judicium domesticum* of the Roman household as his standard, the legislator would prefer the role of the juniors to be a silent one. "Show your hand, but hold your peace" might have been the directive given to the younger members of the chapter. But quite the contrary. "Speak your mind, Brother, we are listening." We find that the juniors, the degrees of humility notwithstanding, are invited to state their views.

Perhaps in this St. Benedict is reflecting his authority, Cassian, who frequently champions the cause of youth. "The competency of old men," Cassian quotes Abbot Moses as saying, "is not to be measured by their grey hairs. Ancients, grown old in lukewarmness and ignorance . . . claim authority over youth, not through the holiness of their lives, not through the strictness of their observance, but merely through the respect due to their old age." St. Benedict returns to this idea in his sixty-third chapter, where he points out that God made use of Samuel and David in their youth to communicate His will. In his own monastery at Monte Cassino the saint associated as much with St. Placid and St. Maurus, juniors in the habit, as with the seniors, and we can assume that this was not solely because their company was congenial.

The final point to be noted in the passage quoted is the reference to the abbot's appreciation of what is "best." In chapter the abbot will hear many good views, but what he is to listen for is the opinion which has more of God's will in it than the others. He is not to wait for the expression of the view which happens to be his own—as though the expression of it gave him the excuse for enforcing it—but rather keep his mind open to the infusion of light. If the abbot comes before the chapter with his mind made up, what is the point of summoning it? Surely the tenor of St. Benedict's injunctions on this subject assumes an abbot who has a mind of his own, but who is ready to change it if he sincerely believes such a change to be God's will. "It is often to the younger that the Lord reveals what is best"—possibly because the minds of the young are more open, less prejudiced, more ready to come to the forum of conventual chapter expecting light. It is the tendency among the elders to receive their brethren's opinions on the hard surface of preconception.

> But let the brothers give their advice with all subjection of humility, and not presume stubbornly to defend their own opinion; but rather let the matter rest with the abbot's discretion, that all may submit to whatever he shall consider best. . . . Let all, therefore, follow the Rule in all things as their guide, and from it let no man rashly turn aside. Let no one in the monastery follow the will of his own heart; nor let anyone presume insolently to contend with his abbot, either within or without the monastery.

St. Benedict, as so often in the Rule, passes from the constitutional to the ethical and the moral. The brethren must know their place, must stifle the tendency to assertiveness, must bow to the decisions arrived at. It is impressive in any monastic assembly to watch this exhortation carried out. The truculent speech strikes the wrong note, is painful to hear, and cannot but do harm to what may be the truly monastic cause by which it is prompted. The vow of *conversio* (or *conversatio*) *morum* should have the effect, even if other considerations have not, of curbing a monk's too natural flamboyance in conventual chapter. The

"monasticity of manners" to which we are pledged should effectively drive from our chapter-houses such expressions of self as
sarcasm, retaliation, veiled criticism, oblique reference to controversial matter not under discussion, low comedy, and personal
infallibility.

The monk, though he may not think of it in this way, is accordingly being "worldly" when in monastic chapter—or for the
matter of that anywhere else—he indulges in oratorical flourishes
and fireworks, displays of ill-temper, cynicism and smartness.
It may not be a sin to be pompous, but to be opinionated may
offend against monastic humility and decorum. Flippancy, again,
may not be a sin, but it may offend against monastic tact and
good taste. To speak at length without necessity is an offence
against charity.

Cassian shows, by citing the edifying example of Abbot Moses,
that prolixity in even the most elevating of public discourses is
to be avoided. "But allow me to say," he quotes from Abbot
Moses, "that since the short space of the night which remains will
not suffice to complete the conference, let us give the time to
bodily rest . . . for it becomes the masters of this virtue of discretion to show by their own conduct the excellency of that upon
which they are consulted . . . so that when speaking with moderation of that virtue which is the mother of moderation, they may
avoid all excess which is opposed to it. The first effect will be
the moderation we observe in the limits and extent of this conference."[1]

St. Benedict notes that in all things the Rule is to guide the
deliberations of conventual chapter. It is the Rule, and not current opinion and practice outside the monastery, that must be
the standard of reference. In the Rule we have a cut and dried
norm to which abbot and community are alike bound by vow.
The abbot, with the help of the community, interprets the Rule:
neither he nor they may discard it.

Once the abbot has interpreted the Rule, pronounced his decision, closed the proceedings, there is to be no criticism either
within or without the monastery. The brethren are to assume in

[1] *Conferences,* 1; ch. 23.

faith that there is no difference between the Rule and the abbot's understanding of it. And sometimes this requires great faith.

Even where the individual monk's reason refuses to accept the abbot's ruling as reflecting the mind of St. Benedict expressed in the Rule, there must be submission in the will. And where there is submission in the will there can be suppression of criticism. Unless this absolute silence is imposed upon the natural inclination to rend apart what has been built into one by the mere human word of another, there can be no true peace in the subject's soul.

Sometimes the knowledge that it is impossible to reverse a superior's decision sends the subject, by way of compensation, into destructive criticism. Even if it never comes out into the open with explicit murmuring, the resistance in the mind is bad and must be worn down.

The motion which you so much hoped would be approved has been defeated? The point in the holy Rule which you felt to have but one meaning has been read in another sense altogether? The brethren whom you counted upon for support have failed to rally?—have even subjected you and your view to ridicule? Nothing could more surely manifest to you God's will. All this is what you have taken on, though perhaps not what you bargained for, when you embraced God's will in preference to your own.

When we take on God's will we take it on in its entirety. If we accept only its foreseen manifestation and not also its unpredictable consequences, we are restricting our acceptance by about half. We are virtually choosing to submit to that aspect of God's will which happens to coincide with our own. We are certainly closing our will to that revelation of Himself which most demands the act of faith. The purest act of faith is that which does not anticipate, does not perceive. "Blessed are they that have not seen and have believed."[2]

In accepting God's will in love and faith, we do roughly the same as when we accept a person in love and faith. Just as we love the whole person, weaknesses and all, so we love the whole

[2] John 20;29.

of God's will, apparent inconsistencies and all. In human love we do not bargain about future possibilities; nor in the love of God should we close our hearts to what we do not know. In either case it is confidence, otherwise faith, that leaves the future open to any eventuality.

We do not like the sufferings resulting from the declaration of God's will—any more than we like the unlovable qualities which we see in those whom we love—but we do not concentrate on the contingent elements. We accept, and love what is essential and significant: we love the whole.

The monk who surrenders to the whole of God's will is not likely to ventilate his disappointments either to his brethren or to externs. St. Benedict's phrase "within or without the monastery" reveals the sad truth that men who have suffered set-backs to their hopes, especially as the result of differences with the abbot, are prone to look for sympathetic listeners. But whether their humiliation has come to them in public during conventual chapter, or in private during an interview with authority, "let no one follow the will of his own heart, nor insolently contend with his abbot." It need hardly be said that to present the stubborn or martyred attitude before those outside is even more reprehensible than to do so with only one's brethren as witness.

But, as already suggested, the whole and only solution to the frustrations endured in the religious life, to the slow sense of disillusion as much as to the quick flash of resentment and rebellion, is faith in the fact of God's will. Nothing else matters. "My Beloved to me, and I to him . . . I to my Beloved, and his turning is towards me."[3] So long as the monk can hold on to the conviction that God's will is ever turned towards him for good and not for idle pain or waste, he has nothing to fear. It is the thought of God's indifference that cripples effort in religion and allows a man's spirituality to trail along on broken wings.

If it happen that less important matters have to be transacted for the advantage of the monastery, let him [the abbot] take counsel with the seniors only, as it is written: "Do all things with counsel, and thou shalt not afterwards repent it."

[3] Cant. 2;16 and 7;10.

This council of seniors is an altogether different thing from the conventual chapter at which the whole *familia* must assemble. It treats of less important subjects and does not carry so strong a power of veto. Its function is either to prepare material for the larger body to decide upon or simply to advise the abbot in questions of domestic order. Each Benedictine Congregation has its own instructions to follow as regards the meetings of such councils, what powers attach to their consent, and how far the abbot is bound by their vote. Necessary as the present-day council undoubtedly is, it certainly reduces the sovereign paternal authority which was given to the abbot in St. Benedict's time. Dom Delatte, speaking from the experience of many years as abbot, says: "We do not think an abbot has anything to regret in the loss of the freedom and initiative of former times. It is enough that present legislative arrangements come from the Church for them to deserve to be well received. Certainly the Church has seen to it that quite a number of matters are beyond the range of the abbot's unaided decision; today a scaled list of subjects exists for the respective attention of the council, the conventual chapter, the general chapter.

"Yet in communities which are wisely governed and which have a good spirit," concludes Dom Delatte, "things go on always much as they did in the days of St. Benedict: a feeling of filial trust causes matters which he knows better than anyone else to be left to the discretion of the abbot . . . and all is done in harmonious concord."

In lumine tuo, the monks might say as they gather for whatever meeting it may be at which they will be called upon to vote, *videbimus lumen.* They certainly have the comfort of knowing that whatever their doubt about the direction of God's will, a light upon which they may rely is the reflected light of their abbot's wishes. An abbot may want the mistaken thing, may force upon the community a measure or a policy which is not at all liked by the brethren; it remains nevertheless true that where on the subject's part there is a genuine inability to decide, the abbot's intentions are normally the surest pointers to follow.

The motion on the agenda-paper may not be sign from heaven,

but at least it has the savour of authority's desire. "We will run after thee to the odour of thy ointments,"[4] we can say—in the knowledge that we are speaking through the human authority to the divine.

[4] Cant. 1;3.

CHAPTER 4

WHAT ARE THE INSTRUMENTS OF GOOD WORKS

For most monks it is not the principle that is in doubt; it is the performance. But it must be the performance that proves the principle or the understanding of the vocation is wasted. Lacking co-operation, the vocation itself is wasted. Unless the impulse that moved the man to give himself to God in religion is continued in day-to-day practice, it would have been better to have received no impulse at all. Since the impulse was a matter of grace, of light, it may even be said that ignorance and blindness were preferable to knowledge and vision. If they had not had a vocation, such souls would not have had sin, but because they knew and saw, their vocation is to them sin.

Vocation, like Christ Himself, is something which is set for the rise and fall of many in Israel. Thus if the routines of prayer and work which make up the religious life are to have any supernatural meaning at all, there must be a swelling desire for union with God which is the end of the whole undertaking. It is to ensure, or at least to promote, this desire that St. Benedict drew up the instruments of good works.

These injunctions, succinct and couched in machine-gun language, are to be understood in their positive and constructive sense. Even where expressed in terms of prohibition they are truly instruments—exhortations, that is, and not merely warnings, deterrents, threats. They suppose a monastic body which is striving to build itself up to its full stature of perfection. Elimination of defects is brought about in exercising, or at least aiming at, "good works."

A superficial reading of the Rule might lead a man to think that St. Benedict's idea was to present a society which would be free from the grosser obstacles to Christian perfection. But the Benedictine life amounts to more than a determined refusal to go back on one's vows. In religion we have other things to do besides not running away from the monastery.

"Freedom from cancer and consumption does not mean that a body is healthy," says F. J. Sheed; "freedom from divorce and birth-control does not mean that a marriage is healthy. A body may be free from major diseases, yet unhealthy and devitalized: so may a marriage." So also may a monastery. To understand health, as the same author goes on to explain, we must study health—"the conditions in which a thing is most fully itself and most abounding in vitality."[1]

As in a human body and a natural family, so in a human soul and a supernatural family: we must study the good proposed and at the same time provide as far as possible the conditions in which the monastic family, and each member of it, may be most fully itself and most abounding in vitality. The chapter on the instruments of good works helps precisely this study.

St. Benedict, having outlined the nature of the society which he wants his monastery to be, now gives the means by which the perfection of that society is to be attained. The monk who lives up to the implications of this chapter has found himself, has found Christ. The monastery which takes this chapter as its monastic gospel has found itself, has become the family of God which it is meant to be.[2]

St. Benedict is not the first in the field with this sort of thing. The idea of presenting "maxims" or "sentences" goes back to the philosophers before Christ. The Rules of St. Macarius and St. Pachomius are largely composed of axioms derived, as most of St. Benedict's are, from the Scriptures. Cassian twice speaks of

[1] *Society and Sanity*, p. 141.
[2] Cf. Eph. 2;19,20.

"instruments" in connection with advancing in virtue, and commentators have assumed that it was from him that St. Benedict borrowed the term.

It is possible that St. Benedict, unlike Cassian, is thinking of the texts themselves—"here are the approved statements about the quest for perfection"—and that his *instrumenta* accordingly mean written testimony. The point is academic. What the saint clearly wants is that his seventy-two injunctions should represent the doctrine taught: each one, as he says at the end of the list, is a tool in the workshop.

> In the first place to love the Lord God with all one's heart, all one's soul, all one's strength. Then one's neighbour as oneself . . . not to covet. Not to bear false witness. To honour all men. Not to do to another what one would not have done to oneself. To deny oneself in order to follow Christ. To chastise the body. Not to seek after delicate living. To love fasting.

Charity, because it is at once all-demanding and all-embracing, comes first. It is the only thing in the world that admits no limits. As such, it is the virtue on which the specifically monastic virtues will have to be built.

Love is given by the whole man, and hence by the whole monk. Divine worship must call upon all the human powers. Heart, soul, strength: each dedicated to God. When the affections have been surrendered, to be directed towards God alone but to be used in relation to creatures if God should demand this expression as part of love's service and sacrifice, then, and then only, has detachment begun in the will. When the soul, rejecting superficial impressions of God, stretches out to God in purity and truth ("I will seek him whom my soul loveth"),[3] then is God loved for Himself alone and not for His gifts. Lastly, God is loved with all the soul's strength when His love is made the object of every power and appetite: "I held him: and I will not let him go."[4]

Love of God is proved by, and cannot exist apart from, love of neighbour. St. Benedict follows up the Law of Moses and Christ's

[3] Cant. 3;2.
[4] *Ibid.*, 3;4.

precept with a word-for-word quotation from St. Mark.[5] Since the life for which he is legislating is essentially the corporate life of the community, the saint will have much to say in amplification of this second instrument of good works.

Because fraternal charity is the theme of this section of the Rule, the first nine instruments give us the motive and range of our duty towards others. (They have not all been repeated above, since they merely echo the decalogue.) On the negative side they forbid expressions of uncharity; on the positive side they demand the elementary, though high, acceptance of the Christian ideal. Monks are not to consider themselves above learning the first principles of Christ's code.

"To honour all men" and "not to covet" come so familiarly and obviously that they tend to be taken as read. In the same way we assume that we in monasteries do not bear false witness. Yet do we never in fact envy the chances, the advancements, the rewards of our fellow monks? Do we really honour all in the community? Are we never guilty of accusing others unjustly?

St. Benedict is providing for a social unit, for a congregation of human beings, and he knows that half the miseries that exist in the social order are to be traced to covetousness, rash judgment, and a want of respect for the dignity of man. Probably more than half the vocational failures—let alone the minor upsets resulting from misquotation of people's indiscreet remarks, from unwise comparison of merit, from low views of people's motives—spring from a neglect of these apparently elementary instruments of good works.

To bear false witness, in the full sense, may be hardly even a temptation to the monk. Nor is he likely to dwell deliberately on the thought of what excellent goods another is allowed to enjoy while he himself is fitted out with what is inferior. Again he does not *dis*honour, in the sense of treating with manifest scorn, his brethren. But what a wealth of difference there is between this and the cultivation of the opposite attitude. Should not a monk aim at being habitually *un*envious, refusing to be jealous of a brother's achievement, or promotion, or response in the form of

[5] Mark 12;31.

a following? Should he not be prepared to drop every form of
backbiting, even the kind that is excused on the ground of lend-
ing interest and amusement to community recreation? Should he
not "honour," which presumably means actively strive to reverence, the members of his community?

Nothing is so damaging to family life as an aptitude for superiority. Brother can isolate himself from brother, each looking
down as from a great height. Both may know in their hearts that
they have manoeuvered themselves into false positions, but
neither will climb down. They come to exaggerate each other's
faults—partly in an effort to cover up their own, and partly to
justify their conduct—and this inevitably leads to harsh con-
demnations expressed to others in the house. The recognition
accorded to one of them is taken by the other as a slight to himself. St. Benedict did well to group these three instruments together. No envy, no overt criticism, no despising a neighbour.

After gentleness towards one's brother, the next thing is stern-
ness towards oneself. In order to follow Christ, says St. Benedict,
one must go against self: no soft living, no evasion of the discipline of fasting. If self-love is the enemy of our perfection, self-
denial is the friend of our perfection and all that leads to it.

Corrupt nature must be punished; the animal will in man must
be bent and trained till it is worthy, as a rational power, to co-
operate habitually with supernatural grace. The body, with its
animal instincts, must be kept in subjection to the spirit.

In his Prologue, St. Benedict stressed the need for a *return* to
God, and a *laborious* return, so it is not surprising that early in
the catalogue of instruments he warns of the strictly ascetical
side of the life. The "good works" are not acquired by holding
out your scapular and watching them drop into it.

The present century has witnessed a marked falling-off in the
matter of penance. Bodily mortification is rarely preached about,
and directors are becoming increasingly shy of recommending it.
But are we to believe that the whole business of "returning to
God" is effected by a vague act of accepting the ordinary set-
backs of every day?

St. Benedict explicitly tells us to chastise the body, to forswear luxury, to love fasting. Is this a piece of pious antiquarianism? For monks to pamper the body, to delight in creature comforts which are just not worldly enough to be sinful, to take elaborate precautions against having to fast, is the kind of monastic anomaly which brings the whole idea of the religious life into disrepute. If loss of prestige were the worst of its evil consequences it would not matter so much, but such unconcern for the earlier Benedictine tradition exposes the individual soul to the danger of losing the monastic spirit altogether. Mortification, voluntary and physical, is the astringent necessary to the health of the soul. Without the antitoxic quality of corporal penance, the monk risks infection from the world: the poison of sin is not kept out of the cloister either by the walls which surround the enclosure or by the general resolve to take everyday trials in one's stride. For the avoidance of the evils which threaten the religious, and by this is meant not only sin but every form of dangerous worldliness, there has to be a combination of love and stern self-renunciation.

While self-love can never be dethroned by penances, at least its tyranny can be checked. The reason why self-love must remain a continued menace to advancement in the love of God is that in fallen human nature it is integral to the essential human desire for happiness. The desire for happiness is not an evil but a good. Mixed up with every legitimate instinct for self-realization, however, is a selfishness which is the last enemy to a man's perfection, and therefore to happiness itself.

Though grace is needed to curb self-will effectively, the compunction which shows itself in voluntary penance, and which is itself an effect of grace, acts both as a sure discipline and as the goodwill offering which most surely invites the mobilization of the forces of grace.

The way to grace is through penance, and the way to penance is through grace. Penance is at once the disposition and the effect. No man can come to Christ unless he is drawn by grace, and the grace of being drawn nearer to Christ shows itself in compunction of heart and desire for amendment. St. Benedict is careful in the wording of his axiom: it is *in order to follow Christ* that the monk denies himself.

Self-denial without Christ is idle. Indeed not only would it be a waste of time and energy but it might be a form of vanity. For a monk to indulge a taste for affliction, in the name of affliction alone, would be no better than to indulge any other taste. Pain for the sake of pain is no good at all; it is an evil.

The monk chastises the body, then, for these reasons: to bring it into subjection to the spirit; to show in an outward and appropriate way that he is sorry for his sins, and is ready to help in atoning for the sins of others; to bear witness to the Passion of Christ. The monk knows that it is solely in virtue of Christ's sufferings that there is any value attaching to his penance. From the infinite store of merit laid at man's disposal by the Passion of Christ, the monk draws the graces which make his own mortifications worth while.

The "delicate living" mentioned by St. Benedict is not normally provided in monasteries, but it can sometimes be procured. The monk who seeks it can usually get permission for it; but he does so at his spiritual peril. Abbots not unnaturally find it hard to oppose those subjects who are bent upon an easy existence—particularly since indulgence in luxuries has a way of so blinding the indulgent as to make them incapable of seeing any harm in their concessions—with the result that physical comfort can come to be preferred before almost anything else.

The fasting which St. Benedict recommends as a corrective to this can be effective only if it is "loved." Where it is resented, fasting quite fails to counter delicacy of living, and becomes a source of bitterness. Sooner or later its discipline is either whittled down till it becomes meaningless or else it is abandoned altogether. To follow our holy Father's mind in the whole matter of renunciation, we have to *want* the recommendations which he puts forward. To love fasting is not to enjoy it; it is to see its point and to want to benefit by its exercise.

More will be said about fasting when St. Benedict's regulations regarding the allowance of food and drink are examined. It is enough to stress here that fasting, like silence and enclosure, is part of the monastic imposition. If a monk's aim is a particular kind of perfection, then going hungry is a particular kind of penance proper to it. Anyway this is what St. Benedict says, and it is not for the individual monk to judge differently.

> To relieve the poor . . . to visit the sick . . . to console the sorrowing. To keep aloof from worldly actions. To prefer nothing to the love of Christ. Not to gratify anger. Not to harbour a desire for revenge . . . to utter truth from heart and mouth . . . to do no wrong to anyone, yea, to bear patiently wrong done to oneself.

The roots of self-love, as we have seen, strike deep. But in the measure that we try to prevent its growth, the practice of the beatitudes and the corporal works of mercy will be accelerated. The man who is genuinely willing to deny himself will find himself increasingly concerned about the poor, the sick, the sorrowing. In the ordinary way it will not fall to the lot of the individual monk to see to the needs of the indigent—this being the duty of the council or particular officials of the monastery— but when the occasion presents itself the brethren should be ready to go without so that the less fortunate should not be in want. In some communities appeals are made for clothing, for example, or for books. It would not be acting in the spirit of this instrument of good works to dismiss such appeals as touching only the bursar or the librarian. Still less would it be interpreting it in its true sense to respond promptly with the sacrifice of clothes and literature, and then to get permission for new things to replace the old.

Nor should the sick and aged be considered the exclusive province of the infirmarian. It is a corporal work not only of mercy but of monasticity to visit the sick. For one reason or another it is possible for the infirm in even the most fervent community to suffer long stretches of loneliness. The brethren are too busy, the cell of the sick brother is too far away, there is my spiritual reading which I must get in, today is the day when we have a choir-practice (or an abbot's conference, or a chapter of faults), so the sick are left to the infirmarian, to their trays, and—worst of all—to their thoughts.

In the work of consoling the sorrowing we are on more intimate ground. Not everyone has the gift, and it requires considerable tact. But compassion remains a duty nevertheless, and is not a requisite emotion merely. It must surely be the experience of everyone in a community that at one time or another a fellow religious comes to him for sympathy. It may be that he comes only to find a listener, and not to get advice or positive help. Every religious man must be ready at a moment's notice, and at inconvenience, to console. He must be ready to go out of his way to seek out, if he sincerely thinks this to be a good and not an officious thing, the sufferer: he must make the Good Shepherd his model here, and leave the ninety-nine calls upon his time, his care, his interest, to bring comfort where he feels it to be needed.

Pity is feeling sorry for someone; compassion is feeling sorry *with* someone. Compassion is one of the most expansive and comprehensive of virtues; true spirituality cannot fail to engender it. Wherever you find monasticism at its best, you find compassion at its most true.

The fathers of the desert were rough men, schooled in austerity, but they valued the virtue of compassion. Of St. Anthony the hermit, an ascetic if ever there was one, Evagrius says: "his conversation, which was seasoned with wit, consoled the sad and reconciled enemies." This saint, who was the pattern for monks in the early history of the religious life, not only showed particular tenderness towards the depressed but further bore out St. Benedict's instruments by "persuading all that nothing should be preferred to the love of Christ."

In holding himself aloof from worldly actions the monk is fulfilling the programme outlined for him in the Prologue and demanded of him by his vow of *conversio morum*. Except as trying to help it, monks may not love the world. The things of the world spell death to the monastic ideal. Neither the pleasures of the world nor its wisdom, standards, opinions or fashions have any place in the monk's life. With St. Paul, the monk should be able to say that the world is crucified to him and that he is crucified to the world.[6]

"It is painful to mention that many pretend to renounce the

[6] Gal. 6;14.

world," says Cassian, "yet change not their manner of living but only their habit . . . if these religious did seriously desire the way of perfection, they would strive with all their energy to attain it; they would strip themselves not only of their earthly possessions but still more of their former affections, cares and anxieties."[7] When St. Benedict speaks of worldly actions he is forbidding the monk other things besides mundane affectations and mannerisms: he is telling his disciples to cultivate a different outlook altogether from the world's—to make spiritual judgments, and so to rise above actions which are of the world.

The principle of putting nothing before the love of Christ is a favourite one with St. Benedict: it comes again in the seventy-second chapter and is implicit in a number of passages relating to obedience. A familiar theme in the writings of the Fathers, it can serve as a practical guide in the whole moral and ascetical life.[8] The man who habitually brings his decisions to the bar of Christ's love, judging every issue as affecting His love for us and our love for Him, must arrive at that delicacy of feeling for Christ's interests which in effect amounts to constant recollection.

The maxims which immediately follow in the list are concerned with keeping the peace in community life. But it should be noted that they aim at keeping peace also in the individual soul. In fact the social peace, if it is to be supernatural as well as social, must spring from the interior disposition. A monk may not be able to help feeling resentful, but if he is not to break out into acts of revenge he must refuse to dwell on his resentment. The cherished hurts of a sensitive nature are as harmful to the spiritual life as the explosions of the more bucolic.

Magnanimity is a condition both of corporate harmony and personal serenity. If the monk is to be a man who keeps aloof from worldly actions, he must also be a man who keeps aloof from bearing malice. If Christian perfection asks of us "to bear patiently wrong done to us," monastic perfection asks no less.

[7] *Conferences*, 4; ch. 20.
[8] Dom Delatte quotes St. Cyprian as providing the words used by St. Benedict.

Not to be proud. Not given to wine. Not a glutton. Not drowsy. Not slothful. Not a murmurer. Not a detractor. To put one's hope in God. To attribute any good that one sees in oneself to God and not to oneself. But to recognize and always impute to oneself the evil that one does.

Turning from relations towards others, St. Benedict shows us the attitudes which make for balance within ourselves. Though we shall never master pride, we can at least make war on it and subdue vanity. Since the humble man is more able to control his animal nature, the next points to be dealt with are the physical appetites.

Later on we shall see how St. Benedict comes out strongly against the drinking of wine in monasteries, but he does not absolutely forbid it. Here, in the instruments, he limits himself to the general principle of moderation. The same temperance is to be shown in eating. These three qualities of humility, restraint in drink, denial of greed, are grouped together by St. Benedict, and it is interesting to note that the hymn for Prime follows the same grouping:

> *Carnis terat superbiam*
> *Potus cibique parcitas:*
> *Ut cum dies abscesserit,*
> *Noctemque sors reduxerit,*
> *Mundi per abstinentiam*
> *Ipsi canamus gloriam.*

The motive, moreover, in St. Benedict is the same as that expressed in the hymn: namely, the glory of God. Man can give glory to God only where there is the right relation between the inward and the outward; only, in other words, where there is integrity of life. The true life of the monk is the life dedicated to the service of God's glory, and in this there is no room for physical excess. To serve God from the depths of his being, a man must be mortified as well as meek.

Sloth is an evil which from the earliest years of monasticism has come in for its measure of attack, exposure, ridicule, and punishment. Sloth has its by-products which are as much to be avoided as the vice itself. Bitterness, murmuring, contempt for the rules, refusal to help out in an emergency, the numberless furtive infidelities which the idle monk indulges in simply so as to escape the hideous burden of extended free time—these are only some of the Dead Sea fruits of sloth.

In the *Paradise of the Fathers* we read of an old monk who was asked what a religious man should do that he might live. "Now the old man used to plait palm leaves into mats, and he never lifted up his head from the work of his hands but occupied himself at all times therewith. And the old man answered and said to him that asked the question: 'Behold what thou seest.' "[9]

From the *Dialogues* we get the well-known phrase of St. Benedict's, *Ecce labora, et noli contristari.*[10] And if this, particularly in its context, needs some special pleading if it is to be cited as an attack upon sloth, there is the incident from the same source which tells of the brother who was as idle in prayer as he was out of it, and who needed to be exorcised before he was put right.[11]

The vice of smouldering discontent is one to which the saint will return in another chapter. Murmuring is a spreading disease; a community can suffer its spirit to be wrecked by the presence of a minority of active grumblers. To see faults and remain uncensorious is virtuous; to look for faults and talk about them is vicious. There is nobody so disedifying in a religious body as the soured, querulous, self-pitying monk or nun. This particular kind of acid seeps through the enclosure wall and can be a cause of sad disillusionment to those outside.

Ultimately the reason why religious people murmur is that they are lacking in trust. If they were to put their whole hope in God (as the instrument following those about murmuring and detracting tells them to do), they would be proof against the disappointments which give them grounds for complaint. The

[9] Bk. 2; ch. 1, 198.
[10] Bk. 2; ch. 6.
[11] *Ibid.*, ch. 5.

soul that can mean *in te domine speravi, non confundar* has little to fear from the temptation to malicious criticism.

To give credit to God for whatever good we see in ourselves, and to take the blame for whatever evil, is in the last analysis only common sense. But these things are not always easy to do, so they are counted to us for virtue. Dom Delatte points out that in St. Benedict's day it was particularly necessary to recall the doctrines of grace and free-will: particularly necessary therefore to stress the soul's dependence upon God and the reality of personal guilt. "Thou hast wrought all our works for us" is the acknowledgment which we must echo from Isaias.[12] "He has filled Sion with judgment and justice," says the same prophet.[13] There is nothing of our own of which we can boast: all has been lent: we owe everything to the Source and Author of all good. Shame at having offended is something which we can call our own; and this, if it is not to lead to discouragement, must be turned to the service of contrition.

> To fear the day of Judgment. To be in dread of hell. To desire with all spiritual longing everlasting life. To keep death daily before one's eyes. To keep guard at all times over the actions of one's life. To know for certain that God sees one everywhere.

Though we may confidently count upon the promises made to those who leave the world at the call of grace to enter religion, we may not rule out the possibility of damnation. The Judgment and its consequences may not be dismissed out of hand. Sin and its consequences still have their bearing upon our calculations. It would be a mistake, for instance, to adopt the attitude of a certain Benedictine abbess who, after questioning one of her nuns on the subject of a retreat-conference, was heard to say with some heat: "Mortal sin indeed! What does he think we are?"

Our dread of punishment need not be morbid to be true. It need not be imaginative or particularly forced. But it should be there—to be drawn upon when loftier motives for right action

[12] Isai. 26;12.
[13] *Ibid.*, 33;5.

fail. The course to be followed is suggested by the sequence of St. Benedict's instruments: the monk should cultivate an ardent desire for everlasting life. But it must be a spiritual desire, not the purely natural desire to escape from the afflictions of this life.

Death, "kept daily before one's eyes," must be waited for in patience. Too repugnant to some, the thought of death is to others too inviting. There must be calmness in the consideration of death or the implied graces are wasted. Detachment from its superficial aspects is in this, as in so much else in the spiritual life, an essential condition: we must want death as God wills it for us, and when God wills it. But want it we may, and let no one tell us otherwise.

Those who "desire with all spiritual longing everlasting life," and who look forward to death as the means towards the fulfilment of that desire, will instinctively "keep guard over the actions of their lives." To the man who lives in terms of eternity it requires no great effort to put temporal affairs in perspective: his actions are not only preserved from the defects of irresponsibility, impulse, passion, but on the positive side are seen to take on a supernatural significance. The spiritually minded man can so "watch over his actions"—because in fact he is watching God —as to direct them in praise towards Him who is at once their inspiration and their end.

This is what we mean when we say that God is in our works, and that our works are performed in Him. Since God, moreover, rewards only His own works, and since works performed apart from God are works of self, it is vital that the actions of one's life be canalized as well as guarded. One's works are material only to the degree that one allows them to be so; there is nothing to prevent them from being spiritual.

When St. Benedict says that we must keep guard over our actions he is directing them towards their proper object, namely God. We watch over our actions because God is watching over our actions—because God is drawing them towards Himself and making them His. Our actions are valuable only in so far as they are His. Nothing done by man alone has any value. To leave God out is man's greatest folly, greatest sin. "Without Me you can do nothing." God looks for His own activity in every work of ours. It is for us therefore to guard our works from ourselves, so that they may be wholly His.

The knowledge that God, "the unsleeping watcher over Israel,"[14] observes our actions should be the greatest incentive to recollection. But it is an idea that has to be understood correctly. Taken in a superficial sense—as, for example, to imagine the eye of God following us about—it would lead to strain, and ultimately to disgust. Taken rightly, *in omni loco Deum se respicere pro certe scire* can lead, according to St. Bernard, to the heights of contemplation. "The exercise which in itself is worth all else," says that saint, "is the continual remembrance of God . . . so that no day nor hour shall not find the servant of God engaged in this work, in the endeavour to make progress or in the enjoyment of divine consolations."

The habit of recollection is not arrived at by force but by grace. Grace, however, demands deliberate and constant co-operation. And though force may not promote recollection, careful management does. We are expected to organize ourselves, to plan our day ahead, to make use of our opportunities, to choose out the devices and devotions which help us, and make serious efforts to avoid whatever is found to distract. "All the days of thy life," said Tobias to his son, "have God in mind."[15]

Certainly the psalmist drew profit from the thought of God's comprehensive presence. If at first he is corrected by the fear which God's presence inspires, he is all the more comforted by the security which he finds in it. "Whither shall I flee from thy face? . . . if I . . . dwell in the uttermost parts of the sea, even there also shall thy hand lead me. . . . And I said: Perhaps darkness shall cover me, and night shall be my light in my pleasures. But darkness shall not be dark to thee." Two verses later he is saying: "Thou hast protected me from my mother's womb; I will praise thee, for thou art fearfully magnified."[16] And in the psalm immediately following: "Thou hast overshadowed my head in

[14] Ps. 120;4.
[15] Tob. 4;6.
[16] Ps. 138;7-14.

the day of battle, O Lord the strength of my salvation."[17] The theme that we are never out of God's sight is returned to by St. Benedict when he makes it an incentive to attention at the Divine Office. The vigilance of God should be the means of stirring the vigilance of man.

To dash down at the feet of Christ one's evil thoughts the instant that they come into the heart. To lay them open to one's spiritual father. To keep one's mouth from evil and wicked words. Not to love much speaking. Not to speak vain words or such as move to laughter. Not to love much or excessive laughter.

Of the above instruments, the first two are to be taken together: instant rejection of evil thoughts, to be followed by admission to a "spiritual father." No sooner does the presence of evil disclose itself in the monk's soul than Christ is called upon for help. Christ's help is again sought through the medium of one who represents Him. The practice of making a manifestation of conscience is a familiar one with the ancients. In the lives of the desert fathers there are frequent references to monks unburdening themselves to their fellow monks—sometimes to obtain absolution but sometimes merely to obtain relief—and Cassian has a passage in the *Institutes* recommending the custom.[18]

The question of "much speaking" and "speaking vain words" can be left till we come to St. Benedict's sixth chapter, which deals with the spirit of silence. The love of "much and excessive laughter" can be considered here, because though the matter of noisy behaviour comes up later (again in the same chapter on silence) it will then be used as an illustration rather than as the main theme.

Clearly St. Benedict does not mean to ban gaiety from community recreation. All religious leaders and founders of religious orders seem to be agreed that lightness of heart is a good thing, and that there should be an exchange of unserious matter between the brethren. Then what does St. Benedict mean? If his words do not forbid jokes, what do they forbid?

[17] Ps. 139;8.
[18] Bk. 4; ch. 9.

The best way to answer these questions is to distinguish between different kinds of laughter, between different kinds of
jokes. Probably what St. Benedict is trying to prevent is the
kind of attitude which is interested only in entertaining others
or in being entertained by others. Those in whom the comedian-
mentality is allowed to grow will give rise, either in themselves
or in others, to the wrong sort of laughter and to the wrong sort
of joke.

There is a certain incongruity about the religious man who
is *always* seeing something funny. In the refectory, in the choir,
in the *statio*, in the library—wherever the brethren assemble—
there will inevitably be occasions for humorous comment; but to
be for ever commenting, and to await the recognition of one's
wit, is to go clean contrary to St. Benedict's fifty-fourth and
fifty-fifth instruments of good works. A sense of humour, carried
beyond a certain point, can be a very great bore.

The gaiety expressed in a monastery should never reach the
point at which a detached lay spectator would feel it was becoming worldly. When monastic hilarity strikes a note which is
common to the club or the bar, it qualifies for St. Benedict's
stricture "excessive."

What St. Benedict, in the company of other saints whether
monastic or not, is interested in is developing an appreciation of
true joy. The soul who has learned the meaning of peace, of
happiness in God, of joy in the service of religion, does not want
to laugh excessively. Such a soul may feel as amused as any,
may see jokes, may be perfectly ready to take his share in keeping the conversation from becoming too solemn, but he does not
surrender himself to the luxury of immoderate laughter. He sees
in uncontrolled amusement an indulgence which is on a level
with any other indulgence, and he would rather not indulge himself.

To some this would appear priggish and smug. But could it be
called priggish and smug to let drop extravagances which the
great—even the great of this world—transcend? The extravagance of laughter is released by the emotion of joy awakened
and thrown off its guard by surprise. The saints had their joy

in control, were never completely surprised. Our Lady cannot be thought of as suddenly surprised into laughter.

Laughter can be prompted also by nerves, by catching the infection of another's mood, by an over-eager desire to please. But the soul of the saint is no more committed to this kind of laughter than it is committed to the laughter of mockery, vulgarity, or the common response of mass hysteria. In none of these instances can we see any relation to the joy of our Lady. Neither she nor her Son can have laughed in the way that men laugh who have not the spirit of God.

Delight in God's creatures, in the happiness He allows to man, is a calm and reverent emotion. St. Benedict's aim is so to restrain the boisterous tendencies in man as to allow for the development of true gladness among the brethren. Enjoyment is not incompatible with the life of prayer; heartiness may be. Buffoonery certainly is.

From what has been said it might be thought that St. Benedict was a forbidding character, rigid and granite-faced. We simply do not know. Though it is true that in St. Gregory's life of him there is no mention of St. Benedict's lighter side—he is never recorded as laughing, for instance, or even smiling—there is abundant evidence of the saint's humanity. Both in the Rule and in the *Dialogues* the tenderness of the man stands out a mile. Here, possibly, is the explanation: where respect for one's fellow human beings is cultivated to perfection, there is no call for ebullient expressions of goodfellowship.

Thus to sum up this matter of laughter in the Rule, we can note the following principles. While joy is a good, finding its origin in the unalterable happiness of God, it is also one of the passions. The human passions, if they are to reflect the pro-passions of Christ, must be subject to discipline. The risible faculty of man again is a good, but its proper object, which is laughter, has, like the objects of other appetites, to be regulated. Where there exists in nature an appetite, there exists also an appropriate satisfaction. If there is an instinct in man to laugh, there must be funny things to laugh at. There are—in plenty. But they must be seen in perspective, against the background of more significant realities. Where this focus of vision has become habitual—and we have seen that the whole business of attaining to a sense of true proportion is a matter of responding to Truth itself in prayer— the necessary controls are found to follow.

> To listen willingly to holy reading. To apply oneself frequently to prayer. Daily to confess in prayer one's past sins with tears and sighs to God . . . Not to fulfil the desires of the flesh; to hate one's own will. To obey in all things the commands of the abbot, even though he himself (which God forbid) should act otherwise. . . . Not to wish to be called holy before one is so, but first to be holy that one may be truly so called.

Reading, the *lectio divina* which will be dealt with at length in a later chapter, was intended by St. Benedict to occupy on an average four hours of a monk's day. But this *lectio divina* meant private study, pursued at one's own pace and meditatively. The fifty-sixth instrument of good works may refer to something else, to spiritual reading held in common. There was the time immediately before Compline when the brethren assembled to hear a chapter read from an approved author or from Scripture, and there may have been other occasions as well which would justify the use of the word "listen."

But whether St. Benedict has in mind public or private reading, he clearly means it to be closely linked with the exercise of prayer which is mentioned next in the order of instruments. Spiritual reading is not an end in itself, but it is something more than a means of avoiding the waste of time.

That the saint himself read widely and seriously is seen from the easy way in which quotations slide into the text. So naturally are his own words dovetailed into Biblical passages that it is not at once easy to recognize the difference. In the Rule there are quotations from Genesis, Exodus, Kings, Isaias, Ezechiel, Daniel, Tobias, the sapiential books (particularly Ecclesiasticus and Proverbs), Psalms (between sixty and seventy references), the Gospels, all the Epistles except Hebrews, and the Apocalypse.

So far as non-Scriptural literature is concerned, we learn from

Dom Cuthbert Butler's *index scriptorum* which accompanies his edition of the Rule that St. Benedict quotes explicitly ten times from Cassian, and that he uses this authority as his source in no fewer than eighty places. There are parallel passages between St. Benedict's Rule and the Rules of St. Pachomius, St. Macarius, St. Basil. "Of the Western rules," says Abbot Butler, "he uses that of St. Caesarius of Arles, and the letter (211th) of St. Augustine, which was later called his Rule; this is definitely cited several times." Dom Butler further shows, with ingenuity, that St. Benedict wove three separate sermons of St. Leo into one piece, and that he had also a working knowledge of St. Cyprian, St. Jerome, Sulpicius Severus, and, apart from the example given, St. Augustine. There is a citation also from the *Acts of the Martyrs* and an idea is suggested by one of the Festal Letters of Theophilus attacking Origenism. St. Benedict's familiarity with the *Paradise of the Fathers*, the *Histories of the Solitaries of the Desert of Egypt*, the *Sayings of the Fathers* and the *Questions and Answers of the Holy Men* is shown in a number of allusions and stylistic similarities.

In the *Dialogues* St. Benedict is described as "sitting alone at the monastery gate, and reading."[19] So intent must the saint have been on his reading that even in the height of the emergency which followed, "the holy man rose not from his reading but called upon the brethren to bring the man [a Goth named Galla] to receive his benediction."

If the painter Spinello Aretino six times shows St. Benedict either holding or reading a book, it is not because the artist's imagination failed to find anything better to put instead. Since Aretino is to the *Dialogues* what Giotto is to the life of St. Francis, we can assume that he has caught, in his Florentine murals, the authentic spirit of St. Benedict. The wonder-worker, the father, the judge, the man of prayer—he is there as each— and, as suggested, the reader and student.

Prayer rises out of reading as song rises out of music. Reading is the most appropriate prelude to prayer. To the degree that

[19] Bk. 2; ch. 31.

"faith is from hearing,"[20] prayer is from reading. Just as hearing does not complete the work of faith, so neither does reading complete the work of prayer. Grace works through hearing and reading: from then on the soul must take the work to a new level. On the new level grace again works, and the soul again is moulded by what is learned.

The word of God is communicated to the soul by reading, and is in turn referred back to God again by the soul in prayer. God rejoices in His own word. The soul needs to be fed by the manna of the Scriptures—"not in bread alone doth man live, but in every word that proceedeth from the mouth of God"[21]—so that the most significant of his acts may be expressed in the accents of God.

"The written law is our firmament," says St. Augustine, which means that under its cover we live out our earthly lives. The word of God, studied and applied and acting as the inspiration of our prayer, is the element or setting of our human existence. It is of the created order, but stands above the world. We may not hide from the law of God, nor cheat it. God's revelation is comprehensive.

It is St. Benedict's intention before all else to form his monks as men of prayer. His approach in the Rule is practical rather than mystical, giving guidance on the choral recitation of the Divine Office and leaving the matter of private mental prayer to the direction of the Holy Spirit and the attraction of the individual soul.

Phrased as it is ("to apply oneself frequently to prayer") the instrument under review supposes a prayer which is not strictly of obligation—certainly in regard to set times—and which is presumably not vocal. In his twentieth, and again in his fifty-second chapter, St. Benedict outlines the monk's attitude towards interior prayer. Both passages suppose a direct and simple prayer. Association implies the same here, where the required frequency can be taken to denote devotional rather than liturgical prayer.

[20] Rom. 10;17.
[21] Deut. 8;3. So important is this text that it is quoted by our Lord when tempted by the devil (Matt. 4;4 and Luke 4;4).

We get frequent glimpses in the *Dialogues* of St. Benedict in the act of prayer. Not only does the saint apply himself to prayer on occasions of emergency, as when he raised the dead boy to life[22] or when he cast out a devil,[23] but is frequently mentioned as "praying in accordance with his custom,"[24] "going forward to the chapel to pray,"[25] "making his prayer to Almighty God about midnight."[26] These are incidental references to incidental occasions: the experience in prayer which throws light upon St. Benedict's interior life as a whole will be examined on a later page.

Just as reading promotes prayer, so prayer develops the habit of compunction. Father Merton defines compunction as "a grace by which God draws us to Himself, causing us sorrow for what we have done, aversion from what we are, and fear of what we may yet become." This gives us exactly the disposition required by St. Benedict's fifty-eighth instrument. A mere notional assent to the corrupt nature of man is not enough. "To confess in prayer one's sins with sighs and tears" implies heartfelt regret for personal failure, acknowledgment of guilt, and sincere desire to begin again in the service of love.

The point about compunction is that it does not stop short at remorse. It is not just a sad flat lake. It is more like a spring. Compunction causes the whole being to rise up to God in hope and love. The psalms are full of this true contrition which transforms the soul's attitude from helplessness and despair to complete confidence in the power of grace.

In his Lenten sermons St. Bernard reminds us that compunction is a source of strength. It frees us from our own self-confidence, from our own supports and superficialities, and concentrates our effort in the right direction. When we begin to recognize our weakness, we become strong. Power is made perfect in infirmity. Compunction shows us not only what sinners we are, but what fools we are. With this knowledge we can have

[22] Bk. 2; ch. 32.
[23] *Ibid.*, ch. 16.
[24] *Ibid.*, ch. 27.
[25] *Ibid.*, ch. 30.
[26] *Ibid.*, ch. 35.

confidence that the foolish things of this world has God chosen to confound the wise.

St. Gregory distinguishes between *compunctio timoris* and *compunctio amoris*. Once we have raised the first to the level of the second we have learned the vanity of earthly things. Those creature satisfactions which lured us into sin are exposed for what they are. We are now in a position to detach ourselves from them. Lacking a more or less habitual compunction we are always more or less at the mercy of the creature's attraction. The absence of compunction, says St. Basil, is a sign of tepidity.

Again we find deliberate planning in the sequence of the instruments: from compunction St. Benedict leads on to detachment, denial of self-will, obedience. The assumption is that true sorrow for sin *delivers* us from self-will, *subjects* us to ready obedience. Untrue sorrow, on the other hand, enslaves us further to self-will by making us bitter, exasperated with ourselves, unwilling to make the effort. Untrue sorrow is ultimately the enemy of obedience.

Strictly speaking one cannot "hate one's own will," but one can hate having it. One can suspect its motives, veto its unreasonable demands, employ every variety of discipline in the work of its education. The primary discipline is that of obedience.

Whether or not the abbot happens to live up to his office, the duty of the monk remains the same. If the abbot's lead is a good one, so much the better. But in the final analysis it is what he tells you to do that matters. An artist may be a good or a bad man in private life; it is what he does with his brushes in the studio that concerns his followers in the art-school.

The desire to be thought holy is human and wrong, but it is also so instinctive to the would-be saint that it can hardly be detached from the desire for sanctity itself. But if the soul trains the focus of desire beyond even personal holiness to God Himself, there is less room for these reflex considerations. Where there is a self-constructed norm of sanctity, there is inevitably a tendency to check up on results. It is on results, that is to say on the external, that others are expected to pass their favourable judgments.

What St. Benedict is trying to prevent in this sixty-first instrument is the attitude of mind which says: "You see what my practices are; you see the sort of holiness I am aiming at; you see the kind of life I have chosen to lead. Well then?"

The next nine instruments go over again the teaching contained in some of the earlier ones. They relate mostly to fraternal charity. In one of them, the sixty-third, mention is made for the first and last time in the holy Rule of chastity. Chastity is so much part of the religious obligation that St. Benedict evidently felt no need to single it out for special attention.

Nor need the two concluding instruments delay us long. The seventy-first ("To make peace with an adversary before the setting of the sun") only adds the practical recommendation to the general doctrine of peace and reconciliation; the seventy-second ("Never to despair of God's mercy") is the final rounding-off of St. Benedict's whole teaching on compunction, forgiveness, hope.

The implication in these last injunctions is the single principle of charity with its twofold application. It is as though St. Benedict were saying: "Nothing may be allowed to disturb the harmony either of the community or of the individual soul. If animosities flare up, they must be stamped out the same day; if anyone feels he has completely failed in his vocation, he must know that he can still go on loving God and that God has not ceased to love him. A monk who has offended against all the virtues spoken about in the above list of instruments still has the mercy of God to draw upon."

Having come to the end of his list, the saint adds an epilogue which is of immense significance. In its closing lines it states as categorically as anywhere else in the Rule what are the distinguishing notes of Benedictinism.

> Behold, these are the tools of the spiritual craft, which, if they be constantly employed day and night, and duly given back on the day of Judgment, will gain for us from the Lord that reward which He Himself has promised—"which eye hath not seen nor ear heard; nor hath it entered into the heart of man to conceive what God hath prepared for them

that love Him." And the workshop where we are to labour diligently at all these things is the cloister of the monastery and stability in the community.

The first part of this, except for the quotation from Isaias and Corinthians, comes straight from Cassian. "The artisan does not provide himself with tools necessary for his trade," says Cassian, "that they may remain idle; he does not hope to derive profit from the mere possession of them. No, he seeks by their means to make himself master of his art or trade. It is the same with us in our profession. Fasting, watching, meditation . . . are not themselves perfection but the instruments by which we may acquire perfection."[27] Perfection is there, apparently, for the asking; all that is needed is grace and continued labour. The promised reward may be looked upon not only as an incentive, a bait to attract our self-interest, but as an inspiration which will supernaturalize by anticipation our human endeavours.

That these works are to be performed "in the cloister of the monastery" and under the aegis of stability is the specific feature. Enclosure is not merely a matter of monastic topography; nor is stability merely a matter of monastic congruity.

The idea of enclosure for monks goes back to the earliest days of monasticism. The whole point of a cloister and a cell is that people stay in them. They are designed to provide an enclave for the undisturbed pursuit of perfection. The world is kept out and the activity is kept in.

"On one occasion there was an assembly, and all the old men were asked: 'What opposition is the mightiest against the monks?' And they all agreed that there was none stronger than that which would make a man leave his cell and depart, for when this is overcome, all the rest can quite easily be overcome and brought low."[28]

" 'Flee ye, O brethren,' said Abbot Macarius. And one of the old men asked, 'Whither can we flee farther than this desert?' Then Macarius laid his hand upon his mouth, saying: 'Flee in this manner,' and straightway he went to his cell, shut the door,

[27] *Conferences*, 1; ch. 7.
[28] *Paradise of the Fathers*, Vol. 1; 23.

and sat down."[29] Enclosure may not be as fundamental as stability, but it is an insurance towards it, the most appropriate manifestation of it, and the best way of keeping it.

Enclosure does not guarantee stability any more than stability guarantees enclosure; but the two go together, they are parts of the same ideal. By keeping enclosure a monk conserves energy for God which is otherwise dissipated. Enclosure is the wall of stability, self-possession, recollection. Apart altogether from the monastic and ascetical aspects of it, enclosure has a therapeutic value: restless minds are steadied by it, and, provided the restrictions it imposes are accepted in the right spirit, a soul to whom extroversion would be fatal can become settled.

It was the lack of religious enclosure in the sixth century that called for measures from St. Benedict which were then novel and extreme. We have seen what the saint thought of wandering monks; we shall see, when we come to the vows, what St. Benedict expected of those who applied to join his community. All that we need to note here is that monastic stability means the will to remain steadfastly in the monastery of profession until death.

What St. Benedict makes the material of a vow he wants to make the substance and character of Benedictine spirituality. This is his individual contribution to contemporary monasticism as well as his reaction against its current abuses. Here, in stability, is something which St. Benedict does not take over from Cassian or Basil or Pachomius. It is something which will create a new outlook, impose new standards, develop a new spirit. It will also of course, as the evolution of an ideal must, give rise to new problems and account for new failures.

So long as the unfortunate consequences resulting from a principle are accidental—and there are principles even in the Gospel which, if not properly responded to, can give rise to unfortunate consequences—the ideal remains intact. Stability is the characteristic ideal of Benedictinism.

[29] *Ibid.*, 30.

CHAPTER 5

OF OBEDIENCE

Christian perfection is summed up in Christlike obedience. Monastic perfection is nothing more, nothing less. Perfect obedience assumes the law of love, and is the ground of moral and spiritual conduct. By being subject to man in the further subjection to God—and this not out of compulsion but out of love —a soul shares the mind of Christ as closely as is possible in this life.

In St. Benedict's chapter on obedience, the first virtue to be mentioned is not obedience itself but humility. It will be seen how, particularly in this and the seventh chapter but also throughout the Rule, St. Benedict speaks of obedience and humility almost as though they were the same thing. The two virtues are shown to interact, giving rise to the same kind of virtuous action. St. Benedict treats obedience and humility as combining to form a single and settled outlook which covers the whole range of monastic obligation, rather than as separate virtues to be exercised on specific occasions.

If pride is responsible for the fall of man from grace, humility goes a long way towards restoring the original position. Just as pride and rebellion are one in the fall, so humility and obedience are one in the restoration. Is it by humility or obedience that a man surrenders his will in the monastic life to another? It is by each equally, acting as cause and effect. In the *Acta Sanctorum* obedience and humility are described, in reference to St. Majolus, as the "sacraments of monastic observance." Hildebert, the biographer of St. Hugh, is quoted by Dom van Houtryve, as saying that obedience and humility are the principal virtues of Christian morality. [1]

The principle which governs Christian obedience is given in the space of two verses by St. Paul. "Every soul must be submissive to its lawful superiors; authority comes from God only, and all authorities that hold sway are of his ordinance. Thus the man who opposes authority is a rebel against the ordinance of God, and rebels secure their own condemnation."[2]

But besides the need for maintaining the right relationship between the ruler and the ruled, there is the need to maintain the right relationship between the monastic superior and the monk. The peace of the monastery depends upon it. The peace of the individual monk depends upon it. There can be neither social nor spiritual tranquillity where there is resistance. Subordination to Christ seen in authority is for St. Benedict the only way to harmony, recollection, love.

> The first degree of humility is obedience without delay. This becomes those who hold nothing dearer to them than Christ, and who on account of the holy servitude which they have taken upon them . . . just as if it had been commanded by God Himself are unable to bear delay in doing it. It is of these that He says: "At the hearing of the ear he hath obeyed Me." And again to teachers He saith: "He that heareth you heareth Me."

The opening note of obedience, then, is promptitude. But the promptitude thought of here is not just punctuality. It is the kind that is habitual. The soul is ever on the alert because the will of God is always being sought. The actual call of obedience provides the occasion of finding God's will. The command is the signal, not the substance. Obedience was not invented merely for the maintenance of good order in the house.

Having told how obedience shows itself in action, St. Benedict goes on to define the subjective attitude which inspires its acts.

[1] *Benedictine Peace*, p. 174.
[2] Rom. 13;1,2.

He shows how the monk must borrow from Christ the motive of his conduct. In the seventy-first chapter he speaks of the *bonum obedientiae;* the whole good of it derives from Christ.

"The true lover of Christ always thinks Christ, speaks and venerates Christ, does not doubt that Christ is everywhere present to him," says the monk John Tritheim; "such a one forgets himself, for his mind and desire are wholly with Christ."[3] We shall see the same principle applied when St. Benedict comes to consider the official and social relationships within the monastery. To the Christ-centred soul, selflessness and obedience become first nature.

In the realization of the monastic ideal, which in one form or another is charity, there has to be the subordination of one lot of elements to another lot of elements. The "firmament of the law" covers different altitudes. But at each level the significant authority is the same, and the motive must accordingly be the same in the obedience given. The firmament is not only that of law but that of love. Which means that the law is love.

Though monastic obedience is one in direction, it is twofold in expression. We obey the word of the abbot and the word of the Rule. The word in either case, though not of course on the same level as the revealed word of God in Scripture, is the expression of God's will. And like the revealed word of Scripture, the word of authority brings peace to those who fully respond to its implication. The word of authority carries with it health. "Say but the word, and my soul shall be healed." A command is not a test, merely, or a correction; it can be a cure. *Obediens loquetur sanitates.*

> Such as these therefore, leaving immediately all that is theirs and forsaking their own will, with their hands disengaged and leaving unfinished what they were about, with the ready step of obedience follow by their deeds the voice of him who commands . . . they live in community and desire to have an abbot over them. Such as these without doubt fulfil that saying of the Lord: "I came not to do Mine own will, but the will of Him who sent Me."

[3] *Homilies,* 8.

Since St. Benedict in these passages clearly has in mind obedience to a person, as distinct from obedience to the written Rule, we can follow him in taking this aspect of the duty first. The point which immediately stands out in this connection is that the abbot's rule is desired by the community. Granted that the monks are true monks—that they not only want to forsake their own will but are also ready to show it by an unhesitating response to the living voice which commands—they will see the necessity of being under one man. They will ask for one who will represent divine authority to them, and who in turn will be their representative.

When laying on a fellow monk the burden of abbatial office, says Dom Besse, the brethren "contract in his regard the strict obligation of aiding him through prayer, through patience, and through an obedience of the heart. If it turns out that his rule displeases them, they have only themselves to blame." The same Benedictine writer goes on to say that " a man would be wanting in loyalty if he tried to burden another, perhaps the victim of his own choice, with a responsibility which is his own."[4]

Disloyalty is bad enough when the object of it has been imposed from without, but when we have asked to have an abbot over us and have got one—even if he is not the man whom we had hoped to get—the disloyalty is worse. Obedience in the world to a secular authority is in some ways harder than obedience in religion to an abbot. Disloyalty to a tyrannical master where no explicitly supernatural relationship is involved would at least be reasonable. But in the cloister there is no such excuse. Not only do we know all about authority, but we have put this particular extension of it where it is.

Disloyalty towards one's abbot stands at one extreme, flattery at the other. Both amount to the same thing: a want of faith in the recognition of his position. Without faith, the abbacy is seen simply as a post to be filled or a power to be reckoned with. Perhaps it is even seen as a power to be bargained with. Flattery, persuasion, pretence: these things run clean contrary to the spirit of obedience.

[4] *Le Moine Bénédictin*, p. 87.

Now that he has accounted for the spirit which must animate our obedience, St. Benedict lays down instructions about its performance. The qualities which he is to consider here are external rather than internal, but they will be seen to depend upon the monk's disposition of soul rather than upon his discipline and deportment.

> This very obedience will then be acceptable to God and sweet to men if what is commanded be done not fearfully, tardily, nor lukewarmly, nor with murmuring, nor with an answer showing unwillingness . . . it ought to be given by disciples with a good will, because "God loves a cheerful giver."

If our submission is to be *acceptabilis Deo*, which is the primary purpose of it, it must be given generously. To delay the act until the last permissible minute, to perform it with obvious indifference, to grumble while doing it, to act the martyr, to show by its slapdash execution that we think the task beneath us, to leave it unfinished and to come running back for permission to abandon it altogether, to pester authority: these are the qualities which render our obedience unacceptable to God.

A religious who would not dream of committing an act of frank disobedience will cheerfully perform many acts which evade, and so indirectly run counter to, obedience. He will try to get an assurance from his abbot that his own interpretation of the command is a reasonable one, he will advance every sort of excuse for the non-fulfilment of the duty, he will persist in his incomplete obediences until the command is withdrawn and he is free again. A superior cannot as a rule hold out against the overt blackmail of an imperfectly obedient subject.

For the perfection of obedience, St. Benedict wants to see, besides acceptability to God, the quality of "sweetness to men." The saint may mean here that the only way for anyone to find the yoke of obedience sweet is to perform its acts unhesitatingly, ungrudgingly, unevasively, and so on; or he may mean that a monk's obedience will be agreeable to others only if the work is accompanied by the required signs of generosity. Perhaps St.

Benedict means both. Both, in any case, state cenobitic obedience in true terms.

Thus in the first place a man has a right to find happiness in subjection. If self-will is the cause of unhappiness, the surrender of it to the will of another must bring peace. The more perfectly the acts which result from this subjection are performed, the happier is the subject. Acts which are disagreeable in themselves, and from which the subject may shrink, can bring to the man who handles them properly true satisfaction.[5]

As to how one man's acts of obedience affect his fellows in community, a different law is seen to apply: the communication of virtues. The individual has obligations, positive and negative, towards his brethren, separately and collectively. The collection of monks in a monastery amounts to more than the juxtaposition of individuals under one roof. While the social ideal is paramount, there is also the physical factor to be considered: the adjacencies involved in community life call for a host of practical responsibilities. The smoothness or unsmoothness of one man's obedience will closely touch his neighbour's.

Our obedience will be agreeable to men, to our brethren, under given conditions. It is for us to supply those conditions. The common good of the monastic family is attained by the co-operation of separate members. This is what the cenobitic society stands for; this is its whole meaning.

"You ought to strive to draw others to God with you by whatever you believe has benefited you or increased your merit," says St. Gregory; "you should long to have companions in running in the way of God's commandments, and if you wish to reach the throne of His Majesty, beware lest you perish before Him in solitude."

The bride in the Canticles sings of the Beloved that "Thy name is as oil poured out: therefore young maidens have loved thee."[6] The unction of Christ, at its most fragrant in His obedience, is not stored up but poured out. The secret of His name is disclosed, and has attracted the youth and beauty of the human

[5] *Ambulabam in latitudine, quia mandata tua exquisivi.* (Ps. 118;45.)
[6] 1;2.

race. Our obedience in community, taking its character from
Christ's, must have about it that winning quality which draws
others closer under the same yoke.

> If the disciple obey with ill-will . . . although he fulfil
> the command, yet he will not be accepted by God, who re-
> gards the heart of the murmurer. And for such an action he
> shall gain no reward; nay, rather, he shall incur the pun-
> ishment due to murmurers unless he amend and make
> satisfaction.

And with that, St. Benedict closes his chapter on obedience.
Whether to the voice of the abbot or to the word of the Rule,
the monk's good will is absolutely essential. For the monk to
restrict his response to one or other of the twofold aspects of
authority would be to undermine the whole principle of his obedience. *Cum bono animo* he offers his dual—rather his combined
—sacrifice.

Sacrifice offered in a spirit of pride or bitterness is of no use
to God. If they are celebrated in the wrong way, God hates our
fasts and new moons. "Behold in the day of your fast your own
will is found,"[7] says Isaias in scorn of the religious man whose
obedience to the Law is diverted. Observance to the letter,
whether of the Law or of the Rule, is a waste of energy unless it
comes from a heart that is right with God.

Monastic obedience, then, supposes a willing and joyful service
which aims at the perfection of love. The obedience which sees
its function in terms of service under constraint is not the obedience of St. Benedict. An illustration from the *Dialogues* can be
taken as a symbol of this. St. Gregory tells how a certain hermit-
monk named Martin managed to keep faithful to his purpose
only by means of an iron chain which bound him to the walls of
his cell. When St. Benedict heard of this he sent him word that
"if thou art a servant of God, let no chain of iron constrain thee
but be bound instead by the chain of Christ."[8]

A false devotion to the holy Rule can equal the legalism and

[7] Isai. 58;3.
[8] Bk. 2; ch. 16.

formalism of the Jewish Church in the time of Christ. It can be used in opposition to the other obedience, the living voice of authority which interprets the holy Rule. "Is this such a sacrifice that I have chosen? . . . if thou wilt take away the chain out of the midst of thee, and cease to stretch out the finger and to speak that which profiteth not . . . the Lord will fill thy soul with brightness . . . then shalt thou be delighted in the Lord, and I will lift thee up above the high places of the earth and will feed thee with the inheritance of Jacob thy father."[9] The inheritance of our fathers, both Jacob and Benedict alike, is the reward of obedience.

Obedience given in faith to abbot and Rule is the primary expression of monastic service. It is at once the foundation and the culmination of monastic perfection. "Obedience practised as a manifestation of our reverence for God," says Dom van Houtryve, "becomes part of the cult of religion. It can also come under charity in so far as it is an expression of our love of God. Understood in this way, the whole life of obedience acquires a remarkable grandeur and largeness. It is the glory of the true monk. It puts him in his right place with respect to God; it grounds him in truth. And it is the glory of man to be in truth."[10] The same author concludes his reflections on obedience with these words: "Let us do perfectly what we have to do at the present moment, in obedience and love. That is the secret of security, of freedom, of light, and of true peace."[11]

[9] Isai. 58;5,9,11,14.
[10] *Op. cit.*, p. 75.
[11] *Ibid.*, p. 78.

CHAPTER 6

THE SPIRIT OF SILENCE

In time, St. Benedict stands between two epochs; in place, between two traditions. He was able accordingly to hand on the wealth of the earlier patristic age to generations which would have to wait a long time before they could claim to have rediscovered the same spirit; he was able also to give to the West what had been built up by the East. Before he wrote his Rule, St. Benedict had studied, in Rome itself, the accepted interpreters of the Church's law and doctrine; he had also practised a way of life which as nearly as possible reflected that lived by the monks of Egypt and Syria. With his written Rule he was to graft the best of one inheritance upon the best of another. The result of his experiment was the Western monasticism which has been lived ever since.

The differences between the two traditions, though this is only to suggest them in their roughest outline, might be seen as follows: from the Roman side came St. Benedict's ideas of the family life, of the abbot's position as father and ruler, of the precedence in the monastery, of moderation in matters of penance, of the need for order and regularity, of respect for all forms of authority; from the Christian East came the saint's insistence on silence, zeal, mortification, humility, enclosure, recollection.

While it would be an over-simplification to say that the ascetical aspect of the Rule derives from its Eastern influences and its social aspect from its Western influences, it might justly be

claimed that the ancients of the Thebaid would have been as
much dismayed by the concessions allowed by St. Benedict as
the monks of Lerins or Vivarium would have been dismayed had
they been asked to imitate the desert fathers.

Chief among the ascetical practices borrowed from the earlier
monasticism of the East, then, is that of silence. St. Benedict's
teaching is that the cenobite needs it no less than the solitary. It
is a discipline, certainly, but not only a discipline. It is a means,
admittedly, but if it can become identified with recollection it
can be classed as one of the ends—though one of the relative ends
—of the monastic life.

> Let us do as says the prophet: "I said I will take heed to
> my ways that I sin not with my tongue; I have placed a
> watch over my mouth; I became dumb and was silent, and
> held my peace even from good things." Here the prophet
> shows that if we should refrain even from good words for
> the sake of silence, how much more ought we to refrain
> from evil words . . . therefore on account of the importance
> of silence, let leave to speak seldom be granted even to per-
> fect disciples, although their conversation be good and
> holy and tending to edification.

At first sight St. Benedict's regulation appears somewhat repressive. He seems to be saying in effect, "If you cannot talk
without the likelihood of sin, better not talk at all." But this is
not the way his mind works. If the passage is examined, particularly if it is examined in the light of the many other references
to silence which are to be found in the Rule, a more positive
principle is discovered. St. Benedict is concerned not so much
with the evil of talk as with the good of silence.

Silence was in the world before noise, and what St. Benedict
wants is a return to silence. Silence is a thing in itself; it is not
the mere absence of conversation. In the element of silence the
soul is free to raise itself to God. In the soul that loves silence,
both within and without, the silent working of grace is given
greater liberty.

It is because silence is such a liberating force—almost, one
might say, a creative force—that men have been urged in every

age of religion "to refrain even from good words." It is as if good words are weighed against silence, and found to be of less value. Certainly for the monk, who is not a preaching religious, silence is more eloquent than speech. If a monk is called upon to preach, his sermons must come out from the treasury of his silence.

Seen in this way, silence is the viaduct of a monk's apostolic as well as his ascetic spirit. Having built up, with its principles of abstraction and solitude, the monastic habit of mind, silence indirectly transmits the fruits of the training to other souls and to God. There is the closest possible connection between silence, charity, and worship.

Thus the reason why St. Benedict gives only grudging consent to conversation within the monastery is that if edification is its sole excuse, then to abstain from conversation for the love of God is more edifying still. That St. Benedict did in fact allow periods of recreation at which the brethren were free to talk to one another is clear both from references in the Rule itself and from a number of incidents recorded by St. Gregory in the *Dialogues.*

Thus for example the prohibition contained in the forty-eighth chapter of the Rule "let not one brother associate with another at unsuitable hours" would be without point if there were no hours that were suitable. In Lent, again, the brethren are told that their conversations are to be fewer and more restrained. Though the apparent contradiction cannot altogether be explained away, it would be reasonable to conclude that while there were no daily periods of recreation in St. Benedict's time such as there are in Benedictine monasteries today, the silence was not intended by the saint to be perpetual.

It is interesting to follow the way in which St. Benedict's *rara loquendi concedatur licentia* has been interpreted in the course of Benedictine history. There is no mention of regular recreation in Paul Warnefrid's commentary, which dates from the eighth century, and it is very unlikely that St. Benedict of Aniane would have introduced it in the monasteries over which he ruled at the beginning of the ninth. Yet by 1000 A.D. the custom was, according to Dom Morin, widely established. Later at Cluny, when Udalric was drawing up that monastery's customary, there were two periods in the day when the community might talk: the morning recreation lasting half an hour, and in the afternoon only a quarter of an hour.

In the effort to discover St. Benedict's mind on this subject of conversation among the brethren, we may perhaps see a hint in the distinction which he makes between *taciturnitas* and *silentium*. The former means a disposition, the habit of not talking, the recognition of the need and the spirit of silence; the latter means the physical fact of quiet. If St. Benedict can be sure of forming the habit in his monks, he knows that he need not worry about the fact.

The word *silentium* is used only four times in the Rule, and then not always in its absolute sense. Complete silence must be observed during the night, during the summer siesta, in the refectory, and while the brethren leave the oratory: this is the application of his terms *summum silentium* and *omne silentium*. When he speaks of *silentium* by itself he means, according to Dom Cuthbert Butler, the kind of silence which is not broken by talking "in a subdued voice."[1]

In Benedictine houses today widely differing customs as regards the times allowed for talking are found to obtain. Apart from these stipulated periods, the Benedictine day is meant to be spent in silence. Apart from the places where talking is allowed, the Benedictine monastery is meant to be a house of silence. Whatever else St. Benedict meant in his regulations on this matter, he certainly never meant his cloisters to ring with the sound of voices.

Thus the monk would do well to be guided by the rules suggested by St. John Climacus, who says that monks should leave their silence only when charity, necessity, or real utility require it. A monk should strive "not to speak without permission, and even with permission briefly and with moderation."

[1] *Benedictine Monachism*, p. 290. This work and Dom Morin's *Ideal of the Monastic Life found in the Apostolic Age* have been freely drawn upon in this historical digression.

Certainly if we took our principles as regards silence solely from authorities like St. John Climacus, Cassian, St. Nilus, and others whose doctrines St. Benedict was clearly following, we would have cause to feel ashamed of having fallen so far below the primitive standard in practice.

For consolation it may be noted, however, that even St. Basil allowed occasional interruptions of the silence which was such a feature of his rule, and that St. Pachomius prescribed a short morning session each day at which spiritual matters might be discussed. So even in the ages of early monastic enthusiasm the outlet of speech was not entirely banned.[2]

It is written: "In much speaking, thou shalt not avoid sin"; and elsewhere: "Death and life are in the power of the tongue." It becomes the master to speak and to teach, but it is for the disciple to be silent and to listen. And therefore if anything has to be asked of a superior, let it be done with all humility and subjection of reverence, lest he seem to say more than is expedient.

The picture of community recreation suggested here is a little forbidding: the elderly fathers holding forth and the juniors meekly dumb. But perhaps St. Benedict is being too strictly loyal to Cassian from whom, almost word for word, he has taken the passage. Clearly what he wants to avoid is the unseemly situation in which a young voice is found to shout down the opinion of a senior. No one, be he an ancient or a novice, should attempt to hold the floor: both the conversation and the interest should be kept general.

It is accordingly in the interests of humility as well as in the interests of recollection and good order that silence be studied by the brethren. "If thou wishest to acquire the power to keep silence," said Abbot Poemen, "think not within thyself that thou art doing the works of spiritual excellence, but say rather 'I am not even worthy to speak.' "[3]

[2] See Delatte, *op. cit.*, p. 93, who cites Dom Besse, *Les Moines d'Orient*, to whom Dom van Houtryve also makes frequent acknowledgment.

[3] *Paradise of the Fathers*, Vol. i; ch. 1,45.

Pride and loquacity go together: humility makes for quiet. The vain man is talkative because he hungers for attention, because he wants everyone to know what he thinks, because he has no interest in other people's views, and, perhaps most of all, because he is afraid that if he keeps quiet he will have time to learn what he is really like. The humble man shrinks from much talk because he cannot honestly believe that he has anything significant to contribute. It is not because he is afraid of committing himself, or of making a fool of himself, that the truly humble man cherishes his silence. He cherishes silence because silence is his proper element, and because his soul expands in it more than it would in conversation.

Where some talk too much because they think too much of themselves, others come to think too much of themselves because they talk too much. So either way St. Benedict is right to insist on the virtue of silence.[4] Silence is virtuous both because it inspires other virtues—humility, recollection, self-restraint—and because it crowns them. It is virtuous also, and still more, because Christ gave us an example of it.[5]

Silence, like every other good, has its obverse side. It can be misconceived and misapplied. It can be the easy refuge of the lazy temperament, it can become an affectation, it can engender egotism and harbour resentments. It can make a man bitter, introverted, unwilling to face reality and life. St. Nilus says that to keep outward silence while burning with inward disgust and uncharity is worse than to keep up conversations all day. But the same saint says also that well-instructed monks speak rarely, and that "ignorant ones are always talking, but do not know what they are talking about." The evils are attendant only, not of the essence. Silence, despite the abuses to which it is liable, remains a good. If it is a good for all, it is pre-eminently a good for monks.

[4] St. Thomas does not enumerate silence among the virtues; it is virtue by analogy and by implication only.
[5] The Fathers have seen in His infancy, in His love of solitude during His ministry, and in His answer to Pilate evidences of Christ's desire to give an example of silence for our sake.

Even when talking to the abbot, St. Benedict lays upon the monk the obligation of reserve. The warning *ne plus videatur loqui quam expedit* is not only to safeguard the superior from garrulous subjects but also to prevent disrespect, assertiveness, self-importance in the subject. Excess is always a mistake and nearly always a sin. Immoderate outpourings to one's abbot must inevitably express so much of self as to rank as pride. A monk must cultivate the habit of being brief: it will spare him many faults against charity, dissipation, vainglory, loyalty towards the community, and it will also prevent him from becoming a great nuisance to everybody.

But as for buffoonery or silly words, such as move to laughter, we utterly condemn them in every place; nor do we allow the disciple to open his mouth in such discourse.

St. Benedict could not be more emphatic. If we are left in any doubt on the regulation of silence in the saint's monastery, we have here the clearest possible directive on the subject of the kind of behaviour suitable and unsuitable to monks: jollification is banished *aeterna clausura* and *in omnibus locis*. The word *damnamus* is more than "we prescribe unsuitable"; it strikes the authoritative, the pontifical, note. "We rule it out altogether" would be more the meaning.

Laughter may be a good medicine, but it is a bad drug. Certainly for a monk it is a medicine that must be constantly looked at and prevented from becoming a habit. Too much laughter can break down barriers which a soul may have taken years to build —barriers against the world, against distraction, against gossip or obscenity.

When the shepherd in the Canticles went down into the garden to see the fruits of the valley and to "look if the vineyard had flourished" he was forced to admit that he could not tell. His visit of inspection was a failure. "I knew not" is his sad confession; "my soul troubled me for the chariots of Aminadab. Return, return, O Sulamitess; return, return that we may behold thee."[6] Laughter and unrestrained gaiety have a blinding and

[6] 6;11,12.

blunting effect. Our perceptions in spiritual matters become less keen. The chariots, rattling along on their noisy wheels, trouble us. We are forced now to cry again and again to the bride that she may return.

To the extent that the soul is serene the light of grace can be reflected. If the surface is troubled, the shimmering effect is due not so much to the light as to the dancing of the waters. The lake of the soul may sparkle with laughter, but is this always because of the light of grace? It is not only misplaced cares that busy the soul, and rob it of tranquillity; it is also misplaced mirth.

CHAPTER 7

OF HUMILITY

Dom Delatte says of this chapter that "it is justly regarded as the finished expression of monastic spirituality." Certainly it can be made to cover every aspect of Benedictine life, interior and exterior, and of all the chapters in the holy Rule is the one that most clearly reveals the spirit of the legislator.

This seventh chapter, moreover, has had more written about it than any other. This is not only because both Dom Mège and Dom Martène were caught up in their respective commentaries by the de Rancé-Mabillon-Bossuet wrangle about fictitious humiliations, but more because every commentator since Paul Warnefrid seems, partly by pillaging from his predecessor and partly by hitting upon new facets of the virtue, to have built up the figure of St. Benedict as *humilitatis doctor*.[1]

After an introductory paragraph consisting of three quotations from Holy Scripture linked together—with his own explicatory sentence ("teaching us that all exaltation is a kind of pride against which the prophet shows himself to be on his guard") to help them out—St. Benedict makes his own specific opening in the following terms:

> Whence, brethren, if we wish to arrive at the highest point of humility and speedily to reach that heavenly exaltation to which we can only ascend by the humility of this

---

[1] It will be noticed that this present book is as guilty as any other in the matter of pillaging.

[1] Bk. 2; ch. 35.

present life, we must by our ever-ascending actions erect such a ladder as that which Jacob beheld in his dream, by which the angels appeared to him descending and ascending. This descent and ascent signify nothing else than that we descend by exaltation and ascend by humility. And the ladder thus erected is our life on earth . . . the sides of the same ladder we understand to be our body and soul, in which the call of God has placed various degrees of humility or discipline which we must mount.

In this paragraph St. Benedict shows what is the most potent force of religious behaviour. The interaction of grace and the human will co-operating with grace is the generative principle of charity, of Christianity, of monasticism. Where the human will is acting unselfishly, with confidence not in its own action but in the action of grace, you have the virtue of humility in operation.

The theme of ascending and descending, which is repeated in his introduction, is only another way of expressing St. Benedict's doctrine of true and false happiness. There are two sorts of exaltation, and if you are looking for the one which is realized only in the next life, you must do without the one which is realized in this. When you are really prepared to sit for the rest of your days at the bottom of the ladder, you find yourself being carried up it.

The difference between the good and bad angels was the difference between humility and pride. The good go up Jacob's ladder, the bad come down it. The humble mount upright, the proud drop headlong: it is the paradox of the unimportant looking dignified, and the important looking absurd. The same idea is expressed in the *Magnificat*.

The heavenly ladder symbol, Dom Delatte points out, is much used by early writers. With different applications it provides allegorical interest for St. Basil, St. John Climacus, the author of the Passion of SS. Perpetua and Felicity, and Cassiodorus.[2]

[2] Interpreted strictly, the ladder in Joseph's dream (Gen. 28;12) represents the movement to and from the earth of God's messengers. The angels are good angels, not some of them good and some bad.

Though Cassian does not mention the ladder, he gives a gradated scheme by which the soul is seen to mount in humility to God.

It is the unwillingness to climb down and be like everyone else in subjection that constitutes pride, whether spiritual or human; so it is the willingness to stay small, and even look small, that gives its value to the performance of ordinary actions. The common life of the monastery is a discipline primarily because it is humbling. Obedience is always humbling, but it is doubly so when offered together with everyone else and in connection with routine observances which afford no scope for ostentation and heroism.

Spiritual pride has to be broken down by the acceptance of ordinary ways of prayer, of a reputation for ordinariness, of the fact that in religion one is no better than very ordinary people living in the world. Straightforward natural vanity has to be broken down by applying the conclusions arrived at—by following out the implications of St. Benedict's twelve degrees.

St. John of the Cross says in the *Ascent* that "the state of divine union consists in the soul's total transformation in the will of God, so that there is nothing contrary to the will of God," and that "when the soul rids itself totally of that which is repugnant to the divine will and which conforms not with it, it is transformed in God through love." The soul's every movement is actuated by—is indeed identified with—the will of God. This is the ideal proposed by St. Benedict no less than by St. John of the Cross, and as the means towards its realization St. Benedict offers his twelve degrees of humility.

"While the king was at his rest, my spikenard spread wide the scent of it," says the bride. "A bundle of myrrh," she adds significantly, "is my beloved to me."[3] The soul must be at rest if there is to be union. The scent of its calm and of its detachment from self is spread abroad by the spices of virtue. There is suf-

---

The idea is that God sends graces to men and that the use made of these graces is reported back to Him. "My word shall not return to me void," says Isaias 55;11. St. Benedict and others interpret the ladder dream in an accommodated sense.

[3] Cant. 1;11,12.

fering involved in this state of love—there is myrrh as well as sweetness in the coming of the king who is at the same time the beloved—but it is a suffering that is gladly endured. It is even looked forward to. Accordingly the first thing that the novice-master is instructed by St. Benedict to examine in the candidate for the monastic life is "whether he truly seeks God, is zealous for the *opus Dei*, for obedience, and for humiliations."[4] The qualifications *ad obedientiam, ad opprobria* are the myrrh, without which the union with the beloved in this life to which the whole purpose is directed is impossible. The degrees of humility are not pious consolations.

Though St. Benedict nowhere says that his degrees must be studied one at a time, and that the disciple should not proceed to the next until he has mastered the one before, the whole point of casting the chapter in its graded form is to suggest order. The soul is expected to attempt all degrees at once, seeing in their arrangement more a challenge to serious effort in the acquisition of humility than an exact plan which leads inevitably to a crowning perfection.

The thought is expressed by Cassian, who quotes Abbot Nesteros as saying: "There are in the world many arts and sciences, most of which are useless save for the conveniency of this present life; yet all have a method by which they may be acquired. If these arts and sciences have a fixed and established system by which they are to be learned, how much more should our religious life have its appointed rules and principles? . . . If you have a sincere desire to ascend to the higher and more excellent part of our spiritual science, not prompted by vainglory but by the wish to purify your interior, you will be inflamed with ardour to possess the sixth beatitude: Blessed are the clean of heart, for they shall see God . . . so let me beg of you to be earnest in your application to whatever regards morality, or the practical part of the spiritual science, without which you can never ascend to that purity of contemplation which is given to those who have attained to perfection."[5]

[4] Ch. 58.
[5] *Conferences*, 14; 1 and 9.

St. Benedict's treatment of humility under twelve heads is imitated by St. Thomas, but where the Rule proceeds from the internal to the external, the *Summa* starts with the external and spiritualizes the acts as the degrees follow one another.[6] Also the general conception is slightly different in the two saints, St. Benedict looking upon humility as the disposition which colours all relationships and covers all circumstances, St. Thomas looking upon it as a virtue distinct from other virtues and as having a function proper to itself.

For St. Benedict the monastic virtues of poverty, obedience, indifference to comfort, frankness with superiors, the willingness to sink one's theories and suppress one's singularities are all the outcome of the spirit of humility. Humility is the reason why they are reasonable. Humility makes them worth practising, and perfect when practised.

> The first degree of humility, then, is that a man always keep the fear of God before his eyes, avoiding all forgetfulness; and that he be ever mindful of all that God has commanded and that those who despise God will be consumed in hell . . . keeping himself at all times from sin and vice, whether of the thoughts, the tongue, the eyes, the hands, the feet, or his own will; let him thus hasten to cut off the desires of the flesh.

The thing begins in the heart and mind; it is not just a matter of behaving with modesty. A man must have a right understanding of God's relation to His creatures; his humility must be built upon realism and not sentiment. If humility were the product solely of the intellect or solely of the emotions, its acts would be lamentably incomplete. Neither a notional assent to the fact of man's insufficiency nor the glow of feeling oneself to be abject is, by itself, enough. There must be the sincere desire to show one's dependence upon God by proving it with interior and exterior works.

The first requirement, then, is an awareness of God's justice. The monk may never forget that God expects to be taken at His word. Unless he is "mindful at all times" of the consequences

[6] II. II.,q.161,a.6.

of sin and vice, his self-esteem will grow and ultimately get the better of him. It is only humility that can counter the continual pressure of our natural self-assertiveness. St. Benedict's idea is that when the arrogance of a man is kept under by humility, the positive attraction of the love of God will be free to make itself actively and effectively felt.

Just as the works of natural creation are drawn by the law of gravity towards the earth's centre, so the works of spiritual creation are drawn by the law of charity towards the heart of charity itself. Once freed from its material weights, the soul responds according to its very nature to the gravitational drawing of charity. The soul can feel the pull of love even before the weights and shackles are struck off, but for the magnetic influence to take effect the life of the senses must be subject to the life of the spirit.

Humility, keeping watch over the appetites, surrenders "the thoughts, the tongue, the eyes, the hands" to the dominion of grace. So far as in him lies, the monk "cuts off the desires of the flesh" and keeps himself from the tyranny of "his own will." This is humility's effective contribution. It is as far as it can go. From here it must be God who takes over. Man humbles himself —so far so good, and this is our concern—and it is for God then to exalt him.

The more the soul yields to this grace of humility the more effectively and rapidly does the further grace of exaltation come into play. The passivity of the humble soul is caught up in the activity of grace. Raised thus to a level unattainable by mere human effort or by the force of discipline alone, the soul comes to the free exercise of a spirituality that transforms everything that it touches.

"The subjection of every appetite to the reason," says Dom Maurus Wolter, "cannot but bring about peace of soul. Almost all disturbances, displeasures, anxieties, and disputes arise from our concupiscences, so that by restraining and calming them we may establish a most gratifying concord with ourselves and with our neighbour."[7]

[7] *Elementa*, ch. 4, quoted by Dom van Houtryve in *Benedictine Peace*, p. 195.

St. Thomas, in the article already quoted, gives as the root and principle of humility the reverence which the soul has towards God. It is only the humble man who recognizes what is due to God, and who finds in every department of his life the means of rendering it. Community life spells it to him, regular observance spells it to him, his prayer and his mortification are expressions of it.

After some further exhortations to keep alive the sense of God's presence and the thought of His retributive justice, St. Benedict enlarges upon a theme which is constantly recurring in the holy Rule: the conflict between self-love and the signified will of God.

> We are indeed forbidden to do our own will by Scripture, which says to us: "Turn away from thine own will." And so too we beg of God in prayer that His will may be done in us. Rightly therefore we are taught not to do our own will if we take heed to the warning of Scripture: "There are ways that seem to men right, but the ends thereof lead to the depths of hell."

Reason and Scripture together prove the wrongness of self-will and the rightness of humility. Humility is truth; self-will is the desire for something false. When the false is consistently sought, the self that seeks becomes confused and loses its true identity. It becomes a false self seeking a false good. What seems right and to be desired turns out to be wrong. Selfishness has warped the judgment and laid the soul open to delusion.

"The good of human virtue consists in the order of reason to man's end," says Father Merton. "The most important virtues are the theological, which have man's last end as their object. But second to these are the virtues which order man's reason to his end. This *ordinatio* is established above all by legal justice. But humility subjects us to it." *Ordinationi facit hominem bene subjectum humilitas in universali quantum ad omnia.*[8]

Where the end is lost sight of in the welter of more immediately desirable means, anything can happen. St. Benedict's quo-

[8] *Summa*, II. II.,q.161,a.5,c.

tation from the book of Proverbs comes as a shock. But it is not so alarming when we realize the true nature of the threat. It does not mean that a man, having followed a course in all good faith, will wake up one day to find himself in hell. "So it was the wrong course after all." What it means is that the man who has chosen to call evil good and good evil has so misdirected his desires that inevitably he ends up where his desires take him. "Go not after thy lusts," we read in Ecclesiasticus, "but turn away from thy own will."[9]

> Let us be on our guard, then, against evil desires, since death has its place close to the entrance of delight; wherefore the Scripture commands us saying: "Go not after thy concupiscences." Since therefore the eyes of the Lord behold good and evil, and the Lord is ever looking down from heaven upon the children of men to see who has understanding or is seeking God . . . we must be on our watch, brethren, lest, as the prophet says in the psalm, God should see us at any time declining to evil and becoming unprofitable.

The presence of God must have been an abiding reality to St. Benedict: again and again he gives it as the element in which the monastic life is lived. The divine presence gives form to what are otherwise purely human acts. Performed under the eyes of God, every detail of religious observance is strictly a religious observance—is an act of religious worship.

If form can be defined as principle made actual in outward symbols, then the outward symbols of obedience, of fidelity, of fraternal charity, of prayer and penance are *informed* by the principle of the divine presence. Moreover it is humility that recognizes this presence—as it is this presence that deepens and strengthens humility.

The outward signs of inward humility which are required by St. Benedict in the later degrees will thus be the realization of the principle expressed here in the first. In each of the twelve degrees God's presence is the idea which, under one or other aspect, emerges in terms of sensibility.

[9] 18;30.

Man perceives before he performs. God "looks down upon the children of men to see who has *understanding or is seeking Him.*" The knowledge of this fact evokes an idea in our minds which, acting through the will, sets the spur to action. Then we do, in truth, understand and seek. His presence is thus not only the element in which our lives are led, not only the form which is given to the works we do, but is also the driving power which keeps us moving in the right direction.

The warning contained in the concluding words of the quoted paragraph shows that the recognition, taken merely by itself, of God's presence does not guarantee either humility or fidelity. We have to be constantly on our guard against declining to evil and becoming unprofitable.

> The second degree of humility is that a man love not his own will nor delight in gratifying his own desires, but carry out in his deeds that saying of the Lord: "I came not to do Mine own will but the will of Him who sent Me." And again Scripture says: "Self-will has punishment but necessity wins a crown."

Since this degree repeats much that has been either said or implied already, the commentators have jumped at the chance of discussing the second of St. Benedict's quotations. Nowhere, despite the designation given to it, does it appear in Scripture. Explanations are not wanting, but to the inexpert they savour of special pleading. Whatever its source, the phrase "necessity wins a crown" must surely mean that works performed under sanctions which are inescapable, but which have been imposed upon us by our own choice, are blessed with God's reward. Coming immediately after the words "self-will has punishment" the statement implies more than that we should make a virtue of necessity. The juxtaposition suggests the further idea of voluntary necessity. "The selfish and the selfless," St. Benedict is making some undiscovered authority say, "are recompensed at opposite extremes."

> The third degree of humility is that a man for the love of God submit himself to his superior in all obedience; imitat-

ing the Lord, of whom the apostle saith: "He was made obedient even unto death."

In his fifth chapter St. Benedict says that "the first degree of humility is obedience without delay"; in this seventh chapter he puts obedience in the third degree. But there is no real contradiction in this; it is merely that in his earlier mention of obedience he is claiming its primary importance in relation to humility. In the present chapter, where he is splitting up humility into sections, he allots a particular place to obedience in relation to other expressions of the virtue.

In coming back time and again to the humility-obedience combination St. Benedict is followed by perhaps his most illustrious disciple in the history of Western monasticism, St. Bernard. *Nihil mihi occurrit quod utilius possitis audire:* it is for him as for St. Benedict the foundation of the monastic life.

Not only when he is dealing with the subject specifically, as in *De Gradibus Humilitatis*, but also in his sermons *De Diversis* and *In Cantica Canticorum*, St. Bernard stresses the need for, and the connection between, the two virtues of humility and obedience. The monk who is expecting to find nothing but pure mysticism in the sermons on the Canticle will discover frequent injunctions to go back again to what might seem to him the elementary virtues.

The argument is that once the human will is perfectly subject to the divine will, it must want what is willed for it by superiors. And this is humility as much as it is obedience. "The perfection of humility is seen in the absolute subjection of our will, as is only right and proper, to the divine will." There can be no other foundation to spirituality than this, and neither St. Benedict nor St. Bernard is above repeating himself in its restatement.

In his *De Gradibus Humilitatis* St. Bernard makes it clear at the outset that the object sought is not one or other virtue as though it were an absolute, but Christ. Absolute truth is both the end and the way to the end: Christ alone fulfils man's every desire and at the same time provides the sustenance required for the journey towards Him. The concluding paragraph of St. Bernard's first chapter on the degrees of humility gives a description of the virtue which would be hard to equal anywhere in spiritual literature.

St. Benedict is careful to insert the phrase "for the love of God," which makes the whole difference to obedience. Charity is the guiding consideration. When submission to a superior is given in charity, it no longer dictates terms. Lack of charity restricts both obedience and humility to a service which satisfies the obligation outwardly, but which cannot either advance the soul or please God.

The monk obeys "for the love of God" when he gives up his own ideas and adapts himself to the immediate mould. The common good, a particular necessity, the trial of an individual's faith: any of these things or a dozen more may influence a superior to issue a command. The response goes straight to God when the subject denies himself the luxury of holding to an opinion of his own.

Thus in the terms of this third degree of humility, the monk must remain always flexible, always ready to see the will of God in the unexpected call of authority. He must be willing to sublimate what he conceives to be a personal call to something higher if he learns through the word of a superior that the objectively lower course is the one which God wants followed. Certainly he may cherish in his soul the call to even the most exalted heights, but he must know at the same time that perhaps God does not want him to proceed any further with them. God gives us lofty aspirations, and we are meant to keep them, but if He gives directives through the medium of an external authority which suspend the realization of these holy desires, which even destroy the chances of their ever being realized in this life, we cannot go wrong in bowing to His will as signified in the word of the superior.

If this were not the case, and if we had always the right to judge by our own light, would there be any point in obedience at all? Would we not always advance the claim of following a higher good? Would not our interior calls and inspirations multiply? We would end up with no other voice to obey but our own.

The fourth degree of humility is that if in this very obedience hard and contrary things, nay even injuries, are done to him, he should embrace them patiently with silent consciousness and not grow weary or give in, as the Scripture says: "He that shall persevere to the end shall be saved" . . . and showing how the faithful man ought to bear all things however contrary for the Lord, it says in the person of the afflicted: "For Thee we suffer death all the day long; we are esteemed as sheep for the slaughter." And secure in the hope of the divine reward they go on with joy, saying: "But in all these things we overcome through Him who has loved us."

This degree is the logical religious development of the one that went before: it accounts for the occasions which raise rightly directed obedience to heroically performed obedience. It is not a question here of interpreting a superior's wishes in an heroic manner; it is a question of fulfilling the superior's wishes however uncongenial they are to self. The heroism lies not in the histrionics but in the fidelity. Truly heroic obedience may demand the sacrifice of what a superficial view might see as heroism.

Silent endurance is worth more than any quantity of voluntary demonstration. The whole point of heroic obedience is that it is necessary and not optional. Like martyrdom, which cannot be refused under pain of apostasy, heroic obedience is a necessary obligation voluntarily underwritten in the act of taking the vows of religion: it cannot be refused under pain of disobedience.

Commenting on the fourth degree of humility, Dom Delatte has this to say: "Combine these three: the difficulty of the object commanded, the difficulty that comes from the authority, the difficulties which we make for ourselves, and the result may be too much for our nature, which at length is stifled and exasperated. There are some who cultivate this frenzy, who lose their heads in it, and draw from it the germ of resolutions which upset and dishonour their whole life."[10]

[10] *Op. cit.,* p. 115.

St. Benedict allows, as we shall see later, that there may be occasions when what is commanded is not only repugnant to nature but impossible of accomplishment. But even in such rare cases, which are to be handled in a particular way, there must be patience, serenity, resignation. St. Benedict's *tacita conscientia*, translated above as "with silent consciousness," speaks volumes. The interior smouldering of a nature not wholly sacrificed to the service of obedience must be ruthlessly stamped out. So also must the nervous agitation which, if indulged, can become a neurosis. A man can dwell upon the hardness of his lot, turning round and round in his mind the reasons which prove how unfair it is, till in the will he has virtually laid down the cross altogether. And it is by the will that the cross has mostly to be borne.

It is in situations of this sort that the monk will have to draw upon the patience of Christ and the stimulus provided by the Scriptures. "Stand fast in the faith, do manfully, and be strengthened. Let all your works be done in charity."[11] Hearing this text at Matins every ferial day of the week, the monk should feel encouraged to persevere, whatever happens, in the service of love which he has undertaken.

Moreover *until* the monk has made his own the verse quoted by St. Benedict from the forty-third psalm, and has got himself into the Messianic frame of mind whereby he too is under the shadow of death all the day long and lives as a sheep destined for the slaughter, he will always find himself trying to shuffle out from under the burdens of religion. While there is nothing morbid about it, the ascetic side of the holy Rule aims at forming in the consciousness of the monk the idea that he is sentenced: his life is a glad and voluntary self-conviction. He has charged himself with sin, he has pleaded guilty, and is now under constraint for the rest of his life awaiting the final release. A monastic vocation is a serious business. Like this, a monk accepts with gratitude and a certain surprise the joys that come to him; the trials he accepts as what he bargained for.

But always in the process, as St. Benedict says, the monk goes on in the "happiness and security of hope, saying: 'In all these

[11] I Cor. 16;13,14.

things we overcome, through Him who has loved us.' " The monastic life is neither a matter of quiet enjoyment nor a matter of supine acquiescence; it is something which for its fulfilment in the crowning happiness of love requires grave determination and positive, active courage. To approach it with any other view is to approach it frivolously. You might just as well form a judgment of it from books composed of pictures showing beautifully tonsured monks sitting in sunlit cloisters with illuminated tomes open on their laps. St. Benedict nowhere uses the superficial, the picturesque, the romantic or the comfortable to attract souls to the monastery—or to keep them there once they have entered it—but instead we find him constantly stressing the more serious aspects of the life. The attraction must be to the cross, to Christ and Him crucified, or it can not be guaranteed genuine. The words which follow in the text show this clearly enough.

> And so in another place Scripture saith: "Thou hast proved us, O God; Thou hast tried us as silver is tried by the fire; Thou hast led us into the snare, and hast laid tribulation on our backs." And in order to show that we ought to be under a superior, it goes on to say: "Thou hast placed men over our heads." Moreover, fulfilling the precept of the Lord by patience in adversities and injuries, they who are struck on one cheek offer the other.

Our constancy must be proved at every point or there is nothing to show that we are constant. The trial of our strength may make us feel weak and miserable, but without such a trial we would remain weak and deserve to be miserable. At least while in the purifying fires that temper our nature we have the knowledge that all this will one day give place to perfect peace. When our Lady said to Bernadette: "Je ne vous promets pas de vous vendre heureuse dans ce monde" the significance is lost if we interpret it stressing "I did not *promise*" instead of giving the emphasis "in *this* world." If all Christians are meant to take the long view and have confidence in ultimate happiness, certainly all monks should be habitually aware of this perspective.

It is God, according to the psalmist, who has let us fall into the snare and who has burdened our shoulders with tribulation. "Very good," says the well-trained disciple; "not only is it what I deserve, but if I keep my wits about me I can so use this present discipline as to provide me with the best possible preparation for eternal life: I can unite my afflictions with those endured by Christ." The further implication in St. Benedict's words is that if the worst comes to the worst in our trials of obedience, we can always comfort ourselves with the thought that over our heads now are mere men, but that this state of affairs will not last for ever. God has placed them over our heads for a time, but eventually our heads will be free of them and will be under Him alone.

> The fifth degree of humility is to hide from one's abbot none of the evil thoughts that beset one's heart nor the sins committed in secret, but humbly to confess them.

In the pre-Benedictine history of monasticism—witness Cassian and St. Basil who urge the practice as being part of the discipline of the monk; witness also a number of incidents in the *Paradise of the Fathers* which show how common the practice was—these manifestations of conscience were subject to a looser control than St. Benedict, coming later with his ideas of a patriarchal society, intended them to be. St. Benedict wants his monks, as members of a family, to be perfectly open about themselves with their father. It is not here a question of sacramental confession, but of the avowal of hidden faults to the abbot in private conversation.

Though undoubtedly an expression of humility, the custom admits of misinterpretation and abuse. A monk, eager to comply with the letter of the text, may make his manifestation in the correct form yet withhold the real motive which has led him to make it. If it is not vainglory that has prompted him, it may well be a certain cunning which seeks to forestall an obedience or a punishment. Before abasing himself in the terms of the fifth degree of humility, the subject should assure himself that neither the desire to stand high in the abbot's estimation nor the fear of being loaded with a difficult obedience is influencing his action. Looking at it from the abbot's side, such declarations from his subjects will have to be treated with the utmost care. He will have to make up his mind whether the admissions spring from a sincere wish for pardon and direction, from self-deception, or from the intent to mislead. In any case he will refrain from forming his judgment of the man solely on the evidence presented. Nor will he allow what he has heard to influence his behaviour towards either the confidant himself or any others whom the confidences may affect.

Because of the problems to which it gives rise, the practice of revealing matters of conscience to the superior is not viewed by the Church with the same enthusiasm as it was by St. Benedict. Religious superiors today are not allowed to exact manifestations, and even to act as regular confessor to members of his community is now forbidden to an abbot. But the subject is still free to gain the merit of the fifth degree of humility, and benefit by the advice he receives as the result of it, so long as he delivers himself of his disclosures in the mood envisaged by St. Benedict.

The sixth degree of humility is for a monk to be contented with the worst and meanest of everything, and in all that is enjoined him to esteem himself a bad and worthless labourer, saying with the prophet: "I have been brought to nothing, and I knew it not; I am become as a beast before Thee, yet I am always with Thee."

In English the phrase "to be contented with" has come to mean "to endure without complaint." But surely St. Benedict's meaning is that the monk is positively glad when occasions of living poorly present themselves. If he has learned the lessons taught by the earlier degrees, he will jump at the chance of proving his nothingness by enjoying the least rather than the greatest. He will even look out for the less favoured position, the more menial occupation; he will avoid the platform, the limelight, the shower of honours.

It is seldom that a monk belonging to a community that has been established for any length of time is called upon to endure "the meanest and worst" in the way of material things, so perhaps this degree of humility can be more suitably applied to the endurance of frustrating circumstances. To find oneself left with the most boring occupations, or to have to stand by without recognition while others are advanced, can aptly fulfil St. Benedict's conditions. "I have been brought to nothing . . . yet I am always before Thee": I must develop a liking for the lowest place.

But there can be a snare even in this. I can come to develop a taste for the lowest place as such, for the meanest and the poorest articles because they are mean and poor. By the inverted snobbery to which the most devout are liable, I can wallow in the luxury of poverty: I can become an aristocrat in neediness. It is thus that the degrees of humility are turned the wrong way round, becoming steps of pride.

> The seventh degree of humility is that he should not only call himself with his tongue lower and viler than all, but also believe himself with inmost affection of heart to be so, humbling himself and saying with the prophet: "I am a worm and no man . . . it is good for me that Thou hast humbled me, that I may learn Thy commandments."

This degree is immediately connected with the one before, not only securing the sincerity of our protestations of unworthiness but also extending the disposition beyond the acceptance of things *vila vel extrema* to the whole of life itself. Humility is incomplete until the conviction, borne out by experience and actual humiliation, is arrived at that we are entirely despicable. God allows us this sense of being less than the dust so that we may have absolute confidence in Him.

When our whole trust is in the power of God, and when we are habitually aware of our powerlessness in His service, then we can begin to "learn Thy commandments." Then we can begin to taste something of true peace. True peace means freedom, and it is the commandments which make us free. *Ambulabam in latitudine, quia mandata tua exquisivi.*[12] When humility has taught us trust, and trust has taught us humility, then we can move freely about His law and enjoy peace in the peace which He enjoys.

[12] Ps. 118;45.

*Meditabar in mandatis tuis quae dilexi . . . memor fui judiciorum
tuorum a saeculo, Domine, et consolatus sum.*[13] Humility, law,
trust, freedom, peace: they are all bound up together.

In St. Bernard's analysis already referred to, this degree of
humility is discussed chiefly in regard to what is opposed to it,
namely arrogance and presumption. Often the best way of determining an ideal is to see it inside out; often the best judge of
character is the man who can see the caricature. Thus a monk
who has failed to absorb the spirit of this degree, who still thinks
himself to be someone, will as inevitably push himself forward as
a bubble of air inevitably pushes its way to the surface of the
water: it is in his nature to do so.

Such a man may oppose humility by showing himself as a
straightforward thruster—manoeuvering himself into the more
coveted offices in the community, behaving and talking with too
great assurance—or, more subtly, by refusing to defer interiorly
to the opinions of others and to the accepted way of doing things
in the community. This latter attitude of mind provides the material for the next degree, which follows in close association.

> The eighth degree of humility is for a monk to do noth-
> ing except what is authorized by the common rule of the
> monastery or the example of his seniors.

This puts a stop to both the overbearing manner and the un-
submissive judgment. By now St. Benedict supposes a monk who
is so far independent of self as to be indifferent in the choice of
what means are to be preferred in the pursuit of monastic perfection. The common custom of the monastery is to be his guide,
the will of the brethren.

There must be many who feel that this is the hardest degree
of all to practise. They know that it means the sublimation of
every personal conception of the monastic ideal, the resolute
abjuration of every outlet that is not recognized by the community as usual, the desire to sink oneself—and not for the love of a
quiet life but for the love of God—in the general interpretation
without a trace of either singularity, wistful misgiving, dramatiza-

---

[13] *Ibid.*, vv. 47,52.

tion or sense of secret orthodoxy in the midst of prevailing error. Accordingly it does a monk no good to lose himself in the crowd and follow carefully the example of his seniors if inside himself he is saying, "I happen to be right in my understanding of St. Benedict's Rule, but just to show what respect I have for the common life I will keep my views hidden and adapt myself to the brethren's mistaken ways."

What St. Benedict wants in this degree is that the monk should plunge himself into the flow of community charity, not that he should paddle in it for the sake of appearances. Unless the monk allows himself to be carried by the current, he might just as well stay at home and have a bath on his own. In this particular simile, where the waters of charity circulate through the community, the brethren determine the current.

The sanction given by St. Benedict to the common rule of the house and to the standard set by the seniors might well be used against him: it might, taken out of the context of the Rule as a whole, be made into an excuse to condone abuses. To read the eighth degree in such a sense would be to discount a hundred other passages where fidelity to regular observance is stressed. What St. Benedict is looking for here is the individual monk's conformity with the best elements in the monastic family, not with the worst. The monk is being told not to strike out an individual line, whether in the cause of relaxation or reform, but to eliminate self-interest in looking to the highest interests of the whole. The highest interest of all is charity. All political, partisan, aesthetical, social and devotional tendencies or programmes must be subjected to the ultimate test of charity.

The many are likely to know more about charity than the one. Those who have matured in the religious life are likely to know more about charity than those who have lately joined. The Canticle of Canticles, which is all about charity, speaks of "threescore valiant ones [who] surrounded the bed of Solomon, the most valiant of Israel and most expert in war . . . because of the fears in the night."[14] Solomon felt safe among his many veterans. The monk has reason to fear the illusions which are magnified in

[14] 3;7,8.

isolation and in the dark. In fighting against the many he may be fighting against God. "It is not good for man to be alone."[15] Left to himself he may see good things, but see them in wrong proportion. He is safer when he humbles himself, accepting "the valiant ones who surround him"—the bodyguard of tradition, example, and experience.

The ninth degree of humility is that a monk refrain his tongue from speaking, keeping silence until a question be asked of him, as the Scripture shows: "In much talking thou shalt not avoid sin," and "The talkative man shall not be directed upon the earth."

This and the two degrees which follow can be taken together as giving St. Benedict's practical legislation on the subject of the spirit of silence discussed in the sixth chapter. It is no good having a deep reverence for silence if you are ready to break it for the lightest reason.

The connection between silence and humility is close. Indeed the two cannot but go together. The reticence which is the sign of humility is not sterile and negative: it is positive enough to impose restraints. The first thing to be restrained is speech. If silence were nothing more than the painlessly delivered child of inertia, there would be no supernatural value about it whatever.

The sequence of St. Benedict's thought is simply this: the humble man is the one who can distinguish between the real and the superficial, between the essential and the accidental; to him the necessary is so important that the unnecessary must be restricted. The humble man, therefore, refrains from speech until necessity obliges him to use it. Even then he uses it sparingly, and with the desire to get back to the silence which is his proper element.

But what constitutes necessary conversation? Clearly there are occasions when, even during times and in places of silence, a monk has to speak. There are also occasions when it would be conceivably possible to put off speaking until a time allowed for it, but when to do this would be highly inconvenient. Is the monk

---

[15] Gen. 2;18.

in such cases to keep silence? It is here that the preceding degree of humility will come into play: he will decide by referring to the practice of the more responsible members of the community.

In clinging obstinately to his interpretation of the letter of silence a monk may find himself in danger of losing the spirit of charity. If it is not good for a man to be alone in his community, it is equally harmful for a monk to be alone in his idea of silence. His observance of silence should be such that it attracts others to silence. If it disturbs the recollection of others by making them want to break it, there is probably something wrong with it. The monk whose silence is so singular that it exasperates his brethren is defeating the end of silence. Such a monk will be the last to admit it, but his silence is being to him too a distraction and affectation, an obstacle to interior and exterior charity.

Yet somehow, despite the exaggerations which threaten it, silence must be preserved. Must, in charity and self-denial, be built up. It does not happen of itself; it is not a void. A monk has not satisfied his obligation towards silence even when he has hollowed out spaces from the material of his day. A space may be a waste space, which is worse than not being a space at all. The monk must so make use of his leisure as to create the disposition for prayer. This is a positive work. It is the primary function of silence, to dispose for prayer. Understood in this way, silence and recollection are so mutually assisting as to become almost convertible terms. The signal for silence is the summons to the practice of the presence of God.

> The tenth degree of humility is that he be not easily moved and prompt to laughter, because it is written: "The fool lifteth up his voice in laughter."

If the presence of God gives us the cue to the foregoing degree, it can be taken all the more surely to provide us with the reason for this one. The question is more than merely that of monastic good taste; it has the further reference to the monk's essential interior life. As a means toward securing outward tranquillity in the house, the regulation has its value; as a safeguard to the soul's personal relationship with God, however, is its value chiefly to be appreciated.

The lack of humility implicit in *facilis ac promptus in risu* becomes explicit in what laughter so often gives rise to. Ostentation, playing to the gallery, eagerness to hear the answering laugh, resentful disappointment when this applause has been denied: all this is of the vanity of the world.

St. Bernard, as might be expected, attacks in strong terms the tendency in monks to levity; he gives a whole chapter to *inepta laetitia*. His degrees of humility contain such expressions as *verba resonant ampullosa . . . pueriliter hilarescit . . . in signis scurrilitas . . . pronus ad jocum . . . per cachinnos* [guffaws] *excutitur*. This fatuous gaiety, which is the enemy of the tenth degree of humility, renders a man unfit, according to St. Bernard, for the grave affairs of life. The appearance of being constantly amused, which the facetious affect, is both empty and misleading. "Nothing reveals true misery," says St. Bernard (though in another place)[16], "so much as untrue joy."

St. Bernard accounts for much of the falseness in religion to curiosity and lack of modesty. If monks were more indifferent to excitement and experience, less interested in matters outside their immediate monastic concern, they would not have to dissemble. But because they want to taste the pleasures of the world as well as those of religion, they act the polished entertainer in one company and the rough ascetic in another.

A religious man may not be so susceptible to outside influence as to have no identity of his own. He should not take his colour from the association of the moment, or he will find himself simply at the mercy of circumstance. His inability to resist atmosphere and suggestion will lead him inevitably to adopt a manner which is entirely foreign to his religious profession.

> The eleventh degree of humility is that when a monk speaks he does so gently and without laughter, humbly and gravely, with few and reasonable words, and that he be not noisy in his speech as it is written: "A wise man is known in a few words."

[16] *On Grace and Freewill*, ch. 5.

After giving us two degrees that are for the most part negative, St. Benedict gives us one that is mostly positive. Except for
the concluding sentence, which tells us not to be loud in our
talk, the passage makes concrete suggestions. The key word here
is "reasonable."

By reasonable speech we may understand two things: first, as
already treated above, that there is reasonable cause for suspend-
ing silence; second, that what is said is a considered statement and
not the first thing that comes into the speaker's head. Without
having to be sombre in his utterances, a monk is expected to show
a certain maturity in his conversation: his talk must not be wild
and irresponsible.

Allowing that to misread the eleventh degree might lead to
the idea that the perfect monk in St. Benedict's opinion is the
one who is either so gentle and soft in speech as to be quite without spirit, or else so grave and circumspect as to be quite without
humour, it remains true nevertheless that the words chosen by
our holy Father denote emphatically a subdued tone and a brief
delivery. If the eleventh degree does not mean this, it means
nothing at all. You may say that it does not apply to the modern
idea of community recreation, that it has been dispensed from,
that St. Benedict surely never meant, etc. But you cannot say
that the words as they stand do not demand the greatest strictures
in the matter of verbal communication between brother and
brother.

Turning from St. Benedict to St. Bernard, we find that the
disciple has more to say about the abuse of silence than his master.
Though he did not demand from his monks absolute and perpetual silence—he wrote in one of his letters that *inhumanum
est hominem in taciturnitate semper esse et non loqui*[17]—St.
Bernard took care to insure that what conversation there was in
the monastery should be sober and short.

In St. Bernard's thirteenth chapter on the degrees of humility
there is a stinging description of the monk whose unhumble spirit
causes him to spurn the rules of silence. The garrulous monk
gives opinions unasked, anticipates with a ready answer un-

[17] To Hildegard, Abbess; letter 366.

spoken enquiries, interrupts others in the middle of what they are saying, goes on talking after the signal has been given for a return to silence, even gets permission to go on with his story afterwards and complains that the time of recreation is too short.

One of the faults which we shall most often have to confess will be failure to live up to the standards of religious silence set us by our monastic forefathers. So long as we do not condone our weakness, justifying the denial of St. Benedict's "gently and without laughter, humbly and gravely, with few and reasonable words," we shall maintain ourselves in the authentic tradition. It is better to admit inconsistency between ideal and practice than to wipe out the ideal or to try, by argument and excuse, to reduce it to the level of our observance.

The twelfth degree of humility is that the monk, not only in his heart but also in his very exterior, always show his humility to those who see him: that is in work, in the oratory, in the monastery, in the garden, on the road, in the field, or wherever he may be, whether sitting, walking, or standing, with head always bent down, and eyes fixed on the earth; that he ever think of his sins . . . saying in his heart what the publican in the Gospel said with his eyes fixed on the earth: "Lord, I a sinner am not worthy to raise mine eyes to heaven."

This, the last, is perhaps the most difficult degree to explain. But there is no reason on that account to try to explain it away. Dom Jean de Monléon, whose book *Les XII Degrés de L'Humilité* is a masterly treatment of the subject, and who is careful to avoid extremes, cites instances from the lives of the saints which illustrate on the one side the value of gravity in bearing and on the other the necessity of appearing always with a pleasant expression. He gives quotations from the writings particularly of St. Gregory of Nazianzus and St. Francis of Sales to show the need for flexibility in conduct. But neither of these great Doctors of the Church were Benedictine monks. If his words are to be believed, does not St. Benedict ask for something a little more rigid?

For the regulation of monastic conduct it is best to consult specifically monastic authorities. No one could be studied to better advantage in matters monastic than St. Bernard; and on this matter of custody of the eyes and moving with restraint St. Bernard has a good deal to say.

Again St. Bernard is found to fix his attention rather upon the negative than upon the positive side of the question, but this is only the better to build up towards the constructive principle at the end. *Si videris monachum de quo prius bene confidebas, ubicumque stat, ambulat, sedet, oculis incipientem vagari, caput erectum, aures portare suspensas, e motibus exterioribus hominis immutatum agnoscas. Vir quippe perversus annuit oculo, terit pede, digito loquitur, et ex insolenti corporis motu recens anime moribus deprehenditur.*[18] And again the saint accounts for all this on the same grounds of unchecked curiosity. *Nam curiositati pes vagus et indisciplinatus oculus famulantur* and *evidenter proinde curiositati pietas adversatur, et quem illa a corde evocat ista revocat.*[19]

But it should not be thought from the above quotations that St. Bernard is against all joy; still less against the sense of companionship which comes of a well-ordered community life. His argument is that self-discipline in external behaviour makes for, and is the sign of, true hilarity and peace. Thus in his sermon on St. Malachy, he says: *Risus aut indicans caritatis, aut provocans. Rarus tamen et ipse. Equidem interdum eductus, excussus numquam: qui ita nuntiaret cordis laetitiam ut ori gratiam non minueret sed augeret.* And this he bears witness to in the concrete case by adding about St. Malachy that *Nempe, quod non mediocri laudi inter sapientes ducitur, oculus ejus in capite ejus nusquam avolans nisi cum virtuti paruisset.* In his own life, St. Bernard bore out the doctrine: biographers of the saint are unanimous in saying of him, as biographers say also of St. Francis, that his very walk was a preached sermon, and that he radiated joy and the sweetness of love. His custody of the eyes was such that he did not know there was a window high up over the choir where he had attended the Divine Office for years, did not know

[18] *De Gradibus Humilitatis,* ch. 10.
[19] *De Diversis,* sermon 14.

that his journey on horseback had taken him past a lake, did not know that the bottle in front of him in the refectory contained oil.

To take another monk-saint—not a follower of St. Benedict this time but a master from whom he derived much of his monastic doctrine—St. Basil has this to say about the training of the senses and religious deportment generally: "Souls, enclosed as they are in bodies, cannot communicate without accepting the services of the senses . . . it is thus that they see, hear, and talk; it is thus also, as if through windows, that one comes to see their nature. No one could judge the beauty of another's soul, because it is hidden in the body, unless he were able to divine from that other's actions what good there is in the power which produces them; he is able to contemplate the soul as in a glass."

For St. Basil, clearly, every outward gesture of the monk is an indication of his spirit. The two, outward and inward act, cannot be separated. It is not an unsmiling expression as such that these authorities look for in their disciples; it is simply that they want to assure themselves that the disciples are seriously pursuing perfection, and that the virtue of humility is keeping them from extravagance.

And so on down the centuries: insistence upon details of manner together with a still greater insistence upon motive. "How beautiful art thou" is the praise which the shepherd in the Canticle gives to the outward form of the spouse, "besides that which lieth hid within."[20] After the multitude of similes which signify the fairness of what meets the eye, it is what lies hidden within that is taken for truest beauty.

Not only has motive been stressed, but in the course of monastic history there has been an increasing call for the sign of joy. What at first might seem to be equivocal—this simultaneous demand for religious gravity and religious gaiety—in fact provides no contradiction. The contradiction comes in where there is either forced solemnity or forced hilarity. It is interesting to find Dom Guéranger, as stern a disciplinarian as St. Benedict would

[20] 4;1,3.

have wished, writing to Dom Wolter on the absolute necessity of cultivating a spirit of joy in his community.

But head always bent? Eyes ever cast down? The mind constantly occupied with the thought of guilt and the dread of judgment? For answer we have again St. Bernard: "How, after the revelation of himself to himself, can a man lift up his eyes and walk with head erect? . . . the soul can find no motive more effective for humility than a knowledge of itself as it really is . . . and obtaining this knowledge how can it be otherwise than humbled?"[21] But humility is truth, not gloom. Together with the humiliation of seeing oneself comes the relief of knowing at last that one's whole safety lies in the mercy and love of God. Here is peace, here is joy. While the monk goes about with his sense of guilt, not presuming to raise his head in the confidence born of achievement, he is glad of heart and singing interiorly for the joy of his discovery.

But may he never sing outwardly too? Must his composure be such that he never runs, never kicks off the heads of dandelions, never throws his dirty washing across the floor? St. Benedict's "wherever he may be" is unambiguous, but it is better to humble oneself and expand one's movements occasionally than in the name of humility to live under a strain that may become insupportable. So long as humility is served, and the details of the twelfth degree are respected wherever possible and not scorned, the monk is fulfilling St. Benedict's intention. He may not be fulfilling it perfectly, but he would be fulfilling it less perfectly while in a constant state of tension.

Certainly the twelfth degree would rule out haste, and the same prohibition is echoed later in the twenty-second chapter where the brethren are told to come in the mornings promptly to choir *cum omni tamen gravitate et modestia*. Hurry and fuss kill recollection stone dead, and can offend also against charity. It is better to come late for an office than to speed like a tornado through the *statio*. Not to arrive on time breaks only one rule, and that the minor one of punctuality, whereas to sweep to the immediate duty in a frenzied fear of being late frustrates the purpose of several rules.

[21] *Sermons on the Canticle*, 36;5.

There would be some excuse—since he is new to the principles of recollection, and also because novitiates seem to allow little margin—for the novice who runs from his cell to ring the *Angelus,* from manual labour to lay out the vestments, from the sacristy to pick up his books for a choir-practice; less excusable is the father who races from the choir, dives into his vestments, and scuttles to the altar to say Mass.

"Saint Benoît recommande de veiller particulièrement à garder cette mesure," says Dom de Monléon, who, it must be repeated, is not a rigorist: "*au travail,* parce que l'application à la besogne risque de la faire perdre aisément, et avec elle le sentiment de la présence de Dieu; *à l'oratoire,* à cause de la sainteté du lieu, et pour ne pas tomber dans la même faute que le Pharisien de l'Evangile; *dans le monastère,* c'est-à-dire: sous les cloîtres, au réfectoire, dans les escaliers et même dans le secret de la cellule, où l'on pourrait être tenté de se croire seul et d'oublier que Dieu nous voit. Il n'est pas permis de s'en départir non plus *dans le jardin,* si l'on descend y prendre quelque délassement, ni *à la campagne,* si l'on va travailler dans une terre éloignée; ni *dans le chemin,* si l'on part en voyage."[22]

All the ordinary circumstances of the monk's life are covered by the above passage and by the paragraph from St. Benedict which it amplifies. More will be said in another place about the need for custody of the eyes when outside the monastery. Here it is only necessary to add two comments: first that it would be wrong to treat with contempt *any,* however trivial they appear, of St. Benedict's rules for external conduct; second, that in keeping them the great thing to avoid is hypocrisy.

For a professed monk to despise as elementary the practices inspired by this chapter in the Rule and taught in the novitiate —for example, to keep the hands under the scapular (or if you are a Carthusian to keep the hands in the sleeves *outside* the scapular), to walk along the sides of the cloister, to sit upright and not cross the legs, not to go upstairs two steps at a time— would be to show pride. In the work of perfection even the details count.

At the other extreme there is another kind of pride—that of

[22] *Les XII Degrés de L'Humilité,* p. 310.

false humility. *Gloriosa res humilitas,* says St. Bernard, *qua ipsa quoque superbia palliare se appetit, ne vilescat . . . si ad hanc superbam humilitatem non leviter flectitur,*[23] and he quotes from Ecclesiasticus: "The furnace trieth the potter's vessel."

In his every exercise, whether of worship or discipline, the monk will have to guard against the hundred subtleties of vainglory. "La fausse modestie est le dernier raffinement de la vanité," says La Bruyère, "elle fait que l'homme vain ne paroisse point tel et se fait valoir au contraire par la vertu opposée au vice qui fait son caractère; c'est un mensonge."[24]

> Having therefore ascended all these degrees of humility, the monk will presently arrive at that love of God which, being perfect, casts out fear: whereby he shall begin to keep, without labour and as it were naturally and by custom, all those precepts which he had hitherto observed not without fear, no longer through dread of hell but for the love of Christ and of a good habit and a delight in virtue. Which God will vouchsafe to manifest by the Holy Spirit in His labourer now cleansed from vice and sin.

This concluding paragraph reiterates the promise made in the Prologue. Love will take the place of fear; love will establish the soul in unbroken service. But it means a laborious climb: the monk is alluded to here not as a "brother" or a "disciple" but as a "labourer"—*operarius.*

Yet once the ascent has been made, the work is performed *absque ullo labore, velut naturaliter ex consuetudine.* This is so simply because by now God Himself is fully in the work and in the performance: the element of self has been eliminated. By the gravitational attraction which we examined at the beginning, the soul, together with its every activity whether interior or exterior, is being drawn towards its centre—towards its proper object which is God. It is St. Benedict's teaching that humility both allows for this action of grace, and, in that the virtue is itself a grace, brings it to perfection.

The whole process rests, then, on the soul's ready co-operation

[23] *De Gradibus Humilitatis,* ch. 18.
[24] *De L'Homme,* no. 66.

with the grace of being humbled. *Omnis qui se exaltat humili-abitur, et qui se humiliat exaltabitur.*[25] Our self-esteem must sink to nothing or we shall never be made capable of rising to meet the summons of love. Lifted by the power of grace we are enabled to plumb the depths of our own inadequacy. It is thus that our two individualities, the one naturally proud and the other supernaturally humbled, cross one another on what St. Benedict calls the ladder of Jacob.

[25] Matt. 23;12.

CHAPTER 8

OF THE DIVINE OFFICE AT NIGHT

After setting the direction of his disciples' minds, St. Benedict arranges the affairs of their day. First among the duties to be performed, in order both of importance and of time, is that of the Divine Office. Nothing could be more practical than the way in which he opens the subject—starting straight off on the question as to what hour Matins is to begin, and going on with regulations regarding what psalms are to be said—but for the sake of approach we here anticipate some of the saint's teaching on the Divine Office which will be met with in later chapters.

It is not until chapters nineteen and twenty that we are told of the dispositions which we should bring to the exercise of prayer. The key phrase *nihil operi Dei praeponatur*, which gives the whole Benedictine conception of the matter, does not come until the forty-third chapter. In chapter fifty-eight "zeal for the *opus Dei*" is laid down as one of the essential qualities to be judged evident in the novice seeking profession. When it is noted also that to be excluded from choir is taken to be one of the most severe punishments that can be imposed upon a monk, and that faults in the recitation of the Divine Office are penalized, we can form an estimate of the influence which the liturgy of the choir is designed to have upon Benedictine spirituality.

When enumerating the instruments of good works, St. Benedict alluded briefly to the necessity of prayer. When he comes to treat of it expressly, as now, it is the liturgy that claims his first attention. The *opus Dei* does not represent the sum of Benedic-

tine prayer—because the strictly interior life is assumed throughout the Rule to be integral to the monastic vocation—but it is
taken to be the characteristic work of monks and contemplatives. It is significant that St. Benedict devotes no less than
thirteen out of his seventy-three chapters to this work of common worship in choir.

But neither the primacy of place nor the thoroughness of the
treatment given to it should incline us to believe that the *opus
Dei* is the sole work of monks. If monks existed for nothing else
but attendance at the Office, they would tend to waste the time
spent outside the choir and to become preoccupied with ritualism
when in it. The Divine Office gives the impulse to the rest of the
life; all other works take their character from this first and most
indicative monastic duty. The *opus Dei* is comprehensive, not
exclusive.

A more ample discussion of this subject may be left till St.
Benedict draws attention in the holy Rule to its points of principle and practice; here in these preliminary chapters it will be
necessary to note only his method of arrangement and various
facts affecting the Divine Office in the course of history.

In winter-time, that is from the Calends of November
until Easter, the brethren shall rise at whatever shall be
calculated to be the eighth hour of the night; so that having
rested till some time past midnight, they may rise having
had their full sleep. And let the time that remains after the
Night Office be spent in study by those brethren who have
still some part of the psalter and lessons to learn.

St. Benedict divides the year differently, according to whether
he is legislating for the Divine Office, for manual labour, or for
meals. From the point of view of the Divine Office the year falls
into two seasons: from the Calends of November until Easter,
and from Easter until the winter observance is begun again. From
the point of view of labour, and the time for reading, the year is
divided into three parts: summer, winter, Lent. From the point of
view of the refectory, and the hours at which the brethren eat,
St. Benedict recognizes four seasons: summer, winter, Lent,
Paschal time.

Taking Dom Berlière and Dom Cuthbert Butler as our authorities in much of what follows,[1] we can conclude that the monk's day in St. Benedict's time began during the winter at about two or a quarter past two in the morning. This was roughly "the eighth hour of the night." The Night Office—or "Matins," which is the current monastic term and as such will be used hereafter except where the translation of the text requires the older usage—began as soon as possible after the call. This was followed by certain prayers and the interval referred to for study or the preparing of lessons. Then, some time between half-past five and six, came what in St. Benedict's day was called *matutini* or *matutinum officium* but what we call Lauds.

In the summer the horarium is, as we shall see, quite different. St. Benedict's intention is to time the Divine Office according to the length or shortness of the nights, altering even the composition of the Hours in order to allow for considerations of light and sleep. St. Benedict keeps to the same frame, but adjusts the psalms and lessons. Neither in winter nor summer did the brethren go back to bed between Matins and Lauds.

Allowing that the monks went to bed immediately after Compline, which was said in winter at about six and in summer half an hour later, there would have been enough sleep to satisfy the normal need. But only just enough. The Rule does not favour sleep as a luxury. During the summer half of the year an hour or so is taken off the time given to sleep at night, but to compensate for this a period of rather more than an hour is allowed for a siesta in the afternoon after the chief meal of the day. The practice observed in some monasteries of getting up during the night for Matins was based on a faulty reading of the Rule (so Martène): broken sleep was not part of St. Benedict's plan. According to recent scholarship the time for rising varied apparently throughout the year between the hours of half-past one at the earliest and three o'clock at the latest.

As to how the caller of the community was himself called we have no accurate information.

[1] Berlière, *L'Ascèse Bénédictine*, pp. 52 ff., and Butler, *Benedictine Monachism*, pp. 275 ff. Dom Justin McCann's *St. Benedict* and T. F. Lindsay's *St. Benedict* have also been plundered.

The phrase *meditationi inservatur*, taken together with *psalterii vel lectionum aliquid indigent*, as accounting for the time spent between Matins and Lauds should be noted. Calmet suggests that the verb *meditari* in Low Latin has no particular religious connotation and that it may mean to learn by heart. But if it means no more than this, why does St. Benedict bring it in at all? If committing the psalms and lessons to memory is what we are to understand by the term, St. Benedict has said as much already in requiring those who are short in these subjects to catch up on their study.

Though there is no prescribed period of mental prayer in the holy Rule, would not this interval between the two morning offices be the best time for it? We know that St. Benedict's monks did in fact pray mentally, and that the saint himself was much given to it. "While St. Benedict leaves great scope to individual inspiration in the matter of private prayer," says Lindsay, "he clearly points the way to the heights of contemplation. Whatever form their active life may take, and however deeply they may be engaged in manual labour or study, Benedictine monks are expected by their founder to aim at nothing less than the advanced prayer of the mystic."[2] Thus because the habit of interior prayer demands a daily exercise—since no activity can be maintained without the repetition of its specific act—we can assume that room was made in the timetable for a prayer that was not vocal but contemplative.

That *meditationi inservatur* may imply an interior exercise is further suggested by negative evidence—the employment of those brethren who would not be occupied in learning psalms and lessons. No alternative is proposed, and since every other part of the day is carefully legislated for, it is not unreasonable to suppose that they are to be engaged in prayer. While these, the more advanced or better educated, are at whatever devotions they feel drawn to follow, the rest will be set to meditating on material supplied by the liturgy.

But from Easter to the aforesaid Calends of November, let the hour for the Night Office be so arranged that after

[2] *St. Benedict*, p. 169.

a very short interval, during which the brethren may go out for the necessities of nature, Lauds, which are to be said at daybreak, may begin without delay.

During the summer half of the year, then, it is sunrise and not the hour of the night that governs the distribution of offices. In May, June, and July the interval between Matins and Lauds will last hardly any time. But if during these three months Lauds takes place at about four o'clock, the interval will lengthen as the November Calends approach.

We get a hint—even from this preliminary chapter on the Divine Office, and it will appear more clearly later on—that the horarium of the day is determined by the liturgy. With the work in choir as their fixed pivot, the other duties of the house will group themselves as best they can and according to the balance of *labor* and *lectio*. This is not to say that St. Benedict planned to use the Divine Office to peg down the occupations of his monks; it is rather to say that within the framework of his day, the Divine Office is the least movable feature. Neither the timetable nor, as we have seen, the Office itself is absolutely fixed, but the only factors which can be allowed to alter the position of the primary obligation are the seasons of the year or the considered wishes of the abbot.

Thus far St. Benedict and the practice of his own monks in his own time. But what of the monks who came after him—who used a different Matins and Lauds, and who followed definite rites in the observance of the delay between the one office and the other?

Monasteries in the time of Charlemagne, for instance, were following the Roman and not St. Benedict's arrangement of the Office. The communities which served basilicas in Italy and Gaul throughout the eighth century did the same. It was not until the time of St. Benedict of Aniane in the ninth century that the *opus Dei* as outlined in the Rule was restored. The break with the original tradition may have been due either to the destruction of St. Benedict's own monastery of Monte Cassino in the late sixth century by the Lombards or to a passage in the Rule where he says in so many words that if anyone has a better distribution of psalms to offer, "let it be followed."[3]

Regarding the gap between Matins and Lauds, Paul Warnefrid speaks explicitly of reading and "keeping vigil." He says also that to prevent the brethren from slipping away to bed at this time, the abbot should propose to his monks certain difficult problems which will keep them searching for a solution until the signal is given for the next office. Perhaps we see in this the first draft of what was later to become a *casus*, or theological disputation, to be held by the community gathered together in chapter. As an evasive tactic such a suggestion resorted to by an abbot might today be held suspect. It is to be wondered how even in Warnefrid's day it could have been judged strong enough to keep the monks out of bed. St. Benedict of Aniane makes use of no devices for keeping his monks on their knees—or at least on their feet—at this hour. The Monastic Capitulary of Aachen forbids the monks "to return to bed in the interval after Matins unless it happen that they have risen before the appointed hour." The monks of Cluny frankly resumed their sleep after Matins, getting out of bed again for Lauds at dawn; but then they seem to have begun Matins earlier than the Rule of St. Benedict required. Monks of later times, Dom Ménard observes, employed this morning respite according as devotion prompted or as the wish of the abbot dictated.

If we go back past Benedictine history to the monks of the desert, we come across a prevailing opinion as to the spiritual wastefulness of allowing the first supernatural exercises of the day to be interrupted by bodily rest. "So when the canonical prayers have been duly finished," says Cassian, "everyone returns to his own cell . . . and again all offer with great earnestness the same service of prayer, as it were their special private sacrifice; nor do any of them give themselves to rest and sleep . . . till the brightness of day succeeds the labours and meditations of the night."[4] That the word "till" in the final sentence does not mean that the monk may go to bed at break of day after an early vigil

[3] Ch. 18.
[4] *Institutes*, Bk. 2; ch. 12.

is seen from a passage in the chapter which follows next in the text: "wherefore to the canonical vigils there are added these private watchings, and they submit to them with the greater care, both in order that the purity which has been gained by the psalms and prayers may not be lost and also that a more intense carefulness to guard us diligently through the rest of the day be secured beforehand by the meditation of the night."[5] So as to maintain the principles expressed above, Cassian lays down in greater detail the regulation of morning observance.[6] The two books of the *Institutes* here cited must surely have helped St. Benedict to draw up his scheme of Benedictine liturgical worship.

Now that the Rule has determined the times at which the first two strophes of divine worship are to begin, he will go into the question of their composition. Without considering yet the exceptions in the way of feast-days, the ninth chapter will tell what material is to be used for the ferial office during winter; the tenth will do the same as regards the ferial office in the summer. Since the headings given to the chapters on the Divine Office do not always tally with the subject matter of which they treat, it is as well that we should know in advance what is proposed.

[5] *Ibid.*, ch. 13.
[6] Bk. 3; ch. 5.

CHAPTER 9

HOW MANY PSALMS ARE TO BE SAID AT THE NIGHT HOURS

The bulk of these chapters which deal with psalms, antiphons, responses and hymns can be left to the liturgists. Research has brought to light much that relates both to St. Benedict's sources and to the adaptations of his liturgical scheme at the hands of later legislators. To follow, and still more to pass judgment upon, the processes of the experts would require more than the present work presumes to undertake. In these pages not only will considerable sections of St. Benedict's text be left out, but the notes which attempt to explain whatever remains will be confined to summarizing the information which has seemed to be relevant.

In winter-time, after beginning with the verse *Deus in adjutorium meum intende, Domine ad adjuvandum me festina*, let the words *Domine labia me aperies, et os meum annuntiabit laudem tuam* be next repeated thrice. Then the third psalm with a *Gloria;* after which the ninety-fourth psalm is to be chanted with an antiphon, or at least chanted. Next let a hymn follow. Then six psalms with antiphons.

Liturgists are doubtful about whether the first half of the above is what St. Benedict actually wrote. Assuming it be authentic, the text as it stands would make St. Benedict's Matins or Night Office begin as it begins today. Certainly if he introduced the opening *Deus in adjutorium* it was an innovation, because though the invocation was a favourite one with the monks of

Egypt it does not appear in any pre-Benedictine liturgy. The *Domine labia me aperies* from the psalm *Miserere* occurs also at the beginning of the Roman Office, though its threefold repetition is again a Benedictine interpolation.

The third psalm, chosen because of the reference to being called by the Lord from sleep, gives time for late arrivals to be present at the invitatory. This invitatory, the ninety-fourth psalm, is to be rendered with some solemnity. St. Benedict wants it to be chanted "with an antiphon, or at least chanted."

When St. Benedict says that a psalm or a group of psalms must be chanted *cum antiphona* he means more than that there should be an antiphon at the beginning and the end as we have it today: he wants the antiphon repeated after each verse or group of verses. Psalms which he wants rendered *in directum* or *sine antiphona* still have their antiphon at the beginning and end; it means merely that the refrain is eliminated.[1] Our existing liturgy follows this course.

A distinction must be made between antiphons and responses. When St. Benedict speaks of *responsoria* being sung (as he does in the text to be quoted below), he means the choir to repeat in unison the phrase inserted between the verses or group of verses chanted by a single voice. Thus for example the invitatory, as we have it today, is both antiphonal and responsorial: it is given out by a cantor or cantors, and taken up at intervals by the choir, who repeat the antiphon. In St. Benedict's scheme, however, it is not so much the psalms as the lessons that are punctuated with *responsoria*. What we now call a *breve* is also in this sense responsorial.

> These [six psalms] being said, and also a versicle, let the abbot give a blessing. And all being seated in their places, let three lessons be read by the brethren in turn from the book on the lectern. Between the lessons let three responsories be sung . . . let the divinely inspired books, both of the Old and New Testaments, be read at the Night Office, and also the commentaries upon them written by the most renowned, orthodox, and Catholic Fathers.

[1] Compline is the exception, and is treated separately.

Putting a versicle and response between the two main features of the Divine Office, namely the psalms and the lessons, is not St. Benedict's invention. It seems to have been customary in both East and West, linking one phase of the liturgy with another.

It seems likely that the abbot's blessing before the lesson—no mention is made of an absolution such as we have today, and although there were three readers involved the blessing appears to have been given only once—was not a fixed formula. Smaragdus, who is the earliest commentator on the Rule after Paul Warnefrid, and who wrote in 820, gives a specimen of the kind of blessing in use and adds "or any other of this sort."

While the lessons were being read at the lectern, the brethren remained seated. They stood to their feet only for the *Gloria Patri* at the end of the third responsory.

Points both of ceremonial and of construction find their parallels in other liturgies and other Rules. The ancient Jewish rite combined psalmody with readings first from the Law and then from the exponents of the Law and from the Prophetical books. Later on, Christian monasticism in the East, taking over from the synagogue, determined for the ferial Office a fixed sequence of psalms and lessons: two nocturns of six psalms each, and readings to divide the nocturns.

In the same two books of the *Institutes* quoted at the close of the foregoing chapter, Cassian describes a liturgical Office which was followed in his day in Egypt. Here the ceremonial and arrangement were alike very simple: while one monk chanted the psalms, his brethren remained silent and seated. At intervals the community rose and prostrated; after a pause of varying length one of the elders present prayed aloud. The Egyptians preferred listening to singing, and it was only at the end that all joined in aloud. What mattered for them was the act of uniting themselves mentally with the cantor or celebrant, and with one another.

Palestinian and Syrian monks observed a more corporate ritual as regards the chant. But even here the psalmody was not sung wholly in unison, the main work being still left to the monk who intoned and recited. "After standing and singing three antiphons, the monks sit on the ground or on low seats and answer three psalms which are sung by one monk taking the duty in his turn."[2]

St. Caesarius, only one generation before St. Benedict and writing for monks in Gaul, composed an Office which was more elaborate than that of either Egypt or Palestine. It is believed that in his version the antiphonal method was introduced—a refrain between each verse or set of verses. Here also responses and hymns are found to figure. The psalmody would probably have been rendered on some simple system; the hymns again would have had a melody of their own. St. Aurelian, almost contemporary with St. Caesarius, gives nearly the same arrangement for his own monks and nuns. Arles was well served in the matter of religious. When St. Caesarius died in 543, St. Aurelian succeeded him in the episcopal see. Both men wrote Rules for, and themselves presided over, monasteries which numbered hundreds of subjects. St. Aurelian died in 549. It is estimated that the Rules of St. Caesarius and of St. Aurelian were written about twenty years before the Rule of St. Benedict.

Meanwhile at Milan the liturgy was being observed with greater solemnity than at any of the monastic centres in Gaul. The Ambrosian chant was rendered with harmonics, and with a greater range of modulation than hitherto attempted elsewhere. The singing was alternated, choir with choir, and the psalmody was treated both antiphonally and responsorially. It was here that the *Gloria Patri* was introduced as a doxology—the intention being to combat the Arian heresy—together with special anthems which gave more attention to the hymnal side of the Divine Office.

So once again we find St. Benedict occupying a position halfway between East and West. His *opus Dei* is less monotonous and austere than the Offices celebrated in Egypt, Syria, and Palestine. It is less varied and flamboyant than those of Italy and Gaul.

---

[2] *Institutes*, Bk. 3, ch. 2. This is perhaps the place to mention that Cassian, the early authority on Eastern monasticism, and whose *Conferences* and *Institutes* are so frequently drawn upon by St. Benedict, was himself a monk of the West. He belonged to a monastery at Marseilles. He hoped that by writing of the Egyptian monks, those especially of Scete, he would be able to guide the communities of Marseilles and Lerins towards a more primitive and ascetic ideal.

How it compares with contemporary Offices further west than Gaul, namely in Spain, we do not know. That monasteries existed in Spain before St. Benedict's time is well known, but nothing has yet been discovered about a pre-Benedictine Spanish liturgy.

Further north too, in Ireland and Wales, monasticism was well established before the sixth century. Following the Eastern rather than the Western pattern in their way of life and general ideal, these Celtic monks would almost certainly have favoured the more simple Office. But again nothing definite—beyond the fact that a very great number of psalms were said every day—has survived about Celtic liturgies.[3]

> After these three lessons with their responsories let six more psalms follow, to be sung with an *Alleluia*. Then let a lesson from the Apostle be said by heart, with a verse and the petition of the Litany—that is *Kyrie eleison*. And so let the Night Office come to an end.

Six more psalms. Always the staple of liturgical prayer will be psalmody. The day when someone in authority decides that the psalms are out of date—the day when he claims to have discovered a surer way of expressing the virtue of religion—that will be the day to say good-bye to liturgical worship. And certainly the monastic choirs would very soon be silent.

When St. Benedict says that the psalms of this second nocturn are to be sung with an *Alleluia*, he may either intend them to be treated as we treat them today, with the *Alleluia* as an antiphon at the beginning and end, or else with *Alleluia* interposing every now and again.

The "lesson from the Apostle" is short enough to be said by heart, and has become what we now call the "little chapter." St. Benedict's words seem to imply that whatever the set paragraph was, it might be chosen at the abbot's discretion. But this

---

[3] "In Ireland and Wales there were large monasteries, each numbering many hundred monks. The eremitical life was much in vogue; and these Irish and Welsh hermits, notwithstanding all difficulties of climate, rivalled successfully in their fasts, austerities, and vigils their compeers of Egypt and even of Syria." Butler, *op. cit.*, p. 19.

is only a guess, based on the practice then current with regard to the longer lessons recited between the nocturns. The abbot or traditional usage determined both the books to be read and the length of the passages to be quoted. Certain factors contributed to an early stability in this matter of the lessons to be read at Matins. Thus particular seasons had their appropriate books, and the length or brevity of the particular lesson came to be measured by the time allowed between its recitation and the beginning of Lauds. That the lessons were considerably longer than they are at present is known from a number of sources. At Cluny, according to Calmet, the whole of Genesis was read in one week, and the whole of Isaias in another.

Following the short lesson recited by heart came, as we have them today, first the versicle with its response and then the *Kyrie eleison*. St. Benedict does not say so, but probably this "litany" which begins with *Kyrie eleison* was something which went on for some time. Certainly the Rules both of St. Caesarius and of St. Aurelian refer to the custom current in monasteries of the West, and it is believed that the *Pater Noster* which we have in our own Office formed part of these concluding devotions. In view of what he says three times over in his eighteenth chapter about a collect coming at the close of the day hours, we can assume by analogy that St. Benedict meant the traditional prayer to come also at the end of Matins.

CHAPTER 10

HOW THE NIGHT OFFICE IS TO BE SAID IN SUMMER

In the modifications of the Office as celebrated during the winter half of the year, there is to be no reduction either of the number or of the antiphonal rendering of the psalms. The psalter, which, as we have seen, was the common prayer-manual of the ancients, is the essentially monastic and cenobitic prayer required by St. Benedict and retained by the monks of today.[1] Our summer arrangement of Matins is exactly the same as St. Benedict's.

From Easter to the Calends of November let the same number of psalms be recited as prescribed above, only that no lessons are to be read from the book on account of the shortness of the nights: but instead of those three lessons let one from the Old Testament be said by heart, followed by a short responsory, and the rest as before laid down; so that never less than twelve psalms . . . be said at the Night Office.

It is significant that St. Benedict chose rather to shorten his Matins in the early morning than keep it the same length and cut out one of the other hours later in the day. If considerations apart from the liturgy had been uppermost in his mind, the need for work in the daytime would have justified such a course. But having chosen to keep Lauds at the hour of dawn, and to inter-

[1] See Dom Ursmer Berlière's *L'Ascèse Bénédictine*, pp. 183 ff.

sperse the day with separate meetings for prayer, he had either to get his monks up earlier in the morning or curtail the office of Matins. It must be remembered that St. Benedict was tied to no canonical regulations in the matter of his liturgical allocations. Had he wished he could have followed the Pachomian order, bringing the monks together for prayer at dawn, at noon, at sundown and at midnight. Instead he broke up the day into smaller sections, giving always the best times, rather than the most convenient, to God.

"We are not religious for the Work of God *and* for study," says Dom Delatte, "any more than for manual labour; for then our condition would be far inferior to that of the secular clergy who are directly concerned with souls. We do not deny that a contemplative can and should study; we do not dispute that erudite labours may be lawfully undertaken and successfully accomplished by monks. We content ourselves with the affirmation that the proper and distinctive work of the Benedictine, his lot and his mission, is the liturgy."[2]

Several statements in the above-quoted passage forestall points connected with Benedictine polity which must be studied at greater length. It has been placed here at this stage in the book partly because it reaffirms the liturgical postulate, and partly because its claims regarding works suitable to monks might well be borne in mind while other aspects of the holy Rule are under review.

[2] *Op. cit.*, p. 134.

CHAPTER 11

HOW THE NIGHT OFFICE IS TO BE SAID ON SUNDAYS

From the earliest Christian times, Saturdays and Sundays have had their distinctive regulations. Pachomian monks, for example, went on Saturdays to the village nearest their monastery to assist with seculars "at the offering, and to receive the blessing." On Sundays the priest and his deacons came from the parish church to sing the conventual Mass in the monastery. Not until the custom of ordaining priests from among the monks was introduced would there have been more than one conventual Mass a week. On days which were not Sundays or feasts, the monks appointed for the week would go round the cells giving the signal for the general assembly, the *synaxis*, which was presided over by the superior and which comprised psalmody, readings from the Scriptures and prayers. This ritual of St. Pachomius, with its weekly processions back and forth, was the pattern for the monastic life at Atripa under Abbot Schenoudi.[1]

Cassian too has information to give on the distinctions made in Egypt between Sundays and weekdays. "They use a more solemn and longer service of psalms and prayers and lessons . . . and hence it results that, owing to the addition of the lessons, there is no diminution of their devotions."[2] In his *Conferences*

[1] See Dom van Houtryve, *op. cit.*, p. 125.
[2] *Institutes*, Bk. 3; ch. 11.

he quotes Abbot Serenus as saying, at the close of his discourse, that the brethren must get in some sleep before the dawn, "and then we will go together to church, for the observance of Sunday bids us do this."[3] In Egypt the monks received Holy Communion only on Saturdays and Sundays.[4] In Gaul the custom seems to have been to communicate daily.[5]

> On Sundays let the brethren rise earlier for the Night Office. . . . When six psalms have been sung and all are seated in their proper order, let four lessons with their responsories be read from the book as before. And to the last responsory only let the reader add a *Gloria*, all reverently rising as soon as he begins it.

Summer and winter the same arrangement holds for the Sunday Office. Although a good deal of time is saved which would have gone to manual labour, the added solemnity of the chant entails an earlier rising. The whole day, beginning sooner, is turned over to reading, private prayer, and the *opus Dei*.

The point is made by St. Benedict that the brethren sit in choir according to their rank in the community. He will return to this question of seniority later on, demanding a due regard for precedent which is typically Roman. In chapter, in the refectory, in assuming various weekly duties, the brethren are placed as they are at the work of God—according, that is, to their time in the habit. There are exceptions to this rule: those who come late to an hour must move to the lowest place, and those whose reading aloud is not to edification miss their turn.

Having sat during the lessons and the first three responses, the whole choir rises for the *Gloria* which is added to the fourth. What the practice was in St. Benedict's time with regard to the *Gloria* at the end of the psalms we do not know. We can presume, however, again on grounds of analogy, that wherever the *Gloria* occurred the choir stood and bowed. This is the almost universal practice in monasteries today.

[3] 7; ch. 34.
[4] *Institutes*, Bk. 3; ch. 2.
[5] *Ibid.*, Bk. 6; ch. 8.

After further instructions about the Sunday psalms, antiphons, versicles, lessons and responses which bring us to the end of the second nocturn, St. Benedict indicates a variation to be observed.

> Next let three canticles from the prophets be said, as the abbot shall appoint; which canticles shall be sung with an *Alleluia*. . . . Let four more lessons from the New Testament be read as before; and at the end of the fourth responsory let the abbot begin the hymn *Te Deum laudamus*. After the hymn let the abbot read the lesson from the Gospel, while all stand in awe and reverence.

So on Sundays and feasts, when there are three nocturns, the number of psalms remains the same (fixed always at twelve throughout the year); the three canticles do service for the psalter in forming the material of the third nocturn. What is interesting is that the abbot may choose them at will.

The *Te Deum*, then as now, is intoned by the abbot. The common custom today is for the community to turn towards the altar for this. The *Te Deum*, the Gospel of the day, the *Te decet laus* and the prayer bring Matins to a close. Since they are the most solemn features of the ceremony, they fall to the abbot's prerogative. *Cum honore et tremore* the choir listens to the voice of Christ's representative as the word of God is read.

There has been much controversy among scholars as to exactly how St. Benedict's Office ended. The terms used in the holy Rule admit of various meanings. Since it has not been thought worth while to go into these details here, the dubious passages in the text have been frankly omitted. St. Benedict finishes this chapter by providing for the unfortunate occasion of a late start. If— which God forbid, he says—the brethren oversleep, the lessons and responsories must be shortened. Care will have to be taken to prevent such an accident, and the neglectful caller of the community must make satisfaction in choir before his brethren for the fault which has curtailed the common prayer of the house, and so deprived Almighty God of what is His due. St. Benedict insists that it is God who has been primarily slighted by this carelessness. *Digne inde satisfaciat Deo in oratorio.* The brethren

may or may not have been inconvenienced by the circumstance
—according to the way they happen to look at it—but the loser
in the late rising is God. Penance is therefore performed *in front
of* the community—as much to warn them of the consequence of
neglect as to show common courtesy—but *to* God.

CHAPTER 12

HOW THE OFFICE OF LAUDS
IS TO BE SAID

This chapter is simply a continuation of the preceding one: it deals only with Sunday's Office. In the chapter following we shall be told of the ritual to be observed during the week. It is because St. Benedict is so anxious that Lauds should begin *incipiente luce* that he treats it separately from Matins. In other liturgies, the Ambrosian for example, where the two offices ran consecutively the combined service could be looked upon as a unit.

As an act of worship Lauds has a more clear-cut history than Matins: the rites connected with praying at daybreak came to be stabilized long before Matins settled into a fixed frame. In giving special attention to Lauds, its composition as well as its place in the day, St. Benedict was reflecting a tradition already some centuries old.[1]

> At Lauds on Sunday let the sixty-sixth psalm be said straight on without an antiphon. After this let the fiftieth psalm be said with an *Alleluia*, and then the hundred and seventeenth and the sixty-second. Then the *Benedicite* and psalms of praise, a lesson from the Apocalypse said by heart, a responsory, a hymn, a versicle, a canticle out of the Gospel, a litany, and so let it come to an end.

Has he forgotten the *Deus in adjutorium* or is he purposely leaving it out? Opinions vary, but since the main argument in

[1] Cassian's not very clear reference in his *Institutes*, Bk. 3; ch. 4.

favour of a deliberate rejection is based on the natural link between Matins and Lauds, the second office being regarded as
complementary to the first, it would seem reasonable to suppose
that St. Benedict, who held a different view, would have wanted
to make a fresh start with Lauds. Another reason why the omis-
sion may be judged accidental is that the symbolism involved in
the idea of Lauds would make the words *Deus in adjutorium
meum intende* particularly appropriate. The praise of Lauds is
intended to celebrate the victory of light over darkness. What
could be more fitting than that, at the moment of dawn, the faithful should invite the Lord to hasten on His way? In a sense each
night is an Easter Vigil, each dawn a herald of the Resurrection.
*Deus in adjutorium meum intende, Domine ad adjuvandum me
festina.*

The first of the psalms to be recited in this office is the sixty-
sixth which, because of its shortness, is to be taken slowly: like
the corresponding psalm at Matins it gives the brethren time to
settle down. Then the *Miserere.* Why this penitential note in an
office which, as its name proclaims, is all praise? Perhaps the
reason for it is the same as the reason for having the *Miserere* at
the end of one year and the *Te Deum* at the beginning of
another. We first express our sorrow and ask pardon; then we
break into songs of praise and joy. In some liturgies, notably that
of St. Caesarius but in others besides, the *Te Deum* did in fact
figure during Lauds; this in turn was followed by the *Gloria in
excelsis.*

The psalms chosen to succeed the *Miserere* are chosen carefully: the first because it is the psalm particularly of Easter, the
second because it refers to having waited early upon the Lord,
the third—which is not properly a psalm at all but a canticle—
because it blesses the Lord in all the works of His creation, and
the remaining psalms of praise from which the office gets its
name.

But it should be added that this selection was not originally St.
Benedict's. The office of Sunday Lauds had taken definite shape
by the time St. Benedict entered the field: East and West—witness Cassian and St. Caesarius respectively—the composition was

almost the same. It is where psalmody is left for lesson, responsory, hymn, versicle and whatever followed, that varieties of usage are found. The only feature which can almost certainly be attributed to St. Benedict is the introduction of the "canticle out of the Gospel"—the *Benedictus*. If we have St. Benedict to thank for this enrichment of Lauds, we have him to thank also for the corresponding addition to Vespers of the *Magnificat*. The rest of the office is as outlined in regard to Matins.

CHAPTER 13

HOW LAUDS ARE TO BE SAID
ON WEEKDAYS

At first sight the reader of the holy Rule is tempted to think that the handling of these regulations regarding the psalms to be said at the various hours might have been done more shortly. But for one thing St. Benedict is leaving nothing to chance, and for another a full treatment is found to be the only practical one. With Sundays quite behind us, we are now launched upon the consideration of Lauds on the ordinary feria.

In his opening paragraph St. Benedict repeats the directions which he gave to the first part of Sunday Lauds; it is only with the third psalm that the ferial office begins to differ from the Sunday's, and from then onwards it differs considerably. The psalms remain the same in number, but different psalms are chosen for each day. The saint makes special provisions for Saturday, when the exceptional length of the Canticle of Moses requires readjustment elsewhere in the arrangement. The enumeration of psalms finished, regulations are laid down about the necessity of following the Roman rite concerning canticles and about the rest of the office until its customary conclusion.

The reason for borrowing from the Church in the matter of canticles at Lauds, while allowing to the abbot their free designation at Matins, is that the Roman rite recognized only psalms at Matins. Though St. Benedict did not feel bound to adopt the liturgy of Rome as a whole, he clearly felt that where his and Rome's were contiguous he should defer.

The office of Lauds and Vespers, however, must never conclude without the Lord's prayer being said aloud by the superior, so that all may hear it, on account of the thorns of scandal which are wont to arise; so that the brethren, by the covenant which they make in that prayer when they say "Forgive us our trespasses as we forgive them that trespass against us," may cleanse themselves of such faults. But at the other offices let the last part only of the prayer be said aloud, so that all may answer "But deliver us from evil."

Said secretly at other offices, the *Pater Noster* is made into a public act at morning and evening. The emphasis at morning is "give us this day our daily bread," and at evening "forgive us our trespasses as we forgive them." At one time it was thought that St. Benedict was the first to insist on having the prayer said aloud, but now the general opinion seems to be that the custom was current at his date.

CHAPTER 14

HOW THE NIGHT OFFICE IS TO BE SAID ON SAINTS' DAYS

This is one of the chapters in the holy Rule which consists of only a single paragraph. Short as it is, both textual critics and historians of the liturgy have had a good deal to say about it.

This is also one of the chapters where the title and the subject-matter do not absolutely correspond. From the wording of the heading, it might be supposed that Matins alone would come up for treatment; but the text seems to assume Lauds as well.

On the festivals of saints, and all other solemnities, let the Office be ordered as we have prescribed for Sundays: except that the psalms, antiphons, and lessons suitable to the day are to be said. Their quantity, however, shall remain as we have appointed above.

Dating long before St. Benedict's time, the liturgical calendar for secular churches numbered more saints' days than were celebrated in monasteries. Monastic choirs seem to have commemorated very few. It would seem that in the East devotion to the saints was practically a private concern—laudable but optional. The martyrs had their votaries, and certain local saints were kept in high honour by the clergy and faithful, but it would not have been considered usual for religious communities in Egypt, Palestine, or Syria to appoint special days in their liturgical calendar on which to pay homage to special saints. Devotion to the saints in early monasticism was shown more by making pilgrimages to their shrines and relics than by keeping their anniversaries in the Office.

Little by little, as Dom Delatte points out,[1] monastic Offices came to be enriched by what was copied from the observance in secular churches. As time went on and monks were ordained to the priesthood, the contact between monastery and parish drew closer. Monks who went out to serve souls in the neighbourhood brought back ideas, devotional and liturgical, which finally became incorporated into monastic usage. St. Benedict himself, despite his summary handling of saints' days, gave particular prominence to two favourite saints, St. John the Baptist and St. Martin of Tours. In honour of each he built a chapel when he came to Monte Cassino. Also it is over the relics of saints that he would have his disciples pronounce their vows. The monk who is above honouring the saints is not in the authentic Benedictine tradition. Those who hold the purity of the liturgy in such esteem as to be unable to include in their spirituality a devotion to the Church's holy ones, recognized or unrecognized, are in danger of worshipping a system instead of leaving the system free for the worship of God.

After mentioning saints' days, St. Benedict adds *vel omnibus solemnitatibus*. But solemnities, pertaining to Christ, take precedence over the festivities of the saints. As solemnities the commentators count the following: Christmas, Easter, Epiphany, Pentecost, and then, Thursday, Friday, Saturday in Holy Week, and the Ascension. Among saints' days they distinguish between those of greater and lesser rank. Only to the feasts of the first rank do the commentators allow the application of the present chapter in the Rule.[2]

For these more solemn occasions then, whether of feasts *de tempore* or *de sanctis*, the sequence already appointed for Sun-

---

[1] *Op. cit.*, p. 164, where he cites as his authority H. Delehaye, S.J., *Les Origines du Culte des Martyrs*, ch. 3, pp. 109 ff.

[2] See Sister M. Alfred Schroll, O.S.B., *Benedictine Monasticism as reflected in the Warnefrid-Hildemar Commentaries on the Rule*, from which much information has been taken both here and in other chapters of this book.

days is to be followed: the same number of nocturns, lessons, responsories. But this is where the similarity ends, because St. Benedict makes it clear that the psalms, lessons, and antiphons are to be "proper to the day." Four great commentators (Calmet, Mège, Martène, Delatte) wrestle with the meaning of *ad ipsum diem pertinentes* in the context of St. Benedict's explanation. Since there can be no certainty in the matter, the best, and certainly the most interesting, way of approaching the matter is to see how the same problem was being met in other liturgies. The Ambrosian rite included a completely separate catalogue of psalms, lessons, and antiphons for feast-days. So did the Roman; and since in Rome were kept feasts of martyrs not celebrated elsewhere, the days in the week which saw the ferial office must have been few. In Jerusalem "the psalms and antiphons are always appropriate," writes the pilgrim Eucheria of an observance already traditional by the time of St. Benedict, "both those said at Vigils and those of the Morning Office; likewise those said during the day or at Sext and None and at eventide; all are so apt and significant that they suit the occasion."[3] In the liturgy drawn up for his monks and nuns by St. Caesarius in his Rule (only twenty years, it will be remembered, earlier than St. Benedict's), special legislation is accorded to the greater feasts of the year such as were commemorated universally, to saints' days, and to days dedicated particularly to the martyrs.

On the above evidence, the words *ad ipsum diem pertinentes* would justify the translation given to them—"proper to the day," that is to the feast. Those who take the phrase to mean "proper to the ferial office of the day" base their argument on St. Benedict's explicit statement in his eighteenth chapter that the entire psalter must be said in the week. If festal psalmody is of frequent occurrence, how can this be done? And there the dilemma has to be left, still with its question mark.

[3] *Peregrinatio.*

CHAPTER 15

AT WHAT TIMES OF THE YEAR
ALLELUIA IS TO BE SAID

This is again one of St. Benedict's briefer chapters. The only reason that can be suggested why it forms a chapter of its own and was not incorporated into the eighth, ninth, or tenth, is that it regulates for the day hours as well as for Matins and Lauds. When he has got this chapter behind him, St. Benedict can devote himself to the exclusive consideration of the Divine Office beginning with Prime and ending with Compline.

From the holy feast of Easter till Pentecost, without interruption, let *Alleluia* be said both with the psalms and responsories. From Pentecost until the beginning of Lent it is to be said every night at the Night Office with the second six psalms only. But on every Sunday outside Lent let the Canticles, Lauds, Prime, Terce, Sext, and None be said with *Alleluia*. Vespers, however, with antiphons. The responsories are never to be said with *Alleluia* except from Easter to Pentecost.

As an expression of holy joy, the word *Alleluia* goes back to the Book of Tobias.[1] In the psalter it occurs at the head of the psalm *Confitemini Domino* as giving the cue to what is to follow.[2] St. John mentions it in the Apocalypse as being the refrain of

[1] 13;22.
[2] Ps. 104.

praise which runs through the song of the just in heaven.[3] It is not a mere exclamation. The Hebrew, rendered literally, means "All hail to Him who is." The "who is" of the *Alleluia* echoes the title which is above name as we find it in the Lord's injunction to Moses: "say to the children of Israel: He Who Is hath sent me to you."[4] "I am who am"—eternal, self-existent, infinite, independent Being. It is to Him who is the source of all being that creation worships with its *Alleluia*.

The actual sound of the word can be held to signify, as Calmet puts it, "a kind of acclamation and a form of ovation which mere grammarians cannot satisfactorily explain; wherefore the translators of the Old Testament have left it untranslated, and, in the same way, the Church has taken it into the formulas of her liturgy." As such it appears in the four most primitive Christian liturgies of the East: those of St. Mark, St. James, St. Clement, and St. Chrysostom. The only difference in its Eastern and Western use is that where Rome and Gaul excluded it during Lent, the churches of Jerusalem, Antioch, Constantinople, and Alexandria kept it the whole year round. In the Eastern Church the *Alleluia* was heard, and is still, even in Masses of the dead. St. Jerome, to whom it is the cry of victory over sin and death, claims it as a right at the Christian Office of the Dead. *Sonabant psalmi et aurata temporum reboans in sublime quatiebat Alleluia*, he says of his sister Fabiola's funeral.

In the monastic liturgy as observed in the Thebaid, we have Cassian describing how the second nocturn of the night office, "verse after verse being evenly enunciated, the chanter finished the twelfth psalm with a response of *Alleluia*, and then, by his sudden disappearance from the eyes of all, put an end to the service."[5] Also of the Egyptian monks Cassian says in a later chapter: "They observe this with the greatest care, namely that no psalm should be said with the response of *Alleluia* save those which are marked with the inscription of *Alleluia* in their title."[6]

[3] 19;1,3,4,6.
[4] Exod. 3;14.
[5] *Institutes*, Bk. 2; ch. 5.
[6] *Ibid.*, ch. 11.

Thus St. Benedict has ample precedent for his use, both in and out of Paschal time, of *Alleluia*. From Easter until Pentecost it is the only antiphon which he recognizes, and from Pentecost until the beginning of Lent—Septuagesima is of later origin —it is the ferial antiphon for the second nocturn. In this latter connection it was probably St. Benedict's intention to have it repeated in the course of the psalms.

Since every Sunday is taken to stand for Easter Sunday, and because *Alleluia* is a shout of glory, there is a more generous scattering: the three canticles in the third nocturn at Matins, the first psalms after the sixty-sixth at Lauds, and the psalms of Prime and the little hours—all are at least begun and finished with their antiphon of *Alleluia*, and possibly in some of these instances interspersed with it as well. Outside Paschal time it is only Vespers that has its own antiphons. At no season of the liturgical year is Compline recited with antiphons, whether *Alleluia* or other. Nor is there any indication that *Alleluia* figured, as it does now (except when *Laus tibi Domine Rex aeternae gloriae* takes its place from Septuagesima until Easter), at the introduction of any of the offices.

CHAPTER 16

HOW THE WORK OF GOD IS TO BE DONE IN THE DAY-TIME

Regarding Lauds as still part of the night office, St. Benedict now examines the offices which belong to the day. The day proper begins with Prime—witness the prayers which relate to the beginning of the day, the duties of the day, and to the successful conclusion of the day—so it is with this office that we must first concern ourselves.

Prime became a canonical hour only at the end of the fourth century. Cassian refers to prayers and psalms of which it was composed but does not give the name of Prime; to him it was a new devotion which had not yet settled down into the scheme of the liturgy. The name of Prime is recognized by the time of St. Caesarius, so St. Benedict is not introducing either a new hour or a new name.

Whatever may be said about making up the mystical number required by the psalmist, Prime seems to have owed its origin to the tendency on the part of monks to sleep straight through from the end of Lauds till the signal for Terce. Prime was invented to get them up.[1]

There seems to have been some idea in early monastic times that those who had attended Lauds at the right time were not obliged to come back again for Prime. Prime came thus to be regarded as the morning prayers of those who had been dispensed from the morning office.

[1] See Pargoire, *Prime et Complies*, quoted by Delatte, *op. cit.*, p. 171.

It is significant that Prime was incorporated into the monastic Office before it was accepted by the secular churches. Perhaps it was not until the Benedictine influence had begun to spread that the position of Prime became solidly established as an hour equal in dignity with the rest.

Certainly by the time of St. Benedict of Aniane there was no mistaking the importance of Prime in the conventual day. It was more than morning prayers for late risers, more than a device for preventing the brethren from thinking that Terce (at 8.30 in summer, 9.00 in Lent, 9.30 in winter) was the next thing they would have to worry about when once Lauds was done.

Allowing then that in St. Benedict's, Paul Warnefrid's, and St. Benedict of Aniane's days the horarium was as it appears in the Rule, at what time would Prime have been celebrated and how did the brethren employ their time after Lauds until the signal was given for Prime?

In their respective schedules already referred to, Dom Berlière allows half an hour between the end of Lauds and the beginning of Prime; Dom Cuthbert Butler gives an hour to an hour and a half. Thus Dom Berlière puts Prime at 6.30 in winter and 4.30 in summer. Dom Butler makes the time for Prime six o'clock in Lent, and accounts for the longer period all the year round between Lauds and Prime by making greater allowance than Dom Berlière for the southerly latitude of Monte Cassino. Dom Butler suggests that this hour or more was given to mental prayer.

"A document thought to be a report on the discipline of Inde, the model monastery ruled by St. Benedict of Aniane," says the Benedictine nun, Sister M. Alfred Schroll, in her book *Benedictine Monasticism*, "prescribes that the interval between Lauds and Prime should be of such length that the brothers may conveniently pray before each of the altars, and prepare themselves so that when they depart from Prime they may be ready for reading or for the work enjoined on them. In the biography of St. Benedict of Aniane written by a contemporary, it is related that he introduced like practices among his monks. As a consequence he has been generally accredited with the origin of the custom of making miniature pilgrimages, as it were, from altar to altar."[2] The same authority cites Paul Warnefrid's commentary (thirty or forty years before St. Benedict of Aniane) as evidence for the ritual of chanting psalms in these early morning processions from altar to altar. Warnefrid, on the grounds that the Rule knows no such custom, is neither for nor against it. "The origin of the practice appears to be more remote than has generally been thought" is the present-day conclusion; "beyond this vague reference, the commentaries make no reference as to the manner of passing the interval between Lauds and Prime; from what has been said it would seem that the time was left to the disposal of the individual monk to be used for his private devotions."[3]

> As the prophet saith: "Seven times in the day I have given praise to thee." And we shall observe this sacred number of seven if, at the times of Lauds, Prime, Terce, Sext, None, Vespers and Compline, we fulfil the duties of our service . . . at these times therefore let us sing the praises of our Creator for the judgments of His justice . . . and at night let us arise to praise Him.

In their desire to arrive at the significant figure of seven, different early legislators have enumerated different hours. Cassian, coming before the introduction of Compline, made up the number by including the Night Office. St. Basil, also earlier than the date of Compline, got round it by dividing the noon prayer into offices before and after the midday meal. Others again had other systems of computation. For St. Benedict, with his Compline, the number seven was secured without having to borrow from the night. Later on in Benedictine history the offices and semi-liturgical devotions so accumulated that it must have been difficult for those who practised them to make the required calculation.

In legislating for what we call the "little hours," St. Benedict was doing no more than his immediate predecessors: he simply took over the offices current in both secular and religious litur-

[2] P. 114.
[3] *Ibid.*, p. 115.

gies. What psalms he wanted said at these offices we shall note below when he himself specifies them.

Until shortly before St. Benedict's time, Vespers (the office of *Lucernarium*) was generally observed as the concluding office of the day. But somewhere about the middle of the fifth century the practice grew up among monks of the East of reciting various psalms before closing down for the night. This must have spread westwards before long, because modern scholarship recognizes the canonical hour of Compline as being in existence before St. Benedict wrote his Rule. If Benedictines can no longer credit their holy Father with having invented Compline, they can still account him responsible for its existing form in the monastic Office.

So, to conclude, it is clearly St. Benedict's intention, in line with earlier liturgical legislators, to space out his offices in such a way that they cover not only the waking hours of the day but also, as far as possible, the watching hours of the night. *Et nocte surgamus ad confitendum ei.* "The *opus Dei* does not merely place the psalms upon our lips haphazard," says Père Bouyer in his book *The Meaning of the Monastic Life;* "it makes their recitation correspond with the different hours of the day. After what has been said of the psalms taken in themselves, how easy it is to recapture their meaning, fresh each day, as it is conveyed by the hour at which we say them and the choice this hour has guided."[4]

[4] P. 187.

CHAPTER 17

HOW MANY PSALMS ARE TO BE SAID AT THESE HOURS (OF THE DAY)

This chapter comes as a necessary corollary of the one before. It is as if, having arrived at this stage, our holy Father remembered that he had not fulfilled in the text what the title of chapter sixteen had proposed; instead of telling us what the hours were to consist of he had told us only of how many there were to be. So now, having got as far as giving us the list, he must go on to the question of their content.

At Prime let three psalms be said, separately, and not under one *Gloria*. The hymn at this hour is to follow the verse *Deus in adjutorium* before the psalms are begun. Then at the end of the three psalms, let one lesson be said, with a versicle, the *Kyrie eleison* and the concluding prayer.

An exception to the above rule of three psalms at Prime will be met with when Sunday comes up for treatment: the arrangement on Sundays is to have the first part of the hundred and eighteenth psalm divided into four sections, each with its *Gloria* at the end.

The office as it stands in the Rule is a short one, no longer than one of the *hores minorae*. But very soon it acquired prayers and readings which, if not part of the canonical Office, came to be identified in the monastic liturgy with this hour of Prime. The dedication of the day's labour, the reading of the martyrology and of the holy Rule, various prayers for the dead: these customs seem to have been universally accepted in monasteries by the end of the ninth century.

"The morning chapter, a daily assembly of the brotherhood, took place immediately after Prime. It is not formally mentioned in the Rule, but its chief functions are either expressed or implied in the Rule. The universal establishment of the chapter in the monastic life of the Carolingian age is evident from contemporary consuetudinaries. Assuming that the recitation of Prime required twenty to thirty minutes, we are led to infer from a remark of Hildemar that the chapter assembly consumed about one half-hour daily: 'By the time Prime has been chanted and chapter has been held, the first hour will be nearly spent.' "[1]

Writing still of the eighth and ninth centuries, the Warnefrid period and later, the same authority says further: "References to the chapter, scattered throughout the commentaries and contemporary accounts, indicate the main purpose which it served. A public reading, of which a chapter of the Rule formed a part, was held, and this was probably followed by a few words of instruction by the abbot; matters for consultation were discussed; transgressions of discipline were acknowledged and public corrections were administered; the duties of the day were assigned; and articles of clothing were distributed as needed. In fine it was a sort of clearing house for the family affairs of the community—spiritual and temporal, instructional and remedial."[2]

With the versicle *Pretiosa* at Prime, the night silence is judged to have come to an end. This rule of strict silence from Compline to Prime is of ancient origin. Though neither St. Pachomius nor Cassian knew Compline, both of them are emphatic on the necessity of absolute silence during the night. "No one may speak to another at night-time," says St. Pachomius in the forty-fourth chapter of his Rule. "And so when the psalms are finished and the daily assembly is broken up," says Cassian, "none of them dares to loiter ever so little or to gossip with one another."[3] From Prime onwards the silence, though maintained where reasonably possible, is relaxed.

[1] Schroll, *op. cit.*, p. 115.
[2] *Ibid.*, p. 116.
[3] *Institutes*, Bk. 11; ch. 5.

Terce, Sext, and None are to be sung in the same way: that is the verse, the hymn proper to each hour, three psalms, the lesson and versicle, *Kyrie eleison* and the concluding prayer. If the community be large, let the psalms be sung with antiphons; but if small, let them be sung straight through.

St. Clement of Alexandria bids the faithful pray three times a day in honour of the Blessed Trinity. At the third, sixth, and ninth hour the Church is invited to praise the Lord, and in so doing to show that it has not lagged behind in the tradition established by the Jews who prayed at these times in their synagogues and in the Temple. As to how solemn these *hores minorae* are to be in their performance, both for modulation and antiphonal rendering, the determining factor will be the strength of the community.

Let the Vesper office consist of four psalms with antiphons. After the psalms a lesson is to be recited; then the responsory, the hymn and the versicle, the canticle from the Gospel, the litany and the Lord's Prayer and the concluding prayer.

St. Benedict's is an interesting variation on the usual and earlier celebration of Vespers. The earliest form of Vespers, though admittedly bearing little enough resemblance to the office as we know it and as St. Benedict required it, is the ceremony which included the *Agape* and even the celebration of the evening Eucharist. It was, in short, as near as possible a reproduction of the Last Supper. If None, the third of the lesser hours, took place at the ninth, then Vespers took place at the twelfth hour—at about six in the evening when the star *Vesper* appeared and when lamps were lit.

Vespers or *Lucernarium* is placed by St. Basil, St. Gregory of Nyssa, Cassian and others among the offices of the night-time; it had its own lessons which may even have been as long as those of Matins to which it acted almost as a prelude.

With Lauds coming as the complement of Matins, and Vespers as its overture, it was natural that the two offices should be so constructed as to balance one another. Thus St. Benedict is careful to see that the *Magnificat* of Vespers corresponds to the *Benedictus* of Lauds, and that the *Pater Noster* is said aloud at each (though not aloud at the other hours) and in the same relative place. That it was St. Benedict who made these changes is suggested by the fact that St. Caesarius, who as we have seen was at the most only two decades earlier, still kept to the old *Lucernarium* as it had been drawn up in the East.

Let Compline consist of the recitation of three psalms to be said straight on without antiphons; then the hymn for that hour, one lesson, the versicle, *Kyrie eleison*, the blessing, and the concluding prayer.

Compline is a distinctive office. It conforms neither to the grand pattern of Lauds and Vespers, nor to the varied character of Matins, nor to the businesslike simplicity of the little hours. Where at Prime the hymn comes before the psalms, at Compline it comes after. It has resemblances to each office but exact parallels to none. There is, however, this feature which Compline has in common with Matins as appointed by St. Benedict—it ends with a blessing. Since the blessing is not mentioned as concluding the other offices, we can suppose that St. Benedict meant the monk's day to begin and end under the sign of the cross and in the name of the Blessed Trinity.

CHAPTER 18

IN WHAT ORDER THE PSALMS
ARE TO BE SAID

In spite of the ground covered in the foregoing chapters, it will be noticed that the only office for which St. Benedict has issued specific instructions as to what psalms are to be said is Lauds. So he has still to establish the psalmody of each other hour of the day office, and in this he will trace the sequence through the week. For our present purpose in this book it will be enough if we follow him at a distance, making summaries at the natural stopping places of St. Benedict's long chapter.

Starting with Sunday at Prime, the saint provides for that hour so long a psalm (the hundred and eighteenth) that when its first four sections are found to be more than enough for one office, the rest will serve for the little hours not only of Sunday but of Monday as well.

This leaves St. Benedict free to start the psalter on Monday at Prime. He does so, but he cannot get far because he has already borrowed the third psalm for the opening of Matins, the fourth for a psalm at Compline, the fifth for one at Lauds on Monday. He pursues the order as closely as possible, however, for the rest of the week, finishing on Saturday at Prime with the nineteenth.

Next he regulates for the little hours on all days except Sundays and Mondays. Here he breaks away from the order of the psalter, appointing nine psalms which are all much the same length and which can easily be said by heart.

This brings us to Vespers. Following the Roman and Ambrosian Offices, St. Benedict starts off with the hundred and ninth psalm on Sunday and ends with the hundred and forty-seventh on Saturday. Not all the intervening psalms have been available for this, because some have done duty in other hours.

At Compline he wants the same psalms to be repeated every day, Sundays and weekdays alike. Since Compline is to take place in the dark this arrangement suggests itself. The rest of the hour, though it is not mentioned here, is short enough to be delivered by heart.

Having disposed of the day hours, St. Benedict turns to the psalms of Matins. Here the direction is simplicity itself: all the psalms left over from the preceding allocations are to be distributed in their order over the seven nights of the week. So as to secure the stipulated twelve psalms a night, the longer psalms may be divided and counted as two.

All this now concluded, St. Benedict seems to breathe a sigh of relief. He winds up the chapter with a smoothly flowing paragraph which, revealing something of himself, returns us to his former approach.

> Above all we recommend that if the arrangement of the psalms be displeasing to anyone, he should, if he think fit, order it otherwise; taking care that the whole psalter of a hundred and fifty psalms be recited every week and always begun afresh at the Night Office on Sunday. For those monks show themselves too slothful in the divine service who say in the course of a week less than the entire psalter with the usual canticles. Since we read that our holy fathers resolutely performed in a single day what I pray we tepid monks may achieve in a whole week.

St. Benedict is not, in the first sentence of the above, inviting irresponsible alterations of what he has planned at such labour and such length. It is rather that he is leaving room for authorized development. In the history of Benedictinism advantage has been taken of the saint's liberality: some communities have reduced, others have expanded, St. Benedict's measure. One psalter a week, together with the canticles consecrated by monastic custom, may constitute a wise mean on paper, but it can be variously inter-preted when applied in choir. What St. Benedict is trying to do is to put within the reach of the average religious an Office which future authority may see fit to amplify or modify. If changes should be proposed (is the implication), it must be borne in mind that the psalter is something which everyone ought to be able to manage in a week, and that what experiments are made should regard this minimal brother's capacity in preference to that of the liturgical zealot. There is room, after all, for supplementary hours and Offices to be recited by those who feel the attraction and who obtain the abbot's permission.

CHAPTER 19

HOW TO SAY THE DIVINE OFFICE

This and the next chapter come as a spiritual rider to the preceding eleven. They outline the attitude of mind with which to approach the whole duty of prayer, public and private. If he can get his disciples to bring to their interior exercise as well as to their choir attendance a disposition which combines awe, simplicity, compunction and purity of intention, the saint knows that he has nothing more that he need teach them about the spiritual life. He can then go on in his Rule with matters of discipline: in the light of their prayer the monks will be enabled to see the inwardness of outward things like observance and punishment.

We believe that the divine presence is everywhere, and that the eyes of the Lord behold the good and the evil in every place. Especially do we believe this without any doubt when we are assisting at the work of God.

Thus here again, as in the exercise of humility, it is the omnipresence of God that inspires the monk in his choral worship—and at the same time encourages him to keep up his unceasing struggle against distractions, against the sense of wasting time, against the dismay which he will feel at making no sensible progress.

If religion is nothing else but man's response to the drawing of God, then religion will find its fullest expression in the response of worship. Worship is the virtue of charity placed directly in relation to God who Himself is charity. Thus if it is charity that man seeks above all to express when he prays, and if it is to the plenitude of charity that he addresses himself in his prayer, then charity is vitally present *cum ad opus Divinum assistimus*.

It is the presence of God, His beauty and His truth, that elicits from His human creatures the moral virtue of religion. By exercising the virtue of religion man orientates himself towards God: he disposes himself towards rendering to ultimate Goodness, Truth, Beauty, the homage that is His due. What the philosophers may term Essential Being, what the mystics may term His sovereign eminence recognized only in union, remains always the formal object of our stumbling attempts at worship—His infinite excellence as it is in Him alone. *Tu solus Sanctus. Tu solus Dominus. Tu solus Altissimus.*

The infinite excellence of God, independent of man, reveals itself to man in any number of ways: by nature, by study, by contact with others, by argument and example, and above all by grace. Once the necessity of religion has dawned upon the soul, whether it has come by way of human reason or by the blinding light of faith, there is not just one more moral virtue to be practised—namely the virtue of religion that had not been practised before—but there suddenly appear many virtues, all to be directed along the channel of charity towards the one end, God.

In discovering the virtue of religion, the soul discovers the real meaning of justice, fear, fortitude, humility, piety and the rest. The soul discovers also the essential need to pray, and particularly to pray in sacrifice. Prayer and sacrifice, indeed, are seen as the logical and necessary consequence of justice: God must be served for His great glory, thanked for His great glory, atoned to for the outrages done to His great glory.

Thus the monk, who knows about God's existence and who recognizes His sovereign rights over His creatures, must want to express this knowledge and this submission in the most immediate way possible. He will want to dedicate himself in a special way to the expression of these attitudes. He will want to use his physical faculties in the service of this expression, and he will know that in their exercise a still more immediate and intimate relationship with God is being realized: outwardly and inwardly he will be tending directly towards union with God.

In heaven, says St. Augustine, satisfied love sings the hymn of praise in the plenitude of eternal enjoyment. Here below, yearning love seeks to express the ardour of its desires: *modo cantat amor esuriens tunc cantabit amor fruens.*[1] It is in the *opus Dei* that the Benedictine particularly formulates the desire. It is in the *opus Dei* that the presence of God, known to be everywhere, is particularly recognized.

Let us then ever remember what the prophet says: "Serve the Lord in fear," and again "Sing ye wisely," and "In the sight of the angels I will sing praises unto Thee." Therefore let us consider how we ought to behave ourselves in the presence of God and of His angels, and so assist at the Divine Office that mind and voice be in harmony.

Again there is here the reminder about the need in our spirituality of a holy fear. If St. Gregory makes irreverence one of the signs of a soul's deterioration, we should be on our guard against taking our choir duties too lightly. It is all too easy to discount the external aspect of the liturgy to the extent of contempt for rubrics, chant, and monastic good manners. If our love of God is not strong enough to correct this weakness, our fear ought to be. We are not asked to show a cringing servitude—in which there would be affectation—but a loving service. It is one thing to serve and it is another thing to be servile. Service does not exclude fear; indeed it assumes it. But the fear which love and service look for is filial rather than servile.

Quoting the psalmist, St. Benedict would have us sing *wisely*— adding that we must *consider* our actions. It is a thoughtful as well as a reverential service that we must render. *Ut mens nostra concordet voci nostrae.* "The monk must devote all his efforts to penetrate the letter of the psalms," writes Père Bouyer, "in order to acquire the spirit. The study of the psalter, the initiation into a psalmody which comes from the heart, is one of the monk's

[1] Sermon 255.

great tasks."[2] It is a formidable task. So also is it a formidable
task to discipline our actions, bringing them into line with the
required ceremonial. But the *opus Dei* requires of us formidable
tasks. The body and the mind—which means the voice, the eyes,
the movements, together with the thoughts, desires, emotions—
must be in harmony. Only so will the prayer of the Divine Office
flow back evenly to Him from whom it comes. "So shall my
word be which shall go forth from my mouth: it shall not return
to me void."[3]

The Divine Office is at the same time the word of God for man
and the work of man for God. It is God's revelation of Himself
in human accents; it is man's debt repaid to Him in the medium
of sacrifice.

The Divine Office is the re-presentation of "the continual
holocaust offered on Mount Sinai for a most sweet odour of
sacrifice to the Lord,"[4] the *sacrificium laudis* of the psalms and of
the holy Mass itself. In the chant the monk endeavours to bear
witness to that verse of the *Laudate pueri* psalm which says *a
solis ortu usque ad occasum laudabile nomen Domini.*[5] Office to
office, day after day, the continuity is maintained. For his encouragement in the labour of maintenance, the monk knows,
though he perhaps seldom feels it, that participation in the Divine
Office does not consider the glory of God to the exclusion of all
else: his work in choir strengthens his own soul and benefits the
whole mystical body of the Church.

"Like the sacraments," says Guardini, "God's word is spiritual-
corporal: like them it is meant to nourish the spirit in flesh-and-
blood man, to work in him as power. The saving God who came
to us was the eternal Word . . . the same mystery continues in
the living word of liturgical proclamation, and it is all-important
that the connection remain vital."[6] This psychosomatic element
is not the whole, nor indeed the first, aim of the monk as he

---

[2] *The Meaning of the Monastic Life*, p. 180.
[3] Isai. 55;11.
[4] Num. 28;6.
[5] 112;3.
[6] *Besinnung vor der Feir der heiligen Messe*, p. 13.

approaches the most important work of the day. The first aim is to think of God and not of self. But in directing his whole self, *psyche* and *soma* alike, to God, he must know that if he is faithful enough in the exercise he will come eventually to the forgetting of self in the further praising of God.

CHAPTER 20

OF REVERENCE AT PRAYER

This chapter treats of the whole activity of prayer, pointing out first the principles which govern it and then applying the principles to the actual exercise. The principles remain the same whether applied to liturgical or private prayer, but since liturgical prayer has been already discussed it is private prayer that particularly engages St. Benedict's attention here. This chapter in the holy Rule should be taken together with the fifty-second, which, while legislating specifically for the oratory, confirms the instructions given here about prayer. Both chapters derive largely from Cassian's ninth conference. If we are looking for an exposition of Benedictine spirituality, we can find it as clearly formulated by Cassian before St. Benedict's time as by critics and commentators who have come after it.

If, when we wish to make any request to men in power, we presume not to do so except with humility and reverence, how much ought we with all lowliness and purity of devotion to offer our supplications to the Lord God of all things? And let us remember that not for our much speaking but for our purity of heart and tears of compunction shall we be heard.

From the above paragraph, the following list of requirements can be made: humility, reverence, purity of devotion (which may mean either the unelaborate approach of the truly devout who use the simplest prayers, or the singleness of purpose which prays without selfish motive), integrity, contrition. It makes a formidable catalogue, assuming dispositions which already themselves assume a measure of perfection. But this is only what might be supposed: the desire to dispose for prayer is already prayer; the endeavour to set the soul to acquire the necessary virtues is already to advance; the supplication for grace is already a use of grace. Grace, attracting the soul to all these dispositions and emotions and virtues, is helping the soul to will and to accomplish. In the process of accomplishment, grace will so train the soul as to reduce the multiplicity to simplicity.

Where at first there is the conscious effort on the part of the soul to pray with humility, reverence, compunction, and so on, later there is felt to be a more comprehensive activity: grace is seeing to it that the diversity is making for unity, that the separate dispositions are swallowed up in charity. All virtues are one in charity; charity reproduces itself in all the virtues.

But there must be signs to prove the authenticity of the inspiration. And when we examine them, these signs turn out to be precisely the qualities which St. Benedict wants to see. Without reverence there is no verifying the soul's desire; without humility no proof that the soul will accept the will of God when it reveals itself; without compunction the vice of presumption would be hard to distinguish from the virtue of perfect trust.

To lack any one of the dispositions demanded by St. Benedict would be to put prayer on an uneven, indeed on a false, foundation. Each of them plays an essential part in the interior life. Since, in connection with the Divine Office, we have discussed the question of reverence, and since humility has had a chapter expressly devoted to it, the subject still needing attention is compunction.

Compunction is something more than remorse for past sins. It is an habitual awareness of the tendency to sin. It has a twofold thrust: it keeps alive a sense of guilt with regard to previous failures; it warns of weakness in the face of future temptations.

Nor does compunction's work stop here; if it did, it would have a negative function only. Compunction views both past and future in terms of God's mercy. The soul, conscious of personal insufficiency and seeing itself powerless to remedy what it sees, puts complete trust in the power of grace.

Compunction is objective and realist. It does not have to fancy guilt. The guilt is *there*, and compunction views it in the light of truth. There may not be the scorching shame which accompanies remorse, but the resolution which results from compunction is likely to be more effective. Compunction moreover leads to sympathy with others, gratitude to God, a wider understanding of divine Providence.

Where remorse, self-pitying and often tending towards despair, works its emotion inwards so that it can become to some an obsession, compunction on the other hand works towards God. Compunction is just as much aware of evil as remorse but sees it chiefly in relation to God rather than to self.

Those who imagine that the soul of compunction is the soul of misery have failed to understand the matter. Compunction has nothing to do with self-appointed misery—which more often than not is, like indulged scrupulosity, a defense against conscience. Remorse may be an escape, a reflex action, a device to screen guilt; compunction cannot be other than the expression of humbled love.

Far from inducing depression in a man, true compunction makes for peace and joy. Based on the right kind of fear, it proceeds to the right kind of joy. "The fear of the Lord is honour and glory and gladness and a crown of joy," says Ecclesiasticus; "the fear of the Lord shall delight the heart. . . . With him that feareth the Lord it shall go well in the latter end, and in the day of his death he shall be blessed."[1] St. Benedict's spirit is close to the spirit of Ecclesiasticus, as can be seen in the parallel understanding of power and responsibility and humility and compassion, but nowhere do the two writers meet more surely than in their understanding of fear. "The fear of the Lord driveth out sin" is the doctrine of Ecclesiasticus, echoed by St. Benedict; "for he that is without fear cannot be justified: for the wrath of his high spirits is his ruin."[2]

[1] 1;12,13.
[2] 1;27,28.

In one of his sermons on the Canticle, St. Bernard has this to say of the relation between joy, fear, and perfection: "Happy are you if your heart be filled with this threefold fear: so that you fear when you have received grace, still more when that grace is lost, most of all when it has been regained . . . and you will deserve the blessing of Christ which shall turn the water of your poor nature into the wine of gladness, until the time when your charity, being perfected, will cast out all fear." Later on in the same sermon he says: "He who fears thus neglects nothing; for how can negligence enter into that which is wholly filled? That which is capable of receiving something more is not absolutely full. For which reason it is not possible to fear and at the same time to indulge in thoughts of pride. There is no place for pride to enter your mind if it be filled with holy fear. And it is the same with other vices: they are of necessity excluded by the fulness of this gracious fear . . . fear without love is but pain and suffering, and love, when perfected, casts out fear."[3]

With these two virtues of compunction and love, then, the vices are repudiated and the virtues assumed. The combination is accordingly the required disposition for prayer. But St. Benedict reminds us further that "not for our much speaking" shall we be heard. It is "purity of heart" that qualifies, not weight of words.

In the foregoing chapter on how St. Benedict wants the Divine Office to be said, we saw the necessity of integrating the outward with the inward. If the liturgy is, to use St. Bernardine's term, *totius Ecclesiae os*, then contemplation might be called *totius Ecclesiae cor*. The body is one; it is only that its life is expressed in different movements. The essential activity is the same, but expressed by different members in their own appropriate medium. Here, in this present chapter, we are considering the prayer performed *in puritate cordis*—in private prayer generally, but as finding its fruition in contemplation.

For St. Benedict, basing his interpretation of prayer on Cassian, the purpose of the monastic life is habitual recollection leading to perfect union with God. Dom Cuthbert Butler gives the epitome of Cassian's doctrine as taught in the ninth conference(and

[3] 54;11,12.

therefore at one remove St. Benedict's doctrine also) where he sums up the second chapter: "the aim of every monk and the perfection of his heart tends to continual and unbroken perseverance in prayer—an immovable tranquillity of mind—lasting and continual calmness in prayer: for this are all the other exercises of the monastic life undertaken." The third, fourth, fifth, and sixth chapters of Cassian he condenses as follows: "purity of prayer is to be attained only by purity of heart and mind and life, and the one will be proportionate to the other."[4]

Should the objection be raised that you cannot define a tradition by looking to an authority which belongs to another tradition there is the witness of the Benedictine St. Gregory, who in the generation following St. Benedict would have been well qualified to interpret our holy Father's mind on the subject of prayer and the monastic purpose. "A monk is nourished only by the practice of contemplation, rejoices with tears in the hope of heavenly rewards, forgoes even the things he is allowed to have, strives to converse intimately each day with the Lord, does not disturb his mind with any care of the passing world but always expands it in expectation of heavenly joys. The monk has no other desire than to attach himself to God in such a way that the soul loses all taste for anything else, spurns other occupations, longs fervently to see the face of the Creator, and knows how to endure the sadness and burden of corruptible flesh."[5]

The only possible conclusion to be derived from all this is that St. Benedict, while leaving his disciples free to follow their own attractions of grace, is understood by his first biographer to propose to them the heights of contemplation. Certainly unless the strictly interior life is very seriously pursued, there will be nothing to justify the terms used and the picture drawn by St. Gregory. St. Gregory, no less than St. Benedict before him and St. Bernard after him, allows for all the claims which the active life may make upon the monk's time. The original postulate nevertheless holds good. The Benedictine life, the specific vocation, is contemplative.

[4] *Op. cit.,* p. 63.
[5] *Homil. in Ezechiel,* 1,2.

God must be invited, in the sense formulated by St. Gregory, to take full possession of the soul. Self-will, with its hundred subterfuges and falsified motives, must be repudiated. Prayer is to be resorted to not as a means of promoting either self-esteem or a sense of security, but simply as a means—and the most direct means—of giving glory to God. When God's glory is accounted by the soul as being of greater importance than its own advancement in prayer—as being more important indeed than anything else in the world—then it may be supposed that the Holy Spirit will take over the soul's entire direction and order its outward religious life accordingly. Then it may be supposed also that in actual practice the prayer will tend towards an ever-increasing simplicity. *Non in multiloquio sed in puritate cordis* are St. Benedict's words. Not only will outward and verbal discourse in private devotions cease to attract the soul, but the more inward discursive activity produced by the faculties of the soul will give place to an exercise of greater tranquillity, simplicity, and unity. The prayer of faith will replace the prayer of feelings, imaginations, affections, acts. This is surely the prayer which St. Benedict, centuries before systems had been invented and an idiom developed to deal with them, meant when he wrote of "purity of heart" and "purity of intent." Prayer was still an uncharted land in his day, its soil yielding an unlaboured plant.

Thus far St. Benedict's concept of prayer and its method or lack of method. It is a concept which exactly reflects the psalmody: mood for mood the two prayer activities correspond. Articulated in the psalms are compunction, confidence in God alone, longing, praise and reverence; unarticulated in words but present in the soul are the same emotions and intentions. There is an essential unity in contemplation.

The principle which we know from the Rule is in line with the practice which we know from the *Dialogues*. That St. Benedict was a man of contemplation is abundantly clear. His initiation and training began as far back as the period spent in solitude at Subiaco. Each of his miracles is preceded by time spent in prayer, he is found engaged in it by Theoprobus to whom he foretold the destruction of the monastery,[6] he is seen while experiencing

[6] Bk. 2; ch. 17.

a mystical transport by Servandus the deacon,[7] and he died in the act of "breathing forth his soul to God in prayer."[8] He is known to have spent whole nights in prayer.[9] Certainly the illumination described in Gregory's thirty-fifth chapter leaves no room for doubting the quality of St. Benedict's contemplation: he was clearly the recipient of the highest mystical graces. Freed from limitations of time and space, the saint seems to have been able to take in the whole universe at a single glance. Seen thus in light, in the new dimension of the spirit, creation appeared to him as it appears to the Creator. "The whole world, compacted as it were together, was represented to his eyes in one ray of light," says St. Gregory. The biographer goes on to explain to Peter the Deacon, the other character in the dialogue, the nature of the grace: "To a soul that beholdeth the Creator, all creatures appear but narrow; for, should we partake never so little of the light of the Creator, whatsoever is created would seem very little; because the soul is so enlarged by this beatific vision, and so dilated in the divine perfections, that it far transcends the world and itself also. The soul thus rapt in the light of God is in its interior elevated, lifted above itself . . . easily comprehending how little that is which before it was not able to conceive. . . . What wonder then if he who was in mind exalted above the world was able to see that world in one view? But whereas I said that the whole world, compacted as it were, was represented before his eyes, it is not meant that heaven and earth were straitened by contraction, but that the mind of the beholder was dilated, so that it might, rapt in the sight of God, behold without difficulty that which is under God."[10]

Though the saint himself seems to have prayed for long periods at a stretch, he was careful not to impose the same burden on his monks. The time factor is secondary to the cultivation of the desire. St. Benedict knows that if he can get his disciples to value prayer and want to practise it, he can leave it to the Holy Spirit

[7] *Ibid.*, ch. 35.
[8] *Ibid.*, ch. 37.
[9] *Ibid.*, ch. 5.
[10] *Ibid.*, ch. 35.

to invite a lengthening of the actual exercise. If the doctrine is assimilated, the monks will themselves want to prolong their prayer times.

Therefore prayer ought to be short and pure, except it be perchance extended by the inspiration of divine grace. But let prayer made in common always be short; and at the signal given by the superior, let all rise together.

The flexibility of Benedictine spirituality is nowhere shown better than here. The whole matter depends upon "the inspiration of divine grace." One brother is not to feel inferior if grace does not prompt him to protracted devotions; nor is the brother who believes that he is being called to spend longer in prayer to feel superior. The point is that when they are required by the custom of the monastery to pray together, they should be made by the superior to start and finish at the same time. The period allotted for prayer in common should be short for two reasons: first, because allowance should be made for the weaker rather than for the stronger constitution and attraction; second, because the more interior the exercise, the more liberty must be allowed to the soul in the performance.

The mental prayer that is practised for so long at a time as to be a weariness must inevitably end up sterile and wasteful. Those who cannot manage longer at prayer than the minimum fixed by the rules of their congregation have ample opportunity of compensating in one way or another. Prayer is not confined, after all, to the time spent in the act of formally addressing God from a kneeling position.

St. John Chrysostom says how a soul should be as ready to pray in the marketplace as in the oratory, when sitting among friends as when attending services in church. The interior cry of love can still go up to God, he says, when there are no doves for the sacrifice, when there is neither wood nor fire nor knife nor altar. The soul itself is the altar and the sacrifice and the Temple.[11]

If the monk cannot have unceasingly upon his lips the syllables

[11] *De Anna Sermo*, 2 and 4.

of prayer, St. Pachomius would have him practise prayer in his heart "while going from his cell to the oratory, from the oratory to his cell, while fulfilling an office; before, during and after work in the open, and even while lying awake in bed."[12]

In the last analysis what God wants of the monk is what he wanted of Abraham—that he should "walk before me, and be perfect."[13] The contemplative life, the Benedictine vocation, can mean nothing more nor less than this.

[12] Quoted by Dom van Houtryve, *op. cit.*, p. 150.
[13] Gen. 7;1.

CHAPTER 2I

OF THE DEANS OF THE MONASTERY

St. Benedict, who has no great liking for the office of prior, sets great store by the authority vested in the deans. Though working under the abbot and prior, the deans are given considerable responsibility and, in their respective fields, wide discretionary powers. To them is entrusted, subject to the general supervision of the cellarer, the division of labour. They are responsible also for securing discipline in the community.

Neither the term nor the function is proper to St. Benedict: Eastern monasticism knew both (witness St. Jerome and Cassian as quoted by more than one commentator), while the immediate source of St. Benedict's legislation in this chapter seems to have been St. Augustine.

> Should the community be large, let there be chosen from it certain brethren of good repute and holy life, and appointed deans. Let them carefully direct their deaneries in all things according to the commandments of God and the orders of their abbot. And let such men be chosen deans as the abbot may safely trust to share his burdens; let them not be chosen according to order, but for the merit of their lives and for their learning of wisdom.

What would St. Benedict call a "large" community? Allowing that abbot and prior would be enough to maintain good order in a house of twelve monks—which was the number at Subiaco and Terracina under St. Benedict's rule—the appointment of a dean to every ten members suggests that a community of twenty monks would be considered by St. Benedict large.

Ideas about what is the right size for a Benedictine community have varied with the centuries. Warnefrid puts forward the number of twelve for the ideally constituted monastery. Hildemar, while agreeing that twelve would be enough for the desert or for lonely regions, wants to see a greater number in monasteries which are anywhere near cities.[1] Certainly the monasteries of the Middle Ages can have felt no obligation towards the mystical and apostolic number of twelve. St. Benedict of Aniane's community at Inde (Cornelimünster) numbered forty-four monks; Corbie, the house to which Hildemar himself originally belonged, had as many as three hundred and fifty professed brethren; at Fulda during its peak period there were two hundred and seventy.

In the sixty-fifth chapter St. Benedict comes back to the question of deans, explicitly confirming the hint contained above concerning their appointment; the choice lies within the abbot's prerogative. "If possible," says St. Benedict when reviewing the post of prior, "let all the affairs of the monastery be attended to by the deans, as the abbot shall appoint."

As to what affairs the deans were required to attend to we have little information in the Rule itself; the commentators, however, supply the details. "The duty of deans," says Warnefrid, "is to exercise custody over their subjects. If the latter are not corrected, then the deans are to report to the abbot . . . what is understood with regard to the deans is applicable likewise to the *circatores*. Thus when the abbot is not present there ought to be a prior in his place with equal authority; and if the prior is absent a dean should fill the position."[2] At Inde a dean, even if he were not a priest, might give the blessing to the readers in choir.

Martène distinguishes between the duties of the deans and those of the *circatores*. A dean, from the military *decurio*, presided over his deanery of ten in the refectory and dormitory, and at manual labour: he gave permissions and administered correc-

[1] See Schroll, *op. cit.*, pp. 54 ff.
[2] *Ibid.*, p. 61.

tion. A *circator* had no immediate subjects, but was a roving invigilator who might admonish any of the brethren whom he happened to find transgressing.

As the Benedictine idea grew, and as the whole thing became more elaborate, the position of dean became more important. The major dean occupied a place in the refectory next to the prior; deans were put in charge of granges and farms; a dean might represent the abbot at ecclesiastical and even civic assemblies. All the more necessary then that St. Benedict's conditions be justified in the choice of deans: *boni testimonii et sanctae conversationis . . . secundum vitae meritum.*

Not only would example prove more effective than any other factor in the maintenance of order, but so far as concerns the dean himself a ripened experience of spiritual things would be a safeguard against the distractions of the office. Neither seniority nor administrative ability need necessarily determine the choice. The qualities to be looked for in a dean are fidelity in observance, discernment of souls, wisdom and tact in the expression of correction.

Though the two may coincide, it would be a mistake to identify the role of dean with that of councilor. A councilor advises, a dean supervises. A councilor is more concerned with matters of policy, finance, building projects, and the suitability of subjects for profession; a dean is more concerned with religious practice and instruction. Perhaps because the dean's activities bring him in closer relation to the brethren—the councilor's lying rather in relation to the abbot—there is danger of pride in the possession of a deanery. St. Benedict takes this into account.

> Should one of them, being puffed up with pride, be found worthy of blame, and after being thrice corrected refuse to amend, let him be deposed, and one put in his place who is worthy. And we order the same to be done in the case of the prior.

CHAPTER 22

HOW THE MONKS ARE TO SLEEP

In placing this between two chapters which would seem to pair off well together, St. Benedict appears to judge that any aspect of the common life is important enough to justify an interruption of the sequence. Or it may be that having treated of deans, he goes on to treat of the domain where the authority of the dean is most likely to be exercised. The dormitory, perhaps even more than the refectory or library, is a place of studied behaviour.

If it be possible, let all sleep in one place; but if the number does not permit of this, let them rest by tens or twenties with the seniors who have charge of them. Let a candle burn constantly in the cell until morning. Let them sleep clothed . . . and thus be ready, so that when the signal is given they rise without delay, and hasten each to forestall the other in going to the *opus Dei*, yet with all gravity and modesty.

That the monks in St. Benedict's own monastery slept *omnes in uno loco*, we gather from a reference in the thirty-fifth chapter of the *Dialogues*, where St. Gregory tells of the visit of Servandus to Monte Cassino. *Largius erat habitaculum in quo utriusque discipuli quiescebant*, which suggests that there was a dormitory for visiting monks as well as one for the community. St. Benedict is described in this chapter as standing at the window of the dormitory when seen by Servandus.

The practice of allowing monks to occupy separate cells did

not come in until long after St. Benedict's time. To sleep in common was considered as much part of the cenobitical life as to pray, work, and eat in common. St. Caesarius, with the generality of Western monasticism, knew only the open dormitory without screens or curtains. Where the East was taken as the model, as at Lerins for example, the monks enjoyed greater privacy, but it is probably not until the hermit life came back to monasticism with the Carthusians and the Camaldolese that each monk had his four walls of cell. The reformers from the Cluny and Bursfeld movements denounced the use of private cells for monks, but since they allowed partitions in the dormitory—a cubicle to each monk—the condemnation strikes an unreasonable note.

Eventually, with the increasing emphasis on study, the Benedictine tradition changed, and St. Benedict's original plan was sacrificed to the claims of uninterrupted labour in the cell. What the monk lost in the way of primitive simplicity he gained in the way of solitude and recollection, and if work in the cell has taken away from work in the open cloister, the compensating advantages may be held to have justified themselves. "Not to break completely with monastic antiquity," says Delatte (from whom, together with Schroll, the information contained in the present chapter is mostly taken), "the cells were closed by a simple screen, or else the door had a small aperture with a movable shutter, while the name of 'dormitory' was preserved for the corridor on to which the cells opened; and, finally, the light which St. Benedict says should burn until morning was faithfully kept in this same corridor all through the night."[1]

The idea of sleeping in one's clothes was not so surprising as it would be now. It was in keeping with simplicity and poverty, it was in the monastic tradition, and it ensured the minimum of delay between the caller's summons and the brethren's arrival in choir. Also since the habit stood for the supernatural character of the life, the sleeping as well as the waking hours were to be spent in the dress which symbolized conversion from the world.

In his fifty-fifth chapter St. Benedict tells us what should constitute the monk's bedding: mattress, blanket, covering, pillow.

[1] *Op. cit.*, p. 201.

According to Calmet the foundation of the bed, the *matta*, was a thing of rushes or straw. Hildemar allows, which Calmet does not, horsehair. Warnefrid says that at Monte Cassino feather mattresses were allowed to the sick. In the tenth century at Farfa the straw mattresses were overhauled once a year by the cellmaster or *camerarius*, who provided also a new woolen blanket, a bolster, and a sort of quilt composed of skins stuffed with hay or straw.

As soon as the signal was given for getting up, the monks went at once—presumably leaving their washing until later in the day—to the oratory. St. Benedict is careful to qualify his word "hasten" by saying that the procession from dormitory to choir must be *cum omni tamen gravitate et modestia.* No lying in bed followed by a last-minute dash, no running through the cloister, which would militate against subsequent recollection in choir, no flippancies at that early hour, above all.

> And when they rise for the *opus Dei*, let them gently encourage one another, because of the excuses of the drowsy.

This final injunction has puzzled the commentators. Does it mean that the *summum silentium* is to be broken by whispered exhortations among the brethren? Surely not. A heavy sleeper can be "encouraged" without the use of words. In present-day Benedictine houses, where the monks sleep one in a cell, the occasion when a brother is "encouraged" to get out of bed seldom presents itself. Sometimes the caller on his rounds may have to stimulate wakefulness, and sometimes a novice is sent out of choir by the superior in order to summon a latecomer, but whatever the necessity the use of words should be avoided. Monks should regard the *summum silentium* as inviolable save in cases of sickness, charity, and the strictest emergency.

CHAPTER 23

OF EXCOMMUNICATION FOR FAULTS

There is much to be said for the theory that this and the next seven chapters of the Rule made up a separate directory for the use of the abbot and those in authority under him. Looked at from the point of view of the subject, these eight chapters afford little material for meditation: a penal code may be useful enough for reference, but can scarcely act as an inspiration.

As a general introduction to this section of the Rule which gives the legal structure of the monastery, it is to be noted that St. Benedict divides the faults committed by monks into two classes, light and serious; he then classifies the serious faults according to the degree of obstinacy which follows their discovery. In the matter of punishment St. Benedict recognizes four different applications: verbal reprimand, corporal punishment, spiritual suspension, excommunication. These various categories will be dealt with below.

If any brother shall be found contumacious or disobedient or proud or a murmurer, or in any way opposed to the holy Rule and the orders of his superiors, and a contemner, let him according to our Lord's commandment be once or twice admonished by his seniors. If he do not amend, let him be rebuked in public before all.

The question here is not of stray weakness but of deliberate resistance to authority. Nor is it the sudden expression of an imperfectly tamed spirit, the deliberate transgression on the part of an emotional and headstrong nature, that St. Benedict has chiefly in mind. The saint aims at correcting the tendency; he wants to find a way of training the character according to grace. Whatever the particular kind of punishment employed, the main thing is to bring the rebellious subject into the frame of mind which will itself get rid of murmuring, open opposition, disobedience.

Private admonition, repeated if necessary, is the first in the order of means to be adopted. The responsibility of administering reproof must rest with one who holds some sort of official rank; for an equal to issue warnings would not only be unbecoming but would be liable to have the effect of entrenching the difficult brother in his bad disposition. If the private appeal fails, then a correction is to be addressed to the culprit in public.

Where the obstinacy persists, a third stage is reached; here it becomes necessary to resort to either corporal punishment or spiritual excommunication. The alternative between being put under physical restraint and being deprived of spiritual association with the rest of the brethren will depend upon a condition for which the recalcitrant monk alone can answer:

> If he do not correct himself, let him be subjected to excommunication, provided that he understand the nature of the punishment. Should he however prove froward, let him undergo corporal chastisement.

Following St. Benedict's arrangement of dealing with the various degrees of excommunication in separate chapters, we need treat here of bodily punishment only—and that very briefly since its interest is purely historical. Instructions relating to imposed fasts, confinement to the cell, beatings of one kind and another came down to St. Benedict from the rules of earlier legislators. In the light of his predecessors' legislation, St. Benedict's recommendations are moderate indeed. Nor was he the last to speak of coporal chastisement. St. Benedict of Aniane drew up a document called "Methods of Penance," and he was by no means the sole exponent.[1] In the seventh and eighth centuries, and possibly later, codes of penance were issued which gave what can only be called scaled tariffs of faults with their respective penalties. These were the centuries of specialized privations and flagellations. To the modern mind it appears strange to think that saints imposed these penances upon their subjects, but it must be recalled that the discipline and the rod were not exclusively monastic weapons: decrees were issued by more than one Council of the Church insisting that for certain offences clerics were to be beaten.

St. Peter Damian was the first to introduce the discipline as a voluntary and self-inflicted penance. From Camaldoli the custom spread, and what was once an affliction to be endured at another's hand became in monastic usage a purely private action.

To conclude this section of St. Benedict's penal legislation it should be observed that when the saint mentions public satisfaction for faults he does not mean that others outside the conventus will be witness; it was enough that the brethren should be present. The chapter-house would be the scene of public rebuke and sentence. To be debarred from taking part in community exercises would affect choir and refectory, but as we shall see in the next two chapters the essential punishment here is social and spiritual rather than physical and local.

[1] The Rule of St. Fructuosus is not above sentencing a guilty monk to a hundred lashes. St. Columbanus allows up to two hundred lashes, provided that no more than twenty-five are delivered at one time. The Rules of St. Pachomius and St. Caesarius also make provision for punishment with the rod. The earliest pictures of St. Benedict show the saint with an instrument of penance in his hand; and in one of the Aretino murals he is seen administering penance to one of his monks.

CHAPTER 24

WHAT THE MEASURE OF EXCOMMUNICATION SHOULD BE

However exactly on paper the punishment is measured to the crime, in fact it will have to be governed by the particular case. St. Benedict makes it clear that the judgment of the abbot must override classifications of guilt and atonement. In the saint's opinion it is better to risk getting an arbitrary decision from an irresponsible abbot than to bind subject and superior alike to an inflexible system. Here, as in other places where he qualifies his enactments with the clause about the abbot's decision being final, St. Benedict removes from the disgruntled monk the opportunity of appealing to the text of the Rule against the sentence passed upon him.

> The measure of excommunication or chastisement should be meted out according to the gravity of the offence, the estimation of which shall be left to the judgment of the abbot. If any brother be found guilty of lighter faults, let him be excluded only from the common table.

This is the minor conventual excommunication; the major excommunication, incurred by faults which St. Benedict does not specify but which assume material and formal gravity, is dealt with in the chapter following. *In levioribus culpis* refers to acts of indiscipline and not to moral lapses or sustained disobedience. This graded excommunication is not peculiar to St. Benedict.

Earlier monastic legislation knew the distinction, though not always with the same accompanying details.

A monk falling under the less serious excommunication might attend the choir with his brethren, but was not allowed to play any personal role in its performance. Thus he recited with the rest, but intoned "neither psalm nor antiphon . . . nor shall he read a lesson until he have made satisfaction." Customaries issued in later ages insist that the lesser excommunicate sit apart from the brethren in choir, and do not come up for the kiss of peace. Nor would they be incensed by the thurifer or given holy water by their neighbour on coming in to an office. The major excommunication, as we shall see, goes much further than this.

Exclusion from the common table was no very great hardship. Outwardly it meant no more than having one's meals later than the rest of the community, and perhaps being served with food of a poorer quality. The punishment lay primarily in the break which it denoted with the family life. Food is a symbol of social unity, and even though monastic meals are taken in silence the brethren come in closer contact with one another over their eating than over their working.

For a monk to be cut off from the social side of the cenobitical life is not as bad as to be cut off from the choral or sacramental sides, but it is bad enough to represent an essential loss. These penalties of expulsion may not be in force today, but the point about excommunication which must always be pertinent to monks is how far a man may harm his vocation by virtually excommunicating himself.

Without going against the letter of obedience, a monk may find himself drifting further and further from the community until he is, for all practical purposes, using the monastery merely as a shelter for the practice of his own private spiritual life. Meticulously obtaining permission for every exemption from the common exercises of the house, careful to justify his action with the loftiest of motives, such a monk is not serving his brethren but making them serve him. He might just as well be giving glory to God in an hotel.

By private arrangement he gets out of taking his turn at the

solo duties in choir, and at serving and reading in the refectory.
With a splendid show of humility he explains that he is so bad
at these things. With an edifying regard for recollection, he finds
them distracting.

The monk who lets his individualism run away with him will
even want to be served with special food in the refectory. Where
there would be the merit of obedience if this had been imposed as
a punishment by superiors, there is now the guilt of singularity.
It is the same in the matter of being absent from the community
meals: the penalty of eating after the others have finished might
have a salutary effect when commanded, but when chosen by
oneself cannot but be harmful.

There are monks who, in order to procure what they imagine
their health requires, will persuade their superior to allow them
out on foraging expeditions. They will, with permission, keep a
store of provisions in the cell. It is thus not only the community
life that suffers; enclosure, poverty, obedience, and indeed all the
monastic virtues suffer as well.

There can be few punishments more severe than that which
the isolationist monk imposes upon himself. Unconsciously he
condemns himself to the miseries of selfishness, and loneliness becomes his portion. His indifference to the feelings and needs of
others hardens, and since he is present at the community assemblies only in body there is no immediate reason why the falsity of
his position should ever be brought home to his spirit. The normal
lines of communication are out. The flow of graces proper to
the cenobitical life is, if not actually dried up, reduced to a
trickle.

"Let no one work for himself," says St. Augustine, "but let all
your works be in common, and may they be performed with all
the greater zeal and more fervent alacrity than if you were carrying them out for yourselves. 'Charity seeketh not her own'; she
places the common good before her own interests." Though St.
Augustine was not a monk, he might well be writing here for
monks. Certainly nothing could be more destructive of the
Benedictine ideal than a free-lance approach to spirituality.

This shall be the rule for one deprived of fellowship at the common table: he shall intone neither psalm nor antiphon in the oratory, nor shall he read a lesson until he make satisfaction. Let him take his meals alone . . . so that if for example the brethren eat at the sixth hour let him eat at the ninth, if they eat at the ninth let him eat in the evening, until by proper satisfaction he obtain pardon.

It is not the mere fact of men being in one place at one time that is the concern of this legislation and of its corresponding punishment. You can assemble a crowd by waving your arms or ringing a bell. You can punish a man by making him eat *with* his fellows just as well as you can punish him by making him eat by himself. Nor is it altogether a question of disgrace—the threat of isolation publicly recognized driving a man to take more part in community activities—but rather it is a question of stressing the monk's dependence upon the particular society to which he belongs by profession. All this legislation is concerned with enlisting common effort towards a common purpose. There is all the difference between a crowd and a community. A mob may be animated by a common aim, but in a monastery men are united in a common charity.

The idea of a monastery and the idea of a community should amount to the same thing: a monastery is a place where people of the same mind live in unity, and a community is a group of people who use the monastery as it is meant to be used. Men come to a concert in one way, and to choir in another; they come to a restaurant in one way, and to a refectory in another; they come to a court in one way and to a chapter in another. It is a matter of the will.

"If you do not have unity in willing one thing and not willing another," says St. Columbanus, "it is better for you not to live together." The common choice of one thing supposes the common rejection of another thing, and this free election, far from narrowing it, widens the soul's horizon of charity. The charity of a religious house is not a closed circle but an open circle. Its centre is Christ, and like the rings on the surface of a lake which widen when a stone has been dropped into the water it expands over the whole area.

It is from this ever expanding circle of charity that the monk excludes himself when he decides to follow his own bent against the common spirit. By plunging his will into the common will, a monk is drowning his lower self and at the same time finding his true self in the will of God. In order that this understanding of the common will may be fruitful, and not merely provide an easy escape from the struggle to keep alive his own ideals, the monk must follow it for the right reason. The common will is not a superstition or a convenience. It is not that it happens to be common among the brethren and that it offers the invitation to be common also to the individual monk. Its value lies in the fact that it represents the will of God.

We come to sink ourselves in the common good not by pretending to ourselves that it is what we want, but by believing firmly that it is what God wants. God may not show us that it is what we have been looking for all along, what is best for us, but He does show us that it is what He wills us to follow.

The common will of the community, endorsed by the will of authority, is for us the will of God as well as the will of our fellow monks. To withhold our will from this will is to withhold ourselves from the will of God. If a man is what he wills, he must see that his will conforms.

Thus if I decide that the policy of the house is not for me, and that I may accordingly form a policy of my own, I am not merely out of sympathy but I am out of communion. I am placing myself outside the family, I am repudiating the graces peculiar to the cenobitic life as a whole and to this particular family's interpretation of it. I may still be entitled to active and passive vote, to my stall in choir and to my place in the refectory, but I have no just claim upon either the safeguards or sanctifying influences of the specific vocation within the vocation.

But such a break with the spirit of the monastery of profession would not come about either unconsciously or in a mood of resentment. It supposes a cool determination to sever the connection. A monk may feel out of step with his community, unable to toe the party line, even bitter towards the system which demands his co-operation, but so long as he identifies himself with the general will of the family into which he has been adopted and from which he cannot, save by formal expulsion or dispensation be disassociated, he is still a member of the body and the veins have not been cut. He may be a bad conductor (if the change of metaphor may be allowed), but he is not dead matter. However parlous his state, such a one should know from these chapters in the holy Rule about punishment—even if his experience of the religious life did not teach it to him every day—where his safety must lie. St. Benedict's concluding line to the chapter gives him his cue: *usque dum satisfactione congrua veniam consequatur*.

CHAPTER 25

OF GRAVER FAULTS

St. Benedict's treatment of punishment affects not only the delinquent himself but the other monks' attitude towards the delinquent. Without special authorization, the brethren may not consort with the excommunicated monk. They must pray for him, but they may not hail him with a blessing. Besides impressing the seriousness of the situation upon the monk thus isolated, the measure must act as a warning to those who have not had occasion to suffer a like sentence.

Let that brother who is found guilty of a more grievous offence be excluded both from the table and from the oratory. Let none of the brethren consort with him or speak to him. Let him be alone at the work enjoined him, and continue in sorrow of penance remembering that dreadful sentence of the apostle: "That such a one is delivered over to Satan for the destruction of the flesh that his spirit may be saved in the day of the Lord."

Exiled from his brethren, the monk under sentence is not freed from the obligation of work. But he will have to work at a distance; he must not be allowed to contaminate the others. In later Benedictine centuries there were cells especially reserved for the unruly members of the household, and here the abbot or his representatives came with their appeals to the man's better nature. Left thus to himself for long hours at a time, a monk might be expected to come to a more submissive state of mind. He would argue that if the imposed solitude of a monastic sentence could be so bitter, what would be the loneliness of a soul condemned to live for ever without charity? The brethren, for their part, would be given cause to humble themselves with the thought that no man, even though he be in the way of perfection, is safe from sin.

Let him take his portion of food alone, in the measure and at the time that the abbot shall think best for him. Let none of those who pass by bless him, nor let the food that is given him be blessed.

Severe as all this seems to us, it is nothing like as severe as the treatment handed out to those who offended in the times before St. Benedict. A horror of sin goes with the sense of the supernatural, and in those ages when the faith was strongest there was a corresponding sense of penance. Guilt finds different remedies in different generations, and in our own generation the remedy of solitary confinement and compulsory fasts would be judged unsuitable. Perhaps when the psychologists have had their say, the experiment of going back to the ancients will be tried. Perhaps the monk of the future who is found to be difficult will not be sent to cool his head in a nursing home but, as his ancestors were before him, will be put to work by himself in the cell. It is surely a commentary on our time to see obstinate and unhappy religious living as invalids among seculars when the Rule offers solutions which we are too squeamish or too sophisticated to accept. Perhaps this is part of our penalty—that the unrepentant among us are passed by *nec a quoquam benedicantur*, and that the meals are served without a blessing. Thus, in the devious operations of divine Providence, do religious rules manage to get themselves kept. But all things being equal, it is better that they should get themselves kept in a monastery than in a clinic.

CHAPTER 26

OF THOSE WHO, WITHOUT LEAVE OF THE ABBOT, CONSORT WITH THE EXCOMMUNICATE

The point of this short chapter is twofold: its first aim is to secure for the brother under punishment a real and not a merely nominal separation; its second aim is to refute among those who are not under punishment any false idea about charity.

If any brother presume without the abbot's leave to hold any intercourse whatever with an excommunicated brother, or to speak with him, or to send him a message, let him incur the same punishment of excommunication.

What St. Benedict wants to stress is the supernatural character of the remedy. Neither the guilty nor the innocent would learn the inwardness of this legislation if the isolation were subject to repeated interruption. Any exchange, whether of signs or notes or whispered speech, brings the thing down at once to the level of schoolroom banishment. Suspension of this sort must be taken seriously and supernaturally—by all three parties concerned, namely the guilty, the innocent, the abbot—or it is useless.

Both the seriousness and the supernatural character of the punishment are secured by the obedience which imposes it. We have seen how fatal is that excommunication which has no sanction from authority; we see now that it is obedience which is not only the channel of grace to the man undergoing punishment but also the yardstick by which the brethren's charity towards him may be measured.

It is not that obedience opposes charity, and is given first place; it is rather that charity is tested by obedience, and that the two virtues complement one another. St. Benedict is not telling his monks to suspend their charity for the sake of discipline. He is not even telling them to suspend their charity for the sake of their wayward brother's soul. He is telling them to practise their charity towards him by doing what they are told in their brother's regard.

To contravene St. Benedict's enactment on the grounds of showing compassion for the stricken brother would be to commit a sin of pride as well as one of disobedience. It would be showing that one knew better than authority, better than St. Benedict and the Rule. While the law of charity is universal, there are occasions when the law of obedience must come in to point out the application.

On pain of incurring the same excommunication, the brethren are forbidden access to the brother who has transgressed: this goes one step further than Canon Law which imposes a lesser excommunication upon any who associate with those under the greater excommunication. There can be no doubt of the significance which was attached by St. Benedict to the anathema: since one rebellious monk living under the same roof as the others can spread the same spirit, none may come in contact with him without incurring the same guilt. The nature of the punishment is conditioned by the nature of the contagion.

Nor may a well-intentioned brother, quoting St. Paul, become an outcast in bringing forbidden consolation to the excommunicated member. It is one thing to risk social ostracism in bringing the life of Christ to a soul, and another to risk the life of Christ in bringing social consolation.

Guarding against what might appear excessive severity in the provision of this chapter, St. Benedict in the ensuing chapter shows how solicitous the abbot must be for the salvation of the sinner. It would be a mistake to form an opinion of our holy Father's character on the findings of his penal legislation, but even were we to do this there would be evidence enough of his humanity in the care which we shall now find him showing for the misguided among his monks.

CHAPTER 27

HOW CAREFUL THE ABBOT SHOULD BE OF THE EXCOMMUNICATE

So important is spiritual and moral health that the abbot must feel more responsible towards restoring it among those who are spiritually and morally sick than towards preaching it among those who are well. This is the Gospel doctrine, and it is taken as a basis of St. Benedict's legislation.

Let the abbot take care with all solicitude of offending brethren, for "they that are whole need not a physician, but they that are sick." To which end he ought to behave in every way as a wise physician, sending as it were secret consolers to sympathise with him—that is to say some brethren of mature years and wisdom . . . who may induce him to make humble satisfaction, and comfort him that he be not overwhelmed with excess of sorrow, but as the Apostle saith; "Let charity be strengthened towards him," and let all pray for him.

There is reason to believe that St. Benedict's text has been added to, and that the reference to the secrecy of the negotiations was not in the original. Allowing that the monks knew their Rule, how could the measure escape recognition for what it was? The brethren on their side, and the delinquent on his, would have been in no doubt as to the regularity and openness of the procedure. The only element of secrecy that could come into the matter would be in the choice of consolers, and perhaps here it would have been well for both the abbot and the consolers themselves to maintain a discreet silence about the mission.

These provisions for the reclaiming of obstinate religious are not so obsolete as might appear at first sight. Though it is fortunately rare enough that a superior has to send one monk to win back another to grace, it is not unknown that a go-between is instructed by authority to drop hints and suggest remedies. Not every abbot feels confident of his persuasive powers, and though he may know he will be obeyed if he issues a formal command, it may help him considerably in his dealings with difficult subjects to know that he can count upon the tact and charity of some senior monk to do the work of persuasion for him.

The abbot's concern with regard to the unruly monk should be not so much to punish the man as to eradicate the fault. If the sanctification of the sinner is the aim, then the form in which the punishment is dealt out and the means used in gaining the soul will follow. With the graces of his authority to draw from, the abbot should not have great difficulty in choosing the best way of approach. St. Augustine states the principle where he says that the religious superior is "happy not in dominating by authority, but in serving by charity."

Unless compassion for the soul that has failed is truly supernatural—unless it is extended as to Christ who by His Passion has caused failure to be one of the primary means of sanctification—it will be at best an emotional pity and at worst condescension. When charity is the whole motive, the abbot's mission, whether conducted in person or through the medium of another, cannot but be a channel of grace to the offender.

It is significant in this connection that the rest of the brethren are urged to pray for their brother's change of heart. Human pity is not enough in their case, any more than it is enough in the case of the responsible authority. Compassion is something which comes only with faith—with faith fed by prayer.

If compassion were a trick of the imagination it could be acquired by conjuring up pictures of the crucified Christ, and working into this mental image the features of the sufferer. But to identify Christ with the sufferer implies something deeper than

this. Such a mental projection would, for some, be a difficult
thing to do; it would certainly be a difficult thing to keep up.
True compassion passes from the image to the reality, from the
symbol to the thing symbolized. Charity takes the soul from the
evidence of Christ's love for man to the actual exercise of Christ's
love for man.

It is the same wherever the Christ-life is substantially and not
just superficially re-lived. Grace works inwardly from the expression to the experience, from the proofs to what is proved.
Love has to be expressed by signs, but the signs are not the whole
of love. Neither the messengers nor those who go about Jerusalem are satisfying to the loving soul. None but the Beloved can
satisfy the soul.[1]

The compassionate brethren must accordingly direct their
prayer and their sympathy in such a course as will reproduce
Christ's love for sinners. The ultimate persuasion must be Christ's
love. All other reasons which point to the need of showing compassion for the sinner are incomplete: every argument must lead
on to the one act, the one conclusion. If one man in a community
is to help another, it will be in the measure that he has the mind
of Christ towards him.

The effort to acquire the mind of Christ inevitably enlarges
a man's charity: his soul expands in compassion. The word
"magnanimous," which has come to mean "forgiving," has its
origin in the *magna anima* which is made so by Christ and finds
its pattern in Christ. The abbot, whom St. Benedict repeatedly
refers to as Christ's representative, has more need than anyone
to develop the virtue of magnanimity.

> For the abbot is bound to use the greatest care with err-
> ing brethren, and to strive with all possible prudence and
> zeal not to lose any one of the sheep committed to him.
> He must know that he has undertaken the charge of weak
> souls and not a tyranny over the strong. And let him fear
> the threat of the prophet wherein God says: "What you
> saw to be fat, that you took away to yourselves; and what
> you saw to be diseased, that you cast away."

[1] Cant. 3;3-5.

Commenting on the above paragraph, Delatte has a passage which is worth quoting in full. "Nor should he [the abbot] ignore the excommunicate and abandon him to his passions and wounded pride, saying, 'I cannot help it. If he wants to persevere in his rebellion, why, let him do it! I cannot give him my own will instead of his own.' Obviously you have not died for him or you would not throw him over so readily. 'Yes, but he irritates me. He is so bitter and disloyal.' He is all the more your concern. You are not a prince or an executioner."[2] The same commentator quotes St. Augustine on those who have charge of souls: "Their care should be the cure of men rather than men who have been cured. They must endure the faults of men so as to cure them, for a plague must be endured before it can be cured." Christ not only went after sinners to save them, but took sin upon Himself. Each member of a religious community, and still more the head of the religious community, should be ready to make sacrifices for the straying brother. To the abbot particularly is the Gospel simile pointed out:

> Let him imitate the loving example of the Good Shepherd, who, leaving the ninety-nine sheep on the mountains, went to seek the one that had gone astray, on whose weakness He had such compassion that He vouchsafed to lay it on His own shoulders, and thus bring it back to the flock.

Having brought the wayward brother back, the abbot's responsibility is not over. The whole aim of a superior is not to see that nobody runs away but to see that all are saved. The care of souls is not a holding operation merely; it holds in order to develop. The abbot who congratulates himself on his deathbed as being able to hand over to God the full numerical strength of his community has still a question to answer before the congratulation is echoed in heaven. "It is not enough for the abbot simply to conserve his flock," says Bernard of Monte Cassino in his commentary on the Rule, "he should be concerned to urge it on to useful acts and to increase its virtues."

[2] *Op. cit.*, p. 223.

CHAPTER 28

OF THOSE WHO, BEING OFTEN
CORRECTED, DO NOT AMEND

The opening paragraph of this chapter is a repetition of what was enjoined on an earlier page of the Rule—namely that impenitence is to be treated with the lash. If, however, neither strokes from the rod nor the sentence of excommunication can bring about the reform, there is the final threat to be promulgated. And if the threat is not listened to, it must be put into execution—*jam utatur abbas ferro abscisionis*. Leaving out the repetitions, we can condense the chapter as follows:

> But if even then he [the delinquent brother] do not correct himself, or perhaps, which God forbid, puffed up with pride even wish to defend his deeds, then let the abbot act like a wise physician. If he has applied fomentations and the unction of his admonitions, the medicine of the Holy Scriptures, and the last cautery of excommunication or corporal punishment, and if he see that his labours are of no avail, let him add what is still more powerful—his own prayers and those of all the brethren that God may work the cure of the sick brother. But if he be not healed even by this means, then at length let the abbot use the sword of separation, as the Apostle says: "Put away the evil one from you." And again, "If the faithless one depart, let him depart," lest one diseased sheep should taint the whole flock.

St. Benedict knows that you cannot keep a man to the service of God by nailing him against his will to the cross. The reluctant victim will only kick his cross to bits, and so give scandal to those who are doing their best to stretch themselves upon their own.

We have instanced already the case of the hermit Martin who was urged to bind himself to his solitude by the chain of Christ and not by a chain of iron.[1] The *Dialogues* afford other illustrations which give us St. Benedict's conception of the service of religion as a service of love. But love's lessons have sometimes to be learned through suffering. Those sufferings which are imposed by obedience are the stuff of monastic sacrifice. Those punishments accordingly which the discipline of the Rule exacts are the appropriate material of penance.

Again there are chapters in the *Dialogues* which have their bearing upon the sterner side of the remedies applied by our holy Father to the difficulties of his monks. We read of how Exhilaratus was given the shock of his life for his deception when he had hidden a flagon of wine.[2] We read of two nuns who were excommunicated, and who were admitted to heaven after their death only when St. Benedict had interceded for their souls.[3] We read of the rod bringing to his right mind the brother who, in defiance of the common practice, shortened his mental prayer.[4] We read how St. Benedict imposed upon a cleric whom he had delivered from diabolical possession the duty of never eating meat.[5]

Two further instances may be quoted from the *Dialogues*, but this time with reference not so much to the punitive side of what we have been discussing as to the risk a monk runs who cuts himself off from the brethren. To show us how much we depend upon the brethren, upon the abbot, and upon our religious profession, St. Gregory tells of the young monk who, without the abbot's blessing and from sheer weariness of life, left the monastery for the world. Having made the journey, he died on the day of his arrival at home. Buried among seculars, the monk's body was

[1] Bk. 2; ch. 16.
[2] *Ibid.*, ch. 18.
[3] *Ibid.*, ch. 23.
[4] *Ibid.*, ch. 4.
[5] Bk. 2; ch. 16.

twice forced to the surface and exposed for whatever conclusions the passers-by might draw from the event. Only when St. Benedict's help had been sought, did the earth retain the corpse.[6] The other account is of a monk who wearied of the monastic life to such an extent that, after repeated requests to St. Benedict for secularization, he was allowed to go. Scarcely had he left the enclosure when the forces of evil, taking physical shape, so terrified him that he cried out for help and was led back by his brethren to the monastery.[7] It all goes to show that for monks there is no safety apart from union with the community and submission to the abbot. It also goes to show, as indeed we have twice seen insisted upon in the text of the Rule, that the brethren must support one another and pray for one another. A monk should be able to say with the deepest meaning the verses which are put upon his lips for five days of the week at Terce: *Propter fratres meos et proximos meos loquebar pacem de te; propter domum Domini Dei nostri quaesivi bona tibi.*[8]

[6] *Ibid.*, ch. 24.
[7] *Ibid.*, ch. 25.
[8] Ps. 121;8,9.

CHAPTER 29

WHETHER THE BRETHREN WHO LEAVE THE MONASTERY ARE TO BE RECEIVED AGAIN

This is again a chapter which has stirred the speculation of commentators. Putting aside variant readings, we content ourselves with the accepted text, which, until the interpolators began to interest themselves, admitted of but a single interpretation. Nothing could be clearer than this short chapter which can here be printed in one paragraph.

If any brother, who through his own fault departs or is cast out of the monastery, be willing to return, let him first promise entire amendment for the fault for which he left; and then let him be received back into the lowest place, that thus his humility may be tried. Should he again depart, let him be taken back until the third time. But let him know that after this all way of return is denied him.

Monastic legislation regarding expulsion (or departure) and re-admission was not uniform either before or after St. Benedict's time. St. Basil was more strict, St. Isidore was less. St. Bernard kept to St. Benedict's ruling; Peter the Venerable was for receiving the renegade monk however often he failed and applied again for admission. It is curious to note that leniency is more often found among the ancients, and in the ages of extreme severity, than in later centuries which have made humanity their rule.

The wording of the text makes it clear that St. Benedict was anxious to stretch his law as far as it would go in the guilty man's favour. He did not want the subject to close with the concluding words of the previous chapter. So on two conditions he allows the monk to come back.

Frank admission of guilt is the first condition. Clearly this is a *sine qua non*, and the abbot will have to take the man's word for it that the retractation is sincere. If there is doubt, the abbot is evidently expected to act upon the individual's protestation of good faith. Indeed in such cases there will always be an element of doubt, and if superiors do not give their home-coming subjects the benefit of that doubt they are going against the spirit of the Gospel as well as against the spirit of the Rule.

The difficulty arises where a repentant monk is seen to take the blame, and even take the consequences, but where he is felt to be missing the complete conversion of heart which is the sole guarantee of perseverance. This is where the abbot, and those responsible for the man's direction, must not only exercise great confidence but also inspire great confidence. They must know that a conversion which lacks a full understanding of the implications can, with the help of grace, be worked upon until it develops the necessary supernatural depths. Souls that have been estranged alike from the sacraments and the community life will perhaps be incapable of grasping the significance of the demand. They may have to get themselves acclimatized to the life of prayer before they can again take on the life of the spirit at the level of the spirit.

For this reason St. Benedict makes it his second condition that the monk who returns to the monastery after expulsion or flight is to begin at the lowest place in the community. He has to learn the elements of the religious life as though he were a novice. In the case of the lesser excommunication there is not this condition —either during his suspension or after his re-establishment—and the reason is that the offender has never broken with the house of his profession. In the case of the greater excommunication the banished monk is deprived of membership and therefore of rank.

But a distinction must be noted between flight and expulsion.

The monk who leaves his monastery, whether with all the necessary permissions and dispensations to try his vocation in another order or else by simply disregarding his vows and walking out, is, if he seeks re-admission and shows signs of true humility, to be given his second and even his third chance. On the other hand the brother whose ways have been proved incorrigible, and on whom the sentence of expulsion has been pronounced, enjoys no such confidence. Indeed according to the earliest text of the Rule, and certainly according to current legislation, a return to his own community is denied to such a one.

But on this point tradition has been far from uniform. In the eighth and ninth centuries custom not only allowed the re-admission of the expelled monk but, viewing the enactment as a correction rather than as a final severance, provided for it. "The brother who has passed through the six preceding stages of correction without amendment," writes Schroll, drawing upon the evidence provided by Warnefrid and Hildemar, "is considered 'incorrigible,' and as such is subjected to expulsion. This step was not looked upon as final, however, in the sense that there was no possibility for the offender to return. On the contrary, expulsion seemed to be merely another way of bringing him to repentance; his return was not only expected but encouraged."[1] Hildemar is quoted in an exhortation to the abbot whose concern for the expelled or excommunicated brother must guard against the likelihood of death taking place while the monk is under sentence.

For us at the present date of Benedictine history the disputed question of the rebel monk's return is not a practical one: canonical legislation has closed the way back for those whom authority has once sent out. Rejection from the community supposes in our day a fault so grievous and lasting as to rule out the possibility of a new start. The Church has decided that while every sort of risk may be taken in the name of charity, it is not charity but the reverse of charity which exposes souls to occasions of sin.

[1] *Op. cit.*, p. 94.

CHAPTER 30

HOW YOUNG BOYS ARE TO BE CORRECTED

This is the last of the chapters which have to do with correction, and since it refers not to monks but to boys who are under the care of monks it touches the present purpose only indirectly. Since it is not our aim in these notes to support a particular policy, the controversial question as to how far it is the business of monks to run large modern schools must be left to the men of debate and propaganda. Education in St. Benedict's monasteries, not in ours, is the immediate concern. If our holy Father's mind with regard to the training of the young can be ascertained, the principles should be applicable whether or not the development as found among several contemporary Benedictine congregations has run away with the original intention.

Every age and understanding should have its due measure. As often therefore as boys, or those under age or such as cannot fully understand the greatness of the penalty of excommunication, commit faults, let them be punished by severe fasting or sharp stripes in order that they may be cured.

This is not the only chapter in which the young are mentioned. In the thirty-seventh chapter a plea is made for indulgence towards them, and in the thirty-ninth their physical needs are taken into account. The young are mentioned in four other chapters besides (the forty-fifth, fifty-ninth, sixty-third, and seventieth), but only to say that they must be kept firmly in their place.

Abbot Butler, in his *Benedictine Monachism*,[1] and Abbot Delatte, in his *Commentary on the Holy Rule*,[2] are agreed as to the stages between infancy and maturity recognized in early Benedictine history. "Children" and "boys" means anything up to fifteen. Warnefrid classifies children below seven as *infantes*, those between seven and fourteen as *pueri*, those between fourteen and twenty-eight as *adolescentiores*. Fourteen was the age at which Roman boys left off wearing the short toga.

Considering the number of times when young people are mentioned in the holy Rule, it is surprising to find no explicit discussion of the training they received. Nor do the early commentators help us here. All we know is that these boy oblates and *alumni* came to choir with the community, had their places in the dormitory together with the rest, joined the brethren in the refectory where they were given special consideration, and owed obedience to a master deputed to their care.

"The educational advantages which the oblate system offered are easily recognized," writes Schroll. "The commentators indicate roughly," the same authority explains, "what subjects were taught in the *schola magistri*. When learned guests come to the monastery, the abbot should call one of the boys and, by way of a test, tell him to go and speak with the guest about the chant, the *computus*, grammar, or some art. In the meantime the abbot, unobserved by the boy, should note the manner in which he speaks and acts in the guest's presence. After the departure of the guest, the boy should be admonished if he was careless in speech, or too timid or too forward."[3]

It is further suggested (by the same source of information using Warnefrid, Hildemar, and the Murbach Statutes) that these boy oblates and *alumni* learned the elementary arts during the hours when their seniors were engaged in *lectio divina*, that they studied the psalms and the Rule, which they were expected

[1] P. 323.
[2] P. 231.
[3] *Op. cit.*, pp. 126-7.

eventually to know by heart, that they practised reading aloud, and that they were trained (anyway in the monastery of Inde) in the use of a purer Latin than that to which some of the more rustic neophytes were accustomed.[4]

That all this refers to an alumnate consisting of boy monks or oblates, and not to a secular institution, is implied not only by the character of the observance and course of study which they were expected to follow but also by various enactments which recognize the two quite separate systems of education. Thus the forty-fifth canon of the Capitulary of Aachen forbids, in the early part of the ninth century, that any school be formed in the monastery except one for the training of oblates. In the same century there were schools at St. Gall and Reichenau which catered frankly for lay students. How the conflicting views were resolved we do not know; the fact is mentioned here merely to show that the school for the training of young monks was one thing and the school for the training of young laymen was another.

Omnis aetas debet proprias habere mensuras, says St. Benedict. And if Hildemar is a reliable authority to go by, the measure of courtesy insisted upon in his time is more important than the measure of punishment imposed. The young religious were told how to bow to their seniors on entering the refectory, how they were to stand while the others sat down to eat, how they were to be particularly careful of their manners when eating at the abbot's table and with guests. Hildemar gives a list of salutations to be observed on the part of the young when addressing their elders: the greetings are sealed according to the rank of the one addressed. Before a king, according to the arbiter, the well-bred monk prostrates.

This chapter brings to an end the group of eight chapters which, in the opinion of Abbot Herwegen, formed a special supplement for the use of superiors, and which, in the final draft of the Rule, were given by pure accident the place which they now

---

[4] The distinction, which will be discussed in its proper place, between *oblati* and *alumni* was that while the former were professed monks the latter were bound by no tie of vow. Both groups normally followed the same observance.

occupy. Whether Abbot Herwegen's conjecture is accepted or not, the space devoted in the Rule to the punishment of offenders is considerable. But as we do not judge health by hospitals nor housing by hotels, so it would be a mistake to judge St. Benedict's monks by the penal aspect of the Rule under which they served. We must avoid what Sir Thomas Browne calls "a fallacy in duration."

CHAPTER 31

OF THE CELLARER OF THE MONASTERY

It is clear from this and other chapters in the holy Rule that St. Benedict considers the cellarer to be the most important person in the monastery after the abbot. In giving him greater prominence than either prior or novicemaster St. Benedict might be thought to place too much weight upon the material side of the life when he should be concerned much more with the spiritual formation of his monks. But to see the matter in such a way would be to see it in false perspective. The office of cellarer is to be understood as a spiritual rather than as a material and administrative office. The immediate cares of the cellarer may have to do with things domestic and financial, but the main care—both on St. Benedict's part in legislating and on the cellarer's part in carrying out his responsibilities—is spiritual. If the cellarer loses sight of the supernatural he becomes a manager merely. So long as he views his office in the terms laid down by St. Benedict he is proof against the charge of debasing his vocation and making for himself a worldly career in the monastery.

Let there be chosen out of the community as cellarer of the monastery a man wise and of mature character, temperate, not a great eater, not haughty nor headstrong, not offensive or dilatory, nor wasteful, but a God-fearing man who may be like a father to the whole community.

The term *cellarius* is borrowed not from Cassian but from St. Pachomius. Though other names are given to the office, both in early monastic literature and in current usage, the word, "cell-arer" will here be used throughout. In the history of the cenobitic life the function of the cellarer has always been the same, namely to provide for the temporal administration of the community, and, though St. Benedict does not say so in as many words, the appointment comes from the abbot and not by vote. The abbot is expected to consult the seniors of the monastery in his choice of men for the key positions in the monastery (see the sixty-fifth chapter), but having listened to the opinions of others he is free to elevate or depose as he thinks best. The early commentators are unanimous in amplifying the principles given in the Rule: the cellarer received his orders from, and was responsible to, the abbot; from whom he received his authority. Where the *camerarius*, the deans, and other local officials came under the prior, it is clear that the cellarer had to render account only to the abbot.

The qualities required in the man who must look after the temporal affairs of the house are not inconsiderable. He will have to possess a social as well as a religious sense, and a readiness to submit as well as a readiness to give orders. He will have to surrender his time, his preferences for this or that kind of work, to the common need of the community. More truly than in the case of any other member of the household, the cellarer is the servant of the brethren. But he is a servant with a difference: he is in the most real sense the minister.

The concept of the cellarer which exists in the minds of many, whether within or without the religious life, is one which represents the man of the world. We perhaps do not picture a figure so obvious as the miser with his moneybags and sly expression, but there is often in our minds the image of an adroit financier. We must know that when St. Benedict says of his cellarer that he is to be *sapiens et maturus moribus*, he does not mean wise in the sense of worldly-wise or mature in the sense of having outgrown his youthful idealism. He means that the cellarer should possess a good judgment, should be provident and considered in his administration.

The holy Rule warns against impetuosity and obstinacy in the

cellarer, seeing in these qualities the clearest evidence of pride.
Since the whole of St. Benedict's teaching is based on the twofold
foundation of humility and charity, the requirements in the case
of the most important people in the community are necessarily
bound up with these virtues. *Non elatus, non turbulentus, non
injuriosus . . . sed sit sicut pater.* Far from being a man of the
world, the cellarer must be a man essentially of the cloister: his
spirit of religious poverty must forbid waste either in his own life
or in the lives of his brethren. It will always be the temptation of
a cellarer to be lavish in some things as it will be his temptation to
be parsimonious in others; he must remember that magnificence
in a religious is as bad as miserliness—probably worse because its
vulgarity is patent to all, and disedifies.

But as a check on either prodigality at one extreme and avarice
at the other, the cellarer has the thought of the abbot's supervision. If the relation between the two offices is what it should
be, the principles of poverty are secured, or at all events safeguarded, by the practice of obedience.

> Let him have the care of everything, but do nothing
> without the leave of the abbot. Let him take heed to what is
> commanded him. Let him not sadden his brethren. If a
> brother ask him for anything unreasonably, let him not
> treat him with contempt and so grieve him, but reasonably
> and with all humility let him refuse what he asks for
> amiss. . . . Let him have especial care of the sick, of the
> children, of guests, of the poor, knowing without doubt
> that he will have to render an account of all these on the
> day of Judgment.

It is never easy to deny the request without hurting the feelings of the one who requests it. So the cellarer must possess sympathy and tact. Again St. Benedict comes back to the need for
humility: the apologetic refusal can sometimes be more acceptable than the routine assent. Irritation, exasperation even, must
always be a standing menace to the man who has to listen to
complaints and demands, whose work is for ever being interrupted, who is likely to be surprised at inconvenient hours and
from unpredictable quarters, whose arrangements are liable to be

either blocked by the incompetent or misinterpreted by the suspicious, but if such a man is to preserve his sanity, let alone his peace of mind, he will need to be habituated to the recognition of the supernatural.

To the groups mentioned in the Rule as coming under the care of the cellarer, commentators add that of the serfs or monastery servants. Over these, as over the infirm, the young, guests, and the poor, the cellarer is to exercise a solicitous authority. He is exhorted to visit the infirmary frequently and correct any want of attention on the part of those who are deputed to attend to the needs of the sick and aged; he is to arrange about the times at which the boy oblates are to eat, and the measure of food to be provided; he is to co-operate with the guestmaster in seeing that those who come to the monastery are entertained according to their degree; he is to keep close touch with his various helpers (*manipuli*), and to see that they do not neglect their respective departments.

"The key position of the cellarer," says Schroll, "and his influence for good or for evil in the monastery is thus expressed: 'Through the cellarer many vices may be nourished or cut off in the monastery. It is well that he [St. Benedict] stipulated what kind of man he ought to be, for he realized the great good which would follow if the cellarer of the monastery were wise, and the great danger which would threaten were he unwise.' "[1]

His sphere of authority touching so many, the cellarer's outlook must inevitably have its effect outside as well as inside the monastery. St. Benedict reminds him that for every class of person with whom he comes in touch, the cellarer will have to render an account on the Last Day. St. Benedict has told as much to the abbot, and the fact that he repeats the warning to the cellarer is proof of the strictly supernatural view of the principle of human contact which he wants developed in his monks. The officials of the house are not to restrict their care of others to the fulfilment of human justice; they are to cultivate compassion. Without a true feeling for the sick and the poor as repre-

[1] *Op. cit.*, p. 63. References for the quotation are given as Paul Warnefrid, p. 310 and Hildemar, p. 373.

sentatives of Christ suffering, the "charity" performed is a thing of duty merely. Monks are meant to be more than humanitarians. This is not to say that compassion has to be felt emotionally; it is to say that it has to be practised supernaturally.

The experience of compassion is like the experience of humility: it is something that comes of the knowledge and love of Christ. It is not something that has to be worked up inside oneself: it is something that grows inside oneself until there is nothing of self in the expression of it. It is primarily the work of grace; it is the result of Christ forming Himself in the soul.

A piteous sight may move one to tenderness, just as the sight of one's sins may move one to humility and self-reproach, but the essential virtue in either case is the more interior and more constant disposition which is built up by the action of the Holy Spirit. The compassionate soul habitually longs to suffer with the suffering—is not just stirred to pity as the occasion presents itself. The humble soul habitually longs to take the lowest place with the lowly—is not just stirred to self-condemnation as the occasion presents itself. Pity can easily become mere patronage; not so compassion. Self-condemnation can easily become self-dramatization; not so humility.

Compassion is not something which a man sees in himself—except at those times when he makes the mistake of giving himself the credit of possessing it—but rather it is a light by which he sees something in others. It is the light by which he sees more of Christ.

So too in the case of humility: it is not a quality the growth of which is watched by the soul possessing it; it is the quality by which the comprehensive work of grace is increasingly seen.

> Let him look upon all the vessels and goods of the monastery as though they were the consecrated vessels of the altar. Let him not think that he may neglect anything . . . and let him not presume to meddle with what is forbidden him . . . let such things as are necessary be given and asked for at befitting times, that no one may be troubled or grieved in the house of God.

Again there is, in this attitude towards the *vasa monasterii*, the same insistence upon looking under the material object for the spiritual significance. Just as the poor and sick are to be treated as extensions of Christ, so the ordinary working tools of the house, as well as the more valuable possessions, are to be handled as things dedicated to Christ. Everything in the house of God, from the chalice to the teacup, is sanctified by reason of Him who is served.

This idea of monastic property being sacrosanct is strong in the early religious rules. St. Basil speaks about the "consecrated" character of all things appointed for the use of monks, even going so far as to say that the misuse of them is a form of "sacrilege." Cassian illustrates his point about the sacredness of monastic property with the following story. "During the weekly service of a certain brother, the cellarer passing by saw lying on the ground three lentil beans which had slipped out of the monk's hand as he was hastily preparing them for cooking. Immediately he [the cellarer] consulted the abbot on the subject, and the monk was adjudged a pilferer and negligent about sacred property . . . the offence of his carelessness was pardoned only when he had atoned for it by public penance."[2] Later in the same chapter Cassian explains that if monks do not own themselves they cannot own what they hold in fealty to Him whose property they are. "Wherefore if anything whatever has once been brought into the monastery, they [the brethren] claim that it must be treated with the utmost reverence as a holy thing . . . even in the case of things which are considered unimportant or regarded as common and paltry, so that if they change the position of these things, and put them in a better place, or if they fill a bottle with water, or if they remove a little dust from the oratory or from their cell, they believe with implicit faith that they will receive a reward from the Lord."

Three times in this chapter of the Rule (the entire text has not been quoted since much of it is repetitive) the cellarer is instructed to do nothing without reference to the abbot. To this is now added the warning that the cellarer does wrong to step

[2] *Institutes*, Bk. 4; ch. 20.

outside his proper field of interest and authority. In day-to-day consultation with the abbot about the affairs of the house, the cellarer may be tempted to give advice where it is not asked, may be tempted to assume control of the abbot's mind. It is easier for the cellarer than for any other member of the monastery's executive to bring pressure to bear upon both the abbot and his own fellow officials. Overt blackmail, reinforced by threats of resignation or a breakdown, can make a travesty of the monastic system.

In order to secure to the cellarer a measure of peace, St. Benedict includes the appeal about requests being made of him at befitting times. Since it is our universal tendency as human beings to exaggerate the importance of the situation in which we happen to be involved, this is an injunction which lays itself open to imperfect fulfilment. Members of a religious community should nevertheless respect the cellarer's interior life by presenting their needs not only at convenient hours but briefly.

The words with which the chapter concludes, *ut nemo perturbetur neque contristetur in domo Dei*, have probably figured on the device of many Benedictine monasteries; if they have not, they well might. The demand of authority is to be tempered by the manner of charity. St. Benedict, with his Roman blood and his Roman love for the gravity of the law, can be exacting to the point of severity. But every now and then he betrays an attitude of mind which shows his sympathy with depression, loneliness, homesickness. It is not simply that he knows melancholy to be the bane of the religious vocation; it is that he wants to bring relief to the brethren who suffer from their moods. All in the community must take care to see that none is upset or saddened. The house of God must not wear the air of a penitentiary; it is a place of joy. Anything is better than to let the brethren settle down to lives of gloom. "Let no chain of iron hold thee, but the chain of Christ,"[3] and one of the proofs that it is the chain of the true Christ and not the false is that it is worn without distress and sadness.

[3] *Dialogues*, Bk. 3; ch. 16.

CHAPTER 32

OF THE TOOLS AND PROPERTY
OF THE MONASTERY

This is the first of three chapters which deal with religious poverty. The question of goods held in common follows naturally upon the discussion of the office which is responsible for the goods and their distribution. St. Benedict's method here is to take first the main practical points at issue, and then to develop the theory. But St. Benedict's teaching on poverty is by no means confined to this brief section of the holy Rule: the subject comes up for closer attention in chapters fifty-four, fifty-five, and fifty-seven, where the practice is viewed in greater detail and the principle is reviewed from a different angle.

Let the abbot appoint brethren, on whose manner of life and character he can rely, to the charge of the tools, clothes, and other property of the monastery; and let him consign the various things to their charge, as he shall think fit, to be kept and to be collected after use. Of these let the abbot keep a list, so that as the brethren succeed to different employments, he may know what he gives and what he gets back.

While the direct administration of the kitchen is the cellarer's province, there are departments in the monastery which can be administered by assistants. It may be noted that the abbot and not the cellarer is the one to decide upon the personnel of these assistants. Rather than see his cellarer collect round him monks who might form a party in the community, St. Benedict is willing to risk the overlapping of duties and the possible clash of lesser authority. So long as the power of delegation remains firmly and exclusively in the abbot's hands, there is little likelihood of a faction springing up which might throw out the balance of the whole.

Whether in early times these minor offices were fused or not we do not know; certainly it was found convenient in many later monasteries for the functions of guestmaster and almoner to be performed by one man. We read also of the librarian being at the same time master of the *scriptorium;* the *vestiarius* again and the *camerarius* (who was in charge of weaving, sewing, and supplying textiles and skins) were often the same individual. Pluralism, however, is a bad thing for a monastery, and where it has been practised it has had the grace not to invent a principle to justify itself.

If anyone treat the property of the monastery in a slovenly or negligent manner, let him be corrected; and if he do not amend, let him be subjected to the discipline of the Rule.

Carelessness in a religious betrays a want of training, a want of monastic breeding. The do-it-anyhow attitude shows that the doctrine of God's will has been applied only to the major events of life. If we understand what is meant by "the sacrament of the present moment" we cannot do anything as if it does not matter. We may not be able to do many things perfectly, but it is God's will that we should do nothing listlessly.

Waste, whether in the matter of food, clothes, electric light, fuel, or in the use of less important things such as writing paper, washing and cleaning material, stamps and telephone calls is an offence against a monk's conversion of manners as well as against his poverty. It offends also against humility. It is a vulgarity, and it gives scandal.

Without being fussy, a monk is expected to be thrifty. We would do wrong to accuse of pettiness those saints who wrote their books on the backs of old envelopes, and who lined their habits with newspapers rather than spend community money on warmer clothing.

On the theme of corporate possession our minds tend to inconsistency. Having argued that because we are not gratifying the desire for ownership in the acquisition of what is best, we then treat the goods with less respect than if they belonged to us. The fallacy would be corrected if we truly observed the principle laid down in the foregoing chapter. Whether we are driving a tractor or tying a knot in a shoelace, we are handling something which is ours only because we are God's—something which is ours only in an accommodated sense, and which is so truly God's that a heedless use of it is an irreverence.

CHAPTER 33

WHETHER MONKS OUGHT TO HAVE ANYTHING OF THEIR OWN

In this chapter poverty is considered not so much as a penance but rather as a means towards social unity. The theory is that where there are no distinctions there will be less room for envy. In the ideal community, where all share alike, no one member can exalt himself above the others by display, magnificence, patronage. If such a state was possible among the early Christians as described in the Acts, it should be possible also among monks. Nothing could be more sure than the direction given by St. Benedict in attempting this ideal.

> Above all let the vice of private ownership be cut off from the monastery by the roots. Let none presume to give or receive anything without leave of the abbot, or to keep anything as his own, either a book, writing-tablet, or pen or anything whatsoever; since they [the brethren] are permitted to have neither body nor will in their own power. But let them hope to receive all that is necessary from the father of the monastery.

The poverty of the monastery is different from that of the desert. In the desert the monks aimed at extreme privation. Benedictine poverty may, and indeed should, involve certain privations; what it aims at, however, is the detached use of goods held in common. Nor is Benedictine poverty the same as that of the mendicant orders. Where the begging friar may not know where his next meal is coming from, the Benedictine monk is normally secure in his expectation of three square meals a day. The monks no less than the friars, no less than the poor who have their poverty thrust upon them in the world, must cultivate a sense of continued dependence upon divine Providence. But it would be wrong to think that St. Benedict summoned his followers to walk the way of destitution.

That in St. Benedict's own monastery provisions sometimes sank below the safety level we know from incidents described by St. Gregory in the *Dialogues*. "Almost all the bread was spent," we read in the twenty-first chapter, "so that but five loaves remained for the brethren's evening meal." St. Benedict reproached the community for showing dismay instead of confidence while enduring these straitened circumstances, and told them that next day they would have plenty to eat. "On the morrow were found two hundred sacks of wheat before the monastery gates . . . which when the monks beheld, they gave thanks to God, and by this were taught in their greatest want to hope for plenty."[1] On another occasion the finances of the house were so low that, until St. Benedict prayed for the sum and on the third day received it (with one shilling more than he prayed for), there were not as many as twelve shillings with which to relieve a poor man of his debt.[2] Another instance of how narrow the margin was at Monte Cassino during St. Benedict's time can be seen in the account of the oil that was given to Agapitus the subdeacon. During the period of famine "the man of God gave all that he had in his monastery to those in want, insomuch as there was almost nothing left in the cellar save only a little oil in a glass vessel." The cellarer demurred at the parting with this last item out of his store, and was duly punished for his lack of faith. The oil was presented to the man who had asked for it, and on the same day the supply was miraculously and abundantly renewed.

Though St. Benedict and his monks practised poverty, there is no specific mention of the term "poverty," either as a virtue or a vow, in the Rule. What is stressed is the renunciation of indi-

[1] Bk. 2; ch. 27.
[2] *Ibid.*, chs. 28,29.

vidual ownership. The "poverty" which demands extra labour in the fields[3] is a matter of circumstance not of ideal. The commentators in the same way treat of the evils of acquiring private possessions; they do not make a Benedictine virtue of poverty. It *is* a virtue, and a necessary one to a religious, but it is the kind of virtue which develops out of the given cenobitic state. The given cenobitic state here is conditioned by the repudiation of ownership.

"If private property is held by the monks," writes St. Gregory in a letter to an abbot, "it will not be possible to preserve either concord or charity in the community." The ideal here is not that of collectivism or the welfare state: the ideal is charity through social unity. Where possessiveness is eliminated, amity can be expected to flourish. The Benedictine conception of religious poverty does not stop short, as might be thought from a superficial study of St. Benedict's prohibitions, at equity: it goes on to the use of goods for mutual well-being, and so to the practice of fraternal charity.

If the aim is to iron out distinctions among the brethren, it is not the aim to reduce the life of the monastery to a flat dead-level of uniformity. Ironing out the accidental differences is only part of the process of arriving at the essential harmony. Concord and not regimentation is intended as the final result. St. Benedict is at pains to restrict personal dominion so that possession may be unified—and offered corporately to God.

Thus anything which reflects this ideal of social unity in the monastery is to be encouraged. Even down to the details of the life, the monk chooses wisely when he chooses to act as a member of a body rather than as an independent unit. He will choose, for example, to keep his cowl where other cowls are hanging rather than in his cell; he will clean his shoes with the material

[3] Ch. 48. "If the needs of the place, or their poverty, oblige them to labour at gathering in the crops, let them not be saddened by it; for then they are truly monks, living by the labour of their hands as did our fathers and the apostles." Even here the situation created by the poverty of the monastery is regarded as the exception. The brethren are exhorted to make a virtue of the necessity: the necessity is not a virtue unless they make it one.

provided for all rather than keep a private supply; he will read the periodicals where they are put for common use rather than bear them off to study in solitude; his hair will be cut along with the rest rather than by special arrangement.

In his plea that "the vice of private ownership be cut off by the roots" St. Benedict is echoing Cassian in word, and the whole tradition of desert monachism in thought. The Rules of St. Basil, St. Macarius, St. Caesarius, and St. Pachomius make the same point in almost the same terms, and *The Paradise of the Fathers* gives numberless illustrations of the theme. Leaving aside this wealth of good material, because to make use of it here would strain the subject without adding in significance to what has been said already, we can take St. Benedict's words as they stand and examine the sanctions which he imposes upon tenure *ad usum*.

For giving, receiving, retaining—in other words for the relation between the person and the thing—there must be the abbot's permission. But though this is the necessary condition, it is not always the justifiable excuse. A monk may imagine that by getting permission for a thing he has done all that is required of him when in fact he has far from satisfied the purpose of the regulation. If the end of St. Benedict's enactment is to be served, the monk must assure himself that the reason for asking the abbot's permission is weightier than the reason for doing without the thing asked. The condition depends upon the justification, and not the justification upon the condition.

If a monk could vindicate the right to give, receive, retain— in other words to act as though he were in the world—by the mere external deed which regularized the legal aspect of the thing, there would be nothing but his abbot's strength of mind between him and the considerable acquisition of property. Accumulation is accumulation—with or without permission—and this is what St. Benedict is trying to prevent.

If such is the case with the monk who gets permission, what of the monk who does not? A monk may so stretch his right to "presume" permission as hardly ever to get permission at all. From the liberty which assumes that permission would be gladly granted in the given instance it is no great step to the licence which assumes that permissions are unimportant.

Permissions are important not because of the importance of the thing asked for but because of the importance of obedience. The intrinsic value of the object may increase or decrease the obligation of getting permission but it does not increase or decrease the reason for getting permission. The reason for getting permission lies in obedience and surrender. Accordingly the true value of the material object lies in the spiritual significance which it represents. When the occasion of getting permission presents itself to the monk, whether it is an object or an act that is in question, the entity desired is the occasion either of independence on the one hand or of surrender on the other. It is independence that St. Benedict is attacking in this chapter.

Independence is not cured by having to get permission, but at least it is curbed. As we grow older we seem to grow less fond of asking permission. We do not like the humiliation which apparently cost us so little in our novitiate days. We are tempted to resort to practices of dubious integrity—distributing our requests among different authorities, waiting till we go away before adding to our stock of this or that, sueing for and extending a "general" permission beyond necessity—and so to devalue, if not altogether to spoil, the quality of our obedience.

It is probably in the act of giving, rather than in the acts of receiving and retaining, that we are apt to take a wide margin of interpretation. To give is generally assumed to be an act of generosity, and on the strength of this we imagine that our charity covers a multitude of permissions. But if our giving springs from an independent will, it is essentially a less generous and a less charitable act than that of either receiving in obedience or retaining in obedience.

The freedom to give is one of the most enviable of freedoms, is indeed one of the major luxuries. On that account it must, for the monk, be under discipline. If we give as people give who are in the world, we are exercising the radical dominion which has been renounced in the terms of our adoption: we are reclaiming a right which used to exist but which now does not. Thus when we give as religious we must be sure that the act is performed in the name of religion. Only if what we give is understood to be coming from God more than from ourselves, and in charity is going to God as much as to the one to whom it is given, can the gift have God's blessing upon it. Though the permission may not secure this purity of motive, it is hard to see how the motive can be at all pure without it.

Experience would suggest that the failures in monastic life can be traced to a weakening of the spirit of poverty. Lacking fixed principles about poverty, the monk can find himself giving more and more scope to his possessive instinct until at last the one check upon his independence, namely the check of obedience, is swept away. What is said of the individual religious might be said also of the religious house and the religious order: decline in fervour can be measured by, and can be found to have started by, a decline in poverty. Yet if this is true it is equally true that the first sign of the dawn of spirituality, as of monastic reform, is a deepening sense of religious poverty and of its necessity. It is a wonderful thing to watch the return to poverty—whether in a person, a monastery, a congregation—where before there was indifference to its practice.

> Let all things be common to all . . . nor let anyone say or assume that anything is his own. But if anyone is found to indulge in this most baneful vice, and after one or two admonitions does not amend, let him be subjected to correction.

Scarcity and plenty are held in common. But because this is such a difficult ideal to keep always before the mind, and because from the practical point of view it is inevitable that some things more than others will have to be put aside for some people more than others, St. Benedict foresees trouble. There will be inequality, differences of interpretation, the assertion of rights over objects which are necessary to a particular man's job. The only solution is for everyone to be given what is necessary for his work, and for nobody to hold on to what he has only a steward's claim upon.

Whether it is a question of the things which we need in the exercise of our duties or of the things which come to us from outside in the way of presents, we are likely to preserve the spirit of the Rule if we put off using the object until the superior's wishes have been consulted. It is easy to say that because we cannot do without a particular book or tool, we can take possession of it now and ask permission later. It is easy, at Christmas for example, to look upon a book or some handkerchiefs as our own and make use of them—or even to give these presents away again with every show of religious detachment—before we have consulted authority. Indeed it might be a good thing if sometimes the abbot told us to suspend our use of this or that until he had given the matter deeper thought: such a decision might reveal that we had already entered upon that object's occupation.

Indulgence in the *nequissimo vitio* of possessiveness is contrary to St. Benedict's idea of monasticism precisely because once the will has risen above the human instinct to acquire, the soul is free to mount to God in prayer and in fraternal charity. So long as there is a will to accumulate, to lock up and label with one's own name, there can never be true religious indifference or a true community spirit. In the teaching of religious poverty, as in the teaching of other principles, it is the negative rather than the positive aspects that immediately impress. It is the failures to reach the ideal, as instanced by St. Gregory in the stories of the monk who kept three gold coins and of the brethren who accepted linen as presents from their devout friends, that stand out; but it is the day-to-day success of monastic poverty that matters. Monastic poverty is successful exactly in the measure that it is liberative, directing the soul upwards in the act of love. This basic concept understood, there is no danger that the soul will lose itself in the thicket of dispensations, assumed permissions, deviations and subterfuges. Monks are trained to hold in a loose hand, to be ready at a moment's notice to lay down or exchange. Monks are pilgrims within an enclosure; they travel light.

CHAPTER 34

WHETHER ALL OUGHT TO RECEIVE
NECESSARY THINGS ALIKE

This chapter is to be considered not only as an epilogue to what has gone before but as a prologue to what is yet to come in chapter fifty-five. It is difficult to see what led St. Benedict to leave out here the list of necessary things which he gives later on when treating specifically of what the brethren are to wear. Leaving then, with St. Benedict, the details of a monk's equipment till the wardrobe question comes up, we pursue the governing principle as it appears in the text.

It is written: "Distribution was made to everyone according as he had need." By this we do not mean that there should be respecting of persons (God forbid), but consideration for infirmities. Let him therefore who needs less thank God and be not distressed; and let him who needs more be humbled because of his infirmity and not puffed up by the mercy that is shown to him; so all the members shall be in peace.

It is difficult to talk about discretion without appearing to condone compromise and laxity. Once bring in the diversity of needs in a community according to the differences of health, age, and temperament, and you open the door to individualism. But on the other hand St. Benedict expressly provides for "him who needs more" and "him who needs less." In the desert there was less consideration for the infirm: if you were not able to endure the regime, you might take it as a sign that you were not to become a monk. But in the monastery it is different: if you are not able to endure the regime, you make an act of humility and endure as much of it as you can.

The community is a family and not a regiment; the stronger brethren support the weak and take over the duties of the weak; the weaker brethren are not merely drafted to a unit where less is expected. Those who are strong to endure have no reason to take it upon themselves to rule the rest. For them the duty is twofold: they must show gratitude to God for the powers which He has lent them, and they must not resent the extra labours which their capacity may involve them in against their will.

If the practice of monastic poverty is to a certain extent regulated by the particular needs of particular people, it is also to a certain extent regulated by the particular needs of particular communities. For example, in the World Congress of Religious which met in 1950 in Rome, Bishop Siri came out strongly against smoking, carrying a watch, having a camera, enjoying the use of a car. The question is not so much whether these concessions are contrary to religious poverty as whether in their particular setting they are necessary to the particular community.

Thus monastic poverty must be seen as related to the work of the monastery. Communities whose main work is active and apostolic will have to humble themselves for needing more in the way of material equipment; communities which are contemplative and cut off from the world will be able to carry out a stricter scheme of renunciation. St. Benedict's *et ita omnia membra erunt in pace* might be made also to read *omnia monasteria erunt in pace*: unevenness between monastery and monastery in the observance of poverty is to be accounted for in charity.

> Above all things let not the pest of murmuring, for whatever cause, by any word or sign, be manifested. If anyone be found guilty in this, let him be subjected to the most severe punishment.

St. Benedict appreciates the effect which his doctrine of necessary inequality will have, so at once he follows it up with an absolute ban on the grumbled complaint of the monk who feels put upon. Murmuring, *pro qualicumque causa*, is forbidden to monks. If this means anything at all, it means that even if there is good ground for complaint there is no excuse for murmuring. Under certain conditions, and when couched in a certain form, representations may be made to authority; but this is something quite different from the *malum murmurationis*.

This section which has to do with monastic poverty may be concluded with a summary of St. Benedict's teaching on its theory and practice.

Monks are to free themselves from earthly possessions, and more significantly from the desire to possess, so that they may more completely give themselves to the service of God. The implication is that if the appetite for material things is satisfied beyond the point of reasonable necessity, it will clamour for more, and that this will divert the soul from its true purpose.

Not only is supernatural happiness impossible where there is affection for material things, but so also is natural happiness impossible: the monk, who is expected to be happy as well as holy, must detach himself from the material things which his state obliges him to use.

Thus since even the strictest monks cannot escape from a dependence upon material objects, the only way to enjoy them safely is to hold them in common and to enjoy them in common. This does not mean that community goods may be safely amassed and, so long as they are held in community, enjoyed. It means that in order to destroy the spirit of *proprietas*, the goods which are judged necessary for the general well-being of the monastery, and for the furtherance of the end proposed, are for the benefit of all and at the disposal of all.

Community poverty is not confined to the act of dispossession, either on the part of individual members or of the community as a whole, but extends to the act of sharing whatever is provided. If only a chosen few have access to a telephone, for example, or if some and not others are allowed to gather for coffee at certain times and in a certain place, the Benedictine concept of poverty is being misunderstood.

Though not explicitly stated in the text of these three chapters which we have been considering, the ideal presented is that which finds formal expression throughout the Rule—namely, the example of Christ. The monk embraces poverty as Christ embraced it, as His apostles embraced it.

The monastic poverty that depends more upon what can be obtained from the common store than upon divine Providence is not a true religious poverty. The monastic poverty that is selective, that looks for preferential treatment from the cellarer, that endeavours to "earn" a particular permission, that assumes itself to be above accounting for its acts, that makes things difficult for those who may want to participate in its goods, is no true religious poverty.

The only religious poverty is evangelical poverty. When St. Benedict says *omnia omnibus sint communia* he is thinking of the disciples of Christ. There was a spirit of participation in the early Church which sprang directly from the Sermon on the Mount and from Him who preached it. Leaving aside for a moment the responsibility of those in authority who give their consent to these things, is it in this apostolic tradition for a monk who "has" a television set or radio to invite fellow members of his community to attend a particular programme? Is it in the apostolic tradition for one member of the community to travel first-class, while his brother in religion travels more humbly further down the line?

Offend against poverty and you offend against conversion of manners, against the common life, against humility. Benedictine poverty may not be as real—in the sense of uncomfortable—as the poverty of some other religious orders, or of the needy in the world, but at least it has the Gospel as its inspiration. The source of Benedictine poverty is Christ. Where Christ is the model, the imitation, however miserably inadequate, can be very real indeed. But without Christ, Benedictine poverty can all too easily be a fiction. Or, and this is perhaps worse, it can be a screen.

CHAPTER 35

OF THE WEEKLY SERVERS
IN THE KITCHEN

It will be assumed here, though the assumption is not made by all, that St. Benedict refers to the servers in the refectory as well as to those who help in preparing the food. While the monk responsible for the actual cooking would continue in the job, his assistants take their turn at the less skilled duties in the kitchen and at the work of distribution during mealtimes. Such was the practice in the earliest documented period, and such is the practice today in monasteries where servants are not employed.

Though the regulations to be discussed have nothing to do with the enactments on poverty immediately preceding, it is easy to see a connection. From the idea of common property, St. Benedict's mind goes on to the idea of common service—the members of the family waiting upon one another in the same spirit that they lend to one another. Even down to the detail of exemptions, the principle is the same: uniformity is sacrificed to the particular need. The ideal, again, is Christ. "I have given you an example, that as I have done to you, so you do also. Amen, amen, I say to you: the servant is not greater than his lord; neither is the apostle greater than he that sent him. If you know these things, you shall be blessed if you do them."[1]

Let the brethren so serve each other in turn that no one be excused from the work of the kitchen unless on the score

[1] John 13;15-17.

of health or because he is engaged in some matter of great utility; for thence greater reward is obtained. Let the weaker brethren, however, be helped that they do not do their work with sadness; and let all generally have assistance according to the number of the community . . . if the community be larger, the cellarer shall be excused . . . but let the rest serve one another in turn with all charity.

In times when community recreation was rarely, if ever, allowed, the expression of the family-life ideal was necessarily restricted to acts of mutual service. The monk did not perform these domestic tasks merely because there was no one else to perform them for him. He was encouraged by St. Benedict to see in the week's functions a strictly supernatural opportunity. Nothing could better impress the concept of "household" than the fulfilment of household labours. For this reason, though not for this reason alone, it is a pity that in some communities the monks are waited upon by hired lay help: it means the abrogation of a monastic right. But even where this is the custom we must believe that the merit of obedience to the authority which sanctions it outweighs the merit to which the monks would have been entitled were they able to serve one another. *Quia exinde major merces acquiritur.* Certainly wherever possible St. Benedict's words hold good: *caeteri vero sibi sub charitate invicem serviant.*

Even where opportunity for direct mutual service is curtailed, the ideal of the family life may yet be very adequately served. Indeed if the Benedictine character of the life is to be maintained at all, it must be. Hence the importance precisely, in our day, of community recreation. The dispensation from the normal state of silence was originally granted to monks not because silence was found to be a bore but because recreation was found to be a good. By mixing with one another and enjoying one another's conversation, monks came to have a better appreciation of the family life, of the mystical body, of humanity supernaturalized.

Accordingly it would be as misguided to withdraw oneself from community recreation as to withdraw oneself from one's week of serving or reading or intoning in choir. Monks who

would not dream of refusing to appear in their turn as assistants
at a pontifical ceremony, and so laying themselves open to the
charge of being "untouchable," will readily find excuses for
stopping away from the social life of the house. In the Benedictine idea the social and the liturgical are as closely related to
one another as intellectual labour is related to manual labour or
as the apostolate is related to the arts. The monk who absents
himself from occasions of association with his brethren is withdrawing from a primary monastic influence; he is withdrawing
from a unity, from the whole.

Given that he is present, moreover, the monk must make it his
business to contribute to the purpose of this common recreation.
He is not a passenger, he is not there to be entertained merely.
He must serve—and serve in charity. The essential function is
lost if the brethren fail to co-operate. "We seldom seem to meet,"
said one brother to another at recreation; "I hope that because
you do not often speak to me it does not mean I am out of
favour?" "Of course not," was the reply; "besides, I wish you a
happy feast every year." In large communities instances of this
sort could be multiplied. "How pleasant he looks there," said a
young monk of a senior who was not present when some community photographs were being passed round, "what is he like?
I don't think I have ever spoken to him."

Let him who is ending his week's service clean up everything on Saturday . . . let him hand over to the cellarer the
vessels used in his work clean and in good condition. Let
the cellarer hand them to the one entering on his office,
that he may know what he gives and what he receives. An
hour before the meal these weekly servers shall receive,
over and above the appointed allowance, a draught of wine
and a piece of bread, so that they may serve the brethren
at mealtime without murmuring or excessive fatigue. On
solemn days, however, let them wait until after Mass.

In passing it has been said above that a monk should not consider himself an untouchable—a man never to be asked to do this
or that. But to ask him to wear a cope or hear the nuns' confessions would be to touch him only on one side. A monk may
equally regard himself as untouchable on the other side—he may

resent being asked to give up a particular act of service which he has come to look upon as his own. In order to avoid this kind of attachment, as much as to avoid laying burdens unevenly, St. Benedict provides for the weekly exchange of personnel in the minor duties of the house. With only a week to run, neither the disagreeable task will be insupportable nor the enviable task made matter for *proprietas*.

"He likes doing it, and of course it suits the rest of us" was the explanation given to a visiting monk as to why the same brother went on calling the community every morning at Matins, "so he's been allowed to keep the job." It seems that we can acquire a proprietary affection for almost anything. Convenience may govern a number of these small routine employments—thus it might be a nuisance to change each week the monk who sorts the letters or who sees to the hosts in the sacristy—but generally speaking the less room there is for the sense of their permanence the better.

The cellarer is instructed to keep track of all that has been used in connection with kitchen and refectory. St. Benedict's is an orderly mind, and apart from considerations of waste there must be a clear-cut arrangement which will ensure cleanliness, tidiness, and the feel of Roman discipline. As to these *vasa ministerii*, what were they? Schroll, using Warnefrid and Hildemar as sources, enumerates the following: *scutellae*, open dishes or platters; *lapidea*, stone jars; *scamna*, low tables or benches; *cuppae*, vases for storage; *conchae*, basin-like vessels used for the washing of feet. From the same authority we may gather that those on duty for the week had plenty to occupy them. "In the kitchen was heated the water for laundering the clothes . . . those brothers who prepared this water likewise placed the *conchae* in readiness. The actual washing took place in the cloister. Perhaps the clothes were dried there too. At Hirschau they were hung on a rope in the cloister, and the footgear *(socci)* when washed was placed on the sand of the cloister to dry . . . the linen towels used in the Saturday washing of the feet were washed immediately after this ceremony."[2]

The extra allowance of bread and wine, taken by the servers

[2] *Op. cit.*, pp. 36, 37.

and reader an hour before the community meal, was as much a precaution as a reward. Men who had been up since two in the morning might faint while serving their brethren at the first meal of the day which would normally take place at about noon. But on those days when all would receive Holy Communion at the conventual Mass, the servers and reader would have to fast with the rest.

If St. Benedict is careful to lighten the burdens of the refectory servers, those who are being waited on should do no less. It is not only the servers who should keep their wits about them in the effort to attend to the needs of their brethren; thoughtfulness is almost more necessary to those who are ministered unto than to those who minister. In the refectory we are apt—we, the eaters—to neglect some of the courtesies which are often better observed in the world. Whether from a too careful custody of the eyes or from a too close interest in food, we can keep a tired server waiting with arms outstretched for the sign which will tell him if or not we fancy what he holds.

On Sunday, as soon as Lauds are ended, both the incoming and outgoing servers of the week shall cast themselves on their knees in the presence of all and ask their prayers. Let him who has ended his week say this verse: *Benedictus es, Domine Deus, qui adjuvisti me et consolatus es me;* and when this has been said three times, let him receive the blessing. He who is entering on his office shall then follow and say: *Deus in adjutorium meum intende, Domine ad adjuvandum me festina.* Let this also be three times repeated by all; and having received the blessing let him enter on his office.

This rite, which in one form or another goes far back into antiquity, is designed to remind the servers and the served alike that the works performed in the monastery are, however commonplace, consecrated to God. The act of handing round dishes twice a day for a week may not in itself amount to much—hardly enough, it might be thought, to warrant the addition of yet another ceremony to the liturgy—but it is a question of quality rather than of quantity. The amount has only the value that the quality gives to it. If this is true, then even the most insignificant and menial labours may be raised by prayer to an almost sacramental dignity.

The particular prayers used for the alternation of duties are of Cluniac origin; these in their turn derive their thought from Cassian. The repeated versicles and responses given by St. Benedict are said today, though not all monasteries have retained the custom of placing the rite immediately after the morning office.

CHAPTER 36

OF THE SICK BRETHREN

St. Benedict passes from one expression of service to another. When he has said, in this and the chapter following, how the more exempted members of the household are to be treated, he will come back to the ordinary rank and file in the community and to matters further concerning the refectory. The opening phrases of this thirty-sixth chapter show that it is no mere afterthought which has been wedged in here because of its relation to housework.

Before all things and above all things care must be taken of the sick, so that they may be served in very deed as Christ Himself. For He has said: "I was sick and you visited Me" and "as long as you did it to one of these My least brethren, you did it to Me."

In the effort always to see in human personalities the divine personality of Christ—which is what St. Benedict means with his *ita eis serviatur ut sicut revera Christo*—there is the danger of abstracting too much from the human and so defeating the purpose of the act. Men who are continuously pursuing the supernatural may err in forgetting about the natural. The sick, St. Benedict reminds us, must be served in the person of Christ and Christ must be served in the person of the sick. The point here is not that we have to make an act of the imagination—picturing Christ in this sick man—or even an act of the sensible will—directing the affections through the sick man to Christ—but rather, and much more simply, that we recognize the identification and act upon it. Our action will take the form of ministering to the immediate human object of this identification. And because we in our turn are similarly identified with Christ, our action is His action and our charity is His charity.

"Let this mind be in you, which was also in Christ Jesus. Who being in the form of God, thought it not robbery to be equal with God, but emptied himself, taking the form of a servant, being made in the likeness of men."[1] If Christ takes up our life into His, and if we live His life in our own, then His Passion is reproducing itself in us and our sufferings are being suffered by Him.

Our attitude towards the sick, and indeed our attitude towards *ourselves* in relation to the sick, will be truly supernatural and truly compassionate in the measure that we identify ourselves with the self-giving of Christ. By nature we can cultivate a finite pity; by grace we are endowed with Christ's infinite compassion. Until we have assimilated this doctrine and made it the principle of our works of charity, we cannot look upon the sick and the poor and the afflicted save as either symbols on the one hand or objects of emotional pity on the other. Nor can we, until we have grasped the twofold point of the doctrine, look upon our own dispositions save as the purely personal response to given stimuli.

But let the sick themselves consider that they are served for the honour of God, and not grieve their brethren who serve them by their importunity. Yet must they be patiently borne with, because from such as these is gained more abundant reward. Therefore the abbot shall take the greatest care that they suffer no neglect. And let a cell be set apart by itself for the sick brethren, and an attendant be appointed who is God-fearing, prompt, and painstaking.

Where there is an obligation to act in charity there is a corresponding obligation to be acted upon in charity. The sick must show themselves worthy not only of being treated with kindness

[1] Phil. 2;5-7.

but also of being reflections of Christ who is served in them. Much will depend upon the nature and the gravity of their sickness, but the fact remains that there will always be invalids who seem to be unnecessarily demanding, cross, ungrateful. These are just the ones who are invaluable in a community: they call for the greatest faith, they are those who elicit the purest charity and are responsible for the accumulation of the most merit. Their importunities must be borne with by those in health, their complaints must not be allowed to sadden.

If our compassion is moving along the right lines, we shall be slow to charge the querulous invalid with murmuring. We must make allowance for the vapouring of tried nerves. Commenting on the beatitude *beati misericordes quoniam ipsi misericordiam consequentur*, St. Bernard says that the stages of compassion mount in the order of repentance, self-knowledge, unqualified forbearance and forgiveness. In his *De Gradibus Humilitatis* he pursues the same idea: *et hic est secundus gradus veritatis quo eam in proximis inquirunt dum de suis aliorum necessitates exquirunt, dum ex his que patiuntur patientibus compati sciunt.*[2]

While attention is paid to the sick particularly by the abbot, the infirmarian, and the cellarer, an obligation rests upon all to see that the sick get what they want. If the teaching outlined above carries any weight in a community, those who are confined to the infirmary will not lack visitors. Just as in the refectory it is not only the servers who are expected to watch out for opportunities of providing what is wanted—each brother being ready to anticipate his neighbour's request—so in regard to those, whether ill or old, who are not able to follow the routine of the house: every member of the family is expected to make himself responsible if the occasion presents itself.

In enlarging upon the qualities required for the post of infirmarian, the early commentators state emphatically that a monk and not a layman is to perform the office. The monk-infirmarian, according to Hildemar, might be given lay help in the work of washing and carrying food. Hildemar seems to have seen nothing unusual in the employment of serfs who worked in

[2] Ch. 5.

other departments (as at the mill and on the grounds and in the laundry and farm), so his exclusion of externs from the appointment is intended to be significant: the infirmarian is not a medical man, an expert; he is God-fearing, a man of prayer, understanding, and charity.

The "cell" mentioned in the Rule is interpreted as a dormitory, or even a cloister or wing. In Carolingian monasteries there were facilities for Mass, which the sick could attend in bed. At Farfa the brethren in the infirmary recited together, if they were not too ill to do so, the Divine Office. In the greater houses of the twelfth and thirteenth centuries, the infirmary was often a separate establishment with its own choir, community-room, refectory and kitchen.

Delatte, bringing the subject into its contemporary setting, warns against the tendency to allow monks to seek cure and convalescence among their friends in the world. He further deprecates any idea of having a central clinic into which all the sick of the Congregation could be collected. "Our Holy Father evidently means each monastic family to care for its sick in the monastery itself."[3] It would accordingly seem inconsistent with the spirit and tradition of Benedictinism to send off elderly and ailing monks to nursing homes where they will be expected to remain till they die. The reasons given for this extra-mural care of the sick are certainly good ones: professional attention, suitable diet, freedom from the worry of imposing upon the kindness of the brethren. But do these reasons outweigh the good of being among one's own? A monk should be able to look forward to dying in the monastery of his profession. Certainly he should not be allowed to feel that unless his last weeks are likely to cause little inconvenience to the brethren, he will without doubt breathe his final breath under a secular roof.

> Let the use of baths be granted to the sick as often as it shall be expedient; but to those who are well, and especially to the young, baths shall be seldom permitted. The use of meat, too, shall be permitted to the sick and to the very

[3] *Op. cit.*, p. 260.

weak . . . but when they are restored to health, let all abstain from meat in the accustomed manner.

In Roman civilization much was made of the bath. Private houses had their baths, and monasteries of the West seem for the most part to have followed suit. There were baths at Vivarium where Cassiodorus had his monastery. Commentators mention the use of the *tina* or wooden tub, and the Statutes of Murbach allow the monks to have their baths in *scaphae*, large vats normally used for other things, and in smaller vessels called *copae balneariae*.[4]

St. Benedict's words *quoties expedit* with regard to the frequency of baths came almost at once to be interpreted loosely: we learn that the sick were allowed to have two baths a day if they wanted them. There is no record as to how often those bathed who were in health. All that can be got out of Hildemar is that "for such as become soiled through some work, the baths should be prepared more frequently than for those monks who do not engage in manual labour."

The holy Rule further eases the conditions of the sick by dispensing, though perhaps rather guardedly, from the normal monastic observance of abstinence. The sick and the healthy alike are reminded that this concession is temporary and made on strictly medical grounds: it is not a compensating favour which may be enjoyed a day longer than is necessary. The ordinary exclusion of flesh meat *more solito* from the common meal will be considered when St. Benedict returns to the point in his thirty-ninth chapter.

[4] For details about soap, towels, and combs, see Schroll, *op. cit.*, pp. 39, 40. This authority mentions also the arrangements which were made with regard to laundry, shoe-cleaning, shaving, etc.

CHAPTER 37

OF OLD MEN AND CHILDREN

From treating of the care due to the sick, St. Benedict turns naturally to the care which must be given to those whose weakness comes either from old age or extreme youth. If there are to be dispensations in the monastery—and St. Benedict admits that certain conditions will call for exemptions from the common observance—then let the dispensations be according to rule and not according to whim.

Although human nature of itself is drawn to feel pity and consideration for these two times of life—namely, for old men and children—yet the authority of the Rule should also provide for them. Let their weakness be taken into account, and let not the full rigour of the Rule as regards food be maintained in their regard; let a kind consideration be shown to them, and let them anticipate the regular hours.

St. Benedict is a student of human nature. He knows that we can become sentimental about both old age and childhood. But he knows also that we can become alarmingly hard. We have seen how men whose business it is to pursue the supernatural are often in danger of overlooking the natural; provision must accordingly be made for the needs of those who, though not ill, are yet not strong enough to follow the community exercises. It is not for the elderly themselves, and still less for the young, to interpret the Rule in their own favour. The measure of exemption is in the hands of authority. Once a senior, however high he stands in the community, starts citing his seniority as an excuse for the evasion of his duties, he sacrifices the respect to which his years entitle him.

In the *Acta Sanctorum* it is recorded of St. Bernard of Tiron that when himself a senior at St. Cyprian's monastery, Poitiers, he "looked upon all as his superiors, venerated all as elders, showed respect for them as his masters and teachers, and was obedient to everyone." If those who are growing old in the religious life can cultivate this sort of attitude towards their brethren, they are not likely to be charged with being importunate, boring, evasive when it comes to doing what small duties may be required of them. Age does not entitle a man to being thoughtless, to becoming an object of uncharity to others, to developing habits of unpunctuality and slovenliness. There is dignity in age, and if this is forfeited by selfishness there is little enough left. Naturally, but still more supernaturally, a man should command the finer qualities as he grows older. Certainly he should be able to command the respect of the young.

In Carolingian monasteries special quarters were assigned to aging monks, and it would seem that by this time the concessions allowed by the Rule in the matter of food were allowed the widest possible interpretation. Though the times of meals were advanced, and the quality of food was improved, it seems that for the infirm who were able to eat together the practice of refectory reading was maintained. The question of refectory reading generally will be considered in the next chapter.

If information is sparing with regard to the dispensations extended to the older brethren, who in any case would have had to be treated according to their particular conditions, it is plentiful with regard to the treatment of children and boy oblates. From the sixty-third chapter of the Rule we learn that these *alumni* ate in the community refectory and with the brethren. So it looks as though the present chapter is allowing for food between meals. On this assumption, Dom Ménard's claim that the relaxations mentioned by St. Benedict refer to quality rather than quantity must be taken to apply to what was eaten at the common table and at the regular hour. If supplementary meals were granted to the young, the monastic fare must have favoured those under age on both counts. Paul Warnefrid suggests as a reason for providing meat in the boys' diet that "having been reared with plentiful nourishment, they will not need it when they are older." This would not be everybody's reasoning. Warnefrid and Hildemar agree that the need for supplementary meals should normally cease at the age of fifteen.

In St. Benedict's time such penances as doing without meat and going hungry were much encouraged; they are thought little of today. Perhaps the concessions made by our holy Father to the juniors of the monastic household were designed as much to stimulate a spirit of sacrifice as to express a spirit of humanity. The young do not like being pampered—particularly when they see their elders living hard. The sterner observance required of the community would have acted as a challenge to the generosity of the would-be novices. So the above quotation from Warnefrid may be more subtle than it appears at first sight.

CHAPTER 38

THE WEEKLY READER

In the five pages of commentary on this chapter Delatte cites as many as eleven ancient writers who had something to say on the subject of reading at meals. The quotations show that the usage derives from Cappadocian and not from Egyptian monasticism. Cassian, who as always is the main source of material, accounts for the practice of public refectory reading in terms which are severely down-to-earth. According to him the custom was adopted not so much to raise the minds of the eaters from their earthly occupation (though this motive comes first with St. Basil), but rather for the purpose of "cutting off superfluous and idle talk, and especially those disputes which arise at meals." Without giving reasons for the practice, nor going into the dispositions which the brethren are expected to bring to it, St. Benedict lays down practical regulations as to how it is to be performed.

When the brethren are taking their meals there should always be reading. Yet no one should presume at haphazard to take the book and read; but let him who is to read throughout the week enter on his office on Sunday. Let this brother, when beginning his service, ask all after Mass and Communion to pray for him that God may keep from him the spirit of pride.

Since breakfast did not exist, the Rule refers to what we would now call formal meals. The midday and evening meals are con-

ventual occasions. They are even, with their sung grace before
and after, liturgical occasions. Just as there are to be readings
between the nocturn psalms in choir, so there are to be readings
between the psalms of grace in the refectory. "Monastic tradition," writes Delatte, "adopted this reading at table unanimously.
Often it took the plural *mensis* of the text quite literally, so that
there was reading at first table (at the community meal); reading
at the second table (the servers' meal); reading at the table of the
abbot and guests; reading for the sick; and even at the meals of
monks on a journey."[1] Certainly there can be no question as to
St. Benedict's mind on the matter: *mensis fratrum edentium lectio
deese non debet.*

Since the Rule does not specify, it is left to the abbot to decide
what should be read. Commentators are agreed that the daily
reading in the refectory has from the earliest Benedictine centuries opened with a chapter or chapters from the Scriptures. At
the signal from the abbot, or from whosoever is presiding in the
abbot's absence, the reader changes from the Bible to a work of
biography or history. Though not intended to be matter for
study, the reading is neither intended to be matter for entertainment. The choice of a suitable book may well cause difficulty: if
the reading is interrupted by gusts of laughter from the community, it is too light; if it makes the brethren wince, it is too
controversial; if it appeals to only a few, and those the more
intellectual, it is probably too heavy. The book to aim at is the
one which keeps the majority listening during the meal and
talking about it at recreation afterwards. From the general tenor
of the Rule, as well as from the evidence of tradition, it is edification more than anything else that the refectory book is meant to
promote. Given the right kind of book, and a reader who makes
no demands upon his hearers' patience, a man may sit through
the clatter of a community meal in a state of almost effortless
prayer.

During Lent the reading is traditionally of a more serious and
directly spiritual order. During the time of retreat it is the custom
in some congregations to read the Constitutions and the Decrees

[1] *Op. cit.*, p. 265.

of General Chapter. Before particular feasts of the house, the life of the appropriate saint is sometimes read. Edification: instruction: interest. Never propaganda, never worldliness. From a hint in the sixty-sixth chapter (*hanc autem Regulam saepius volumus in congregatione legi*) we guess that perhaps the holy Rule itself was read at mealtimes. Certainly nothing could better fill the requirements outlined above, nor come as a more fitting sequel to the preliminary reading of the Scriptures.

Nec fortuito casu legere audeat. There must be nothing impromptu about this reading in the refectory, nothing slapdash and left to chance. The function of reader is not to be taken on in a lighthearted spirit; it is one which merits a special blessing in choir on Sunday and which deserves careful performance throughout the week. Together with reading at meals go the duties, either in choir or in chapter, of reading the martyrology, necrology, and daily section of the Rule. It means that for one week a particular set of faculties are put at the service of the community. It may not involve a great responsibility, but it does involve an obligation. It may not win a great reward, but it can certainly be a means of praising God.

If the reader is the servant of the community he should not try to dominate. He is not at the lectern to teach but to read. The *book* may teach, but he may not. Nor is it for him to denounce or to sneer or to amuse. His sole function is to render as smoothly and objectively as he can, without interpretation or artifice, the text in front of him. There is nothing more irritating to an eating assembly than having to listen to a self-styled comedian or to one who gives to the book a meaning all his own. He fails in his duty as reader who uses the office to emphasize his private views, to score points against others among his brethren, to attract applause and awaken admiration. He is not expected to make his reading so lifeless as to sound dull, but he is expected to subdue his natural exuberance. An opinionated reader on the one hand, and a too self-effacing reader on the other, can kill a good book stone dead.

The Sunday rite, taking place in choir, which introduces the reader to his duties and blesses them, is the same today as it was in St. Benedict's time.

Let this verse be said thrice in the oratory by all, he, the reader, first beginning: *Domine labia me aperies, et os meum annuntiabit laudem tuam.* And so, having received the blessing, let him enter on his reading.

The form of blessing used in the ceremony is adapted from one found in Smaragdus. The practice of asking a further blessing in the refectory before each reading can be traced to the twelfth century, and probably owes its origin to a much earlier time. In most houses it is the custom to let the reader give out the title of the book before the signal is given for the movement of the meal to begin.

Let the greatest silence be kept at table, so that no whispering nor voice, save the voice of the reader alone, be heard there. Whatever is required by the brethren for eating and drinking, they themselves shall minister to each other so that no one need ask for anything. But should anything be wanted, let it be asked for by the noise of some sign rather than by the voice.

The obligations resting upon the refectory reader find corresponding obligations in the refectory listener. If the reader may not manifest either a too eager interest or a too obvious boredom, nor may the hearer. It is strange that some who show an admirable self-restraint in the refectory with regard to what they eat show little restraint with regard to how they listen. It is not only the reader who can be distracting to the attention and recollection of the community. Quite against the monastic manners, let alone the spirit of silence, would be any sort of whispered commentary on the reading, any sort of indication by signs and looks that either the reader or the book might have been better chosen. It is all too easy to get a cheap laugh at the expense of the soloist, and those who are safely entrenched in their lines behind refectory tables can by their thoughtlessness have a wounding effect upon a sensitive reader.

In the refectory, as everywhere else, charity and prayerfulness must set the note. Thus it would be inconsiderate to the reader, to the servers, to the brethren who are assembled there to eat in peace, to disturb the refectory with expansive gestures or impatient demands. Charity further demands that those who are read to and waited on be ready to make allowances for what appear to be failures of service. We can err by accusing a reader of affectation when in fact it is a shrinking humility that produces the affected manner; we can find fault with those who are supposed to be offering us second helpings when it fact they are attending to needs which are outside our immediate range.

In some religious orders, and for the purpose of preserving recollection, meals are eaten with the hood up. The custom goes as far back as Pachomian monasticism. St. Benedict's point about the brethren ministering to one another suggests that there is nothing particularly Benedictine in such a practice—the brethren being more likely to notice each other's needs when uncovered than when hooded. *Sibi sic invicem ministrent fratres:* which again implies the exclusion of lay help from the refectory. While it may be found convenient in some houses to accept the services of guests who want to repay hospitality by waiting upon the community, the normal Benedictine practice should be for the brethren to wait upon one another. Shortage of vocations and pressure of work might justify the introduction even of paid labour—the servants assisting only, and not taking over from, the regular monastic servers—but as a permanent arrangement the ideal is clearly, as stated in the Rule, the ideal of monk attending to monk.

Let no one ask any question about what is being read or about anything else, lest occasion be given to the evil one; unless perhaps the superior should wish to say something briefly for the edification of the brethren. The brother who is reader for the week shall receive a sop before he begins to read, on account of Holy Communion and lest it be too hard for him to fast so long. He shall take his meal afterwards with the weekly cooks and servers. The brethren, however, are not to chant or read according to their order, but such only as may edify the hearers.

The reference to the evil one is puzzling. The idea of Satan frequenting monastic refectories for what he can pick up in the way of questions asked by unguarded monks is apt to strike the mind as far-fetched. It is gratifying, therefore, to discover that the reference does not occur in the original text, but is a gloss. *Ne detur occasio*—and we are left to supply "levity" or "annoyance" or "disedification."

In several of the older rules which were consulted, as we have seen, by St. Benedict—notably those of St. Basil and St. Macarius—mention is made of the superior feeling himself free to interrupt the reading and to deliver a short homily of his own. This is a practice which seems to have been completely dropped.

The provision for a *mixtum* to be taken by the reader before the conventual meal has been accounted for on an earlier page: when the community Mass was immediately followed by the principal meal the fast was lifted for those (the servers, the reader, the weak) who would otherwise have had to wait till the second table.

Fratres non per ordinem legant aut cantant, sed qui aedificent audientes. Again this reminder about edification. The system of choosing out good readers from the rest need not at that time have seemed as invidious as it does now to us. In St. Benedict's communities, and in Benedictine communities for several centuries after his period, not everyone would have possessed the necessary education. A stumbling delivery would have been an embarrassment to both reader and read to. It is the common opinion of commentators that the abbot chose out a number of monks who would not be likely to have difficulty with the Latin, and that these took their turn at the weekly duty. St. Benedict thought it better to risk giving offense to the illiterate than to risk giving disedification to the brethren generally.

CHAPTER 39

OF THE MEASURE OF FOOD

Considering how carefully St. Benedict picks his words when handling the subject of food, and how clear-cut his regulations seem to be, it is surprising to discover the extent of disagreement which this chapter has occasioned. No attempt will be made in what follows to justify this or that interpretation of St. Benedict's words: it will be enough to state the various views, the accepted traditions, and then to pass on to where controversy holds less sway.

We think it sufficient for the daily meal, whether at the sixth or ninth hour, that there be at all tables two dishes of cooked food, because of the variety of men's weaknesses: so that he who may not be able to eat of the one may make his meal of the other. Therefore let two cooked dishes suffice for the brethren, and if there be any fruit or young vegetables, let a third dish be added.

The *pulmentaria cocta* mentioned in the text would cover any sort of prepared dish, eaten with bread and cheese. Raw *pulmentum* would be a cold dish consisting of either bread and cheese or fruit, salad, oatcake, and various vegetables. If there were two dishes of cooked food to choose from at each meal, and if a third might be added when the season and the supply allowed, the brethren of St. Benedict's day would have had no reason to complain on the score of quantity or variety. Such a fare would have reflected what was usual in any farming community where agriculture and not livestock was the main concern. Certainly such a fare would have been recognized as considerably exceeding the amount hitherto allowed to monks. Some of the desert fathers ate less in a week than what St. Benedict gave to his monks in a day. But then St. Benedict's phrase *propter diversorum infirmitates* shows that it was not his intention to continue the tradition of Eastern monasticism in the matter of austerity. It was his intention to open the way of monastic life to those for whom the fasts of the ancient ascetics would have been impossible. Putting within the reach of ordinary weak people the mitigated régime of monastic eating, St. Benedict was risking the charge of innovation, of slackness, of cheapening an ideal. Western monasticism is the justification of St. Benedict's decision.

Let a pound weight of bread suffice for each day, whether there be but one meal or both dinner and supper. If there is to be supper, let a third part of the pound be kept back by the cellarer and given to the brethren at the second meal. If, however, their work have been greater, it shall be at the will and in the power of the abbot, if it be expedient, to make some addition, provided that excess be before all things avoided and that no monk suffer from surfeiting.

The "pound weight" of bread has occasioned a wealth of special pleading. The earliest commentators ask whether one may not distinguish between the weight when in the dough and when actually baked? The measure allowed by St. Benedict of Aniane does not agree with that allowed by some of his contemporaries. There is a difference in weight between the imperial and the commercial pound. It seems that not even Rome, with all its genius for accuracy, could guarantee a uniform measure. So it turned out that not even St. Benedict, for all his planning, could ensure a standard loaf which would be eaten daily by his future sons. With nothing fixed and certain to go upon, the decrees of most modern Benedictine constitutions authorize the distribution of bread in the refectory without restriction.

While it is left to the discretion of the abbot to increase the quantity of food, it is still left to the generosity of the individual to use the dispensation as he thinks best. The Rule tells us that an addition to the ordinary fare is to be justified by the exceptional character of the work. It is not to be justified, therefore, merely because the finances of the house can afford the extra cost. The relation between work and food is accordingly an essential and not an accidental one. The relation between cost and food is also an essential one but rather as affecting the particular claim of poverty than the claim of the life as a whole.

Nothing is more contrary to any Christian life than excess, as our Lord says: "Take heed to yourselves lest perhaps your hearts be overcharged with surfeiting and drunkenness." And let not the same quantity be allowed to children of tender years, but less than to their elders, frugality being observed in all things. But all abstain from eating the flesh of four-footed animals, except the very weak and the sick.

Though surfeiting and long hours spent at the table have gone out, it can still be a monastic vice to concentrate too closely upon the subject of food. With too little to keep him occupied, a monk can become obsessed with the thought of the next meal. His body may be spared the heaviness of having overfed, but what about his mind? Frugality is a great safeguard, but it takes the soul only some of the way. From frugality the soul must mount to the positive implication of Christian mortification, must see restraint as the means of recollection.

In forbidding to all save the sick and very weak the eating of meat, St. Benedict was laying down a principle which may or may not be workable to Benedictines of the present day. He was not merely outlining a practice; he was propounding a principle. It was the accepted principle of the time; he had taken it over from his own monastic ancestors. Flesh meat, according to the ancients, heated the blood and stirred the passions. The renunciation of flesh meat did not suggest anything particularly heroic: it was one of the ordinary penances which might be expected of men who had turned to God from the world.

In an attempt to soften the rigour of St. Benedict's abstinence commentators have argued that while the flesh of four-footed animals is explicitly banned, there is nothing against eating the flesh of birds. This reasoning may sound like a quibble—indeed is a quibble—but there is historical grounds for believing that for centuries fish and foul were classified together; neither was judged incompatible with abstinence. Whatever the contemporary view about the biped's meat-content, however, the exclusion of chicken and game from the tables of St. Benedict's monasteries was, excepting only where the sick were concerned, as absolute as the exclusion of beef, pork, and mutton. This was in keeping with the best monastic tradition of the period, drawn from such sources as St. Caesarius, St. Augustine, St. Jerome, and others.

The common monastic fare of fish, eggs, cheese, beans, and different kinds of hearth-cake survived long past the Middle Ages. In most Benedictine congregations today the use of meat is allowed at least four times a week and in some congregations as often as every day not affected by the Church's law. The point at issue is not the rightness or wrongness of meat—still less the rightness or wrongness of a vegetarian diet—but rather the mind of St. Benedict on the subject of self-denial suitable to monks in the refectory. We are at liberty to claim that opinions on these things have changed since St. Benedict's time, but we are not at liberty to claim that St. Benedict meant something which his words did not say.

CHAPTER 40

OF THE MEASURE OF DRINK

This chapter on the amount of wine which may suitably be allowed to monks is in keeping with what we have just been discussing. The same moderate tone is reflected, and there is the same consideration for the weaker brethren. It should be borne in mind throughout any treatment of this subject, whether wine or food is the immediate concern, that St. Benedict is writing primarily for southerners. Italians would not have regarded wine—as we of the north would regard it—as an indulgence. Nor would they look upon the absence of breakfast as a serious deprivation. Where the régime must have made itself most painfully felt would have been on those days when there was only one meal. The quantity of food was enough, and the wine was more than ample. The austerity lay in having to wait so long for it, and in having no further meal to look forward to later on in the day.

"Everyone hath his proper gift from God, one thus and another thus," and therefore it is with some scruple that we determine the measure of other men's living. Yet making due allowance for the weakness of some, we think that a *hemina* of wine a day is sufficient for each. But let those to whom God gives the gift of abstinence know that they shall receive their proper reward.

St. Benedict is clearly appealing to the strong while not letting the weak feel uncomfortable. "If you feel yourself endowed by God with the grace of being able to do without, go ahead with that and my blessing upon it," the saint is saying; "but you must understand that there are some less fortunate." Let those who take advantage of the permission to drink wine do so with a free conscience: they can gain more in humility by a recognition of their weakness than they would ever gain in merit by an assertion of their independence. There is no determining another man's measure—just as there is no determining another man's merit or virtue—so the only wise thing is to let every man follow his own grace in the matter. In giving his monks a wide liberty as to the degree of their voluntary abstinence, St. Benedict is not restricting the opportunity or implication of obedience. He is authorizing their liberty, letting their personal choice come under the cover of obedience. Just as the life of man is lived, in the Augustinian phrase, under the firmament of the law, so the freedoms of the monk are exercised under the firmament of the Rule.

If either the situation of the place, the work, or the heat of summer require more, let it be in the power of the superior to grant it, care being taken in all things that surfeit and drunkenness creep not in.

After St. Benedict's time, superiors were not slow to avail themselves of the power to extend the allowance. We read of something to drink (wine? fruit-juice? beer?) being served after None during the harvest season. Diluted honey was brought out to those employed in haymaking. Extra cups of drink, probably hot, were allowed as early as the ninth century on all occasions when the Office of the Dead was celebrated. To avoid possible abuses in allowing drink between meals, Cluny adopted the practice of having wine immediately after the principal meal of the day. The custom spread north, and we are familiar with the elaborate system of "caritas," "gaude," and "pittance" which developed to the disedification of those who watched the growing worldliness of English monastic houses in the fifteenth and sixteenth centuries.

Although we read that wine is by no means the drink for monks, yet, since in our days they cannot be persuaded of this, let us at least agree not to drink to satiety but spar-

ingly; because "wine maketh even the wise to fall away."
But where the place is such that not even the aforesaid
measure can be supplied, but much less or none at all, let
those who dwell there bless God and not murmur. This
above all do we admonish, that they be without murmuring.

It seems as though St. Benedict's misgivings, already confessed,
are getting the better of him. He wonders whether he was justified in allowing wine at all. He remembers the hard things he has
read about wine being not at all suitable to the religious state.
The *Lives of the Fathers* gives him chapter and verse if he wants
to go back upon his concession. And did not St. Athanasius, in
his account of St. Antony who was the accepted pattern of monastic perfection, say that nobody who was worthy of his salt as
an ascetic would dream of drinking wine? "The nature of wine,"
was Abba Poemen's conclusion, "is not such as to make it useful
to those who dwell in monasteries."[1]

Abbot Cuthbert Butler, treating of the growth of the Benedictine idea throughout the ages, mentions on the same page the
three indulgences of eating meat, drinking wine, and smoking.
"Akin to amenities is the matter of what might be called the
minor luxuries, as smoking. In most monasteries," says Dom
Butler, "smoking is now allowed at discretion. This I believe is
in accordance with the Rule. Not of course that St. Benedict
legislates for tobacco; but in the case of wine he lays down a
principle that covers the case of all such indulgences: '*Licet
legamus*,' he says, 'though we read that wine is not for monks at
all, still as in our days monks will not be persuaded of this, let us

---

[1] *Sayings of the Fathers*, 80. The following stories from the same
source further illustrate the point. "When certain brethren went to
the church during the Easter Festival, they gave a brother a cup of
wine, and when they urged him to drink it, he said to them: 'Forgive
me, my fathers, but ye did the same to me last year, and I was
greatly troubled thereby for a long time.' " (77) "The monks were
celebrating a festival in Scete, and they gave a certain old man a
cup of wine, and he handed it back, saying 'Take this death away
from me.' And when the others who were eating with him saw him
do this, they would also not take wine." (78)

at any rate,' etc."[2] Not all would agree with Abbot Butler that the use of tobacco is in accordance with the spirit of the Rule. Even if the practice of smoking can be squared with what, by the law of analogy, is the accepted interpretation of monastic self-denial, there is still the question of religious poverty by which it must also be judged. If the weight of ancient tradition falls heavy upon wine for monks, the weight of religious poverty would seem to fall heavier still upon tobacco.

If, moreover, St. Benedict leaves it to the generosity of the strong to deny themselves the pleasure of wine, he can be supposed to invite the same generosity where other indulgences are concerned. A monk need not feel that he is guilty of singularity when he refuses the wine that is offered him—he is only doing what the Rule approves—and in the same way his reluctance to smoke should not be taken by his brethren as a criticism of their greater liberty. Liberty, in this context, is the use of the gift according to the mind of the giver. If God has given the gift of abstinence, whether from wine or meat or tobacco, the best way to use it is to abstain from these things for the greater glory of God.

[2] *Op. cit.*, p. 307.

CHAPTER 41

AT WHAT HOURS THE BRETHREN
ARE TO TAKE THEIR MEALS

From the point of view of the refectory, as from the point of view of the choir, the year is divided into clear-cut seasons. St. Benedict takes as his starting-point not Advent, as he would do if he were treating the question liturgically, but Easter. From Easter until Pentecost there is no fast, so there will be two meals a day. The first and principal meal takes place at the sixth hour, the other before sunset. As Pentecost approached, the time for supper would consequently be delayed.

From the holy feast of Easter till Whitsuntide let the brethren dine at the sixth hour and sup in the evening. But from Whitsuntide throughout the summer, if the monks have not to work in the fields nor are harassed by excessive heat, let them fast on Wednesdays and Fridays until the ninth hour, but on other days dine at the sixth. Should they have field labour, or should the heat of the summer be very great, let dinner at the sixth hour be the rule, at the discretion of the abbot.

From Pentecost until (as we shall see) the 14th of September, the arrangement about having two meals a day is the same, except that now every Wednesday and Friday must be observed as days of fasting. On these days the one meal of the day would take place at three in the afternoon. Only heavy field labour and unusually hot weather would give valid excuse for keeping to the normal hour of dinner after Sext. In St. Benedict's very moderate ascetical scheme, the long wait for the first meal of the day—a wait of some twelve hours during a good part of the year—stands out as something specially to be desired. Except for this one rather rigorous fast, the way of life laid down in the holy Rule differed little, according to Dom Morin, from the life of the average Christian layman of southern Europe. All the more reason, then, that St. Benedict's predilection for fasting should not disappear from Benedictine life. Nowhere in the Rule does the saint speak of hairshirts, chains, flagellations—these things came in with the Middle Ages—but he does make a point of keeping hungry for rather more than the first half of the day. If this is the sole exception to the tempered monasticism of St. Benedict, it is a detail which is worth preserving. Later we shall hear him referring to his Rule as this "minimum regulation for beginners," and it was as a "legislator for the weak" that he was alluded to by two sterner sons of his, Benedict of Aniane and John of Gorzia. But when we note the authorities for whom he had the greatest respect we see that they were those who shared, indeed who doubtless gave him, his views on fasting.

"Moses went up fasting to the mountain," St. Basil had written, "nor would he otherwise have dared to approach that smoking hill-top or to go into its darkness unless he were protected by fasting." "No addition at all should be made either to the quality or the quantity of the food," Cassian had written, "but even on the highest festivals we should abstain from those foods by fasting from which we preserve our uprightness on common days." These were, together with those who had collected the sayings of the Fathers, the writers to whom our holy Father owed most in his early schooling. No wonder he did not like giving up his fasts without a struggle: the weather would have to be hot indeed, and the emergency of the harvest acute, if the meals were to be advanced for the convenience of the community.

> From the Ides of September until the beginning of Lent, let the brethren always dine at the ninth hour. During Lent, however, until Easter let them dine in the evening. But let this evening meal be so arranged that they shall not need

lamps while eating, and that all things be finished while there is yet daylight. Indeed at all times of the year, let the hour, whether for dinner or supper, be so arranged that everything be done by daylight.

This brings us to the third and fourth seasons of the refectory year. Strictly it is the Calends of October that mark the beginning of what has come to be called the monastic Lent. The date in our calendar is September 14th, when the Ides of that month are over. From now until the opening of Lent proper, the community meal is to take place after None. Was there anything later than this in the way of a light supper? The Rule does not say so. When the ecclesiastical Lent began, the community must have dined even later; certainly there was here no question of a subsequent meal. If the brethren went to the refectory after Vespers, and if meals throughout the year had to be conducted in daylight, there would have been no time for an additional meal however brief.

What was the principle involved in eating before sundown? There was probably no principle involved at all; the regulation was in all probability severely practical. That the reader should be able to see without a lamp was an advantage, and it would also be easier to wait at table and wash up afterwards by daylight rather than by the light of candles or oil-lamps. The arrangement evidently admitted of exceptions because there is the incident in the *Dialogues* which describes St. Benedict having a meal at which a brother held a lamp. This is easily accounted for, however, since it is clear from the text that St. Benedict was dining late and on his own.[1] Compline is the only community function which traditionally takes place in the dark.

[1] Bk. 2; ch. 20.

CHAPTER 42

THAT NO ONE MAY SPEAK
AFTER COMPLINE

With this chapter a new section of the Rule begins. The
monk's day has been spaced out with reference to the choir and
the refectory; the question that now comes up is how the monk
will use it. Since observance will mostly depend upon silence
and punctuality, it is on these subjects that St. Benedict makes
his present opening. When he has taken steps to secure regularity
of discipline within the house, he will consider the wider question
of monastic work.

Monks should study silence always, but especially during
the hours of the night. And this shall hold for all times,
whether fast-days or not. If it be not a fast-day, as soon as
they have risen from supper let all sit down together, and
let one read of the *Conferences* or *Lives of the Fathers,* or
at least something else which will edify the hearers. But not
the *Heptateuch* nor the *Books of Kings;* for it will not
profit those of weak understanding to hear those parts of
Scripture at that hour; but let them be read at other times.

Omni tempore silentio debet studere monachi. The subject of
silence in the Rule is no mere stop-gap material. St. Benedict does
not come back to it as a convenient way of launching something
new. Though not an end in itself, silence to St. Benedict is the
means to the attainment of almost all the monastic virtues. Rightly

understood it creates the disposition most conducive towards the soul's union with God. "The lover of silence," says St. John Climacus, "is the friend of wisdom, and is continually receiving new light from heaven."[1]

Silence is not an extra in the monastic life, an observance to which a monk may or not feel drawn. It is an essential, it is the condition necessary to all observance. "While he keeps his mouth closed under the discipline of silence," says St. Peter Damian, "the monk lives; if he open his mouth to speak immoderately, he perishes." On this showing the life of grace itself depends upon the cultivation of silence. Without the deliberate imposition of restraint upon the faculty of speech, upon the use of signs, upon even the flight of the imagination which substitutes distracting ideas for distracting words, there can be no true monastic life, no true peace, no spiritual safety.

Silence, if it is to be productive and not sterile, must look to wisdom and light. The silence in which there is no thought is an empty, negative, thing; it is a waste. Where control of unnecessary words leads to training in the direction of thought there is no end to the spiritual possibility. It is related of St. Pambo that his particular exercise lay in the discipline of the tongue, both by the assiduous cultivation of silence and the thoughtful preparation which he made before breaking it. The habit began with the first instruction which he received from one whom he had engaged to teach him the psalms. When his master opened the lesson with the first verse of the thirty-eighth psalm, *dixi: custodiam vias meas, ut non delinquam in lingua mea*, Pambo said quietly, "That will do for today," and went off to think about it. When he had dwelt upon the implications of sinning with the tongue, he came back for more. But his biographer notes that this was not until about six months later.[2]

Especially during the hours of the night St. Benedict wants silence strictly kept. If it be necessary to ask a question or convey information between Compline and Prime, signs or written notes

[1] *Ladder*, 4th rung.
[2] *Lives of the Saints*, edited by Thurston and Attwater, Vol. 7; p. 253.

should be exchanged rather than spoken words. Monastic usage determined very early in history the necessity of absolute silence in the dormitory or cells of the monks. The refectory and library had their aura of silence, but here the silence was necessarily relative. In the same way the church, the sacristy, and the cloisters immediately connected with the church were taken to be places of silence. At Cluny the kitchen, the chapter-house, and the calefactory were also places of silence. St. Benedict does not specify as closely: for him silence is the rule generally throughout the house, and at night a silence which forbids conversation of any sort. The idea of a particular "night silence" is not original to St. Benedict: it is found in earlier rules.

The reading which came immediately before Compline was not just the continuation of the book chosen for meals in the refectory. There was a ritual value attaching to it, making it almost part of the liturgy. Taking place in the cloister or chapter-house, or even in the oratory itself, the study of some ascetical work would have the effect of rounding off the day and providing suitable thoughts before going to bed. It was not designed with a view to keeping the greater part of the community occupied while the servers were either having their evening meal or else washing up. This reading held a privileged place in St. Benedict's mind: all were expected, as we shall see below, to be present.

The reason why certain books of the Old Testament are to be excluded from this brief public reading is simply that the scenes of violence which they describe might keep the child-oblates, or even the more simple and youthful members of the community, awake.

> If it be a fast-day, then a short time after Vespers let them assemble for the reading, as we have said: four or five pages being read, or as much as time allows, so that during the delay provided by this reading all may come together, even such as may be occupied in some work enjoined to them.

We have seen that on the Church's fast-days the brethren went from Vespers to the refectory for the one full meal of the day. So the above must refer to Wednesdays and Fridays throughout the summer, and to all days of the monastic Lent—from the 14th of September, that is, until Lent proper. If Compline is to be the night-prayers of the community, it should not start before all, even the guestmaster and cellarer and those who are helping with the sick, have arrived. There will inevitably be occasions when the sick are too ill to be left, when guests have to be welcomed, and when the cellarer is called away to attend to some domestic crisis. The ideal holds: Compline is for the whole family, and if the whole family is about to give praise to God, then it should come together a little before the time and listen to devout exhortation.

"Till the day break and the shadows recede," we read in the Canticle, "I will go up into the mountain."[3] There is deep significance in the *summum silentium* of a well-ordered Benedictine house. Whatever the distracting duties of the daytime, the hours of the night are kept sacred. What monk does not know the sense of relief with which he closes the door of his cell after Compline? It is not so much what he shuts *out* as what he shuts *in*. In a special way he is able now to belong exclusively to God, and to know that God belongs to him. He has "gone up into the mountain," and until the racket of tomorrow begins again he has nothing to worry about.

[3] 4;6.

CHAPTER 43

OF THOSE WHO COME LATE TO THE WORK OF GOD OR TO TABLE

At first sight it is surprising to find such a long chapter devoted to a not very considerable subject. A study of the text, however, shows us that other things besides punctuality are discussed. This forty-third chapter not only recapitulates much that we have already considered under the head of minor excommunication, but is also a treatise on monastic decorum generally. More important still, it is the chapter which proclaims the primacy of the Divine Office among all Benedictine works.

At the hour of the Divine Office, as soon as the signal is heard, let each one lay aside whatever he may be engaged upon and hasten to it with all speed, and yet with seriousness, so that no occasion be given to levity. Let nothing be put before the *opus Dei*.

The title of the chapter is seen to bracket together the choir and the refectory. It is in these two places that the brethren are most officially a single unit. They may do manual labor together, and they may study together, but while praying and eating they are conventually one. The link is neither wholly natural nor wholly supernatural, but both. Since the natural is always liable to assert itself at the expense of the supernatural, St. Benedict is careful to stress the spiritual side of these corporate community exercises. The summons to a duty in the monastery is a summons of grace. When the duty happens to be a choir duty, the super-natural character of the summons is all the more unmistakable. *Nihil operi Dei praeponatur.*

Promptitude in responding to the signal is of course a familiar theme in monastic literature—St. Benedict could have borrowed his injunctions almost verbally from one of half a dozen earlier rules—but perhaps nowhere is it made so much of as here. The reason is that at the heart of regularity lies the presence of God. For St. Benedict punctuality is more than insistence upon things starting on time: it is an act of necessary courtesy to God. If St. Benedict can convince his monks that observance is really reverence, he has virtually laid the ghost of religious formalism, and, more positively, established the principle of raising routine detail to the level of spontaneous worship.

The will of God may be signified by the sound of a bell, by the rap of a knuckle on a choir-stall, by the notice on a board. The monk must keep himself alert or he will miss his opportunity. It is not only that he must avoid being late—which has only a relative importance after all—but that he must avoid being casual. He must avoid *not* listening to the call of God. "Draw me: we will run after thee to the odor of thy ointments . . . the voice of my Beloved, behold he cometh . . . come from Libanus, my spouse, come from Libanus, come."[1]

The response should become so instinctive and habitual that the human will not only recognizes the divine will without diffi-culty but makes the divine will its own. The human will and the divine will actively co-operate. The soul is no longer the inert material on which the will of God operates; nor on the other hand is it the over-active and selfish agent which uses its freedom with-out direct reference to the will of God. The soul, with God, is now the co-efficient. The soul of the saint, for example—and this is appreciated in the case of our Lady more than in any other—so perfectly responds to the vibrations of the Spirit as to act without the least vestige of self-interest.

Caritas Christi urget nos. Once charity is the motive force of a man's action there can be no further worry about fidelity to the

[1] Cant. 1;3. 2;8. 4;8.

duty of the present moment. Such a man will answer the bell not only in order to serve love, but because it is love inside him that prompts the service. Love is at once the *terminus a quo* and the *terminus ad quem*. Love is the seeker and the sought.

"Our praise is inserted in Christ's praise," says Dom van Houtryve, "so that the grandeur of one Little Hour of the Office lies in the fact that it is rich with the praise of the eternal Priest. It is the prayer of the entire mystical body."[2] Since there is no excellence that can be put above the prayer of Christ, it is therefore strictly true that nothing can be preferred to the *opus Dei*.

Praise is given to God in the name of justice as well as in the name of religion. The Creator has a right to the worship of His creatures, and those creatures whose lives are set apart for the special work of rendering homage owe Him in equity, not merely in generosity, the debt of praise. *Nihil operi Dei praeponatur*. It is man's first duty, a duty that belongs to the whole of man.

It is not a question here of what good works a monk should undertake for God. It is a question of what is *the* good work which is demanded of monks by God. Obviously the monk must study, must work with his hands, must pray in private. But unless as a student, as a worker, as a contemplative he is supported and nourished by the *opus Dei* he is incomplete as a Benedictine. His specifically Benedictine character is moulded by, and depends on, the choir. Each Benedictine congregation, even each Benedictine house, has its own distinctive mission and spirit. History has shown that the Benedictine vocation is a vocation within a vocation. But whatever the diversity of expression, the profession according to the Rule is the profession to the worship of God in choir. The religious vows pledge a man to the service of God; more precisely they pledge him to the service of God in prayer; still more precisely they pledge him to a particular kind of prayer —the prayer performed in common. It is in and through the liturgy that the Benedictine finds the consummation of his relationship with God. You may even say that it is in and through the liturgy that the monk finds his true place among his fellow monks. Without a right understanding of the significance of the

[2] *Op. cit.*, p. 125.

opus Dei in the Benedictine scheme a monk can neither discover himself, nor his brethren, nor what the whole life is all about. Once let him grasp the meaning of his vocation in terms of the Benedictine essential, and he will find his happiness as well as his holiness in the work which gives meaning to the whole. "In the present life there is no happier or truer activity," says Paschasius Radbert in his exposition of the forty-fourth psalm, "than to take part in the Offices of heaven and in the conversation of the Divine Persons; it is then that the soul stands before the eyes of God." "The king has brought me into his store-rooms," the monk can say with the bride in the *Canticles*, "and my spikenard sent forth its fragrance."[3] It is not I who am responsible for the excellence of the act which I perform in choir: it is the king who has brought me here. It is not even the collective effort of the souls who are assembled there that give to our Benedictine choirs their value: the value lies in the prayer of God—the *opus Dei* itself. Because it is primarily the work of God, and only in a secondary sense the work of man, we have the assurance that no shortcomings of ours can alter its essential good. The chains which bind us to the Divine Office are chains of gold, not to be tarnished by any negligence of ours.[4] We may fail in attention, in zeal, in exact performance, but at least we know that for all our defects we are doing something infinitely worth while—something objectively pleasing to God.

Should anyone come to the Night Office after the *Gloria* of the ninety-fourth psalm, which for this reason we wish to be said very slowly and protractedly, let him not stand in his order in the choir, but last of all or in the place set apart by the abbot for such negligent ones so that he may be seen by him and by all, until, the work of God being ended, he do penance by public satisfaction . . . if they were to remain outside the oratory, there might be one who would return to his bed and sleep, or else sit outside and give himself to idle tales, and so give occasion to the

[3] Cant. 1;3,11.
[4] *Ibid.*, cf. 1;10.

evil one. Let him therefore enter and so not lose the whole, and may amend for the future.

Failure to appreciate the ideal must inevitably bring out the unworthy in a monk. For this reason St. Benedict is at pains to prevent latecomers from excusing themselves of further obligations towards the Office. There must be no going back to bed, no whispered offences against the *summum silentium*: all must be arranged so that what is left of good order may be preserved. It is St. Benedict's hope that the public humiliation of taking the last place will be enough to ensure greater care in the future. But this will depend upon whether the purpose of monastic punctuality —which means Whom we are being in time for—is understood.

> At the day hours let him who comes to the *opus Dei* after the verse and *Gloria* of the first psalm . . . stand in the last place as ordered above, nor let him dare to join in the chanting until he have made satisfaction.

Much has been written about the difference between coming late for the night office and for the day hours. Even more has been written about whether or not St. Benedict includes Prime and Vespers among the day hours. The controversy must be left to the learning of the liturgists. The next certain and practical point which concerns us is what happens when a monk comes late for a meal.

> He who does not come to table before the verse, so that all may say it praying together and sit down to table at the same time, must be corrected once or twice if this be through negligence or fault. If after this he do not amend, let him not be suffered to share in the common table but be separated from the company of all and eat alone, his portion of wine being taken from him until he makes satisfaction and amends. He is to undergo the same punishment who is not present at the verse which is said after meals.

Grace is more than a signal to begin eating: it is a conventual prayer. To be late for grace is to interrupt a dialogue. If the children of a family are asking for something in unison, it strikes a jarring note if one member of the family joins in halfway through. The brother who repeatedly fails to arrive when the prayer is beginning has no just cause for complaint if he is made to pray by himself and eat by himself. Having forfeited the blessings which goes with the common meal, he forfeits also the allowance of wine. Is this unfair? If the blessing which is designed to answer a spiritual need is lightly forgone by the unpunctual monk, it is surely fitting that something should be sacrificed which is designed to answer a physical appetite.

It is to be noted that St. Benedict wants his monks to be present for the whole meal, for the grace after as well as the grace before eating. When necessity demands the leaving of the refectory before the end—as it must in the case of those officials who have dealings with externs—care should be taken to regularize the permission. In many communities the monk who cannot stay until the second grace receives his blessing and dismissal bowing or kneeling before the superior. This at least has the effect of reminding all present that the meal is a complete conventual act, and that to shorten it must necessitate the anticipation of what otherwise will be missed. Quite against the spirit of all this accordingly would be the habit of getting up and leaving when one has had enough, or when one is bored with the reading. Benedictine meals are never informal; the refectory is not the same as the dining-room in a club. If a monk treats the community refectory as a man in the world would treat the rooms of an hotel, he might just as well be living in an hotel: he is losing his place in the supernatural household.

> And let no one presume to take any food or drink before or after the appointed time. But if something is offered to anyone by the superior and he refuse it, and afterwards wishes to have what he has rejected, or some other thing, let him get neither this nor anything else till he makes proper satisfaction.

Eating apart from the community meals has always in the history of monasticism been frowned upon. Cassian, Basil, Caesarius— in fact the monastic legislators generally—forbid all eating and drinking, however small the quantity, outside the refectory. The relaxation of this rule almost always leads to abuse. The worst that is likely to result would be private parties among the brethren; the least would be the hoarding of little delicacies in the cell. At times like Christmas and Easter, when monks are liable to be sent presents of chocolate, cakes, and sweets, the prohibition is lifted in some monasteries, provided the necessary permissions are obtained. This would be regarded as a temporary measure only, and quite the exception. More in keeping with the spirit of the Rule would be to hand over presents of food to the cellarer for distribution among the brethren on the particular feast that is being celebrated. To share one's benefits by private invitation savours uncomfortably of exclusiveness and worldliness.

An occasion for the slighting of this rule about not eating outside the refectory is presented during periods of convalescence after an illness. A monk will be tempted, even when he has begun to resume the normal routine of the house, to keep back things like tins of biscuits and bottles of jam which for convenience were left in his care while he was unwell. The monk who has the mind of St. Benedict on the subject of petty luxuries will know how to answer the whispered voice which babbles on about having a little something ready against a rainy day.

CHAPTER 44

OF THOSE WHO ARE EXCOMMUNI-
CATED, HOW THEY ARE TO MAKE
SATISFACTION

In the twenty-fourth and twenty-fifth chapters of the Rule we have read about the faults which incurred excommunication of one kind or another. Though it does not repeat itself in the enumeration of offenses, the Rule deals in the present chapter with matter which is familiar to us from earlier references. The immediate concern is how the excommunicate from the oratory and from the refectory may obtain pardon and be restored to their proper places in the community.

He who for graver offences is excommunicated from the oratory and from the table must, at the hour when the *opus Dei* is being performed, lie prostrate before the doors of the oratory saying nothing. Only let him, with his face on the ground and body prone, cast himself at the feet of all as they go forth from the oratory. And let him continue to do this until the abbot judge that satisfaction has been made. Then, when the abbot bids him, let him come and cast himself at the abbot's feet, and next at those of all the brethren that they may pray for him.

There is a similarity between this monastic penance and the penance enjoined in the early Church upon notorious sinners. For the parish you have the monastery; and though St. Benedict is arranging a purely domestic penance, it is the publicity of it, as in the case of the ecclesiastical excommunications, that hurts.

The penalty leaves nothing out: the penitent may not speak (may not therefore take any part in the liturgy); he may not sit up or walk about; he may not solicit the good offices of his brethren in an appeal to the abbot on his behalf. It is for the abbot to make the first move in the process of reconciliation. When the abbot has signified his willingness to show mercy, the penitent has reached the second stage in his return to favour: there is the acknowledgment of guilt and the appeal for prayers—addressed first to the abbot and then to each of the brethren in turn. Whether the ceremony took place at the entrance of the oratory, in the cloister, or in chapter, we do not know. Certainly in later times, probably on account of the increase in guests and pilgrims, the rehabilitation of those who were making satisfaction was conducted *in camera*.

> Then, if the abbot so order, let him be received back into the choir, in such a place as he shall appoint; yet so that he presume not to intone psalm or lesson or anything else in the oratory, unless the abbot again command him. More-over, at every hour when the *opus Dei* is ended, let him cast himself on the ground, in the place where he stands, and so make satisfaction until the abbot bids him cease.

Even when restored to a place in choir—whether the one he occupied before or lower down—the penitent has not yet finished with his work of expiation. He still performs no solo part in the Office, and there are still these prostrations after even the little hours.

For minor excommunications the discipline is naturally less severe. Faults which have merited exclusion from the refectory only, and not from the choir, are atoned for by light satisfactions made in the oratory and terminated at the abbot's discretion. The abbot gives his blessing, and the incident is closed. The procedure is outlined in the concluding paragraph to this chapter:

> But those who for small faults are excommunicated only from the table must make satisfaction in the oratory so long as the abbot shall command. Let them do so till he bless them and say: "It is enough."

CHAPTER 45

OF THOSE WHO MAKE MISTAKES
IN THE ORATORY

This is hardly more than a pendant to the preceding chapter. As part of St. Benedict's penal legislation it adds little to what we have already considered, but it is interesting because it brings out once again the necessity of countering all the evils that may arise in monasteries with the cardinal virtue of humility. If the saint appears to be over-meticulous in the attention which he gives to light faults, it is only because he sees in the casual and careless approach to rules an evidence of pride.

If anyone reciting a psalm, responsory, antiphon, or lesson, make a mistake and do not make satisfaction, humbling himself there before all, let him be subjected to greater punishment, as one who would not correct by humility what he did wrong by negligence. But children for all such faults are to be beaten.

No one could say that a false pronunciation mattered very much; nor would a monk have to reproach himself interiorly for having given out a wrong antiphon. But the point to be stressed is not the thing done so much as the Person before whom it is done. If it is God before whom we stand in choir, if He is the chief witness to the acts which we perform when we recite and intone, then any imperfection in the rendering is worthy of notice. Again to quote St. Pambo, the man of few words and large thoughts, it was held against him that he never showed interest in the great works that were done by his fellow ascetics nor in the great sums of money that were given by devout laymen to the poor. "Do not ask how much," he said, "but how." As a rider to St. Pambo's advice it might be suggested that we test our fidelity to the standard proposed in choir by examining ourselves on the direction of our effort rather than on the imperfection of our performance. If the ideal is clear, the least imperfection will seem worth correcting.

St. Benedict insists that the satisfaction be made *coram omnibus.* It is not enough that the monk should make an act of humility in his heart. Even if the mistake has not been noticed by anybody, it is still a mistake and must be put right. The monk is not begging the community's pardon, but God's. The superior, standing in the place of God, does not absolve in his own right: he is merely the administrator of either pardon or punishment.

It might be asked why, if faults in choir are to be judged as such on account of their bearing not upon the community but upon God, the monk is not expected to make satisfaction when he suffers a distraction? Is not the *opus Dei* more seriously interrupted by a distraction than by a mispronunciation? The answer is surely that external and internal imperfections require their respective external or internal correctives. Apart from the fact that to get up and make satisfaction would only add to the distraction, there would always be the scrupulous brother who would spend the whole of the Office making satisfaction for what he conceived to be a string of culpable distractions.

Infantes vero pro tali culpa vapulent. Where adult religious can be counted upon to make their satisfactions spontaneously, the boy religious have the matter taken out of their own hands and are beaten. St. Benedict seems to assume that to appeal to a boy's humility is a waste of time. Later on the boy may be expected to understand the point of begging pardon in choir, but in the meantime there is the rod. The rod will prevent repeated lapses, and at least the Office will run smoothly.

The reference to boys being present in choir is confirmation, if confirmation were needed, of the regular attendance, at the Office as at meals, of the entire household. Frequent mention, throughout the Rule, of these *alumni* shows the importance St. Benedict attached to the work of fostering vocations among even the very young. From Warnefrid, Hildemar, Udalric, and others, we learn a good deal about how St. Benedict's idea developed in later centuries. Customaries were drawn up especially to provide for the needs of such a system, and commentators are for the most part agreed upon the wisdom of raising up young monks who have had no experience at all of the outside world. The argument is used that the abbot can rely far more upon those of his monks whom he has watched growing up than upon those who have come to the monastery in later life and with habits already formed. If this gives a rather one-sided view, there is Hildemar's favourite theory that in boyhood the character is instinctively receptive to ideals, to good example, and to the influence of grace. If the right incentives are offered to young people, and if harmful influences are kept at bay, the admission of boys to the habit cannot but be justified. Such was the view which prevailed until the later Middle Ages.

CHAPTER 46

OF THOSE WHO OFFEND IN ANY
OTHER MATTERS

This is the last of the chapters which deal with transgressions and their punishments: by covering all the departments not already touched upon in reference to choir and refectory it tidies up the whole penal section of the Rule and concludes with an exhortation on the interior attitude which the monk should bring to his failures in fidelity.

If anyone while engaged in any sort of work, whether in the kitchen, the cellar, the office, the bakehouse, or the garden, in any craft and in any place, shall do anything amiss, break or lose anything, or offend in any way whatsoever, and shall not come at once before the abbot of the community, and of his own accord do penance and confess his fault, but it be known by means of another, let him be subjected to greater punishment.

Nothing could be more comprehensive. Accidental or deliberate, indoors or out, official or rank-and-file, serious or light: the abbot must hear about it with explanation and apology—and promptly. A hundred practical reasons can be advanced as to why such an arrangement would involve more inconvenience than it could possibly be worth, but the monastic life does not exist to save people inconvenience. It may be a bore for the abbot to have to listen to accounts of petty negligences; it may slow things down if the brethren are forever running off to report the consequences of their inattention and awkwardness; it may lead to invidious distinctions among brethren who are working together and who exercise a joint responsibility with regard to the tools that they use; it may unduly penalize the naturally clumsy, and act as a discouraging break upon zeal and enterprise. We may be sure that St. Benedict envisaged all this and more. Against such possible drawbacks stand the unquestionable goods of humility, detachment, obedience, and sensitiveness to the true inward meaning of property held in common and from the hand of God.

But either because of the growth of Benedictine communities in the centuries following the original foundation or because the ideal was abused, monastic usage established a substitute for the immediate acknowledgment of offences and breakages: the chapter of faults was instituted whereby the confession might be delayed until the more public occasion. In this chapter the monk acknowledges his faults against regular observance, his lapses in choir, his carelessness in the handling of tools, clothes, monastic furniture and goods generally. This development of the original idea gives scope for the added humiliation of having to acknowledge one's transgressions in front of the brethren. In those Benedictine congregations whose constitutions do not legislate for the chapter of faults, or in those houses where the practice has fallen into abeyance, the individual monks are all the more obliged to make their admissions privately to the abbot. It would be more than a pity if this thoroughly Benedictine idea of making known one's formal mistakes and defects were to lapse completely —particularly since it affords to the abbot an excellent opportunity of following up his subject's self-condemnations with a few criticisms of his own. The superior can strike, as it were, while the disposition is warm.

The practice of making "proclamations" in chapter—one monk drawing the superior's attention to another monk's irregularities— has never flourished for long among Benedictines. Only during the ninth century was it accepted as the normal thing for monks, but with the subsequent decline of Cluny the custom was retained only by the Cistercians, who have continued it to the present day. The Cistercians defend the denunciation of monk by monk on the grounds that it fosters the common life and elicits acts of charity. Certainly where tradition and training have combined to frame a policy in the matter, safeguarding the accusations from personal spite, the common life must benefit greatly.

In this whole question of making satisfaction for minor faults, whether the setting of it is the chapter-house or the abbot's cell, and whether the guilty brother accuses himself or is accused by another, the thing to remember is that the practice is designed to be remedial rather than punitive. If the aim is restricted to fault-finding, there can never be much educational value to the act. Granted that the material of the procedure is exterior, slight, non-moral, and confined to purely domestic observance, the danger is to concentrate too much on hair-splitting distinctions of rules and not enough on the rules' purpose. If rules are looked upon as means to perfection and not as ends in themselves, their minute observance is necessarily to be encouraged. But once get the place of rules wrong in the scheme of God's will, and therefore in the scheme of monasticism, and your petty observances become petty indeed.

When Moses was admitted to the presence of the Lord on Mount Sinai, even the sheep and the goats had their part to play in preparation for the delivery of the Law. Moses was to go up to the summit alone, meeting the light within the cloud, while the lesser creatures of God's order had to keep their distance, grazing on the mountain-side. In the fulfillment of our religious obligation we must look to the light itself which issues in the law. When we have recognized the revelation of God, and have come out from the cloud of His presence, then may the lesser creatures of God appear again on their proper level, and we see a renewal of revelation in the created order of nature.

Religious have more reasons than most to remind themselves of St. Paul's doctrine that the law is spiritual and that man is carnal.[1] The commandment which is ordained to life can be to us the means of death. The reason is that we who are carnal can make a carnal thing of the law; we who are petty can reduce the Rule to pettiness. If the law is holy, and if the Rule is holy, why do we

[1] Rom. 7;12,14.

drag down our obedience to the level of scientific compulsion? Why is not our monastic observance supernatural down to the minutiae of its demands? Only when our service of God becomes material does it become, in the pejorative sense, meticulous. The soul who looks fixedly towards the light of God is no longer timidly precise in his fidelity to rule: his is now the exactitude which springs instinctively from a service of love.

> If however the guilt of his offence be hidden in his own soul, let him manifest it to the abbot only, or to the spiritual seniors who know how to deal with their own wounds and not to disclose or publish those of others.

This final injunction has nothing to do with sacramental confession. It refers to what we would now call a "manifestation of conscience." In recommending the guilty monk to unburden himself to his spiritual father or fathers, St. Benedict is only echoing the advice given by countless wise men of the desert. The practice is less favoured today than it used to be (as we have noted in regard to the fifth degree of humility) but there can be no doubt that a monk's relations with his abbot can be vastly strengthened by this kind of admission. For a subject who is uneasy about his spirit, or about a particular line he is taking in the community, to discuss frankly with one in authority the safety of his course—provided there is the sincere desire to learn the truth—brings certainty and peace. The humility which prompts such an act is rewarded with an increase of the same virtue. As a gesture of filial respect it wins confidence where confidence was possibly lacking. As a mortification there can be few things more mortifying than to lay bare the dispositions which no one in the community would have suspected. So long as these open examinations of conscience are not too often repeated, thereby betraying themselves as having something morbid and selfish in their inspiration, they advance the soul in perfection and deepen the sense of community and family. Whatever the fashion in these things, and allowing for differences in national temperament, St. Benedict in his exhortation to the manifestation of conscience knew what he was about.

CHAPTER 47

OF SIGNIFYING THE HOUR
FOR THE WORK OF GOD

This chapter has an afterthought air about it. Not immediately connected which what precedes or follows, it is yet concerned with orderliness and the necessity of working to a strict timetable. The first paragraph is more an admonition to the abbot than a regulation for the observance of the community; the second is a general exhortation addressed to all and framed in terms which follow the pattern of St. Benedict's concluding passages. Though a short chapter, neatly divided into two parts of equal length, the material it contains has given rise to much speculation. Since most of the theorizing turns on points of academic interest—about what itself is theory—we need concern ourselves with no more than a brief survey of known facts.

Let the announcing of the hour for the *opus Dei*, both by day and night, be the abbot's care: either by giving the signal himself or by assigning this task to such a careful brother that all things be done at the fitting times.

In the last analysis the responsibility of day-to-day observance rests with the abbot: no detail is beneath his notice. So for the punctual performance of the Office the abbot must make exact provision, notifying any changes which may have to be made regarding the time, and if necessary seeing to the bells himself. In the actual working out it must seldom fall to the abbot's lot to ring a bell, but St. Benedict would like him to be habitually aware of his obligation.

Since meals fall into their place in the day according to the position of the Hours, there is not the same problem about summoning the brethren to the refectory. The *opus Dei* is the spine of the normal day, and accordingly deserves the greater care. Thus while the Divine Office was heralded *pulsato signo,* which suggests the striking of a gong if not the ringing of a bell, the brethren took their places in the refectory *tintinabulo tacto.* (Perhaps this latter term refers to the intoning of grace?)

Hildemar notes that the only way to insure accuracy in telling the time (*ut horis competentibus omnia compleantur*) is to have a water-clock. Lacking a water-clock, the monastery must be provided with one who knows well how to read the stars and how to calculate from the passage of the sun. Some have thought that it was the duty of the deans to take turn and turn about in watching the whole night through, either scanning the heavens from time to time or else tracing the passing of the hours by means of candles which were notched at regular intervals, till the time came when the dean who was then on guard might rouse the abbot, who himself called the brethren to Matins. The truth of it is we know nothing for certain about how time in the monastery was measured, about how the man responsible for call was himself roused, about the various methods employed in ringing the changes from one occupation to another. All we know is that the abbot was expected to find a way, and to see that it was carried out.

Let those who have been ordered intone the psalms and antiphons, each in his order after the abbot. Let no one presume to sing or to read unless he can fulfil the office in such a way that the hearers may be edified. And let it be done with humility, gravity, and awe; and by him whom the abbot has appointed.

Is St. Benedict recalling the question of the Apostle "how shall he preach unless he be sent"? Without designation there can be no merit of obedience. It is for the abbot to decide who among the brethren can perform public offices to edification, and when he has made his list there is to be no questioning its suitability. Naturally the seniors will head the abbot's rota, but seniority would be no excuse for arrogance. Whatever the function performed, the manner of it must be the same in the case of the senior as in the case of the junior—humble, serious, and awed by the thought of God present in majesty.

CHAPTER 48

OF THE DAILY MANUAL LABOUR

That this is one of the most important chapters in the Rule, and that St. Benedict himself regarded it so, is seen from the careful arrangement of the text. As in the case of the other more significant chapters there is the judicious blending of theory and practice, of doctrine and down-to-earth regulation. Where he teaches, St. Benedict seems to have drawn chiefly from St. Augustine;[1] where he legislates he uses for precedent the rules of St. Macarius, St. Caesarius, St. Pachomius, and perhaps also a letter of St. Jerome's. In general it is probably true to say that when St. Benedict has a policy to propose, as apart from a piece of discipline to enforce, he makes a study of the authorities and borrows freely from the fruit of their experience. For one whom history has hailed as an innovator, St. Benedict is surprisingly traditionalist.

> Idleness is the enemy of the soul. Therefore should the brethren be occupied at stated times in manual labour, and at other fixed hours in sacred reading.

We see from this concise introduction, and we shall see it more clearly as the chapter develops, that manual labour is only

[1] The main source is St. Augustine's treatise *De opere monachorum.* Scholars have also found references to a sermon of St. Augustine's, to two of his letters, and to the *Confessions.*

part of the subject matter to be covered. The time left over from the *opus Dei* will be accounted for in the monastic day: now work that is manual, now work that is intellectual or devotional or mixed. The whole range of Benedictine labour must be investigated. A principle moreover must be discovered in the light of which the multifarious works of a Benedictine monastery may be tested and justified.

Ideas on the work of monks were by no means fixed when St. Benedict came to sift his sources and to decide what tradition he would follow. In the Antonian monasteries of northern Egypt it was thought unmonastic to do work which could not be performed in the cell: to make baskets and weave linen would be considered safe enough, while to tend a garden or keep bees might well interfere with prayer and so have to be dropped. St. Jerome, on the other hand, was scornful of the monk who devoted his whole day to weaving mats and baskets which in any case would be unwoven when finished and begun again. For St. Jerome a monk's work was either toil in the field or study at the desk. St. Basil, representing Greek monasticism in his monastery at Neo-Caesarea in Pontus, required of monastic labour that it should be penitential, useful, and at least not incompatible with prayer. St. Basil's monks accordingly were engaged mostly in reclaiming waste land, hewing stone, cutting wood, draining the soil, planting and dressing vines. But this was Cappadocia and the fourth century. By the fifth century monasteries had become established in Italy and Gaul, their particular work being either agriculture or the development of theological study. (There had been monks in Italy and Gaul before this, but since they followed the Egyptian pattern they had no new ideas to bring to the subject of monastic work.) St. Jerome translated the Rule of St. Pachomius, Rufinus made an abridgement of St. Basil's two Rules, and there were Latin versions of Cassian and the Rule of St. Macarius. With so much to choose from, the monasteries of western Europe showed less uniformity of observance than the monasteries of other areas. As one writer observes (speaking especially of St. Martin's monastery at Tours, Cassian's at Marseilles, Honoratus's at Lerins): "The monasticism which had been imported into Gaul from the

East had not yet become adapted to the conditions of Western life. It was not yet acclimatized, and had not learned to accommodate itself to its new environment. The austerities of Eastern monasticism, though mitigated in some cases, were imitated as closely as circumstances would permit, and the asceticism of the saints of the Thebaid was the goal of the strivings of Western devotees."[2] Thus by the time St. Benedict came to write his Rule the problem of finding a formula which would pull together the widely differing policies as regards work, penance, prayer, enclosure, and other departments of monastic life, was a formidable one.[3]

We have seen that much of the present chapter derived from St. Augustine. While St. Augustine was addressing himself to his essay on the work of monks, the prevailing opinion was that monasteries were houses of prayer and not of work. Monks might give advice to those who came to consult them on spiritual matters, but there was to be no set work for souls. Monks might work about the house, but there was to be no labouring for the open market. Monasteries—and this was the view which St. Augustine set himself to oppose—should be expected to exist on alms rather than to support themselves by work. Since laziness is one of the first enemies of prayer, and since hard work is one of the best ways of doing penance for sin, St. Augustine had no difficulty in finding arguments to support his cause. All St. Benedict had to do was to drive home the principle, and to see that in his monasteries there would be no further doubt about the value to monks of hard, unremitting work.

But before going on to consider what kinds of work are judged suitable to monks we should note that in these early centuries there was very little thought about work as having an apostolic value. Work in the first Benedictine century was felt to meet an essential

[2] Dudden, *Gregory the Great*, II, 78.

[3] Authority for the statements contained in the above paragraph can be found in *The Lausiac History of Palladius, The Paradise of the Fathers*, Dom Cuthbert Butler's *Benedictine Monachism*, pp. 15-20, Dom Besse's *Moine Bénédictin*, pp. 185-195, Dom Morin's *Ideal of the Monastic Life*, passim, and *The Spiritual Life and Prayer according to Holy Scripture and Monastic Tradition*.

need within the monastery, not to meet a need which existed outside it. Work for souls as we understand the term was left to the clergy; the work done by the monk was ordered to his own soul and not to the layman's. Given this direction of purpose—the monk looking inside the enclosure for the field of his activity—the question naturally arose as to which works most immediately related to the end of monasticism and as to how these works could be organized so as not to upset the balance of the rest of the life.

"Cette obligation de travailler pèse à la fois sur l'intelligence et sur le corps," says Dom Besse. "La raison et l'expérience montrent que ni l'une ni l'autre ne sauraient s'en affranchir impunément . . . toutes les Règles monastiques tiennent compte de cette condition de la nature lorsqu'elles ont à déterminer l'emploi de la journée religieuse."[4] But as the same author is ready to allow, it is impossible to define the limits of this twofold necessity. Differences of locality, nationality, temperament, and current need will make it impossible to lay down one rule for all monasteries.

It is clear, however, from the text of the Rule that all things being equal, St. Benedict's preference is for manual labour; study and reading come second. Not only is manual labour treated first after the *opus Dei* in the order of daily occupations, and at greater length than the treatment given to *lectio*, but the best hours of the day are reserved for it. During the summer for three hours in the morning the monks are employed in manual labour, and again between the offices of None and Vespers; during the winter manual labour begins at about the second hour and ends at about the ninth. *Lectio* took up what time was left of the day—about three hours on ordinary days and considerably more on Sundays and feasts and during Lent.

Though it is easy enough on the evidence provided to make this classification, and to speak of so much of the day being devoted to labour and so much to study, it should at the same time be borne in mind that a number of truly monastic occupations, even in St. Benedict's own time, escaped the categories. Thus we know

[4] *Le Moine Bénédictin*, pp. 186-7.

that at Monte Cassino there were those who followed the arts; there were those who were engaged in transcribing manuscripts, in helping with the education of the *alumni*, in building up the library, in clerical work, in attending to guests and sick and poor. All this is work. It is just as much monastic work as labour in the field or the study of the Fathers. The question now is how to regulate and distribute the work so that the interest which it stirs either in the individual or in the house does not take away from the life of the whole. This in effect is *the* problem of monastic employment.

As Benedictine history developed, widely differing solutions came to be applied. In Italy and Gaul, the local as well as the remote apostolate engaged the attention of the monasteries. While monk missioners were being sent out to convert the unbeliever, monk-clerics were serving the basilicas in the big cities, were teaching the chant, were ministering to the sick and poor outside the monastery walls. The original emphasis, which we noted earlier, was beginning to change: the outside need was beginning to dictate the policy. Manual labour, accordingly, was beginning to drop off.

But zeal for the active ministry was not the sole cause for the decline of manual labour among the monks of the West. Even such an ardent champion of the Rule as St. Benedict of Aniane was against too much of it. The monastic day, under St. Benedict of Aniane's reform, was so full of liturgical and devotional exercises that there was little room for more than a routine hour or so of outdoor work. Later centuries added still further obligations with regard to the choir, and we find eventually the Cluniac movement suffering from the same want of Benedictine balance. Always it seems to be manual labour, rather than some other monastic activity, that gets crowded out.

If it was not the liturgy and the active apostolate, it was classical and theological study. Though it is far from certain that Cassiodorus followed, or even adapted to his use, the Benedictine Rule in the monastery he founded at Vivarium, the impulse which he gave to the intellectual life and scholarship had the profoundest effect upon Western monasticism of later generations. Certainly Cassiodorus had more interest than St. Benedict in both secular and strictly theological study, and it was to this tradition that Gallican monasteries reverted when the problem which we have described became pressing.

The earliest monks, in pre-Benedictine times, left no literature worth mentioning. They gave conferences, and went in for dialogues which were virtually debates, but they wrote next to nothing. The literature which comes down to us is simply what the scribes, sitting at the feet of the masters, managed to take down. But with Pachomian and Cappadocian monachism this oral teaching gave place to the written word. In the course of time the written word assumed an importance which had not been attached to the spoken word. It became almost an end in itself, a thing to be studied for the sake of studying it. Monks, particularly when the numbers increased and the majority of vocations were found to come from the more educated classes, devoted their lives to comparing manuscripts, correcting texts, making notes—in a word "specializing." Again manual labour had to go by the board.

Even the great Dom Mabillon himself, defending the Maurist Congregation against the criticism that the monasteries of the seventeenth century were nothing more than schools for higher studies, was frank enough to admit that scholarship might well be a snare for monks. Certainly Mabillon had no illusions about the work-problem and how it was being solved in his own day and by his own fellow Maurists. "Work is not something to be assumed," he wrote, "merely for the purpose of dispelling the boredom of idleness. We cannot be said to have avoided the reefs of idleness when all we have done is to occupy ourselves with trifles." St. Benedict did not introduce manual labor into his monastic day simply in order to kill time. He knew too well that time, if left to itself and not properly used, could kill the monastic day.

What, again, of the pastoral ministry as being work for monks to undertake? As in the case of both running schools (to be examined below) and pursuing patristic, scriptural, theological, and other higher studies, the work of serving parishes has received the blessing of popes and has been taken up by monasteries and congregations of unquestioned monastic spirit. Certainly if Dom Maurus Wolter's wide claim that "all work, provided it does not oppose the aim of the religious life, may legitimately be embraced by Benedictines" can be taken to include work which must necessarily go on outside the enclosure, then parochial work has as worthy a title as any. But though it may be sanctifying to the individual, conducive to recollection even, and of undoubted apostolic value, activity on a parish can hardly be said to reflect the intention of St. Benedict. To meet a particular need, either in the monk or in the neighborhood concerned, there would be nothing strictly contrary to the Rule in a monk living virtually the life of a parish priest for a time: it would carry the merit of obedience, and, provided the monastery is looked upon as the normal anchorage, would strengthen the monk's dependence upon the essential monastic practices which he now has to fulfil on his own. But in no sense can permanent employment in the diocesan field be considered Benedictine.

Would the strictures contained in the above paragraph apply to the work of giving retreats and conferences outside the monastery, to the apostolate as expressed over the microphone and on the screen? Not altogether. For one thing this kind of work would not normally take a monk for long stretches of time out of his enclosure. For another it seems to be a work which was favoured by St. Benedict. Perhaps reluctantly, perhaps willingly, St. Benedict recognized the duty of *contemplata aliis tradere*. Bearing always in mind our holy Father's view of enclosure, which will be examined when the Rule itself considers it, we know from the *Dialogues* that his influence spread beyond the community not only because of his prayer within the monastery but also because of his activity outside it. "By continual preaching, the man of God converted many of the people thereabout."[5] "Not far from the monastery was a certain town in which no small number of souls, by the exhortations of Benedict, were converted."[6] "In that place dwelt certain religious women to whom the servant of God, Benedict, used often to send some of the brethren for the

[5] Bk. 2; ch. 8.
[6] *Ibid.*, ch. 19.

purpose of giving instruction and in order to edify their souls."[7]
"The man of God was accustomed to go to a house not far from
the gate . . . where, when they [himself, his sister, and some of his
disciples] had spent the whole day in the praise of God and holy
discourses, the night drawing on they took their refection
together."[8]

The same willingness to impart to others the graces received,
even at the sacrifice of enclosure, is seen in the lives of the two
greatest monks after St. Benedict, namely St. Gregory and St.
Bernard. The difficulty of combining the two ideals, that of
winning souls to Christ by contemplation within the enclosure
and that of going outside to win them by preaching, is keenly felt
by the great Benedictine Pope. "No one can at the same time
devote himself to the Church's needs and observe wholly the
monastic rule; it would be impossible for him who is daily engaged in these active affairs to keep to the regularity of the
monastery." If this is St. Gregory's experience, St. Bernard's is
little different. It was St. Bernard's constant cry that he was being
torn by the conflicting attractions, the conflicting vocations even.
"It is for the monk to pray and not to preach," St. Bernard proclaimed—but he spent most of his monastic life preaching all the
same. It was not that great monks like St. Gregory and St. Bernard were compelled by the talents which they possessed to leave
their silence and express themselves in activity; it was that the
circumstances of God's will demanded it of them. The compulsion
came from without, supplying them with both the grace to resolve the apparent monastic inconsistency and the genius to
meet the outward need.

But lacking the light and the sanctity of a St. Gregory or a
Bernard, there can be self-deception in a monk's readiness to put
his gifts at the disposal of souls outside. It is one thing to give a
few retreats in the year, and some spiritual conferences to nuns,
and quite another to pursue a whole-time mission. A Benedictine
may not so follow a bent for preaching that there is little to
distinguish his life from that of the Dominican. The monastery is

[7] *Loc. cit.*
[8] *Ibid.*, ch. 33.

not a mere jumping-off place for work among souls. The monastery is the foundation and home. The life that is led outside the monastery—whether while giving retreats, while acting as chaplain to a convent (or even in time of war to a regiment), while doing a course at a university, while ill in hospital—is the exception.

Finally there is the thorny question as to how far education may be judged suitable work for monks. This is another of those subjects which must be seen in relation to historical tradition and contemporary need. To judge it simply on the text of the Rule, or even on certain isolated principles derived from the Rule, would be like judging a meal according to the cookery book and not according to the occasion, the time of the year, the setting, and the guests.

Though the work of running a school presents, monastically speaking, obvious disadvantages, it can at least be done without damage to the principle of enclosure. Against the drawbacks—chief among which would be first the necessity of absenting from choir those most involved in the responsibility, and second the alternation between term and holiday which destroys the idea of keeping up an even pressure—must be weighed such factors as outlet to apostolic zeal, incentive to hard work, the encouragement given to vocations, the opportunity afforded to young people of taking part in the liturgy, and the immediate communication of charity and the spiritual life.

That there is historical justification for education as one of the works suitable for monks is shown by the existence of monastic schools both before and after St. Benedict's time. In Pachomian monasteries boys were educated by the monks, and perhaps even under St. Basil's rule. This may not prove much, but at least it shows that the ancients saw nothing incompatible in the idea of monks teaching. It is true that at that time as in St. Benedict's and for more than a century later, the schools were small and consisted of boys destined for profession in the monastery.

Certainly it was St. Benedict's practice, as we know from the *Dialogues*[9] as well as from the many references to *pueri* and

[9] Bk. 2; ch. 2.

infantes in the Rule, to undertake the education of boys whose parents were worthy and who pressed him to do so. "Certain noble and religious men in Rome began to come to him [Benedict], commending their children to be brought up by him in the service of Almighty God." So a school of some sort, of which Maurus and Placid are described as the most promising among those entrusted to the saint's care, must have been housed in the monastery.

From the sixth to the eighth century we know nothing of the progress of Benedictine education, but in Paul Warnefrid's commentary there are precise instructions as to the management of the *alumni*. The first evidence of an education that was not strictly domestic and claustral is to be seen in an enterprise of St. Boniface's in the latter part of the eighth century, and it is known that Charles the Great made every monastery as well as every cathedral take up the work of preparing boys for careers in the world. Benedict of Aniane, however, reversed this policy, prohibiting as an integral measure of his reform the establishment of schools in all monasteries of the Empire except for the sole purpose of educating *oblati* or future monks. But there were monasteries which resisted this decree, and lay schools survived until Cluny finally put a ban upon the teaching of boys by monks. "By the end of the tenth century," says Dom Berlière, "education had passed from the hands of the Benedictines."[10]

During the later Middle Ages, it became part of the social mission of the greater monasteries, in addition to their many other activities, to revise secular education in the form of local parish schools. These were of course day schools, served by the monks either in the monastery grounds or from the monastery, where the children learned the elements of Latin and the liberal sciences.

After the Reformation, in the early seventeenth century, schools were founded abroad by monks of the English Benedictine Congregation; these schools were transplanted in the nineteenth century to England where they flourish today. The English were not the only Black Monks to take up the work of education. Towards the end of the eighteenth century the Maurists had opened as

[10] *L'Ordre Monastique*, p. 115.

many as thirty secondary schools and six military academies. The Hungarian, the Swiss, the Austrian, and the Bavarian Congregations took on the work of education as one of their first commitments, while the Cassinese Congregation and the Congregation of Subiaco left themselves free to undertake it or not according to the feeling of the individual houses. Nor have the houses in America, whether of the Cassinese or Swiss tradition, pledged themselves to the work of secular education.

One of the interesting features about present-day Benedictinism is the growing appreciation of St. Benedict's original emphases. Always in our history the liturgy was studied and preached, but never with such energy as today. Work for the world by living within the monastery is a doctrine which receives more attention now than it did thirty years ago. Most marked of all is the desire to return to the simplicity of St. Benedict's outlook and spirituality.

Will this affect manual labour? Will the attitude of Cluny towards manual labour—an attitude tacitly accepted by tradition —be modified? It is not unfair to say that apart from one or two outstanding enterprises in one or two congregations, the Black Monks of the eighteenth and nineteenth centuries were little devoted to manual labour. Agriculture, which had passed out of use as the ordinary work for Benedictines when monks studied to become priests in the course of the eighth century, may now be gradually coming back. With the admission of subjects who will not be required to train for ordination to the priesthood but whose vocation to the choir is recognized and provided for, a new phase has developed in Benedictine history. Where a generation ago the farm-hand monk was thought of as a figure out of the Middle Ages, today he is accepted as part of the scene. It is now not only the White Monks who are to be found in the field, the cowshed, the dairy, the workshop and the barns: Black Benedictines are finding their way back to these less sophisticated retreats.

In the face of such diversity as we have described it might be said in conclusion that while all works are of equal supernatural and monastic value if it is God's will that they are undertaken, some works are objectively more Benedictine than others. So long as I know that this occupation is God's will for me, as a monk I fulfil it to the best of my ability: it is my Benedictine duty and I cannot lose on it. At the same time I shall know—and this knowledge should help me to test the manner and spirit in which I perform the work—that my specific vocation is better served, and God consequently more glorified, when I operate within the monastery and in union with the brethren.

The test accordingly is not so much whether the work is "distracting," whether it is "hard," whether it suits me and my idea of monastic work. The test is much more whether I have to do it, and whether I do it in the way laid down by the brethren within the monastery. If this test is answered affirmatively, the work is a monastic work. "Active" and "contemplative" as applying to work are labels only; terms like "God-given" and "in union with the community" tell one far more.

"It is not the presence of activity that destroys the contemplative life of a monastery," says Dom Cuthbert Butler, "but the absence of contemplation." A monk can make himself miserable deploring the loss of his contemplative label when he should be congratulating himself on having been given the grace of living the active life contemplatively.

"It is on the condition of being contemplatives," says Dom Jean de Hemptinne, "that monks will be men of action. If they love God they can be useful workers."

We think therefore that the times for each [labour and reading] should be disposed as follows: from Easter to the Calends of October, on coming out in the morning let them labour at whatever is necessary from the first until about the fourth hour. From the fourth hour until close upon the sixth let them apply themselves to reading.

After so lengthy a treatment of—in its various forms—labour, it will be necessary to delve into the question of reading. If as we have tried to suggest there is something fitting and hallowed about monastic manual labour, there is in the case of monastic *lectio* the added quality which relates directly to prayer. While toiling with a pick or at the carpenter's bench a monk may find himself quite able to pray for considerable stretches of time. But it would be rating manual labour too high to say that this was because of the dignity and sacredness of physical toil as such. The ability to pray while working comes indirectly and as the result of cultivated habit. In the case of *lectio divina* the process is more immediate. Granted that in either exercise the soul is eager to make the most of the impulses of grace, the exercise of studying truth from the pages of a book affords greater scope than would be given in the expenditure of bodily effort.

Thus the guess hazarded above that St. Benedict preferred manual to intellectual labour must be qualified. It is not a question as to which is the more noble, the employment of the body or the employment of the intellect, because obviously a work which engages the higher faculties must take precedence over one which is performed by the lower. It is rather that having regard both to the kind of monks whom he expected to recruit for his monasteries, and the kind of spaces that would exist in the day when he had got the main times ordered for the Divine Office, St. Benedict placed greater reliance upon manual labour than upon study for his communities. It must be remembered that whatever Dom John Chapman's view on the intellectual character of sixth-century monasticism, St. Benedict's monks were mostly drawn from the peasantry. To have allowed the majority in the community to imagine that by working at the kind of tasks which their families were accustomed to, and in the clutter of which they had been brought up, was merely filling in time, and that what really mattered to their holy Father was the work which was done by the privileged and educated few at their desks with their books, would have been disastrous. Far better give pride of place to the kind of humble work which everybody could do, and then make the most of what might be expected—and expected moreover by all, whether educated or not—from the serious cultivation of the objectively more excellent occupation of *lectio divina*.

Unless some such understanding is brought to the order of St. Benedict's day—to the mere spacing of periods, let alone to the balance of values—there must always appear a conflict of emphases. To appreciate the Benedictine way of life it is necessary to see the whole thing as an equally balanced triangle of prayer, work, and reading. Whatever the personal preferences either in St. Benedict's mind or in the individual monk's, and whatever the practical considerations which govern the distribution of hours actually employed in the respective duties, this three-sided frame or foundation is the explanation of the Rule, of the Benedictine vocation, of the tradition which has survived every sort of pressure from without and every sort of false stress from within.

Lectio divina. Does this mean only such reading-matter as relates to God directly, and to faith? Not necessarily. It must be the kind of reading which has God and faith as its object, but as its subject it may have one or other of religion's many aspects. The Scriptures, the Fathers, the liturgy, theology, mysticism, hagiology: there is a wide enough field. It is not so much what to study as how to study it. The purpose is neither to satisfy curiosity nor to exercise the mind in speculation; chiefly the purpose is to dispose for prayer. Reading, properly handled, is the overture to prayer; it can be prayer itself. But if reading is to be the spiritual force which it is designed to be, there must be more than mere co-operation on the part of the reader: there must be discipline, constancy, and the willingness to be influenced by what is read to the point of making alterations in one's life, to the point of making sacrifices.

St. Benedict did not introduce spiritual reading so that we might beguile the hours which were too short for anything more useful. It is not for pious entertainment that we read. *Lectio divina*, like manual labour, is an ascesis. Like manual labour there must be method in it. In the mood of today, system is a little scorned. The best way to kill an enterprise today is to mention its regimentation. But in religion there must be a regimen even if there is not to be regimentation. In reading there has to be order, or the mind will fritter the chances away. Circumspection, careful selection of material, concentration: these qualities sound dull, but they cannot be dispensed with. Merely to ensure getting enough time in the day for one's spiritual reading calls for forethought and effort. Often it requires more courage to address oneself to spiritual reading than to manual labour or mental prayer.

As a corollary to the need for self-discipline is the need to have the sanction of authority for what is read. This is not to suggest that professed monks, unless obliged by the customs of the house, are to consult the abbot on every book that they take from the library; it is rather to suggest that specialized studies should not be embarked upon merely at pleasure and without the blessing of obedience. The situation should not arise in which an abbot finds himself faced with a decision which, had he known of his subject's studies, could have been anticipated long before. To follow an unusual course of study might reflect not only upon obedience and the common life, but also upon detachment and religious poverty. To present to the cellarer a bill for rare books when the occasion to order them might not have come up had superiors known all along what was afoot would be to show weakness in the spirit of poverty.

If monastic reading, intellectual work generally, is to be regularized from above and from within, it must also be ordered in its actual execution. Nothing so destroys the prayerfulness of spiritual study as rush and fuss. Tension is the enemy of *lectio* as St. Benedict conceived it. The desire to read more and more books so as to be fully acquainted with every possible aspect of the subject, the strain of feeling that one should be making notes of everything that one reads, the fever of anxiety lest one's work falls short of another's in the same field: none of this is compatible with the meditative exercise which truly monastic study is designed to be.

Since writing goes well with reading, indeed emerges out of reading, it is worth noting here that no sound monastic writing can be produced in the mood of competition and from a desire for publicity. The rules for a monk's reading apply equally to a monk's writing. A monk, if he will write for the glory of God and not for self-advertisement, must keep his eye on other things besides his typewriter: he will need to look, as above, at obedience, the common life, detachment and religious poverty.

After the sixth hour, when they rise from table, let them rest on their beds in all silence; or if anyone chance to wish to read to himself, let him so read as not to disturb anyone else. Let None be said rather soon, at the middle of the eighth hour, and then let them again work at whatever has to be done until Vespers.

From Prime until the fourth hour, manual labour; from the fourth till the sixth, reading. The office of Terce is not accounted for in this scheme, so was probably recited in the fields during the stretch of manual labour. Sext would be said in the oratory before the principal meal, and after grace all would move off to the dormitory for the siesta. The time of siesta corresponded to the night's sleep, so was observed as *summum silentium*. None, taking place in the oratory a little before the ninth hour from which it gets its name, brought the siesta to an end, and as soon as this office was over the brethren went back to their manual work, which was kept up until Vespers in the evening.

If however the needs of the place or poverty require them to labour at gathering in the harvest, let them not grieve at that; for then are they truly monks when they live by the labour of their hands as our fathers and the Apostles did. But let all things be done in moderation for the sake of the faint-hearted.

Should a full harvest or the exigencies of fruit-picking cause alterations in the normal timetable, the brethren must take it in good part. In the same way if those who for one reason or another are normally exempt should be called upon to help, they must congratulate themselves in faith upon being in the grand tradition: they are real monks as their ancestors in religion were, and their labour is united with the apostolic labours of Paul who was not above making tents and sails, of Peter who was not above fishing and mending nets. It is strange to find in St. Benedict this exhortation to see nobility in labour. Perhaps the West had still to be persuaded that there was nothing necessarily servile in per-

forming the works of slaves. In the East they had always understood that there was nothing unworthy about hard and commonplace work. In the East the husbandman was considered as good
as the next man, as probably better; in the West he was simply
a rustic. In developing the idea of the common life, it was St.
Benedict's aim to bring true values to this issue.

> From the Calends of October until the beginning of Lent
> let the brethren devote themselves to reading till the end of
> the second hour. At the second hour let Terce be said, after
> which they shall all labour at their appointed task until
> None. At the first signal for the hour of None all shall cease
> from their work and be ready as soon as the second signal
> is sounded. After their meal let them occupy themselves in
> their reading or with the psalms.

The winter months will need a revision of the horarium: less
time can be allowed to work out of doors, and the siesta can be
dropped. There is more margin for reading, for preparing the
lessons and psalms of the *opus Dei*. The long evenings make for
greater leisure within the monastery, and either private prayer or
a continuation of the morning's *lectio* fills the gaps. There is to be
nothing pressurized in the monastery, nothing so taxing either
to the body or to the brain as to dismay the faint-hearted. Nerves,
even in St. Benedict's day, had to be allowed for.

> In Lent however, from the morning till the end of the
> third hour, let them devote themselves to reading, and after
> that to work at their appointed tasks until the end of the
> ninth hour. In this time of Lent let them receive each a
> book from the library to be read consecutively and straight
> through. These books are to be given out at the beginning
> of Lent.

With Lent the time allotted to reading amounted to roughly
four hours a day—only a little less than the time allotted at that
season to manual labour. To provide against the excuse of having
nothing to read, St. Benedict sees to it that special Lenten
material is supplied from the monastery library. Whether the
choice is determined by the abbot or by the individual, the custom

of taking out a Lent book obtains today. The book is not to be
skimmed through but ploddingly absorbed from cover to cover.
This is to be taken as part of the Lenten discipline. Perhaps because the Lent book is likely to be stiffer in character than what
is read throughout the rest of the year, or perhaps because the
time set aside for reading it is so much longer, St. Benedict goes
on to make special stipulations regarding the control of the
brethren's *lectio* at this period:

> Above all let one or two seniors be deputed to go around
> the monastery at the hours when the brethren are engaged
> in reading, and see that there is no slothful brother giving
> himself to idleness or to gossip, and not applying himself
> to his reading, so that he is not only useless to himself but a
> distraction to others. If such a one be found, which God
> forbid, let him be corrected once and a second time; if he
> do not amend let him be subjected to the chastisement of
> the Rule in such a way that the rest may be afraid. More-
> over, one brother shall not associate with another at un-
> suitable times.

Surveillance such as is outlined in the above passage does not
recommend itself to the modern mind, but it was doubtless necessary in St. Benedict's time. The seniors in question were not
deans but *circatores*, appointed for a year at a time and responsible for good order inside the house. Paul Warnefrid, who is the
source of this information, says that if the *circatores* do their work
efficiently there is seldom occasion for the brethren to accuse
themselves of having broken the rule. Exactly.

The ban on unauthorized conversations proves again that
there were conversations which were authorized. The term *horis
incompetentibus* supposes *horae competentes*. If the brethren
confine themselves to the period of recreation for their exchanges,
they strengthen the common life and lose nothing in the way of
mutual confidence. To unburden oneself privately at another's
door seldom produces any good result. If an intimate matter has
to be discussed, it is better to discuss it, as St. Benedict advises,
with the abbot or a senior. If it is a matter which needs to be
talked over with one particular person, and him a fellow subject,

it is better to get permission for such a conversation and so gain the sanction of authority to what would otherwise be an irregularity.

On Sunday let them devote themselves to reading, save such as are assigned to the various offices. But if anyone be so neglectful and slothful as to be unwilling or unable to read or meditate, he must have some work given to him that he may not be idle. For weak or delicate brethren let such work or craft be enjoined that they will not be idle and yet will not be oppressed by the weight of labour so as to be driven away. The weakness of such brethren must be considered by the abbot.

St. Benedict is always supremely considerate for those brethren who have difficulty in keeping up with the rest. The suggestion in the above paragraph is that though a monk may not be idle by design he may well become idle by accident. Sustained reading is not for everybody, even if it is only for one day a week, so in default of either education or capacity such potential idlers are to be particularly cared for by the abbot lest they become idlers in fact. It is probably good for most of us to be given work to do which is uncongenial, but beyond a certain point the will can find itself unequal to the demand. Superiors have the unenviable duty of forestalling this point in their subjects, and substituting work for them which is better suited. Temperament has to be allowed for even in the supposedly untemperamental.

From this concluding paragraph to the chapter on work and reading we can see—as indeed we can see from the treatment of the whole subject and from the general tenor of the Rule—that St. Benedict is against the idea of leisure to be disposed of at private inclination: there is not what we would call "free time" in the Benedictine day. Inevitably in any monastery, whether of St. Benedict's day or of our own, there are intervals which the monk may use as he likes; but it would be foreign to St. Benedict's mind that any monk of his should decide every now and then to take a day off. Customs differ in different congregations with regard to this question of holidays, and where superiors explicitly state their wish that the monks should go away at regular intervals for a change there can be no question as to the legitimacy of the practice: the holiday is covered by obedience. Under such conditions it is more meritorious to go away than not to go.

It is when the monk feels drawn to ask for a holiday that the difficulty begins. Is he ever justified—and if so, how often may he apply, how long may his holidays last, how far is he obliged when away to the obligations which bind him when he is in the monastery? These are questions which can only be answered by the authority on the spot. It is for the authority to waive or to confirm the Benedictine principle. Certainly the voice of authority interpreting the Rule can be stronger than the voice of the Rule itself. But if we are looking simply for what may be found in the Rule about holidays, we have reason to believe that St. Benedict was against them. The case is stated with absolute clarity in the sixty-sixth chapter where provision is made for life within the enclosure: *ut non sit necessitas monachis vagandi foras, quia omnino non expedit animabus eorum.*

If St. Benedict referred us to "our fathers and Apostles," saying that when engaged in extra labour and living by the labour of our hands "then are we truly monks," he might choose the same precedents in encouraging us to continue in our monasteries without holidays. We are nowhere told that the monks of Egypt, Palestine, or Syria took holidays. Going back further, we are not told that the Apostles took holidays. Nor can we believe that St. Benedict himself—and after him St. Gregory, St. Bernard, St. Augustine, St. Bede—took time off from the service of God.

Are we to conclude then that a monk may never ask his abbot for permission to go away for a change? No, but the reasons for doing so would have to be very good ones. And the abbot moreover would have to be in the position of appreciating the reasons without being persuaded to see them. The abbot's prerogative, frequently insisted upon throughout the Rule, is not something to be extracted; it is to be used freely and deliberately and when the occasion demands it as an exercise of charity *propter pusillanimes.*

Given these two conditions then, first that the subject views his application not as a request to suspend for a time the terms of his vocation but rather as a means of avoiding what he believes in conscience to be possible disaster, second that the superior is not pressed to give the favourable decision, monks may ask to go away. How they should behave when they are away will be considered in a later chapter. If their request is turned down, *non contristentur, quia tunc vere monachi sunt.*

CHAPTER 49

OF THE OBSERVANCE OF LENT

Since the approach to monastic work and reading, with all the borderline activities implicit in the terms *labor* and *lectio*, is meant to be a spiritual and penitential approach rather than a utilitarian one, the subject of Lent naturally follows what we have just been considering. The physical is given its ascetical value; the intellectual is given its spiritual direction.

Although the life of a monk ought at all times to have about it a Lenten observance, yet since few have strength enough for this, we exhort all, at least during the days of Lent, to keep themselves in all purity of life, and to wash away during that holy season the negligences of other times.

Anyone who reads Dom Ursmer Berlière's *L'Ascèse Bénédictine* will find himself marvelling that after earlier monastic experiments in the ascetical life have been purged of their excesses there is any asceticism left for the Benedictine to practise. History has shown that ascetical fervour is subject to the law of diminishing returns, each successive generation discovering a new substitute for corporal austerity. St. Pachomius, an ascetic by any standard, judged that his master Palamon had somewhat overstressed the need for fasting, thus unfitting himself for the more elevated works of recollection and attention to the word of Scripture. St. Basil, no sybarite either, felt that the ancient

monks in Egypt had made almost a fetish of penance, so instead
of the painful vigils and the voluntary endurance of extremes in
heat and cold he gave his monks useful work to do and encouraged exercises of charity. Cassian, though an advocate of fasting
and an admirer of all things Eastern, was at pains to remind the
monks of the West that in the matter of asceticism it would be
found necessary to make concessions to climate and race. St.
David carried the Egyptian way of life to Wales, and St. Columbanus even outdid the Egyptian standard in the Celtic monasteries
and those which he founded at St. Gall and Bobbio and Luxeuil.
But though these Celtic monks possessed no change of clothes
and slept on the bare ground, their successors had to bow to the
natural conditions of the latitudes where they settled. It is the
same story in the case of the monks of Condat in the Jura, of
Auverne, of Ligugé, of Arles. But in spite of this earlier and contemporary experience, St. Benedict is emphatic: *omni tempore
vita monachi Quadragesimae debeat observationem habere.*

Since not all can keep pace with this doctrine the whole year
through, at least during Lent itself a programme of self-denial
can be drawn up and observed. It is now, during this season when
the whole Church does penance, that the monk must keep the
twofold principle of mortification clearly before his mind: there
has to be atonement for past sin on the negative side, and on the
positive side an endeavour to advance in the love of God. How
this is to be done St. Benedict suggests in what follows:

> We shall worthily accomplish the same if we refrain
> from all sin and give ourselves to prayer with tears, to holy
> reading, to compunction of heart, and to abstinence.

Dom Berlière, who claims that St. Benedict had no intention of
starting something new in the way of monastic life but was
merely legislating for monks who were then living in common
under no set rule,[1] makes Benedictine asceticism consist almost
entirely of silence, stability within the enclosure of the monastery,
and the regimen of prayer.[2] St. Benedict's forty-ninth chapter

[1] *L'Ascèse Bénédictine*, p. 3.
[2] *Ibid.*, pp. 124-129; 159-231.

accordingly comes up for careful treatment by this author. He has much to say about each of the three points raised above by St. Benedict: prayer with tears, holy reading, and compunction of heart.

Orationi cum fletibus debemus. Not only did St. Benedict himself pray in this way ("it was his custom in prayer mildly to weep," says St. Gregory in his account of how St. Benedict prophesied the destruction of the monastery),[3] but the gift of tears seems to have been granted to many of his sons. Dom Berlière instances more than a dozen Benedictine saints to whom this kind of prayer has been ascribed, and though he judges it to be true to the best of Benedictine spirituality he warns against delusion in the matter. On holy reading Dom Berlière has one of the best chapters in the book, giving illustrations from the lives of the saints to confirm his interpretation of St. Benedict's mind. Where he equates "compunction of heart" with particular examens Dom Berlière is less convincing. Surely the essence of compunction is sorrow-with-desire rather than investigation-with-resolutions. The heart of compunction is the heart of Christ. When the soul has sought to live the life of Christ, to reproduce the mind of Christ, to walk in Christ, then whatever the immediate mood or sentiment experienced in prayer is the mood or sentiment of Christ. When Christ tells us in St. John's Gospel that we have no further need to ask *Him* to petition the Father for our needs, He surely means that if we live in Him and if He lives in us the petition already comes from Him to the Father.[4] Through us but from Him. From us but through Him. It is the same in the case of our compunction. If our compunction is true, it is His. If it is not true, it is not worth experiencing or expressing. The fact that in Christ's sorrow for sin there was no element of guilt makes no difference to the fact that our sorrow for sin, occasioned by guilt and inspired by grace, can be united to His. Indeed in this lies the value of compunction. In this lies the value of Lent.

[3] *Dialogues*, Bk. 11; ch. 17.
[4] See John 16;26.

In these days, then, let us add something to the usual measure of our service: as private prayers, abstinence from food and drink, so that everyone of his own will may offer something to God with joy of the Holy Spirit, something beyond the measure appointed to him, withholding from his body somewhat of his food, drink, and sleep, refraining from talk and mirth, and awaiting holy Easter with the joy of spiritual longing.

To the zealous monk it will be a point of honour to go, at *least* during Lent, beyond what his vows demand. Just how far beyond, it will be for the abbot to determine. The areas of mortification are the obvious ones—food, drink, sleep to be curtailed, and private prayers together with serious reading to be increased —but twice in the paragraph St. Benedict reminds us of the spirit of joy in which the renunciations must be made. It is to be noted also that St. Benedict chooses two points from the common life which he wants attended to particularly during Lent: talk and mirth. Mirth and joy are not, in this context, the same thing. If mirth is sobered down as part of the supernatural discipline of Lent, the common life will not suffer. In the same way if talk is restricted for the love of God, the love of neighbour will be deepened rather than weakened. Lent is not meant to provide an excuse for evading the responsibilities of recreating in common. "I may now at last practise charity as I feel drawn to practise it," says the mistaken monk, "which is without reference to my fellow monks."

St. Thomas says that it is more meritorious to love one's neighbour for the love of God, than to love God regardless of one's neighbour. Charity is imperfect if it is unbalanced. The first is inclusive, the second is exclusive. We may not divide charity. Charity is God, and God is charity: and God is not divided.

Let each one make known to his abbot what he offers, and let it be done with his blessing and permission. What is done without leave of the spiritual father shall be imputed to presumption and vainglory, meriting no reward. Everything therefore is to be done with the approval of the abbot.

So hazardous is this matter of external mortification voluntarily undertaken that it must be hedged about with safeguards. The first condition, as we have seen, is that it be performed with gladness of heart. But it must also be performed in the spirit of submission. The clearest sign of the false ascetic is the independent way in which he goes about his ascetical practices: he admits no control, he displays his schedule of austerities, he is arrogant in defending his extreme thesis, he is intolerant of those who feel called to walk by another way. Pride and uncharity reveal the mistaken approach to penance.

The voluntary penance which is practised in monasteries must be conceived in relation to three things: prayer, unobtrusiveness, other people. The penance that is not inspired in the light of prayer will not promote the spirit of prayer; so it might as well be dropped. The penance that is paraded as the most necessary of all virtues will only become an obstacle to the other virtues; so has need to defer to humility and charity. The penance that interferes with the liberty of other people, making them feel uncomfortable or angry or small, is not penance but singularity.

In order to live religiously in community a man must go one better than resisting intolerance of other people and of their views: he must meet them more than half way by respecting them and their views. If necessary he must go so far in their direction as to shed himself and his own views. Greater love than this no man can show, whether in community or anywhere else.

If this means anything at all it means avoiding singularity, independence, didacticism. Though these qualities have sometimes the appearance of being strengths, they are in fact great weaknesses. Vainglory may have a look sometimes of force and bigness, but in fact it is enfeebling and mean. St. Thomas makes vainglory a sin against magnanimity.[5] Magnanimity is a force because it is an aspect of fortitude. Acting from vainglory a man is living on a superficial plane, is performing works which are unreal, is separating himself from truth.

Thus singularity in the religious life is a weakness which draws away the will from its true purpose, which is to find perfection

[5] *Summa*, II. II., q. 129.

in charity. St. Benedict links vainglory and presumption together in the passage under consideration, thereby echoing his own doctrine suggested in the chapter on the instruments of good works: *Non velle dici sanctum antequam sit.* The monk who wants the reputation for sanctity *presumes* to something which he has no right to claim. He is identifying the name with the state, he is leaving out the factor of grace. Without grace to correct and inspire him in his decisions, such a man will act according to the name he has built up for himself. He will be singular. He may have faith in himself but he has not full faith in God. He sins by presumption.

This will account for the way in which St. Benedict comes down so heavily upon any sign of *opus peculiare* in a monk. It is not only the piece of private property that is forbidden but much more the attitude of mind which wants to exercise ownership. The thing retained is a symbol; the acquisitive will is the seat of the trouble. Let the monk have a free hand and he will collect symbol after symbol, he will "please himself," he will be singular.

"Charity seeks not its own, but that which relates to others." The common good is the objective, and the more the common good is taken to be the criterion of action the less room will be left for self-interest, for the desire to take the floor and instruct others, for thoughtless ostentation. St. Basil makes it the sign of the true monk that he "interrogates without over-earnestness, answers without desire to exhibit his wisdom, does not interrupt a profitable speaker nor presumptuously put in a word of his own." Nothing could better illustrate the sense of this chapter nor describe the meaning of monastic courtesy.

CHAPTER 50

OF BRETHREN WHO ARE WORKING AT A DISTANCE FROM THE ORATORY OR ARE ON A JOURNEY

This and the chapter following fit together; they have no essential connection with what has gone before or with what is to come after. Each raises practical questions which elicit conflicting opinions from the commentators. But though they may fail in providing a guide to the conduct of monks who work and travel in the twentieth century, they state a point of view which cannot be mistaken.

Those brethren who work at a great distance and cannot come to the oratory at the proper time, the abbot judging such to be reasonable, should perform the *opus Dei* there where they are working, bending their knees in fear before God. In the same way let not the appointed hours pass them by who are sent on a journey. But as far as they can let them perform them there and not neglect to pay their debt of service.

Since it is the abbot who has sent them out to work, it must be the abbot who decides whether the distance excuses the working monks from choir at any given office or not. The presumption is that *longe ab oratorio* means far enough to involve considerable waste of time, and possibly waste of money too, in the journey to and fro. But from the point of view of the subject the only ques-

tion at issue is that of the abbot's wish. Thus in a climax of the
work entrusted to him, the monk does not have to ask himself
about the material loss or gain which will result from his decision
but only whether the abbot would wish him to stop on or come
back to choir. The one consideration may well clarify the other,
but the first consideration is the abbot's mind and not the mind of
the man on the spot. This admittedly is not the view which the
world would allow; it is the view of faith. Monasteries are
places of faith. The system of acting on "presumed permission" is
regulated by faith and not by common sense. There is a difference
between what is reasonably presumed in the light of faith and
what is presumed solely in the light of reason without reference
to the supernatural.

Moralists tell us that for a religious to presume permission
there must be serious reason to do so, that the competent authority
cannot be consulted, and that the circumstances are reported afterwards. Failing these conditions, the act is one of disobedience
more or less grave according to the relevant matter. In the issue
under review, namely the dispensation from the Divine Office in
choir, the fact that the *opus Dei* is to be said *cum tremore divino
flectentes genua* by those whom obedience obliges to be absent
is proof of the reverence with which it is meant to be treated.
If those who are told by the abbot to stay away are to be so
punctilious in their observance, is there not something more than
a hint to those who are wondering whether or not they need
come back to choir?

From the text it would certainly appear that St. Benedict intended the whole choir ceremonial to be observed when making
up Office. This was the practice in Pachomian and Basilian monasteries, and in some monasteries of today it is the custom still.
When one, or all, of the little hours must be said in the fields, the
monks take up their positions facing one another in two lines and
proceed as in choir.

St. Benedict mentions journeys. But here he allows a wider
margin. "As far as they can," he says, "let them render the hours
in the same way." This may mean at the times when they would
be rendering the hours in the monastery, or it may mean with

the observance of the rubrics as before; or it may mean both. The argument brought against the recitation according to normal performance at home is certainly strengthened by the comparatively late appearance of breviaries. Could St. Benedict possibly have meant his monks when travelling to carry with them the large manuscript books such as were used in choir?

Admitting that in spite of the ease of modern travel we have departed far in our day from the standards set by our ancestors in religion, is there nothing of a practical kind that we can learn from this chapter? From its forthright instructions we can at least learn to pay more attention to the safeguards of recollection in this matter of saying Office when working away from the monastery or when on a journey. By judicious planning we should be able to secure fitting places and times for what after all is our main work as monks. Though we are encouraged to anticipate the hours of the Divine Office—and undoubtedly it is better to do this than to leave them till the last moment when they have to be said one after the other and in a rush—we are not expected to advance the recitations so generously as to make nonsense of the liturgical distribution. It cannot be judged liturgically decent, for example, on the grounds that a busy day lies ahead, to say Compline before breakfast. This is not circumspection but caricature.

The truth is that, good though our reasons may be, once we step out of our normal monastic frame set by the hours in choir we have to walk with infinite caution. The mere fact of working under obedience when away from the monastery does not minimize the need for vigilance. Obedience sanctifies the increased vigilance in much the same way that poverty sanctifies increased detachment, and chastity sanctifies increased purity of heart. The monastic vows and virtues do not excuse from the common duties of the monk, and still less do they cancel one another out. They combine to reinforce the monastic duties. This is seen, in the matter immediately under discussion, how work done outside the enclosure is directly affected by the two other Benedictine vows besides that of obedience. Without a grasp of stability and conversion of manners, the monk working away from home will come to belittle, and ultimately to sin against, his vow of obedience.

Recognition of this unified principle, together with the all-round vigilance which it entails, must animate the monk in all that he undertakes. Such a habit of mind comes of the practice of recollection, which again is essentially linked up with what we are at present considering. It means a recollection and custody of the senses which, as Dom Jean de Monléon insists in his *Degrés de L'Humilité*, may never be relaxed, "ni à la campagne, si l'on va travailler dans une terre éloignée; ni dans le chemin, si l'on part en voyage. Les voyages, et même les allées et venues hors du monastère, sont dangereux pour l'état religieux. On y gaspille aisément ce qu'on a acquis dans la clôture; la multiplicité des choses que l'on y voit, les conversations que l'on y attend, le commerce que l'on est forcé d'entretenir avec les séculiers ont vite fait d'éventer l'âme, si l'on n'a soin de conserver un maintien effacé et un esprit recueilli."[1]

[1] P. 310.

OF BRETHREN WHO DO NOT
GO FAR AWAY

The foregoing chapter arranged for the rendering of the Divine Office when away; this one arranges for meals. The ruling is clear; it is the penalty of breaking the rule that causes some confusion. But, in this chapter as in the other, the main thing is the attitude which prompts the regulation. If this is faithfully interpreted, the regulation will be adequately observed.

Brethren who go out on any business and who expect to return to the monastery on the same day must not presume to eat abroad, even though they be asked by anyone at all, unless permission be given by their abbot. If they do otherwise let them be excommunicated.

This is the whole chapter; its clauses must be separately examined. First it is assumed that absence from enclosure is never a casual outing but always an excursion of some necessity. Such a necessity may be occasioned by either charity, the business of the house, or health. Again the abbot may judge that a day in the open or with secular friends may be, for a particular subject undergoing particular difficulties, a necessary preventative measure: it may be holding off a breakdown. In these circumstances it is for the subject, realizing that Bellerophon has to come down to earth on Pegasus from time to time, to humble himself and accept in a spirit of obedience what is conceded to his weakness.

Next there is the ban on meals taken with layfolk, *etiamsi a quovis rogentur*. Again the title of the chapter must be borne in mind; if the journey were a long one, involving a night or more away from the monastery, it would be impossible to avoid having meals with seculars. For setting out on a day's trip, however, the monk has to provide himself with one of three things: supplies of food from the monastery, special permission from the abbot to waive the prescription in the Rule, or the stamina necessary to go fasting until his return to the monastery in the evening.

An incident from the *Dialogues* so exactly illustrates St. Benedict's mind on this subject as to be worth quoting in full. "It was the custom of the monastery that the brethren, sent abroad about any business, should neither eat nor drink anything outside their cloister. This in the practice of the Rule being carefully observed, one day some brethren upon due occasion went abroad and were forced to stay later than expected; they rested accordingly and refreshed themselves in the house of a certain devout woman of their acquaintance. Returning late to the monastery, they asked, as was the custom, the abbot's blessing. He straightway demanded of them, 'Where dined you?' They answered, 'Nowhere.' To whom he said, 'Why do you lie? Did you not go into such a woman's house? Did you not eat there such and such, drank you not so much?' When the holy Father had told them not only the woman's lodging, the several sorts of meats, the number of cups, they in great terror fell down at his feet and with acknowledgment of all that they had done confessed their fault. But he straightway pardoned them, persuading himself that they would never afterwards attempt the like in his absence, knowing he was always with them in spirit."[1]

Abbot Delatte cites a dialogue held between a monk and his abbot in the *Rule of the Master* where the circumstances are enumerated in which monks should accept or refuse invitations.[2] Dom Delatte further expresses his misgivings about the reasons which monks are inclined to give for eating abroad. "Men sometimes employ the pretext of edification; but is not the edification

[1] Bk. 2; ch. 12.
[2] Ch. 61.

much more real when we are only rarely seen? Would not people of the world be rather surprised that monks should accept invitations so readily? . . . our holy Father wishes that at every instant and in every place the monk should remain a monk, and preserve all that he can of his profession. Let us beware of thinking that once we are outside the monastery it is good manners to walk, look, and act as do men of the world and to be monks only in dress."[3]

"He cannot be a monk," says another Benedictine abbot, Tritheim, "who frequents the assemblies of men. He who delights in cities has not yet tasted the delights of the monastic life. You who are a monk ought not to desert the solitude of the monastery without good and reasonable motive."[4]

[3] *Op. cit.*, p. 326.
[4] *Homilies*, 6.

CHAPTER 52

OF THE ORATORY OF THE MONASTERY

In the case of some of St. Benedict's chapters more is told us of the negative than of the positive aspect of the particular ruling. The positive is frequently taught by implication rather than by explicit statement. Here, in the present chapter, the method is to proclaim the doctrine and then to reinforce it by prohibitions regarding contrary practice. This is shown in the arrangement of the opening sentences.

> Let the oratory be what it is called; and let nothing else be done or kept there.

The oratory is a *locus orationis*, and must be kept as such. We are not left to draw our own conclusions from a description of what the oratory is not. If it is the house of God and the place where He is praised by prayer, reverence demands that the oratory should be exclusively this. It is not to be used as a convenient passage from one part of the establishment to another. It is not an art gallery or a museum. On the grounds that the churches of God are worthy of the noblest adornment, and that the most beautiful works of man's hand find fitting rest in and around the sanctuary, monastic oratories can become show places and so lose something, if not the whole, of their primary purpose.

If it is paying mistaken homage to God's house to fill it up with *objets d'art*, it is not paying homage to it at all to turn it into a

concert hall, a broadcast studio, or a stage set for the use of television. Its peace must be cherished, and to admit the apparatus of
musical or other entertainment is inevitably to disturb its peace.
Furthermore it is one thing to admit a congregation to the service
of God—lay people who want to witness from the body of the
church and take part as far as they can in the *opus Dei* as performed in choir—and quite another to admit an audience that has
come for recreation and distraction.

If St. Pachomius allowed mats to be woven during the psalmody,[1] St. Benedict knows no such custom in his monasteries. If
little meals were sometimes eaten in churches during St. Augustine's time,[2] St. Benedict can be counted a narrow reformer. The
oratory is for one thing only, and *nec ibi quidquid aliud geratur
aut condatur*. Thus to keep any personal belongings beyond the
books needed for the Divine Office in the oratory would be to
offend against this injunction. There is a sacristy outside the oratory where odd objects may be left for a while, and there is a
cowl-room where a hurriedly discarded coat or cloak may be
hung. Neither side-chapels nor the less conspicuous alcoves of
the oratory should be allowed to serve as left-luggage offices or
cloak-rooms.

> When the *opus Dei* is finished let all go out in the ut-
> most silence, and let reverence be paid to God. So that a
> brother who may wish to pray by himself will not be
> hindered by another's importunity.

The withdrawal from choir must be a thing of dignity, of solemnity even. It is to be so performed as to preserve the recollection
of the foregoing hour and to promote further recollection in
whatever work is to come next. To leave choir silently, as the
Rule prescribes, requires a measure of self-discipline. Often if the
Office has been prolonged, the temptation is to skuttle out of
choir as quickly as possible. "Mustn't miss a moment" is a quite
mistaken approach to the Benedictine horarium. Moments need
never be missed if they are spent in God's presence. St. Benedict's

[1] *Regula*, 5;7.
[2] *Confessions*, 6;2.

whole Rule is designed, as already repeatedly stressed, to engender
that setting of soul which looks always towards God.

"We have not been commanded to work unceasingly or to
watch and fast unceasingly," says Evagrius, the Basilian monk of
Pontus, "but the law requires of us in the words of the Apostle
to pray unceasingly." The particular hour which has just been
recited may be over, but the effects of the *opus Dei* go on. The
sound of words is finished but the prayer can go on. Just as in
the act of throwing a stone a man ceases to throw when the stone
leaves his hand, so in the act of praying the Office a man ceases
his effort to produce the sound of it when the final prayers have
been said. But as the stone goes on into the air when the physical
act has ceased, so prayer can go on when the physical act has
ceased.

"I sat down under the shadow of him whom I desired, and his
fruit was sweet to my palate," sings the bride in the Canticles,[3]
but when this phase of the relationship was done there was rest
and silence which might not be disturbed. The voice of the liturgy
gives place to the stillness of recollection.

The reference to "a brother wishing to pray by himself" gives
an indication which must not be belittled. It may reasonably be
assumed that St. Benedict is not thinking here of a visit to the
oratory, spontaneous and lasting no more than two or three minutes, but of sustained mental prayer. This is confirmed by the
paragraph which follows in the text.

> But if another wish to pray by himself, let him go in
> with simplicity and pray, not with a loud voice but with
> tears and fervour of heart. And let him who is not similarly
> occupied be not permitted to stay on in the oratory after
> the *opus Dei*, lest another should be hindered as has been
> said.

From the fourth chapter in the *Dialogues* we know that the
practice of mental prayer as a set exercise was established in St.
Benedict's day. "In one of those monasteries which he had built
thereabout," records St. Gregory, "was a certain monk who

[3] 2;3.

could not stay at his prayers, but, so soon as he saw his brethren kneel and dispose themselves for their mental prayer, he would go out." From the same chapter we learn that this prayer was a daily occurrence and that St. Benedict was accustomed to pray at this time, immediately after the Office, together with his brethren.

So, despite the meagre information about it which can be gleaned from the Rule, there seems to be no doubt about the place which mental prayer occupied in the daily life of St. Benedict's monasteries. "C'était la pratique commune de ses monastères. Il recommande formellement de ne pas prolonger cette oraison en commun, de peur de fatiguer les frères dont le goût pour la prière se trouve déjà épuisé par la longueur des Offices. Ceux que la grâce sollicite vers une contemplation plus longue ont toute facilité de suivre leur attrait; c'est le désir formel du bienheureux Patriarche et une tradition constante de son Ordre."[4]

The gift of contemplative prayer may come through the liturgy, but it is not likely to come through the liturgy alone. The combined work of liturgical and mental prayer disposes the soul for the graces of contemplation. We have noted on an earlier page that to speak of the contemplative life and the active life is often to mislead; it is not misleading to speak of contemplative and discursive prayer. Contemplative prayer is a particular kind of prayer, quite different from discursive prayer, while the contemplative life is largely what we make it.

There are, as Dom van Houtryve observes, many who are incessantly waving the banner of contemplation and who really do very little contemplating. "Contemplation is for them a veil which sometimes covers up a certain indolence, or at least a lack of occupation."[5] The ideal is to preserve the wise balance which makes men who are in the way of contemplative prayer active in God's service, and men who are active by nature and attraction contemplative in their desire. Monks are meant to be men of contemplation *and* action. The terms are not mutually exclusive.

[4] Dom Besse, *Le Moine Bénédictin*, p. 171.
[5] *Op. cit.*, p. 209.

CHAPTER 53

OF THE RECEPTION OF GUESTS

Putting hospitality on the highest supernatural plane, St. Benedict recognizes a twofold necessity: first that of seeing Christ in
all who come to the monastery, second that of preserving the
peace of the community. The balance must be struck between
turning the whole house into a hospice in the name of charity,
and keeping visitors at a distance in the name of solitude.

> Let all guests that come be received as Christ Himself,
> for He will say, "I was a stranger and you took Me in."
> And let fitting honour be shown to all, especially however
> to such as are of the household of the faith and to pilgrims.
> When therefore a guest is announced, let him be met by the
> superior or brethren with all marks of charity.

The duties of hospitality have been stressed in both religious
and pagan literature since long before Christian times. But with
the coming of the Gospel a new motive has entered in, and the
recognition of Christ in the person of the guest is an ideal which
necessarily recommended itself forcibly to early Christian monasticism. When wanderers in the desert were plentiful, and when
the old Eastern tradition of welcoming strangers was strong, the
monks developed a profound sense of responsibility towards all
who came asking for shelter. St. Benedict inherited this tradition,
further amplifying its commitments.

The pilgrim in Italy was probably as familiar a sight as the nomad in the desert. To sleep out under the sky in Italy would have been hardly more agreeable than to spend the night in the open in Scete. Bandits were as numerous in the West as in the East, inns were as scarce, roads were as bad. We are not surprised to learn from St. Benedict (later in this chapter) that in sixth-century Italy "guests are never lacking in the monastery." Two centuries are to pass before Hildemar wryly contrasts the mere trickle of guests in St. Benedict's day with the increasing flood in his own. During the eighth and ninth centuries the numbers of pilgrims, vagrants, travellers of all sorts who sought monastic hospitality were so large that Theodulf's testy pen is found to complain, "If St. Benedict were living now, by God he would close the door against them."[1] But this is no more than the sputtering of an exasperated scholar disturbed at his studies by the importunity of visitors. For the most part the monks of this time, as of other times, were faithful to the traditions.

Fitting honour is to be shown to all, says the Rule explicitly. This is because in all there is something of the image of God, something of Christ. Exception would be made only in the case of those whose presence in the monastery might give scandal. St. Jerome is for keeping out heretics, but perhaps he means combative, vociferous heretics. If today in England we refused hospitality to heretics, we would be sealing off an avenue of approach to the Church; but then we mean the reasonable kinds of heretics who are ready to learn.

Delatte quotes the *Rule of the Master* as demanding security measures in relation to guests: two of the brethren were to sleep in the guest-house and to see that the doors were locked. In those houses where it was still a point of honour not to question their guests on the motives which brought them to the monastery, morning would sometimes find the guest quarters emptied of guests and bedding.

Fellow Catholics are singled out, together with pilgrims, for St. Benedict's special attention. This has the backing of St. Jerome, who warns against the reproach merited by the inn-keepers of Bethlehem. Does this mean that monasteries are ex-

[1] Quoted by Schroll, *op. cit.*, p. 147.

pected to extend hospitality to women? If it does, then special buildings must be provided for them outside the enclosure. This was what was done at Cluny, and there is evidence of the same arrangement in several of our English pre-Reformation monasteries. It became part of the social policy of the monks during the later Middle Ages to shelter Catholics, women therefore as well as men and boys, against feudal injustice and barbarian invasion. Monasteries accordingly became—though in respect to their remote and not to their immediate monastic enclosures—alms-houses, hospitals, hostelries, and havens of refuge generally.

Not only have monasteries from the earliest antiquity been expected to cater for pilgrims who stop for a night or two and then pass on towards the shrine which is the object of their journey, but some monasteries have themselves become centres of pilgrimage—of set purpose attracting crowds to their shrines. Einsiedeln and Montserrat are repeating today what was being done in earlier times at Fulda, Vézelay, St. Augustine's of Canterbury, Bury St. Edmund's and other abbeys up and down Europe.

Indiscriminate hospitality has other drawbacks besides that of risk to property and reputation. One disadvantage is that it is easy for monastic hosts to behave towards the less privileged among their guests with an air of patronage, easy for them to be selective, easy to be guided—which means being ruled—by considerations of class. This is the supreme worldliness: the virtual repudiation of spiritual values.

Why is it that St. Benedict attaches so much importance to the need for filling positions in the community with spiritual men? From the abbot downwards to the doorkeeper, the man who has to deal with people must be a spiritual man. Why not an able man? Why not an abbot who is good with money, and a doorkeeper who can sniff an impostor the moment he sees him? The answer is simply that St. Benedict wants above all to guard against the spirit of naturalism and rationalism. He knows that if his officials are liable to be swayed in their judgments by material and worldly considerations, it means an end to the supernatural life of the monastery.

All who come in contact with the guests, then, and particularly of course the guestmaster, will need to remind themselves of St. Benedict's identification. But if it is not always easy for the monk to maintain the ideal, nor is it always easy for the guest.

The Rule is naturally more concerned about the dispositions of the brethren than those of the guests, but even viewing the matter from the brethren's angle allowance must be made for the guests' imperfect awareness of the role which they are expected to assume. It would be a mistake for the brethren to expect too much in the way of gratitude from their guests, too much in the way of voluntary labour or even of attendance in church at the Mass and at the Divine Office. Most lay guests are wholly ignorant of the inwardness of their status: they do not *know* that they are being received as Christ. To have been welcomed at the door *a priore vel a fratribus cum omni officio charitatis* may have caused the guest some surprise, but unless he has read the Rule or is particularly intuitive he will not see what underlies it all.

> Let them first pray together, and thus associate with one another in peace. But the kiss of peace must not be given until prayer has gone before, on account of the delusions of the devil. And in the salutation itself let all humility be shown. At the arrival or departure of guests . . . let Christ be adored in them by bowing the head or even prostrating.

Readiness to pray, with the monks and in the oratory, is evidence of the visitor's *bona fide*. Allusion in the text to the deceits of the devil may either mean that without prayer going before—without the antitoxin, as it were—the kiss of peace might be given to the devil disguised, or it might mean that the devil could use the kiss as a passport into the monastery without having to endure the ordeal of prayer.

Already by the eighth century the hospitality extended to monastery guests had arranged itself according to whether the visitors were of the nobility, were monks of other houses, were poor. "The commentators appear to be conscious of some departure from the letter of the Rule," says Schroll, and "instead of recognizing that changed conditions demand an alteration in the practice, they attempt to explain the words of the Rule in the light of current practice. The result is somewhat strained and superficial." The result always is; but the same attempt has been made, with regard to one or other practice, all down the centuries. "The principle underlying the practice appears to be based largely on good sense," the same authority goes on, "and allowing for altered times, the practice is not greatly out of harmony with the Rule."[2] So there is probably a valid excuse.

> When the guests have been received . . . let the superior or anyone whom he may appoint sit with them. Let the divine law be read to the guest for his edification, and afterwards let all kindness be shown him. Let the superior break his fast for the sake of the guest, unless it happens to be a principal fast-day which may not be broken. The brethren however shall observe their accustomed fasting.

The custom of submitting the guest to the discipline of being read to almost immediately on arrival was a common one in monasteries before St. Benedict's time. It had a twofold purpose, acting partly as a hint that the ensuing days spent in the monastery were to be regarded as in the nature of a retreat, and partly as a means of drawing the stranger into the community routine and so making him feel more at home.

The *humanitas* to be shown to guests is the term used by Cassian in more than one place, and the fact that the superior is to dispense himself from the ordinary monastic fasts, though not from the fasts of the Church, in his performance of hospitality would indicate that St. Benedict meant the word to be interpreted practically and not as a general exhortation only.

> Let the abbot pour water on the hands of the guests; let both the abbot and the whole community wash the feet of all guests. When they have been washed let them say this verse: *Suscepimus, Deus, misericordiam tuam in medio templi tui.* Let special care and solicitude be shown in the reception of the poor and of pilgrims, because in them Christ is more received. The very fear which we have of the rich procures them honour.

[2] *Op. cit.*, p. 148.

There are passages in the Rule which cause us to admit our poor service, to acknowledge that we no longer even attempt this or that point of observance, perhaps to ask pardon and a blessing, to blush and pass on. This is one such passage. While it is the custom in many monasteries for the abbot still to wash his guests' hands outside the refectory before a meal on the day of their arrival, the ceremony of washing the feet has everywhere been dropped. As Delatte observes, "We must honour our guests, not embarrass them." But it may be noted in passing that the full observance survived at least until the tenth century. Cluny was very particular about it.

The *Rule of the Master*, its date uncertain but roughly in the era of St. Benedict, prescribes a regimen of work for guests who are able-bodied and who stay longer than two days.[3] This is more strict than the observance in Nitrian monasteries, which allowed their guests a week's grace. In later centuries customaries were drawn up which regulated for the employment of the guests' time, for the hours at which they were expected to get up and go to bed, for the amount of silence they were meant to keep. But none of this is in the Rule. Wide discretionary powers are left to the abbot and his appointed guestmaster. The only stipulation made by St. Benedict in the entertainment of guests is that they should eat in a room apart from the community refectory:

> Let the kitchen for the abbot and guests be on its own by itself; so that guests who are never lacking in a monastery may not, coming at uncertain hours, disturb the brethren. Let two brothers who are able to fulfil this duty well be placed in this kitchen for a year. If they need it, let help be afforded them that they may serve without murmuring. On the other hand, when they have not much to occupy them let them go forth to other work wherever they are bidden.

As late as the latter part of the eighth century, and probably later, laymen were not admitted to monastic refectories. The practical and economic difficulties of having two kitchens and two refectories—and if the ruling contained in the thirty-sixth

[3] Delatte, *op. cit.*, p. 338.

chapter about provision for the sick was carried out another kitchen must be added—brought about a compromise: guests and abbot ate in the community refectory but at a separate table. Perhaps they ate at a different hour and were served with different food. But the one kitchen sufficed.

With the simplification just mentioned, the arrangement about kitchen servers came to be altered. The general injunctions, however, still applied: the servers were to work without grumbling, were to be given help when this was necessary, were to be directed to other departments when work happened to be slack.

> Not only with regard to them, but also in all the offices of the monastery let this consideration be shown, so that when they need it help may be given them, and again when they are unoccupied they may do what they are bidden. Moreover, let a brother whose soul is possessed by the fear of the Lord have the guest-house assigned to his care. Let there be enough beds provided there. And let the house of God be wisely governed by wise men.

Again the Rule shows this solicitude for the overworked. More strictly the solicitude is for those who are saddened by the work which they feel to be too much for them. Overwork as such need be no evil; the evil lies in the effect which it may produce on the spirit.

In the same way to be unoccupied, *as such*, may be no evil. It may be the means of drawing the soul to the interior life. The evil lies in the listlessness which it can produce in the spirit. So to avoid the two extremes, the Rule provides for additional help in the one case and alternative employment in the other.

Presiding over the guest-house is a brother who fears God. Only a lively sense of God can protect the guestmaster from the harmful occasions which go with his office. He will often have to be absent from the monk's supreme safeguard, the *opus Dei*. His dealings will be mostly with worldly people who will want him to share their interests and will probably invite him to share their amusements. He will be deprived of the company of his own brethren, and so will miss the kind of social life which is best for him as a monk. His patience will constantly be tried, his recollection disturbed, his periods of mental prayer interrupted. Consequently he will need to be a man of mature spirituality.

Guests who come to a monastery may sometimes see no other monk apart from the guestmaster. The impression which they form of monasticism is the impression conveyed, more often than not, by one man. It is human nature to judge of a movement, of an ideology, of an institution, by the people representing it: we tend to think of the idea in terms of the individual rather than the individual in terms of the idea. Either way you look at it, the guestmaster has more than himself to consider: he is all the time attracting to the ideal or deflecting from it.

It is sometimes the temptation of guestmasters to give too much of themselves to their guests. There are reserves in the soul of the monk which are for God alone, and it is a false charity which urges a self-giving so complete as to leave nothing over for the essential monastic life. It may well be in the plan of God that guests should become attached to the one who interprets for them the ways of the spirit, but it would be rash for the guestmaster to presume that he could safely reciprocate such attachments. There is a difference between being interested in those whom we are appointed to serve, and being absorbed by them.

Another pitfall which lies open to the incautious guestmaster is that of affecting a manner. The manner that is calculated to edify is no less to be avoided than the manner which outdoes the man of the world in worldliness. Each is a sign of untruth, each shows a desire either to cover up what is there or to compensate for what is not there. Another form of pride will show itself in the false humility of roughness. There is an inverted snobbery which makes men of breeding and education play the bucolic. To men of true humility the temptation to an assumed rusticity does not present itself, but to the vain anything and everything must minister to their vanity.

The guestmaster, in order to give to his guests what they come for, has no need to make a cult of anything—whether of scholarship, mysticism, sophistication or their opposites—but has great need to be himself. If, as St. Benedict means him to be, he is a man of God, the apostolate of the guest-house is assured.

> Let a monk who is not bidden to do so on no account associate or speak with the guests. But if he chance to meet them, let him, after humbly saluting them as we have said, pass on, saying that he is not allowed to talk with a guest.

Dom Delatte says of this concluding paragraph to the long chapter about guests that it "gives us St. Benedict's whole mind on the character and measure of our relations with the outside world. Hospitality as here described in this chapter is a duty of faith, since it is our Lord whom we receive in the person of guests; a duty of charity and also an apostolate . . . but St. Benedict would have this inner apostolate harmonize with the essential conditions of our life, so that the practice of charity may never impair peace and observance."[4]

Once granted that prayer is the whole life of the monk, the needs of hospitality find their place in the perspective of recollection, the choir, solitude. "All apostleship demands three things: word, example, prayer," writes St. Bernard to Baldwin, Abbot of Rieti, "and of these three prayer is the most important; it is prayer which obtains the grace and efficacy of word and example."[5] It is precisely to prevent the flood of words from drowning the good effects of example and prayer that St. Benedict makes his provisions in the Rule about the brethren excusing themselves from associating with guests.

A monastery teaches by its prayer and by its life; the words spoken by the monks are incidental. The words of monks are not as powerful as their silence. Unless as monks we believe that there is an apostolic and social value to our prayer, our silence, our solitude, we shall be constantly drawn to leave these fundamental elements of our profession in the effort to reach our neighbour by more direct and active expressions of our charity.

[4] *Op. cit.*, pp. 340-1.
[5] *Epis.*, 201.

CHAPTER 54

WHETHER A MONK OUGHT TO
RECEIVE LETTERS OR TOKENS

The sequence in St. Benedict's mind is surely this: contact with the world through the entertainment of guests leads on to contact with the world through correspondence and the exchange of presents. (In failing to see the connection between this and the foregoing chapter, Dom Delatte misses a beat for the first and only time in his tremendous orchestration.) The monks who are told on one page not to talk with externs are told on the next not to write to them. The rule about humbly saluting such guests as are met in the house or grounds, explaining to them that conversation is not allowed, and then passing on, is echoed in the rule about how to deal with what is delivered at the cell by the generosity of friends.

> On no account shall it be lawful for a monk to receive, either from his parents or from anyone else, or from his brethren, letters, tokens, or any little gifts whatsoever, or to give them to others, without the permission of his abbot. And if anything be sent to him, even by his parents, let him not presume to receive it, except the circumstance have first been made known to the abbot.

As regards presents, given or accepted, the monastic tradition is consistent: the Rules of St. Pachomius and St. Caesarius forbid explicitly all exchanges of this sort, and Cassian, St. Augustine,

St. Jerome and many of the desert Fathers indirectly condemn the practice by pointing out the evils to which it gives rise.

To give is the tacit assumption of ownership, so if a monk has renounced the power to possess he has equally renounced the right to give. Having given everything to God, we have no possessions that we can give to our friends. "Put me as a seal upon thy heart," the Beloved commands us, "as a seal upon thy arm."[1] Not only do our affections belong to Him but so also do the works of our hands. Whatever is given away, however small the gift, must come not from the individual but from the community represented by the individual. If people outside were to imagine that we were capable of personal benefactions, they would be right in wondering about the meaning of religious poverty. The obligation of having to get the abbot's permission to give anything away safeguards the practice; the principle and the spirit can never be altogether safeguarded. Only response to grace in prayer and obedience can give a man the feel of this matter.

For most religious the question of receiving is less troublesome than that of giving. We refer the present to the superior and leave the next step to him. It is true that we can complicate the issue by manoeuvering ourselves into the position of grateful recipients, hinting for this and that from our friends, but the art of indirect persuasion is not confined to the question of accepting presents: it touches most matters which have to do with getting permission. Again the man of prayer will know at once when he is beginning to angle for favours, to edge towards promotion, to canvass for election. Certainly the man of prayer, if he needs a thing, will ask for it of the superior. If it comes to him as a present from outside, he will not hesitate to get permission for it. He will not wheedle. It is a point of monastic etiquette, moreover, that the goods received are not put into use until after the sanction has been obtained. To anticipate the permission is an assumption not only of ownership but of judgment.

So much for presents, but what about letters? Since for most monks the business of correspondence is a great burden and a

[1] Cant. 8;6.

great bore, it may be more a matter of mortification than one of worldliness that is at stake. Be this as it may, the Rule is against a correspondence, and that is that. Allowing that charity and the needs of spiritual direction may legitimately involve a monk in the work of reading and writing letters, we may conclude from St. Benedict's words, as from the monastic tradition generally, that it is no part of the Benedictine vocation to encourage this contact with the outside world. Delusions lie hidden in the mailbag, and it will be nobody's fault but our own if we have to pay the penalty of having persuaded ourselves against the plain meaning of St. Benedict's text.

> If the abbot order it to be accepted, let it be in the abbot's power to appoint to whom it shall be given. Nor let the brother to whom it happens to have been sent be grieved . . . should anyone presume to act otherwise, let him be subjected to the discipline of the Rule.

At first sight this ruling appears to affect the particular case and to have no immediate bearing upon the principle. But perhaps the reason for bringing in the particular case at all is that the principle is emphasized by the illustration. So little claim may the monk lay to objects of personal use—this is the argument—that he would have no right to complain if presents sent directly to him were handed over to others. It is as if St. Benedict is suggesting a hypothetical case as witness to his meaning. Certainly it must be a rare occurrence in any monastery when the abbot says, "No, you may not have this; go and give it from me to that brother over there."

CHAPTER 55

OF THE CLOTHES AND SHOES OF
THE BRETHREN

Opening on a note of humanity and discretion, this chapter
carries over from the foregoing the thought of poverty. Having
just attacked, and not for the first time, the evil of *proprietas* or
opus peculiare, St. Benedict develops the theme by stating what
he regards as necessary for the monk's physical well-being. Not
only is the monk's wardrobe, item by item, investigated but
his bedding also is legislated for, and the conditions to be observed
as regards clothing when the monk is sent on a journey. With its
wealth of detail it is a long chapter, but since some of it has been
commented on already in other connections it can for the most
part be treated briefly.

> Let clothing be given to the brethren suitable to the na-
> ture and the climate of the place where they live; for in
> cold regions more is required, in warm regions less. It shall
> be the abbot's duty therefore to consider this.

Did St. Benedict, then, take it for granted that his Rule would
spread, and that geographical considerations would have to be
allowed for when determining the kind of clothes to be worn by
the monks? Some commentators accept the text in this sense,
advancing it as proof of St. Benedict's wide vision and foresight.
Others suggest that the variations of temperature which exist
between Monte Cassino and other, not far distant, parts of Italy

would be quite enough to warrant the references to *frigidis* and *calidis regionibus*. So we do not know.

If it was the abbot's duty and nobody else's to determine the amount of clothes a monk might have for his use, it is curious to find that at Murbach in the eighth century those who were able to do so made their own clothes.[1] In the same monastery, and for the benefit of those who were inadept in the craft, monks were trained in tailoring so that none might go without. It would have been easier to control the quantity of garments which were received with permission at the hands of the monastery tailor than what was made privately in the cell. Hildemar, contemporaneously, restricts the wearing of fur to those whose condition, in the abbot's opinion, warranted the concession. From Monte Cassino Warnefrid wrote to Charlemagne saying that only the old were allowed to wear the pelisse, but it seems that in the century following (witness the Monastic Capitulary of 817) the permission to wear pelisse and gaiters was extended to all.[2] But there was still, as we shall see, plenty of margin in the matter of dress for the abbot to exercise his right of veto.

> We think, however, that in temperate climates a cowl and a tunic should suffice for each monk: the cowl to be of thick stuff in winter, but in summer something worn and thin. Likewise a scapular for work, and shoes and stockings to cover the feet.

But allowing for differences of cut, colour, and material, there was a distinctive costume worn by monks of pre-Benedictine times, and St. Benedict had no desire to break away from the tradition. The habit has the twofold purpose of warning people in the world what to expect of the man who is wearing it, and of warning the man who is wearing it that he must behave in a particular way. The monk who on the least excuse exchanges the habit for secular clerical dress may not be offending against his

---

[1] *Statutes of Murbach*, Albers, 3;84.
[2] These and other domestic details which will be found in the course of the present chapter are taken from Schroll's *Benedictine Monasticism*, already frequently cited. The relevant pages here are 41-47.

state, but it is not here a question of status so much as of standard. The monk on the other hand who, while avoiding exhibitionism, is reluctant to discard the habit without good reason—and the eighth degree of humility will give him a yardstick by which to measure the reason—can at least be sure that he is hiding nothing of his profession. We should be ready to carry about with us our religious character as others are ready to show the signs of their military, legal, medical or educational callings.

St. Benedict makes the habit consist of cowl and tunic. Originally the cowl was the hood only, covering the head and extending no lower, at most, than the shoulders. But by *cuculla* St. Benedict probably means the whole outer dress with hood attached. Under the cowl St. Benedict legislates for a tunic. Palladius speaks of leather tunics, and St. Pachomius of fleece-lined tunics which were worn also for sleeping in at night. St. Benedict's light-weight tunic was designed with a view to work indoors and out, with the cowl to fit over it as an extra which could be removed when getting in the way.

St. Benedict's is the first mention of the scapular. If the garment was in use before St. Benedict's time, it must have been called something else. It seems to have been a hooded overall or apron, used for work and acting as protection to cowl or tunic. The monks of Cluny—partly on the antiquarian grounds that there was no telling what it was, and partly because their choir duties left them little time for manual work—did not use the scapular.

Of the shoes and stockings mentioned in the Rule little need be said. The word *pedules* is probably nearer to shoes than *caligas* is to socks. What the Carthusians wear today are buskins tied high up the leg and at the foot tucked into loose shoes or boots: this may be much what was worn by the first Benedictines. But there is no knowing, and the controversies on this subject are not made easier when we read that the monks of St. Equitius did their field labour in *caligae* (translated in our text by "socks") which were nailed—*clavatae*.

Of all these things and their colour and coarseness let not the monks complain, but let them be such as can be got in the region where they live or can be bought most cheaply. Let the abbot be careful about their size, that the garments be not short for those who wear them but that they may fit well.

We can believe that any idea of fashion in the monastery was odious to St. Benedict. Earlier writers than St. Benedict had banned the discussion of clothes among monks, and we know from the history of religious orders how harmful to the true spirit can be a preoccupation with the cut, colour, and design of the religious habit. Instinctively we shrink from the picture of a monk with pins in his mouth and a piece of chalk in his hand draping a monastic model with different-coloured materials. St. Benedict's robust approach blows away such conceptions instantly. Always in the religious life the superficial must be left for the real; the aesthetic can be a danger to the true.

If the kingdom of heaven is not in meat and drink, neither is it in white or black. Economy and local supply, not texture and shade, should determine the habit. "Let the habit of the monk be such as may cover the body," says Cassian in a passage which matches that of St. Benedict for its no-nonsense directness, "not such as may foster the seeds of vanity . . . not what may please the fancy, but commonplace, so that it may not be thought remarkable for novelty of colour or fashion among other men of the same profession."[3] In this chapter Cassian goes on to warn against the opposite error of cultivating a coarseness in dress which is ostentatious. He disapproves of a "robe of sackcloth as being conspicuous, and from this very fact will not only confer no benefit upon the soul but rather minister to vanity and pride . . . but even if we hear of some good men who have dressed in this garb, a rule for the monasteries is not therefore to be disregarded."

Fastidiousness is still fastidiousness whether it is directed to good tailoring or bad, to smooth materials or rough. A certain superior once said in the hearing of the present writer: "What an expense to a community these ascetics are—with their homespun habits from Scotland and their boots of undressed leather."

[3] *Institutes*, Bk. 1; ch. 2.

St. Benedict's *vilius comparari* is the bar to which questions of doubt should be brought for judgment; nor should his ruling be prejudiced by the phrase—that last-ditch excuse of the extravagant—"it is cheaper in the long run to buy the best."

In requiring the abbot to keep an eye on the size of the clothes provided for the brethren, St. Benedict reveals not only his own consideration but also the importance which he attaches to consideration in others. Certain hardships can be imposed upon the brethren, but at least they must be spared feeling absurd in clothes which are either too big or too small for them. It was the function of the *vestiarius* to arrange about the ordering of clothes, their storage, and their distribution in chapter. But it was the function of the abbot to see that they fitted the one to whom they were given.

When they are given new clothes, let them always give back the old ones at once, to be put in the clothes-room for the poor. For it is sufficient for the monk to have two tunics and two cowls, as well for night wear as for the convenience of washing. Anything beyond this is superfluous and should be cut off.

Someone has said that the first sign of decay in a religious order is the weakening of poverty. It is always, consequently, the first thing to be reformed. The whole question turns on what, having regard to the particular work proposed and the need of the particular person involved, is superfluous. In the matter of clothes St. Benedict judges that two of everything is enough, and that new clothes do not mean additional clothes. New clothes mean giving back old ones into store.

While the Monastic Capitulary of 817 stipulates that clothes which are neither cheap nor expensive but of moderate value and medium quality be worn by monks, the fourteenth article of the Statutes of Murbach, repeating the clause, goes on to forbid altogether the use of garments made of goatskin or trimmed with silk. Those monks who own such costumes must either wear them out quickly or get them exchanged; no further orders for this kind of garment may be made.

In the same way let them give up their stockings, and whatever else is worn out, when they receive new ones. Let those who are sent on a journey receive *femoralia* from the clothes-room, and on their return restore them washed. Let their cowls and tunics also be a little better than those which they usually wear. They must receive these from the clothes-room when setting out on their journey and restore them on their return.

Femoralia is the word for breeches or trunk-hose. The ancient monks seem to have been divided on the matter of *femoralia*, some allowing them and others regarding them as an unnecessary concession. Even after St. Benedict's time the issue was still being debated, Cluny being in favour and Molesmes against. At Monte Cassino itself their use was optional.

On the washing of clothes there is ample information to be found in the commentaries, but the findings seem hardly significant enough to justify the investigation. No attempt will be made here to trace the tradition of Benedictine laundry.

In commenting on the injunction that those who were sent on a journey should wear better clothes, Hildemar notes dryly that some monks seemed to wear better clothes inside the monastery than what was kept for the use of those who go out. But Hildemar is hard to please, because immediately afterwards he is tilting at those whose shabbiness is a reproach to the community.

In these controversies as to what is fitting for the monk to wear, the detail is inclined to obscure the principle. This is precisely what St. Benedict wished to avoid. For him the issue of monastic dress turned on the much more fundamental issue of worldliness. He did not greatly care what was worn so long as it was not what was worn in the world. "I have put off my garment," says the monk with the bride in the Canticles, "and how shall I put it on?"[4] We have been clothed in the dress of religion, and to put on anything which is not of religion is to go back, if not on our vocation itself at least on the simplicity and singleness of purpose which our vocation demands.

[4] 5;3.

For their bedding let a mattress, blanket, coverlet, and pillow suffice. These beds must be frequently inspected by the abbot because of private property which might be found in them. If anyone be discovered to have what he has not received from the abbot, let him be subjected to the most severe discipline.

Rugged men of Scete and the Thebaid would have winced at the thought of so liberal an allowance; for them the monk's bedding was at most some rushes and a sack or two. But when St. Benedict's list is studied, the resulting bed is none too luxurious. The *matta* was of straw, the *sagum* was a covering of sorts which not until two centuries later became a blanket of wool, the *lena* was a rough over-sheet made of skins, and the *capitale* was a bolster made of straw or horsehair. In the time of Charlemagne, to whom monastic matters had to be reported in detail, it is noted that the sick were allowed feather mattresses and bolsters. Two centuries later again, when Cluny was setting the pace for the Black Monks of the Benedictine following, all restrictions were removed as regards the number of coverings a monk might throw over himself at night. The only stipulation regarding the quality of the bedding was that costly furs were not to be included. The pelt of goat, sheep, or cat was judged permissible.

The inspection of beds on the part of the abbot is an observance which does not recommend itself today. It was, however, part of the monastic routine inherited from the rules of earlier legislators,[5] and would not have been thought unusual in St. Benedict's day. At a time when there were no private cells, the mattress would be one of the few places where a guilty monk might store the things which he would not wish his superior to see.

And in order that this vice of private ownership be cut off by the roots let the abbot supply all things that are necessary: that is cowl, tunic, stockings, shoes, girdle, knife, style, needle, handkerchief, writing-tablets. So that all plea of necessity may be taken away. Yet let the abbot always be mindful of those words in the Acts of the Apostles:

[5] Delatte mentions (*op. cit.*, p. 355) St. Isidore, St. Fructuosus, St. Donatus.

"Distribution was made to everyone according as he had need." Let him therefore consider the infirmities of such as are in want, and not the ill-will of the envious. Nevertheless in all his decisions let him think of the judgment of God.

It stands to reason that if all are allowed what they sincerely need, and if none may have anything over and above, the occasions of envy are removed. Such may be the principle, but in fact it does not always work out so neatly. Those in authority will have to exercise tact as well as consideration. Solicitude for the weak should not be so obviously displayed as to rouse the strong to anger. But even this would be better than rigid uniformity. The authority which reduces all to a dead-level must in the long run defeat, however well-intentioned, its purpose. Any system of government which, in order that they conform to an even pattern and be more ready instruments of obedience, reduces the mental stature of its subjects will have only dwarfs to call upon for service. St. Benedict's plan is to train souls to magnanimity. If his subjects can rise above the petty envies of community life, they can be drawn upon for whatever services he may put before them.

The concluding words of the chapter remind the abbot that the claims of justice, charity, poverty and obedience will have to be balanced and presented as a unity before the throne of God.

CHAPTER 56

OF THE ABBOT'S TABLE

This short chapter has proposed many questions to the historian, to the textual critic, to the ordinary monk for whom the plain words of the Rule are gospel. The controversy is surveyed by Delatte, who, wherever his sympathies lie in the matter of the past, concludes "that the abbot should not now take his meals apart from the community."[1] It would seem again to be one of those issues, so frequently met with in this study, where the weight of orthodoxy is more or less evenly balanced, and where sensible common practice has to call the decision.

Let the table of the abbot be always with the guests and pilgrims. But as often as there are few guests, it shall be in his power to invite any of the brethren he wishes. Let him take care, however, always to leave one or two seniors with the community for the sake of discipline.

As the words stand there can be no mistaking St. Benedict's intention. Unfortunately there is nothing in the *Dialogues* to illustrate St. Benedict's practice. Where St. Gregory mentions St. Benedict having a meal it is always in the refectory and with the brethren.[2] But this does not contradict the explicit statement of the Rule because the incidents recorded in the *Dialogues* may have taken place at times when there were no guests in the monastery.

[1] *Op. cit.*, p. 360.
[2] An exception might be found in the twentieth chapter.

All that can be said is that whenever in history the abbot has decided to abide by the words of the Rule there has been trouble. So much so that more than one General Council of Abbots can be cited as forbidding the abbot to make a regular practice of eating on his own or with guests.

The die-hards who are in favour of the literal interpretation of St. Benedict's regulation support their claim with the reference, from the Rule's fifty-third chapter, to the irregular hours at which guests were accustomed to arrive. This, taken in conjunction with the fact that the superior may break his fast for the sake of the guests, would prove that St. Benedict meant what he said. Again, if the abbot may summon a few of the brethren to his table, leaving some seniors behind for the purpose of keeping discipline, it is more than a presumption that he ate in a place apart and probably also—if the guests were as unpunctual as St. Benedict supposed they would be—at a different hour from the community meal.

There is also the factor of silence being observed at meals while the brethren were listening to the reading. Some have assumed that one of the main reasons why a separate refectory was required by St. Benedict for guests was that this would allow for conversation among them. But if what we have considered on an earlier page is anywhere near the mark—namely, that the guests were to be read to on arrival so as to impress upon them the need to make a sort of retreat, and that this was designed to make them feel part of the place—the argument in favour of segregation, particularly when based on lifting the rules of silence for guests, falls through.

Leaving the theory of it, and avoiding the story of its various reforms, we can say that it is the universal custom among Benedictines today for the abbot to eat in the refectory with the community. In most monasteries there are separate quarters where important guests are entertained; to an occasional meal which may take place here, the abbot is of course free to invite members of the household. Those who are not so invited would show themselves lacking in religious spirit if they resented being left out.

CHAPTER 57

OF THE ARTIFICERS OF
THE MONASTERY

The Rule at this point takes on a slightly different turn. In this and the next two chapters there are economic as well as moral and disciplinary concerns to be considered. What always matters most to St. Benedict is the disposition of the individual monk, but this inward attitude cannot be secured without reference to outward affairs—without reference even to financial affairs. If a man is to spurn money, a man must know about money.

Should there be artificers in the monastery, let them ply their crafts in all humility and submission, provided the abbot give them permission. But if one of them be puffed up by reason of his knowledge of his craft, in that he seems to confer some benefit upon the monastery, let such a one be taken from his craft and be not allowed to exercise it again, unless perhaps, when he has humbled himself, the abbot bid him resume.

A monastery may be expected to collect every kind of person, and St. Benedict assumes that there will be some whose special gifts will have to be enlisted in the service of the community apart from the ordinary service of manual labour. Such gifts will have to be canalized, given a spiritual direction, or they will turn out to be more of a liability than an asset.

The practical condition in the pursuit of a craft is the abbot's approval; the interior condition is humility and submission. The presence of some in the community who are more skilled than the rest poses a number of responsibilities. It rests with the abbot to see that talents are not wasted where they can be fruitfully developed; it rests with the individual craftsmen to see that they do not make their gifts an excuse either for arrogance or for the evasion of the common life; it rests with the others, the less skilled, to suppress envy, to give support to their talented brethren when necessary, and to make allowance for the vagaries of the creative mind.

Any man for whom exceptions are made will feel tempted to take one sort of advantage or another. This must be especially the case when the reason for the exemption from the common lot is the production of something which will be admired. The musician who is taken from the choir in order to play pieces of his own composition at the organ during the Mass; the weaver and the artist who are occupied over their own designs while the rest of the brethren follow the regular work of the house; the illuminator and the carver who are allotted special studios or workshops where they can work independently and perhaps at a distance from the rest: all these will have to take special care. In a sense they are the spoiled children of the family—with all the drawbacks which such a term implies.

In those monasteries where there are enough skilled monks to constitute a school of arts or crafts the advantages are many, and the possible evil consequences envisaged by St. Benedict are diminished. Under such circumstances the artist is less liable to fancy himself as a benefactor to his brethren. No longer the exception, he will have more reason to take part in all the ordinary community exercises. The main danger now is that the artists may get together and make of their workshop a cave of Odollam, an enclave of party feeling.

At the first sign of independence, superiority, patronage in the monk whose taste or professional training has made him a source of revenue to the community, the abbot is enjoined to effect a transfer of labour. The monastery may suffer material loss as the result of such a change, but the individual soul as well as the community will gain. Every now and again it is good for a community to be reminded that the greatest spiritual dividends are paid to the more commonplace undertakings. Certainly it is good for the artists and craftsmen to be constantly reminded of this.

And if the work of the artificers is to be sold, let those through whose hands the business is to pass, see that they presume not to commit any fraud. Let them remember Ananias and Saphira, lest perhaps they, and all who deal fraudulently with the goods of the monastery, should suffer in their souls the death which these incurred in their bodies.

This is to tell us, and the quotation which follows says the same, that the monastery is not a factory. Nor may it be run on lines which even the world would condemn. As a means of support, or simply to provide outlet for the monks, a monastery is perfectly justified in manufacturing goods which are not inconsistent with monastic dignity. But there may be no sharp practice in marketing such goods. In a minute we shall see that neither is there to be competition with the world in the matter of profit. The industry of monks, though it may be paying, is conducted on a different level from industry in the world. Always St. Benedict wants his monks to be acutely aware of the spiritual values contained in material effects, and if this vision is at all lost sight of the consequences are serious indeed. Monks can fall as easily as other people into thinking that the only thing that matters is getting a fair return for labour. From this it is the next step to become obsessed with the thought of profit. Work gets intensified, the target rises, more and more sacrifices are made to successful output. Instead of peace in the monastery there is activity and tension. The security aimed at has shifted from the spiritual to the financial. When this happens, the world has won. Though monks can as easily come to think along these lines as can their counterparts in the world, there is less excuse for monks. The monk farms, teaches, makes various kinds of food and drink which will be sold in shops, prints magazines and books, produces pottery and silk and incense, sells furniture which he has made in his carpentry shop and farm equipment which he has forged on his anvil, but all this has been done with material which he uses in fealty to God. Not even the time he spends on the work is his own. All has been lent to him. All must be accounted for—immediately to the monastery, but no less really to God.

> In the prices themselves let not the vice of avarice creep in, but let goods be always sold a little cheaper than by men of the world, that God may be glorified in all things.

Detachment is one of the first things which people outside look for in the monk. They expect to see a contrast between the monk's and the business man's attitude towards gain. They can forgive a monk if he does not seem to be a man of deep recollection, but they cannot understand a monk who talks always about money. They would rather he talked about food. If the price of things is seen to be the main preoccupation of a monk or of a community, the disillusion will not stop short at the monk or the community: the religious life, and ultimately the Church, will be charged with greed. Time and time again this has been illustrated in the history of religious orders and of the Church. In requiring his monks to sell their wares more cheaply than business firms, St. Benedict was safeguarding not only religious poverty at home but the good name of religion abroad.

CHAPTER 58

OF THE DISCIPLINE OF RECEIVING BRETHREN INTO RELIGION

The chapter coming now under review is generally agreed to be one of the most significant chapters in the Rule. It is long, it contains all the elements which we have learned to recognize as meaning much to St. Benedict, it outlines the kind of training which is to be given to those who apply for membership to the community, and it makes detailed provision for the monk's profession of the three Benedictine vows of stability, conversion, and obedience.

> To him that newly comes to conversion let not an easy entrance be granted, but as the Apostle says: "Try the spirits if they be of God." If therefore he that comes persevere in knocking, and after four or five days seem patiently to endure the wrongs done to him and the difficulty made about his entrance, and to persist in his petition, let entrance be granted him and let him be lodged in the guest-house for a few days.

The would-be postulant arrives, and is not welcomed. He has expected encouragement in his enterprise, and nobody pays him any attention. If he is a man of spirit he will not be put off by a little thing like this, but will go on hoping to be received. If he genuinely believes that God is calling him to the monastery, he will see in the chilly reception a test of his faith. Later on he must learn that God alone can satisfy his desire, so he may as well begin by learning not to trust in anything less than God. He must not come into the monastery on a confidence born of another's affability, encouragement, enthusiasm. His vocation is from God, and not from those in the community who may want him to join them.

Such, at the present day, is the interpretation of St. Benedict's words about *non ei facilis tribuatur ingressus.* In a rougher age a more literal interpretation obtained, and prospective postulants were kept shivering outside. Cassian, St. Basil, St. Pachomius could be quoted at length to show that this idea was not St. Benedict's but that in the monasticism of that time it was the normal thing to try vocations hardly.

From the treatment extended to the candidates who apply, it is evident that St. Benedict had no worries on the score of recruitment. He assumes, as we of weaker faith are less ready to assume, that if God wants the monastery to survive He will send vocations. The anxiety which we sometimes feel about the future of a dwindling community may well be a natural and not a supernatural anxiety. It is right to pray for vocations but it may well be a mistaken zeal which prompts us to go out and canvass them. If we can train ourselves to see the monastery and the people in it from God's angle and not from man's, the question of recruitment falls into proper perspective.

In the East the ancient usage demanded often as long as a year's service in the guest-house under the guestmaster before the transfer was allowed to the novitiate. By the time the novicemaster was entrusted with the care of the neophyte, the danger of misunderstanding—either on the part of the subject not knowing what he was taking on, or on the part of the community not knowing that *they* were taking on—was necessarily reduced.

The state of postulancy is not of ancient origin. It was introduced by the Maurists under the name of "first probation" after a State decree in France had forbidden religious profession before the age of twenty-one. The length of the postulantship is not fixed, nor is it laid down what studies are to be pursued by postulants. The probation of postulants would take much the

same form as that of novices, but the fact that they are not
covered by various restrictions demanded in the case of novices
by Canon Law gives them in most monasteries a more flexible
timetable and a wider opportunity of knowing, and being known
by, the professed members of the community. Postulancy for
monks is not demanded by Canon Law, but the decree *Cum ad
regularem* of Pope Clement VIII (1603) requires of those entering the novitiate that they should possess some previous knowledge of the Rule and vows.

In St. Benedict's time, as we shall see later on in the chapter,
the habit was not given until the day of profession. The novitiate
was spent in lay clothes. Today we recognize no less than three
clothings: the postulant receives one habit, the novice another,
the professed a third. Not until the ninth century were the habit
and tonsure given at the beginning of the novitiate, and even then
the custom was by no means universal until Cluny, a century and
a half later, took it up. St. Benedict himself was given the habit
by St. Romanus, but this seems to have been a purely informal
clothing. Matters were more free for hermits. In delaying the
presentation of the habit till the vows were pronounced, St.
Benedict was following the tradition current in his time and
observed by the Rules of St. Aurelian, St. Caesarius, St. Fructuosus
and others.

> Afterwards let him be in the cell of the novices where he
> shall meditate, eat, and sleep. Let there be assigned to him a
> senior who is skilled in winning souls, who may watch him
> with the utmost care and consider anxiously whether he truly
> seeks God, is zealous for the *opus Dei*, for obedience and for
> humiliations. Let there be set before him all the hard and
> rugged ways by which we walk towards God.

It is to be presumed from the text that the *cella novitiorum*
is to some extent isolated from the rest of the rooms and cells
which constitute the monastery. In the opinion of commentators
the novices of St. Benedict's monastery had their own dormitory,
refectory, study-room, and even perhaps oratory. It is probable
that they were admitted to the common manual labour, and almost

certain that they took part in the Divine Office. The monks of Cluny, again the innovators, seem to have been the first to insist upon novices sleeping in the common dormitory and eating in the common refectory. In choir Cluniac novices occupied, as ours do today, the lower stalls. They were admitted, as ours are today, to the abbot's conferences in chapter but not to those chapter meetings which concern the more intimate affairs of the house or which require a vote.

Because the novices belong to a particular family it is important that they should be brought up in that family, and not in a novitiate house shared by the several monasteries of a congregation or province. Abbot Cuthbert Butler makes great point of this, arguing that in their relations with their superiors the novices must have stability as well as obedience to go upon, and that this essentially Benedictine combination is lacking where local superiors are chosen from different houses.[1]

This brings us to the novicemaster. What are to be, in St. Benedict's opinion, his qualifications for the office? He must be a senior, he must have the gift of attracting souls to spirituality, he must be a man of judgment who can estimate the motives which rule the minds of his subjects, and he must be forthright in laying down the principles of the religious life without minimizing the difficulties. Even on the face of it, it makes a tall order, but when the implications are examined the master of novices will have to be a man of other qualities besides.

From what has been suggested above, in connection with Abbot Butler's objection to a common novitiate, the novicemaster must be one who is imbued with the particular spirit of his house. The training which he gives is not an abstract one, equally suited to any religious order or to any religious house, but is the fruit of his own experience of the religious life as lived in this monastery and not in any other. If his work were confined to instructing the novices in matters of prayer, or in seeing to their religious behaviour and their observance of rules, it would be a straightforward office like that of a form-master or of a prefect of discipline. He would need to be a spiritual man in order to

[1] *Benedictine Monachism*, p. 210.

teach prayer, and he would need to be something of a martinet in order to enforce novitiate rules. But there is more in the office than this. He must embody a characteristic spirit, and seek to develop the same spirit in those who come under him. In order to awaken a particular interest in a particular form of life, he must himself be deeply interested; he must be in absolute sympathy with that particular way of life.

The novicemaster, moreover, has to be working in full agreement with the abbot, whose representative he is and whose doctrine he is expected to teach. The novitiate does not belong to the novicemaster to the exclusion of the abbot. Nor, on the other hand, should it belong entirely to the abbot. Under the immediate direction of the novicemaster, and under the remote control of the abbot working through the man whom he himself has appointed, the novitiate belongs primarily to the house and to God. This is something to be remembered when the possessiveness of one or other superior inclines him to make of the noviceship a private and jealously defended hobby.

That a man should be *aptus ad lucrandas animas* does not mean necessarily that he is to be a man of charm. Charm may help, but it can also be a hindrance in the guidance of souls. Souls who have come under the spell of a winning personality are apt to feel empty and flat when the influence has been removed. No longer exhilarated by the other's manner, a man may come to suspect the doctrine that was so glibly taught. There may be no grounds whatever for such suspicion, and the doctrine may have been in the finest Benedictine tradition, but often on the heels of disillusion come doubts and fancies which obscure the outlines of orthodoxy.

Thus the way in which a man shows himself to be apt in gaining souls is not so much by the exercise of a magnetic power as by the readiness to sacrifice himself on their behalf. The novicemaster who is ever available, always disposed to listen, never dismissive, willing to enter into the mind of the one who consults him, and who refuses to apply a doctrinaire solution to the individual case, which anyway will have elements about it which are unique: such a novicemaster satisfies St. Benedict's conditions.

Selflessness and understanding: these are the qualities which most surely win souls.

Among the supporting qualities must obviously be personal fidelity, not only to the novices and to the abbot, but to the holy Rule. No doctrine sounds convincing if the man who preaches it is disrespectful to the law on which the doctrine rests. Novices, particularly if they are young, must have a personal norm which serves as commentary. They should be able to see this in the observance of their master. "We must choose out some good man," wrote Seneca in a letter to Lucilius, "and keep him ever before our eyes, so that we may live as though he were looking on and do all as though he saw us."

If it is the function of the novicemaster to examine the spirits under him on their true search for God, on their love of the *opus Dei*, on their obedience and their behaviour under correction, it is his function also to take these points for self-examination. Having given a good example in these matters before all, he is in a position to exhort and instruct. "Let us consider one another, to provoke unto charity," says St. Paul, "and to good works."[2]

Si vere Deum quaeret. This must be the first indication of a true religious vocation. The only thing that in the last analysis can test the quality of a man's service and sanctity is his desire for the will of God. If he keeps this desire as the vital constant in his life, subordinating all other desires to it, he is giving all that he can give. Put in such terms the programme appears perfectly straightforward: all one has to do is to go on wanting the highest good. But there are complications even in this, and a complication which is particularly relevant in the novitiate years is that of wanting a higher good which in the God-given circumstances of the life is unattainable. St. Bernard says that precisely in this situation the nature of a man's religious perfection is put to the test.

"Whether he truly seeks *God*." If the higher good which he seeks is found to be in conflict with the will of God which he must seek first, the "higher good" must be sacrificed to God's will. There is nothing higher than God's will. It is Himself. It may

[2] Heb. 10;24.

be that God will want a soul to cling to this idea of a higher good for years, perhaps for the whole of a lifetime, but when this is the case He will want the soul to cling still more to the divine will as immediately manifested.

God leaves much that is uncertain in the unfolding of a man's religious life. In those borderline situations where there is a margin of legitimate decision, the monk will find his vocation tried at its most significant level. It is now that he may learn whether *Deum vere quaeret* or whether he is really seeking himself.

In religion we are mostly spared from rejecting the known will of God, but we can become so wedded to our own wills as not to see the will of God when it is presented to us in an unexpected way. Always choosing what is licit to us rather than what is more perfect, we become set in our ways to such an extent that the ways of God no longer appeal to us. This is now the reverse of the problem described above, where the soul sought only the higher good and forgot about the will of God.

It is in circumstances of this sort, whether the obstacle is the falsely conceived higher good or consistently chosen lower good, that souls lay themselves open to delusions about themselves, about God's will, about their vocation. They have a suspicion that their motives are not as good as they pretend them to be, but they are afraid to look. While the doubt still exists between vincible and invincible ignorance, these souls trust not so much to the grace of God as to habit and to luck. It is important accordingly that the novicemaster should assure himself that from the beginning the novices truly seek God. If they do not seek Him truly, they will ignorantly or vaguely—or, which would be worse, deliberately—seek self.

Si sollicitus est ad opus Dei. This is the second explicit condition of possessing a Benedictine vocation. It should show itself in eagerness to know more about the liturgy, in the care with which the lessons are prepared, in the reverence with which the ceremonies are performed. But these are only the outward signs. The main thing is the assimilation of the *opus Dei* as the nourishment of the life itself. Can the novicemaster always conclude, from the ordinary outward expressions which he sees in his novice, that this is present? Not invariably. The good signs may come from a natural bent for thoroughness, from youthful zest, from a desire to keep up with the rest. Before he can propose his novice for profession, a novicemaster must be confident that there is a deepening spirituality at work in his subject's soul, and that this is integrally connected with, if not actually inspired by, the Divine Office.

Coming new to the religious life, a novice will normally experience within himself an accession of different holy desires. In the Benedictine vocation these desires should find their expression in the liturgy. The *opus Dei* is the unifying principle which embraces and finds an object to a man's proselytizing zeal, his longing for sanctity, his spirit of penance. As the novice enters more closely into the meaning of the Divine Office he realizes that this form of self-expression is both safer and more sure than self-expression in the outward apostolate. He will know that what he is doing in choir is not really a matter of expressing himself but a matter of expressing what God has revealed about *Him*self. Men speak inadequately, whether in choir or in the pulpit, of God. But God speaks adequately of Himself. In choir we hear His word about Himself, and repeat it. We repeat it to Him and it is echoed to others. It is as though God were allowing us in audience to listen to His soliloquy. We are present at this spoken revelation of Himself. Nor is it even that having heard what He says about Himself we go out from His presence and tell the good news to others. It is closer and more immediate than this. Rather it is that in the Divine Office we share His voice and proclaim His name as it comes to us.

Sollicitus est ad opus Dei. But if we are to catch His accent and enter into His thought we must be solicitous. Only if we are eager about His word, shall we be able from our choirstalls to utter truths which will reach the souls of men.

The other required signs are earnestness in obedience and zeal for humiliations. Enough has been said of obedience to prepare us for the further mention of humility. The association was met with in the Prologue, and again in the chapter on the degrees of humility: if a monk is humble he will want to escape from self-will by submitting his will to another, and if he is obedient he will go on learning more about humility. Humiliations and humility may not be the same thing, but in the present context they amount to the same thing. It would be impossible to be zealous for humiliations unless the zeal found its origin in humility.

If the beginner is trained to look upon the Divine Office as an uplifting devotion, he will find himself at a loss when the novelty wears off and his devotion cools. In the same way if he looks upon the humiliations of the novitiate as he would look upon the movements of a game, he will find himself at a loss when called upon later on to take up a work which he feels to be beneath his talent or position. "So let there be set before him all the hard and rugged ways by which we walk towards God." Obedience, the search for God, the discipline of the Divine Office and the humiliation of commonplace work: these things are to be recognized as *dura et aspera*.

"I will seek him whom my soul loveth," resolves the bride, and in her search she asks the watchmen of the city. She knows all along in her quest that his will must mean suffering, but though her beloved is to her a "bundle of myrrh" she goes on searching. Outwardly she may be black with discouragement, discoloured with contempt, but inwardly she is learning that submission in humility and obedience is the appropriate expression of love.[3]

The novicemaster who, fearing to dismay his novices, paints the religious life exclusively in shining colours would be offending against the chapter in the Rule as well as against common honesty. His best course is, while hiding nothing, to exhort his subjects to the virtues of trust and hope. In his instructions on the will of God the approach must be at once realist and idealist: the soul must be invited to look with joy for God's most perfect will—not merely urged to accept with heroic resignation its inescapable manifestations.

Certainly the *dura* and *aspera* of monastic service should have no power to depress. "The surest sign by which to judge of the fervour of any community," says Dom Morin, "is the joy that they reflect."[4] If this is true of the professed, it should be still

[3] Cant.; cf. 3;2,3. 1;12. 1;4.
[4] *Ideal of the Monastic Life*, p. 170.

more true of the novices. *Acedia*, the bane of true joy, has not had time to attack the novice. This weariness in well-doing, which monks in every period of monasticism have had to fight, is a subtle suffering; it has none of the glamour of the more obvious monastic trials. Like other moods it is not recognized at the time as a mood. It fills the soul with disgust and reduces the body to listlessness. It is a *dura* and *aspera* nevertheless, and the novice must be prepared in advance.

> If he promise steadfastly to persevere in stability, after the lapse of two months let this Rule be read in order to him and let him be told: "Behold the law under which you desire to fight; if you can keep it, enter; if you cannot, then freely depart." Should he stand firm, let him be taken to the cell of the novices, and again tried in all patience. After the lapse of six months, let the Rule be read to him again, that he may know what he is entering. If he still stand firm, after four months let the Rule be read to him once more.

Three times during the novitiate year the candidate for profession is required to go into the matter as if from the beginning, and to make a decision. No question here of a routine repetition; it has to be a distinct and deliberate choice each time. This is not simply a measure calculated to cover the authorities if there should happen to be trouble later on. It does, in effect, eliminate the grounds of excuse—at all events the excuse of ignorance—but the threefold study of the Rule, and the subsequent decision to persevere under it until the question of taking vows comes up, is designed also, and more positively, to familiarize the novice with the character of the life which he hopes to lead and also to get him into the way of making responsible judgments.

The repeated presentation of the Rule to the novice, together with the decision to be made, can be traced to earlier Rules. Both St. Macarius and St. Caesarius legislate for the practice. In the English Benedictine Congregation the "perseverance" of novices follows the requirements of the Rule, the novices in chapter or at one of the abbot's weekly conferences petitioning a further period of trial.

Nor is the idea of a year as the time of probation proper to St. Benedict. Apart from those whose Rules we have just mentioned,

St. Fructuosus and St. Ferreolus had judged that this was a suitable length of time in which a man might be tried. Though St. Pachomius knew no fixed novitiate in the communities over which he ruled, it is nowhere suggested that his monks were admitted to profession whenever they felt ready to take the step. In the Middle Ages it seems often to have been left to the abbot to decide upon the length of the novitiate, but today the question is no longer open: Canon Law has ruled that the time between clothing and first profession is to last a year. An abbot may, in an individual case, delay the date of profession if he thinks that the novice is not ready to take vows, but he may not shorten the time of the novitiate.

"Ainsi préparés, les novices entrent résolument dans l'*acies fraterna*," says Dom Besse. "Leur charité dominera toutes les répugnances de la nature, tout ce que les hommes et les démons, par une permission spéciale de Dieu, pourraient entreprendre contre elle. Ils sauront toujours se sacrifier, corps et âme, à leurs frères et à leur abbaye, et se serviront de tout pour resserrer les liens de l'armée et accroître leur dévouement. Quoi qu'il advienne, ils veulent appartenir au monastère, à l'Ordre, les servir et servir l'Église dans la mesure de leurs forces."[5]

> And if, having deliberated with himself, he promise to keep all things and to observe everything that is commanded him, let him be received into the community, knowing that it is decreed by the law of the Rule that from that day forward he may not depart from the monastery nor shake off from his neck the yoke of the Rule, which after such prolonged deliberation he was free either to refuse or accept.

The legal mind of Rome is reflected in the above passage. St. Benedict, drawing upon the experience of his student days, makes the clearest statement possible. The novice has had ample time to consider, has been given the chance of going away, has elected to stay on: very good, he can be received into the community and from now till the day he dies he serves under the yoke.

The consequences of such an act as this can never be fully

[5] *Le Moine Bénédictin*, p. 155.

foreseen. Waiting for his profession day, a novice may know what the effects will be upon his right to possess, upon his status as a social being, upon his freedom of action. But he can have very little idea of the spiritual and psychological effects. Indeed it is right that he should not see much further than what the letter of the Rule outlines, and what the judgment of superiors can reveal. The act must necessarily be an act of faith.

Without trust in God's grace, the act of profession would hardly be an act of religion at all. It would assume that one had the strength of character necessary to fulfil the vows without further help. To pronounce the vows in such dispositions might call for courage, might be a very hard thing to do; it would not be an act of supernatural sacrifice. For the sacrificial act to be pleasing to God the whole of man must be offered. A man must give himself in such a way that his being as well as his body belongs wholly to God; in such a way that his inward activity as well as his outward conduct is surrendered. It is inevitable therefore that in the course of his religious life his hope will be tempted by despair, that his faith and love will be tempted by doubt and disappointment. The faculties of intellect and will can be tested to their fullest extent only when the most vital virtues of the soul, the theological virtues, are threatened.

Until the gift of the whole self to God has been menaced in this way—until, that is, the soul has been tempted at every point of the gift's expression to withdraw from the act of giving—there is no proof that the gift has been unqualified. It is possible for an offering to be sincere as far as it goes, but for one reason or another there are restrictions in the offering. What God wants of those who enter religion in order to serve Him in full perfection is the sacrifice that is unrestricted.

Once He sees that the soul puts no limits to His action, God allows the application of pressure to the most sensitive areas of faith, hope, and charity. But of all this the novice as yet knows nothing. All that the novice has to do is to make his gift of self as complete and sincere as he has the light to make it.

Leaving the treatment of vows until they are given in the text, we can follow St. Benedict's sequence by commenting here upon the incorporation into the community—*tunc suscipiatur in congregatione*. It would seem that originally the novice took his place among the brethren immediately after the year of probation was over. Today the year's novitiate is followed by three years in temporary vows. Monasteries differ as to how much of the time spent in temporary vows is continued under the novicemaster and among the novices, but it would be unusual for a junior monk to join the solemnly professed in less than a year from the date of pronouncing temporary vows.

When his four years in the habit—one spent as a novice proper, three as a junior—are nearing an end, the candidate for solemn profession makes a retreat, is voted on by the council and community, and presents himself for a ceremony which varies according to different congregations. In the English Congregation the junior is summoned before the assembled community, and makes a choice between the habit and a secular suit laid out in front of him. This ceremony takes place on the eve of the profession. At High Mass next day the vows are read out by the junior after the Offertory;[6] the document is then placed on the altar and signed by the abbot and the newly professed in the presence of the community. (The verse *Suscipe me, Domine, secundum eloquium tuum et vivam*, which will be mentioned in the next passage of the Rule to be quoted, and which forms a significant part of the ceremony, will be considered below.) The monk then prostrates on the pall, which symbolizes death to self and to the world, and the litanies are sung by the choir. When the litanies and four long prayers are finished, a new habit is blessed and exchanged for the old one. The monk then receives the kiss of peace, a blessing, and is led back from the sanctuary to his place in choir where he takes up his position among the professed.

The demand for a written statement, signed and witnessed, goes back to the fifth century. St. Benedict's contribution was that of giving to the act both a legal and liturgical character. With him

[6] In most congregations the profession takes place before the Offertory. Peter Boherius, quoted by Martène, is the only commentator who mentions a contemporary custom of placing the profession after the Offertory.

profession became a public and almost sacramental contract, binding the monastery as well as the monk. It is witnessed not only by the abbot and brethren, but by God. It marks the most solemn moment in the life of the monk.

> Let him who is to be received make before all, in the oratory, a promise of stability, conversion of manners, and obedience, in the presence of God and His saints, so that if he should ever act otherwise he should know that he will be condemned by Him whom he mocks . . . Let him write this petition with his own hand (or at least, if he knows not letters, let him affix a sign to it) and place it with his own hand upon the altar. When he has placed it there let him begin this verse: *Suscipe me, Domine, secundum eloquium tuum et vivam; et non confundas me ab expectatione mea* . . . then let him cast himself at the feet of all, that they may pray for him. And from that day let him be counted as one of the community.

From this it would appear that St. Benedict distinguishes between the verbal promise and the written guarantee to abide by what is promised. The novice in St. Benedict's day pronounced briefly his three vows of stability, conversion of manners (*conversio* or *conversatio*),[7] obedience, and then presented the longer petition on paper which was signed.[8] Leaving to others the question of the exact form used, we can turn at last to the vows themselves.

Stability. The promise as understood by St. Benedict was to abide steadfastly in the monastery until death. Its introduction was designed to counter the prevailing tendency among monks to wander from monastery to monastery at will. St. Benedict, though he was the most notable, was only one of the contemporary reformers of monasticism to make stability a condition without which admission to the community would be denied. The Rules of St. Caesarius and St. Aurelian had only recently laid it down that monks belonged to a particular monastery and owed obedience to a particular abbot. Before this Cassian had in a more

[7] See Butler, *Benedictine Monachism*, pp. 134-8, 405.
[8] See McCann, *St. Benedict*, pp. 143-146.

general way attacked the wandering spirit which he saw in some of his contemporaries, and St. Basil had pointed to stability as the only remedy against a system which too easily admitted reasons for the transfer of monks from one monastery to another. Going back farther still we find St. Antony claiming in his statement of monastic perfection the need for three things: stability, study of the Scriptures, and prayer.[9]

In the terms of this vow the monastery is not merely the area in which the monk works out his perfection, nor yet is it the aggregation of fellow monks living under the one roof; it is the unit, composed of place and people, to which those who belong owe particular responsibilities of loyalty. For St. Benedict, as for those who came after him, the monastery meant a local household —a family institution attached to a particular acreage and rooted there.

"In modern Benedictine practice," says Dom Justin McCann, "stability in the monastery is generally extended to stability in the community, and sometimes even to stability in the congregation. The effect is that a monk, though normally living in the actual monastery in which he pronounces his vows, may dwell in a dependency of that monastery or even in another monastery of the same congregation."[10]

What poverty is to St. Francis and his sons, stability is to St. Benedict and to us. Almost all the greatest followers of St. Benedict have had something particular to say about this first vow, and it is interesting to note that almost all of them have had to fight for their stability, defending it either against temptation from within or criticism and attack from without or else against the sheer force of circumstances. St. Bernard defines, and cherishes what he can of it, the *stabilitas in loco* which may not be seen apart from obedience, but which at the same time may not be overruled by obedience.[11] The phrase *stabilitas loci*, which figures in several early forms of profession together with the ex-

[9] *Paradise of the Fathers*, Vol. 2; 163.
[10] *Op. cit.*, p. 145.
[11] *Epis.* 7.

pression *hujus monasterii Sancti N.*,[12] is used by Paschasius Radbert in the middle of the ninth century. Where Warnefrid had used the paraphrase *perseverantia*, meaning perseverance in the monastery, Smaragdus (seventy years later and the contemporary of Radbert) comes into the open with *stabilitas monasterii* and *stabilitas cordis et loci*.

By the thirteenth century the distinction had come in between physical and moral stability. Bernard of Monte Cassino makes stability consist in a "certain persevering constancy of mind"—moral stability—but he reverts to the older idea later on in his *Speculum*, where he says that stability forbids a monk to abandon the state to which he is vowed and to "go forth from the monastery without necessity and the permission of the abbot."[13] Among the Maurists in the seventeenth century there was no insistence upon physical stability. For Mège, Ménard, Martène, stability meant no more than perseverance in the monastic life. Since the Maurists were professed for the congregation and not for the monastery, this indeterminate view is not surprising. What is surprising, however, because he wrote only a little while later, is Calmet's plea for the stricter interpretation: "The most literal meaning is that which understands a stability of place; it was thus that the ancients understood and practised it."[14] Dom Calmet, a monk of St. Vanne and not of St. Maur, managed to escape much of the non-Benedictine influences which were at work in the seventeenth and eighteenth centuries in France.

If then we take stability to mean something more than permanence in the cenobitic vocation, seeing it rather as residence in the house of profession, there arises the question as to when it may be lawful to seek admission to another monastery in pursuit of a higher good. While it is *per se* lawful to apply for permission to follow a more perfect way of life in a stricter monastery, it is in actual practice so often self-will which prompts the application that the best spiritual authorities advise against it. Certainly St. Bernard refuses to admit that there are good enough reasons to

[12] See Butler, *op. cit.*, p. 130.
[13] Ch. 18.
[14] *Commentaire sur la Règle de S. Benoit*, ch. 18.

warrant the change from Cluny to Citeaux. The saint gives as
grounds for his attitude of hostility to the idea: first the harm
done to the monks in the monastery which has been abandoned;
second the principle that in cases of doubt it is safer to maintain
oneself in the position that is known to be bearable than to risk
being placed in a position that in unbearable; third the danger of
delusion and levity of motive.

Further light is shed on this point by the Cistercian monk, Bl.
Guerric, who, writing in honour of St. Benedict's feast, holds
local stability to be integral to our holy Father's conception of
the common life and of monastic authority.

But what, it might be asked, is the monk to do, who, after
prayer and a generous attempt at leading the life of the monastery where he has taken vows, still feels drawn to a life of greater
perfection? Such a man will have to be careful that his desire is
free of discontent with his brethren, with the work of the community, with his superiors and their interpretation of the Rule.
Stability assumes that a monk puts up with such discontent as
part of the sacrifice demanded by the Benedictine vocation.

It may well be in the Providence of God, as we have noted on
an earlier page, that the desire for greater perfection according
to a particular pattern may be a good one—may be inspired by
grace—yet the fulfilment of that desire has no part in God's plan.
God wishes us sometimes to persevere in our hope when it is not
His wish to realize that hope but rather to block it at every turn.

Thus in the case under review, the monk's perfection is more
likely to lie in the direction of surrender to the objectively less
perfect life as led in the existing monastery than in the attainment
of the higher life as believed to exist in the ideal monastery.

To leave the imperfect monastery to which he belongs, and to
join the more perfect monastery to which he does not, a monk
will have to be very sure in his mind that the imperfections of the
one are fundamental and that the perfections of the other are
those which God wants him to practise. The observance of the
first monastery would have to be lax indeed—as in St. Benedict's
own experience the observance at Vicovaro was lax to the point
of abuse and scandal—if the change is to be justified on the

grounds that God's light is revealing itself through the impossibility of living on in the setting provided by divine Providence.

Monks who for one reason or another are unsettled in their communities often make the mistake of identifying perfection with a particular form of observance unattainable here and now. They imagine that somewhere else Benedictines are rapidly finding perfection in a setting ideally suited to precisely the kind of perfection which is exercising such a pull. But surely the essence of perfection is to seek God. So long as it cannot be positively denied that God is there in the monastery, to be served and sought according to the principles of monasticism, perfection is attainable. The soul must search for God among imperfect men in an imperfect monastery: this is his exercise of faith. Perfection consists in surrendering to the limitations at home while retaining the ideals which are believed to better served elsewhere.

Manete in me—not in any idea about Me, or in any setting not devised by Me. God is telling us to see in local stability the surest means of finding our anchorage in Him. If we abide in Him, and allow Him to abide in us, we need have no worry about whether we can safely stop on in the house of our profession without damage to our Benedictine outlook and vocation.

From what has just been said it may be judged that there is another sense in which the term "moral stability" may be used. We have noted the expression in connection with the wider interpretations given to the original conception of stability; we can think of it now as referring to interior constancy, the willingness to counter both in the mind and in outward conduct the restlessness which urges change, to the exercise of a deeper monastic faith.

If the letter of the vow forbids leaving the monastery, either to return to the world or to find relief in some other religious house, the spirit of the vow forbids entertaining thoughts of flight. "Try to repel all restlessness of heart," says the Benedictine writer Blosius, "which chokes true peace, perfect trust in God, and spiritual progress."[15] It can be said categorically that unless the desire for change is proved by submission to wise direction it is a temp-

[15] *Mirror for Monks*, ch. 3.

tation against the spirit of stability. The light which prompted St. Boniface to ask leave to give up one form of Benedictine life and undertake something quite different—and the direction which he received confirming the light—cannot be counted upon by the ordinary monk. The impulses of grace which are granted to the saints do not always create precedents for other people. It would be safer to say with Montaigne that "since I am in no position to choose, I follow the choice of others, remaining in the rut in which I am placed by God. Otherwise I would roll and roll without end."

Unless the tendency to mental roving is ruthlessly curbed there can be no peace in the monk's soul. "A monk cannot long dwell in one place and live in peace," says St. Peter Damian, "if he does not love those things that teach him interior rest." It is often because a man neglects silence and work that he becomes unsettled and begins to look out for an excuse to move. There are always good reasons for dodging behind one's stability and getting away to another monastery, but they are always wrong. The monk who transplants himself almost always does so in shallower soil. And his roots are weaker now.

The suffering involved in trying to live for God alone in the monastery, and in suppressing the urge towards gyrovagy, is probably more sanctifying than the life which would be achieved as the result of a break. "I passed long years where there were a hundred and eighty religious," says St. Teresa, "with whom I lived as though there were only God and myself on the earth." How the common life was affected by this we do not know, but we can certainly see in the admission an example of stability. To wait for further light, to be content to abide by the contract, to persevere in faith, to stifle plans for wandering: this is moral stability. If those who are unhappy in half measures could be persuaded that the price which sanctity demands is the sacrifice which consists in surrender rather than the sacrifice which looks to achievement, they would find happiness as well as holiness within the frame which God has set around them.

If someone reading the holy Rule did not know beforehand that stability was one of the foundations of the Benedictine life, he would almost certainly conclude that this was so before he had reached the present chapter. Stability follows from an understanding of what is meant by the will of God. Without the least taint of quietism or passivity, we can assume that what God hands out to us can be taken as coming immediately from His will. The more we can make our own desire conform with His—which is to say that the more we make His will our own—the more we shall be satisfied with it. If afterwards some other way of serving Him attracts us, we should remind ourselves that God has already opened up one particular way for us and that if He wills us to follow another He must be left to make the arrangements and force the issue.

A monk cannot do everything that is good, following all good vocations. He can do only one good thing, following one certain vocation. If he is determined to try all possible forms of service, now giving up his own form of service to exploit the possibilities of another and now leaving that other in search of yet a third, he will find himself a prey to irresolution and distraction.

"A man who leaves the world and enters once for all a religious order," says Eckhart, "more readily becomes perfect than another who passes from one order to another, however holy he may be. Lay hold of one good way, gathering up into it all good ways, and keep to that one. Do not be afraid of losing anything thereby. No one ever loses anything with God, any more than God Himself ever loses anything. To change one's way is to show an unstable character and an unsettled mind."

Of St. Benedict it was said by a monk of Monte Cassino[16] that he was *fundator placidae quietis.* Though it does not define St. Benedict's stability, nor even refer to it, this phrase gives the feel of it and suggests the fruits of its practice.

Conversion of manners. In its widest interpretation the formula of St. Benedict's second vow means the renunciation of the world and the intention of pursuing perfection according to the monastic tradition. This vow is so comprehensive in character and extent

[16] Alfano, who is quoted by Montalembert in *Monks of the West,* Vol. I; p. 51.

that to narrow its definition is to particularize its application. At once the attempt is lost in a network of examples, explanations, and further attempts to define the subdivisions. If we leave it as "reformation of life" we shall not be far wrong, and the application can be dealt with frankly in a sequence of illustrations which bear out the principle.

As a term *conversio* or *conversatio morum* comes six times in the Rule. It is a little surprising that St. Benedict did not, since this was his favourite authority, take over from Cassian the word *emendatio. Conversatio*, now understood to be the word used in the original text, is a difficult term to pin down. Indeed the earliest forms of profession leave out St. Benedict's second vow, assuming stability to cover its meaning. By the end of the eighth century stability was matter for explicit vow because it is mentioned by Paul Warnefrid in his report to Charlemagne on monastic usage. The vow is here taken to signify "the rooting out of vices and the implanting of virtues."

Dom Justin McCann, for whom the second vow "embraces the whole complex of the precepts and counsels which are involved in the profession of the monastic life,"[17] devotes a chapter to the history and implications of the terms used. Abbot Butler devotes almost as much, and concludes with the formula "monastic life according to the Rule." Abbot Chapman, after assembling a mass of texts, proposes the phrase "monasticity of behaviour." Clearly the discussion is important, because for one thing the other two vows suppose it and to a large extent depend upon it, but the practical conclusions to be drawn from the discussion are more important still. The vague moral principle of striving after greater perfection is not enough; what is wanted is an ideal which will be able to test moral conduct. A monk should be able to know whether or not he is living up to the vow which he has pronounced, when and how he has offended against it, what he must do to reflect it in his every activity as a monk.

For this we must start at the beginning. A man comes to the monastery in order to learn the perfect service of God. If the project is to bear fruit two things are needed: there must be a

[17] *Op. cit.*, p. 145.

cloud of forgetting behind him which hides the world which he has left, and there must be a cloud of unknowing before him into which he is ready to enter for the love of God. By the conversion of his manners the spirit which was of the earth and worldly is transformed into the spirit of Christ. The monk takes a vow proclaiming that he seriously desires, and is ready to further, this process of transformation. He goes forward into the new cloud of faith.

As in the case of stability and obedience, conversion of manners is distinctly personal: particular rather than general and abstract. Thus it would be a mistake to write off the vow as too nebulous for purposes of examination. The point of it is that it is so concrete as to demand for its expression concrete and moment-to-moment occasions.

Taking as the yardstick by which it may be measured the instrument of good works *a saeculi actibus se facere alienum*, the individual monk can examine his response to the vow according to both the letter and the spirit. He will be able to tell whether the standards which were his before he joined the community are his still, or whether he now possesses a quite new scale of values. It is an individual matter, a question of this particular soul's response to the grace of a monastic vocation. There is nothing general or vague or abstract about it.

In the light of such a view—developed in faith and by prayer but brought to bear upon a hundred issues which have little direct relation either to faith or to prayer—the monk can come to see how he stands as regards his recreations, his ambitions, his work, his associations with others both inside the community and out, his interests and opinions.

Am I justified in sharing the worldling's study of the press? Is my liking for sport, theatrical criticism, light reading, food—for any pleasure not immediately connected with the religious life or spirituality—in keeping with my vow of *conversio morum*? Are my judgments of people coloured by considerations of social background, education, worldly success? Does money mean to me what it did when I was in the world? In my way of speaking, walking, sitting, and so on do I suggest the man of God or the man of the world? If in a complimentary sense it may possibly be said of a secular priest that he is a man of the world, of a monk it can be said only in derision.

So it is that whereas the vow of stability brings the monk's mind to focus upon a certain place and a certain attitude towards that place, the vow of *conversio morum* relates to every place and is expected to reflect itself in every attitude. Of the three vows it is the most difficult to keep perfectly, and because it is the most searching in its implications it is the one about which we are the most ready to deceive ourselves.

Obedience. The whole Rule is instinct with the idea of obedience. From the fifth chapter we learn that the submission required of monks is to be interior as well as exterior, that there must be no murmuring, that it must be prompt. From two chapters yet to come, the sixty-eighth and seventy-first, we shall see that "the burdensome or impossible commands are to be received quietly," and that besides being obedient to superiors monks are to be obedient to one another.

"It is the temper of obedience, much more than the actual obediences," says Abbot Butler, "that are of value. This is the fruit and outward expression of humbleness of heart and renunciation of self-will; and these two things are what St. Benedict relies on principally for the ascetical element in his monks' lives."[18]

Where the vow of *conversio morum* looks back in the pages of the Rule to the principles laid down in the degrees of humility, the vow of obedience looks back to the prologue and the fifth chapter. The vows are simply the logical outcome of ideas already discussed. But there is this to be noted, that whereas the first and second vows are unqualified, the third is presented conditionally. The monk promises obedience "according to the Rule of St. Benedict." This form goes back as early as the middle of the ninth century, appearing in Smaragdus and in the records of St. Gall.

St. Bernard, who can never be charged with watering down the obligations of the monk, makes much of this qualifying clause in the text of our Benedictine profession. The obedience, St. Bernard

[18] *Benedictine Monachism*, p. 140.

claims, "is not of every sort but determinately according to the Rule, and to no other Rule than that of St. Benedict. So that the superior must limit his commands to what is right, not in general but according to what St. Benedict established. Obedience is promised not according to the will of the superior but according to the Rule of St. Benedict. No one should be compelled by obedience to what is beyond the Rule which he has professed, much less to what is contrary to it."[19]

The obligations of obedience touch the superior as much as they touch the subject. If the flock must take the food that the shepherd gives them, the shepherd must see to it that only the food prescribed is given. Having stated the principle that the monk is not bound beyond the limits of his vow, St. Bernard goes on to suggest much what St. Benedict will be found to suggest in his sixty-eighth chapter: obey notwithstanding.

Only when the essentially Benedictine life is threatened by obedience may a monk take his stand on the formula of his vow. "I say that the abbot is to be obeyed in all things, yet saving our profession," says St. Bernard. It is the explicit teaching of this saint and doctor of the Church that neither subjection to the abbot nor stability in place may be fulfilled to the prejudice of the other. How is obedience able to excuse the transgression of stability? Since stability is vowed without mention of subjection to the abbot, so it would follow that obedience cannot compel a monk to leave his monastery for work which will keep him permanently away. As a punishment a monk may be sent to another house, but as part of the religious obligation no monk is bound to go out on the mission or on any other enterprise which will deprive him indefinitely of the *opus Dei* in choir, of monastic enclosure, of the common life.

The three vows pronounced by the Benedictine establish the monastic on a social as well as a juridical foundation. More than in the case of either stability or *conversio morum*, obedience to a superior and a written rule is seen to be the basis of the monastic social system. The monastery is a social unit which is kept together

[19] *De Praecepto et Dispensatione*, quoted and abridged by Butler, *op. cit.*, p. 141.

in charity and singleness of purpose by the vows of stability, conversion of manners, and obedience.

Bernard of Monte Cassino shows how each vow opposes a prevailing threat to monasticism and brings the service of God back to the essential cenobitic ideal. By the vow of stability St. Benedict distinguishes his monks from the gyrovagues, by the vow of *conversio morum* he distinguishes them from the sarabaites, and by the vow of obedience to a Rule and an abbot he distinguishes Benedictines from anchorites.

Before leaving the question of vows for a return to the text, we have still to consider the two generally recognized religious obligations of poverty and chastity, which, though not expressly formulated in the Rule are contained implicitly in the monk's profession. Reformation of life assumes perpetual chastity, and obedience—even if *conversio morum* did not—covers religious poverty.

So close is the connection between St. Benedict's vows and those made by religious who do not follow his Rule that some, using Cassian as the medium, have equated the two groups. Thus in Cassian's third and sixth conferences a threefold renunciation is given which comprises the demands made by the religious vows, Benedictine or other. Since self-will and the desire to possess are the first enemies of the religious life, Cassian rates the renunciations of religion in an ascending order towards detachment of heart. The first is the renunciation of material things: this corresponds to the vow of poverty. The second renounces the over-indulgence of the senses and the affections: this corresponds to chastity and conversion of manners. The third renounces all that would come between the soul and the perfect contemplation of God: this, in assuming what has already been said of self-will, supposes the surrender of the will in religious obedience and in stability as the disposition conducive towards union with God in prayer.

Having stated the three vows which he wants his followers to take, St. Benedict goes straight on in the same sentence to remind us that by breaking these vows we mock God. It is more than a question of honour or justice. In this bilateral contract between the soul and God it is a question of divine charity and religion. We give ourselves to be incorporated into the household of God, and to withdraw from that household is apostasy. Apart from legitimate dispensation, there can be no retiring from the position in the family which is given and accepted on the day of profession.

As soon as the agreement has been signed and put on the altar, the newly professed monk proclaims his dependence upon the power of grace in the fulfilment of what he has promised by intoning the *Suscipe*. Sung three times and repeated by the brethren, this verse is the fullest profession of faith in the supernatural character of his vocation that a monk can make. The fact that it is repeated before all, with the *Gloria Patri* added, while the text of the vows with their signatures still fresh is on the altar, gives an unmistakable significance. This singing of the *Suscipe*, because it is more positive, is even richer in implication than the act of prostrating upon the pall. The symbolism of death gives only the disposition, the condition; the words of the hundred and eighteenth psalm state the inspiration, define the direction. Fidelity to what has been promised is so far beyond the capacity of unaided human nature that only confidence in the Lord's guarantee —*secundum eloquium tuum et vivam, et non confundas me ab expectatione mea*—can carry the soul through to the end proposed.

> If he have any property let him either first bestow it on the poor, or by solemn deed of gift make it over to the monastery, keeping nothing of it for himself as knowing that from that day forth he has no power even over his own body . . . let him be stripped of his own garments wherewith he is clad and be clothed in those of the monastery. The garments which are taken from him are to be placed in the clothes-room and there to be kept, so that if ever by the persuasion of the devil he consent (which God forbid) to leave the monastery, he may be stripped of monastic property and cast forth. The petition, however, which the abbot

received on the altar shall not be given back to him, but shall be kept in the monastery.

Abruptly St. Benedict comes down to earth. Property is to be disposed of in favour either of the poor or, in correct legal form, to the monastery. As if to show how little the monk now owns, the clothes that he wears are taken from him. But if money may be given to the poor, the secular dress which was worn before profession is to be kept in the house. No mention is made of the claims of parents in the distribution of goods, and there are grounds for believing that to single out any persons whatever, even parents, as objects of benefaction was judged by early legislators to be an act of *propria voluntas.* "Monastic profession consecrates the whole man to God," says Delatte, "and since his property is in some sort part of him, the best use the novice can make of it is to offer it all to God in the person of His poor."[20] Obviously if a man's parents are in need, as Abbot Delatte admits, his charity should begin with them.

In allowing the monastery to benefit by a candidate's dispositions of estate, St. Benedict is departing from what he must have read in Cassian. Cassian and St. Basil are against receiving donations either from novices or their parents—a precaution against the overt pressure of earlier benefactions influencing decisions later on—but this view is not shared by all who belonged to that period. Subsequent monastic practice endorsed the liberty allowed by St. Benedict.

The chapter's concluding paragraph comes as a sad reminder of the possibility, in this matter of taking vows, of failure. But though the unhappy monk who decides to abandon the monastic life may have back the clothes which he wore when he entered, the document of his profession belongs to the monastery. Nowhere does our holy Father speak of compelling a brother by force to stay. The man has a free will, and if he decides to harden it against grace he must be allowed to follow it.

But if physical restraint is absent from St. Benedict's intentions, moral and spiritual forces may rightly be brought to bear. We

[20] *Op. cit.,* p. 403.

have seen in the chapters on punishment how often the Rule insists that the brethren pray for the delinquent. In the case of the deserter the need is the greater. And we know from the *Dialogues* that "by the prayers of the holy man Benedict" the inconstant monk who left the community "was brought back again to the monastery, promising never to depart" and in the event remaining faithful to this promise.[21]

[21] Bk. 2; ch. 25.

CHAPTER 59

OF THE SONS OF NOBLES OR OF THE POOR THAT ARE OFFERED

The title of the chapter is somewhat misleading; it suggests that the nobleman's son will be treated differently from the poor man's. Nothing could be further from St. Benedict's intention. The only difference, as will be seen, is that there is less to worry about in drawing up the deed for the poor than for the rich. A distinction, however, which is more important than that of financial or social background is one which must be borne in mind throughout the study of this chapter—namely, the distinction between those children who are accepted into the monastery to be taught and those who are dedicated to God in a particular way. The first group are *alumni*, free to leave if they decide not to become monks after all; the second group are *oblati*, destined for the religious life. Both groups follow the conventual life, but it is only of the second group that St. Benedict is thinking here.

Since the Council of Trent the profession of religious under the age of sixteen is invalid; the provisions made in the present chapter are accordingly of no effect. For the sake of linking up St. Benedict's regulations regarding the reception of children with those considered in the previous chapter regarding the reception of adults, the chapter, though obsolete, is worth studying: the same combination of spiritual values and legal forms is to be seen in the account of each profession.

If perchance any noble shall offer his son to God in the monastery, let the parents, should the boy himself be not old enough, make the petition of which we spoke before. And, together with the offerings, let them wrap the petition and the hand of the child in the altar-cloth, and so offer him.

The religious spirit of this opening paragraph, as of the oblation, sets the note for what is to come. The parents of the child are to know that it is to God that their oblation is made; the act is not merely a convenient way of disposing of a younger son. The hand wrapped in the altar-cloth, the solemn moment at the Offertory when the Mass is interrupted to receive the dedication, the public character of the profession: all this is calculated to impress the parent with the seriousness of the sacrifice which is being made.

Commentators are united in pointing to Old Testament precedent for such consecrations to God's service. Samuel, Jephte's daughter, Samson, St. John the Baptist, and our Lady herself: in different terms and at different stages in their early lives, each was vowed to the Lord. Commentators are equally agreed upon the Christian but pre-Benedictine practice of vowing young children to the Lord in monasteries: the custom obtained in Egypt, Palestine, Syria, and Asia Minor. In some Rules, St. Basil's, for instance, child oblates were received on condition that the obligations thus shouldered might not be made matter of vow until later. When the oblate had reached an age when he could be expected to grasp the implication of what had been vicariously undertaken he could either freely ratify or freely repudiate the responsibility. St. Benedict seems not to have cared for such caution.

With respect to their property they must in the same petition promise under oath that they will never either themselves or through an intermediary, or in any way whatever, give him anything or the means of having anything. Or else, if they are unwilling to do this and desire to offer something as an alms to the monastery, let them make a donation of the property which they wish to give, reserving to themselves if they wish the usufruct.

The break with their child is to be no fictional break; the parents are warned that there will be no further control over the oblate's affairs, and the guarantee to avoid interference must be sealed with an oath. The oblate's detachment has to be safeguarded; there must be no room for the cultivation of *proprietas*.

If the boy later on were to be exposed to arranging his affairs, deciding which benefactions to accept and which to reject, he would be as well back in the world.

> And so let every way be blocked that the child may have no sort of expectations by which he may be misled and perish (which God forbid) as we have learned by experience may happen.

Cassian describes the agitation of soul which the expectation of an inheritance occasions.[1] It is Cassian's doctrine, and through this source St. Benedict's, that oblate and parents alike must regard the oblation as a disinheritance.

Whatever the risks attaching to this system of child-oblation, St. Benedict was certainly justified, in two instances at least, when he decided that profession pronounced by the parents in the name of their son was to be allowed in his monastery. St. Maurus and St. Placid were examples of the experiment turning out a success; nor are we told that either Eutychius or Tertullus, the respective fathers, violated on their part the conditions agreed to about gifts and legacies.[2]

> Let those who are poorer do in like manner. But those who have nothing whatever shall simply make the petition and offer their son along with the offerings and before witnesses.[3]

[1] *Institutes*, Bk. 4; chs. 3,4.

[2] In later times St. Bede and St. Gertrude can be counted among those who brought their oblation, made for them in childhood, to the happiest conclusion.

[3] Much interesting historical information about child-oblates may be found in Abbot Delatte's *Commentary*, pp. 407-412. The subject is more briefly dealt with in Mr. T. F. Lindsay's *St. Benedict*, pp. 73-75.

CHAPTER 60

OF PRIESTS WHO MAY WISH TO
DWELL IN THE MONASTERY

This chapter is not concerned with those of the community who are chosen out by the abbot to proceed to the priesthood. Such already professed monks will be the subject of the sixty-second chapter. It is those who apply from among the diocesan clergy that St. Benedict is now considering. At a time when priests in a monastery formed a small percentage of the whole it was necessary, as much for the applicant's sake as for the sake of the abbot and community, to make exact regulations regarding their admission.

If any one of the priestly order ask to be received into the monastery, let not assent be too quickly granted to him. But if he persist strongly in this request, let him know that he must keep all the discipline of the Rule and that nothing will be relaxed in his favour.

The point has been made that in alluding to the "priestly order" St. Benedict includes deacons and bishops: requests, then, from any cleric not trained within the monastery must be treated with this reserve which we have come across in the case of the layman's reception.

St. Benedict is one with St. Pachomius and others in extending to all would-be monks, regardless of their status, a cold hand of welcome. The Church itself does not make it easy for clerics to pass from the ranks of the secular clergy to a religious order.

While admitting the right of clerics to take the habit, Canon Law insists that priests consult their bishop and that the lower clergy do nothing without the sanction of their superior. For a bishop to enter a novitiate, whether of an active or contemplative order, the permission of the Pope has to be obtained.

The early commentators, particularly Warnefrid and Hildemar, are anxious to warn against the dangers of believing a cleric simply because he is a cleric. They suggest that since the advantages offered to the clerics are greater than those offered to the layman, the motives for entering must be all the more severely tested. Despite these misgivings on the part of those nearest in time to St. Benedict, it is difficult to see what, if this present chapter of the Rule was carried out, the cleric-applicant stood to gain.

More reasonable grounds for hesitation would be the argument of experience: men whose spiritual training has been shaped in a particular way find it difficult to adapt themselves to a new mould. But allowance must be made in this question both for the action of grace in supplying a new vocation and for the possibility of an initial mistake in choosing the clerical instead of the monastic state. Neither the priest nor the seminarian has taken a vow of stability, so the process of transplanting carries few of the implications which we have examined in the case of a monk transferring to another monastery or to another order. Nor would it require such weighty reasons to justify it. All that the priest has to assure himself about is whether the attraction to the religious life comes from God or from self. If he genuinely believes that it comes from God, he must ask leave to put it to the test; if, after prayer and self-examination, he discovers his motive to be desire for escape or for a promotion which is likely to be denied him in the diocese, he should know what to do next about it. Certainly it is not for this book, which is addressed to monks, to tell the secular clergy where their duties lie. The holy Rule considers the attitude to be observed inside the monastery towards those without, not that of those outside towards whose within.

The Rule enjoins that nothing be relaxed in favour of the priest who tries his vocation in the monastery, and that when he has embraced the full discipline which he finds there he must dwell upon, and continually purify, the intentions which brought him in:

That he fulfil what is written, "Friend, whereto art thou come?" Nevertheless let it be granted him to stand after the abbot, to give the blessing and to say Mass if so be that the abbot bid him do so. Otherwise let him presume to do nothing, knowing that he is subject to the discipline of the Rule; but rather let him give an example of humility to all.

If the priest is to "stand after the abbot," it can only mean at liturgical occasions when his orders would give him precedence. The regulations made with regard to the novitiate would require the priest-novice to work, eat, and recreate among the other novices. It seems that in certain periods of our history the abbot did not always bid the novice to say Mass, and that the priest had to wait until profession to do so. Where this was the custom, the priest would indeed have had reason to draw upon the virtue of humility.

If there chance to be a question of an appointment in the monastery, let him not expect anything to be granted to him out of reverence to the priesthood but rather according to the time of his entrance. If any cleric [not a priest] should desire to be admitted to the monastery in the same way, let him be placed in a middle rank. But this too only if he promise observance of the Rule and stability.

All that this means is that the priesthood as such can claim no rights in the purely monastic field. Whatever benefits there are that come to monks in their turn, according to the places which they occupy in the community, these the priest may expect along with the other members of the household. The priest's place on the ladder, when it is a question of progression, is determined by the date of his clothing. But St. Benedict leaves himself a wide liberty: the abbot, given good grounds for doing so, can promote a suitable priest or leave him where he is on the list. Having regard to the possibility of envy on the part of the brethren, superiors as a rule show reluctance to advance newcomers. If this "middle rank," *mediocri loco*, is given to those who are in orders but who are not priests, the appointment will have to be made very tactfully. The universal usage today is to give the cleric his place according to his reception of the habit.

CHAPTER 61

OF PILGRIM MONKS, HOW THEY ARE
TO BE RECEIVED

This is the fourth and last chapter on the subject of keeping up the numbers in the community. The idea of recruitment can be distasteful with its suggestion of persuasive letters, platform appeals, ungenerous comparisons, advertisement and partisan direction. While nothing of this worldly method will be met with in the Rule, there is evident in St. Benedict's words a desire to attract souls to the particular kind of service of God which his monasteries are designed to promote. It is not that St. Benedict is trying to market a new commodity in monasticism, and must launch a propaganda drive; it is rather that he is trying to prevent an existing good from going to waste from lack of direction, and at the same time is offering to provide the setting for its fruitful use.

> If any pilgrim monk come from distant parts and desire to dwell in the monastery as a guest, and if he be content with the custom of the place as he finds it, and do not trouble the monastery by any unreasonable wants, but be content simply with what he finds, let him be received for as long a time as he will.

The question of unattached monks constituted, as we have seen, a problem. It was all the more of a problem because many of these monks were genuine; they were not all gyrovagues and sarabaites. At a time when there was no congregation which linked scattered monasteries together, monks would be found on the road from one house to another who were as likely to be potential saints as potential vagrants. There was, until St. Benedict came to preach it, no consistent doctrine about enclosure, stability, behaviour when on a journey. In the East there had been written Rules which had to a certain extent governed the standards of those who followed them, but even here the ideals proposed were left to the generosity of individual interpretation. In the East, again, contact between monastery and monastery in an area—and still more between monastery and monastery under a single head such as St. Antony or St. Pachomius or St. Basil— was closer than anything yet existing in the West. In the West during St. Benedict's time the Rules of St. Caesarius, St. Aurelian, St. Fructuosus, St. Ferreolus and the Master were either just coming into use or had not yet been tried.

In mentioning the monk from *longinquis provinciis*, St. Benedict shows us something of the prevailing conditions in the West. Had local federations of monasteries existed, the need to cater for monk-visitors would not have been so urgent. The abbot would simply consult the abbot of the community from which the visitor had come, and then either send the monk back or allow him to make the first move. But with pilgrim monks and monks who have come from "distant parts" the case would be different. The monk might be in need of direction which it would be difficult to obtain from home, and provided his absence had been approved of by his own superior, why should he not look for light on his problem from the abbot and the brethren who had welcomed him into their company? But in case this view should appear too broad, St. Benedict covers himself in the chapter's concluding paragraph where he insists that the respective abbots should come to an agreement in the matter, and that the exchange is effected not only in the regular form but in religious charity.

It may be assumed that the visiting monk was not lodged in the guest-house with the other guests but was admitted to the daily life of the community. Only by living at close quarters with the brethren would the stranger come to know whether he liked the place or not, whether he fitted in, whether he could ultimately take the characteristic Benedictine vow and "belong." On their side the brethren would want to have experience of their visiting brother before voting on him and accepting him as one of themselves. That stranger monks lived the regular life and were not housed in a place apart we know from the *Dialogues;* the Abbot Servandus, while a guest at Monte Cassino, had a cell "in the lower part of the tower" which was connected with the part where St. Benedict used to pray at night "by an open passage"— *quo videlicet in loco inferiora superioribus pervius continuabat ascensus.* Nor was this proximity a mark of respect due to a visiting abbot: the monks of Servandus's monastery who were with him on this occasion lodged in a "large building where the disciples of both men slept."[1]

As a condition of being treated as a member of the family, the guest must adapt himself to the ways of the family. St. Benedict says that his petition to prolong his stay will be gladly accepted provided the monk takes the place as he finds it and does not make unreasonable demands. Much is left unsaid. Monte Cassino must have suffered from visiting monks who had wanted to change things, who knew just what the community needed, who had travelled and been in other monasteries and had seen things done properly. The surest way for a visiting monk to alienate the sympathies of his hosts is to tell them how much more convenient they will find it if they sing or cook or save money or ventilate and heat the place as he suggests. St. Benedict is right: *sed simpliciter contentus est quod invenerit*—only if he does this will he be invited to extend his visit.

> If however he censures or points out anything reasonably and with the humility of charity, let the abbot treat the matter prudently, lest perhaps God has sent him [the guest] for this very end.

The silence of discretion on the guest's part may be broken only when charity requires it and humility accompanies it. It is not now a question of making demands of, or giving gratuitous

[1] Bk. 2; ch. 35.

advice to, the brethren and minor officials: it is a question of taking up something serious with the superior. Is St. Benedict reflecting upon his experiences in a less happy past—when a humble manifestation from a visiting monk might have spared a subsequent scandal? Could not St. Benedict's failure at Vicovaro have been prevented so? Could not the intentions of the priest Florentius at Subiaco have been made known to him by a discreet guest? Whatever instances there may have been to prompt the above passage, the prompting came chiefly from within: largeness of heart, readiness to learn, docility to the impulses of grace in their unexpected expressions. Only a humble man can ask another to take advice humbly from one who is virtually a stranger.

> But if afterwards the monk wish to confirm his stability, let not such a purpose be denied, and especially since his manner of life could be well ascertained during the time he was a guest. But if during that time he was found to be exorbitant or prone to vice, not only should he not be admitted as a member of the community but he should even be told courteously to depart, lest others should be corrupted by his wretchedness. If however he is not such as to deserve being cast forth, let him not merely on his own asking be received as a member of the community, but even be persuaded to stay.

It would not have been difficult in St. Benedict's time, any more than it would be difficult today, for a monk from another house to influence the members of the resident community. The visiting monk is perhaps made much of, taken out for little walks, listened to if he is an attractive talker. He can either unsettle the brethren with his news of what is going on in the great monastic world outside or he can show them new facets of the ideal. The abbot must gauge the influence and make a choice. He has his own subjects to consider before anyone else's. But even if he decides upon sending the man away, the dismissal should be courteous and not brutal. It is to be hoped, however, that in the terms of the chapter's title the monk will be asked to stay:

> That others may be taught by his example, because in every place we serve one Lord and fight under one King

... but let the abbot take care never to receive permanently a monk from any known monastery without his own abbot's consent and letters of recommendation, because it is written: "What thou wouldst not have done to thyself, do not thou to another."

"Monks are all one," observes Hildemar a shade sententiously, echoing the opening words of the above passage. But for either the visiting monk or the abbot of the monastery which is visited to trade on this unity would be to offend against the spirit of both obedience and stability.

To the modern monastic mind there is something incongruous in the idea of monks wandering out from their communities in search of their true monastic home. Equally unprofessional, despite the reference to *litteris commendatitiis* in the concluding paragraph, is the idea of abbots advising monks of other monasteries to join them. Incongruous and unprofessional, but not entirely out of date. There are monks in our own day who launch themselves on these voyages of discovery, and there are communities which are not above poaching vocations from other houses. The sad part of it is that those who make these mistakes, either in the one direction or the other, are as a rule those who are least likely to be moved by the words and thought of St. Benedict.

CHAPTER 62

OF THE PRIESTS OF THE MONASTERY

The subject-matter now is not recruitment but the order of seniority in the community. Ordination from among the ranks of the brethren will affect the social and hierarchical structure just as much as the introduction into the community of priests from outside. This is not so clearly seen today, when in almost all monasteries it is the normal thing for choir monks to proceed to the priesthood, but it may well be seen more clearly in the future. If the present tendency towards accepting vocations to the choir, as distinct from to the altar, spreads from the smaller to the greater monasteries, there will have to be a closer study of some of the Rule's more neglected chapters.

> If the abbot wishes to have a priest or deacon ordained for himself, let him choose from among his monks one who is worthy to fulfil the priestly office.

First let it be laid down with vigour that the monastic and the priestly vocation can never be in conflict. In a monastery the one complements the other, enriches the other, provides impulse to the other. At the same time they are two quite separate vocations. Where they are found together in the monk, there is matter for gratitude; where they are not found together, there are no grounds for regret or envy. The priesthood is, objectively, a holier state than that of monastic profession. But the point is not which is objectively holier; the point is which does the soul feel most drawn to when the vocation to God's service is beginning to dawn.

If a man enters a monastery, the presumption is that he comes in order to serve God as a monk. Not primarily as a priest but as a monk. The priesthood is something added. It may, if it is conferred, make all the difference. Indeed it should make all the difference. But this does not make the priesthood something which every professed choir monk who is capable of mastering the studies should have. To see it so would not be to honour the priesthood but to cheapen it. Monks who are ordained are ordained for God, for their monasteries, for souls, and for their own spiritual advancement. In that order. Whatever ordination may be to the cleric who is destined for work in the diocese, ordination to the monk is ordered to the spiritual needs of the community. St. Benedict's opening sentences to the chapter give us precisely this approach to the monk-priest: "if one is required by the abbot, let one be chosen who can perform the office worthily." Something added, not something awaited as part of the vocation.

Monastic history shows us how often, in effect, the priesthood was added. St. Gregory encouraged the practice of ordaining monks, St. Eusebius trained monks to work in secular churches, St. Boniface founded seminaries which trained monks as well as secular clerics for the mission. It is Abbot Butler's opinion that by the end of the eighth century "all monks, or certainly most, proceeded to ordination."[1] It may safely be said that during the course of the tenth century it became the established rule that the monks should be ordained. About St. Benedict himself there is no certainty; it has been suggested that he was a deacon. Not until the ninth century, when the Council of Rome decided the matter in 826, were abbots required to be priests. In the Abbey of Saint-Denys twelve years after the Council of Rome, eighty-five out of the hundred and twenty-three monks were either already ordained or else studying for ordination; at St. Gall's half a century later there were only twenty unordained in a community of a hundred

[1] *Benedictine Monachism*, p. 293. Abbot Butler is the authority for most of the historical statements made in this section.

and one monks. Until ordination became the regular thing for monks, there was not only a certain informality about the whole thing—the abbot, himself perhaps not a priest, looking round the community for someone who would make a good priest—but there was far less emphasis upon ecclesiastical study, far less commitment to the works of the ministry.

The change brought about in Benedictine life by this development was profound. As we have seen earlier in this book it had the effect of virtually abandoning agriculture. It influenced recruitment—the unlettered felt less attraction—and gave rise to the establishment of intellectual centres, theological schools, schools of research and specialized scholarship. The problem was now how to prevent monasteries from becoming houses of priests and scholastics living in community. The way in which this problem was met, from the time of Cluny down to the present day, is the history of the various Benedictine congregations which have been founded since the first great break-away of the Cistercians. For centuries it was the Cistercians alone who held to the letter of St. Benedict's Rule.

De suis eligat qui dignus sit. But what if the monk whom the abbot judges worthy does not wish to be a priest? For a number of reasons a man who has entered the monastery for a particular purpose may shrink from the office proposed to him. He may shrink from responsibility, may foresee distractions which he had not bargained for when he made profession, may feel that his imperfections as a monk would be all the more serious in a priest. Both Hildemar and Warnefrid take this contingency into account; Warnefrid briefly, and Hildemar at some length.[2] The conclusion arrived at is that the community should be told of the candidate's unwillingness, and then be invited to give any reason which they may know why the brother under discussion should not proceed to ordination. Failing a report at the first consultation, there is to be a second assembly of the brethren at which the abbot will solemnly "adjure and conjure" those present to manifest what impediments they know which would prohibit the candidate from offering the Holy Sacrifice. If the only result of

[2] See Schroll, *Benedictine Monasticism*, pp. 84-6.

all this is the community's continued silence, the abbot is to confer with each one separately, allowing himself finally to be guided by the opinion of the majority.

On the principle that the selection of some means the rejection of others, we can turn our attention from priests in the community to choir-monks, adult oblates, and lay brothers. Though we read in the second chapter of the holy Rule that the abbot may "make no distinction of persons in the monastery," we know from many later passages (to be found in the present chapter, for example, and in the two preceding chapters) that a man's work in the community—or his training and background, or his particular gifts—made for differences which would have been unavoidable. What St. Benedict wanted to avoid was not variety but segregation. There was to be no distinct class.

We know that before St. Benedict's time there existed in the West, at Lerins and Marseilles for example, monasteries which were composed of monks who were clerics and monks who were laymen. The more literate were naturally entrusted with work which they could do, while the less handled the heavier work. Division of labour but social unity: the common life was preserved. Such monasteries may have employed serfs to help with the rough work, but the serfs were not part of the community as the less literate were part of the community. St. Benedict inherited this tradition and intended to hand it on without modification.

But the tradition was variously preserved. Under our holy Father the brother who was unable to write out his vows and the brother who "could neither meditate nor read" came to choir along with the rest, ate and slept and worked in the fields along with the rest. But under later administration, in the eighth and ninth centuries, the illiterate came to be a community within the community: they formed a group of their own and were given a different life to lead. This marks the first change—from the choir monk, not ordained, to the lay brother.

As monasteries grew, the servants who helped on the farm or about the house tended to join this less cultured section of the community, and their status as monks was recognized: they were the *conversi*. Though the work required of them was frankly and exclusively manual, the brothers were provided with a simplified liturgical Office which they recited in a separate oratory.

At Cluny in the tenth century the life of the lay brother was as exactly planned as that of the choir-monk. But it was quite different from the choir monk's. The Cluniac brother wore a beard while the rest were shaven, was dressed in a different habit, made a separate novitiate, took vows under a different form, and did not vote in chapter with the others. Not only was he a different kind of monk from those whom he served in the monastery but he was a different kind of monk from the lay brother of an earlier time. Instead of driving a team of oxen he was more often than not employed—since field work had long been discarded—in household tasks. He had no standing in the community, nor stake in the place. He could be removed at pleasure to serve as a servant in a grange or other dependency.

In the eleventh century the lay brother system spread from France to Germany where it was further developed by the monks of Hirschau. By the twelfth century it was established everywhere. Offshoots from the Benedictines as well as the many congregations that have been founded since the later Middle Ages have everywhere admitted lay brothers into their communities. The system obtains, though it does not everywhere flourish, today. Under existing conditions of wider opportunities of education, the lay brother state is felt to be in the balance. Vocations which in other generations would have gone to the *conversi* may now in the providence of God be found directed to the choir-monk and the priest-monk state.

As a pendant to the above it is to be noted that the third category alluded to, namely the adult oblate condition, is not inconsistent with St. Benedict's ruling about equality in the monastery. If he allowed infant oblation, our holy Father would certainly have agreed to the reception of those who wished to dedicate themselves in person and in their maturity to God's service.

Since the custom regarding oblates varies considerably in different congregations, and since the existence of adult oblates is not mentioned in the Rule, it would be a mistake to investigate the different manifestations of the practice here. All that need be said is that most Benedictine houses recognize the value of the institution, observing the distinction between internal and external oblates. Internal oblates are those who give themselves to serve a particular community under a rule either for life or for a time, either in the habit or in lay clothes. External oblates are those who are affiliated more or less strictly to the house, and who take part in its liturgical exercises whenever the occasion offers. Both internal and external oblates have to pass through a period of probation before their final acceptance. In the English Congregation there is an additional branch of monastic affiliation, whereby a *confrater* is granted a share in all the prayers, Offices, and Masses of the community for which he is clothed. As in the case of the *oblati*, the *confratres* of a community enjoy the privilege of wearing a somewhat modified habit and of coming to choir.

Let him that is ordained beware of arrogance and pride, and let him presume to do nothing but what is commanded of him by the abbot, knowing that he is now all the more subject to regular discipline. Let him not take occasion of his priesthood to forget the obedience and discipline of the Rule, but advance ever more and more in the Lord. Let him always keep the place due to him according to his entrance into the monastery, except with regard to his duties at the altar, or unless the choice of the community and the will of the abbot should wish to promote him for the merit of his life.

There is little in the above that calls for comment. The Rule is always ready to return to the themes which we know already, and the selection of a monk from the ranks of the community to be priest provides an occasion for stressing the need for subjection and for the constant desire to advance on the love of God. In a case where the abbot is not a priest, and where a clever young man has been ordained, a situation of delicacy might arise. Rapid advancement can lead to a bad manner, and, which is worse, to a spirit of ambition.

It is interesting to note how St. Benedict means the community to have a voice in the matter if promotion is mooted. The brethren are perhaps in a better position to judge the candidate on "the merit of his life" than the abbot, to whom he may have presented himself always on his best behaviour. It is also only fair that if the order of seniority is waived in deference to holiness, the less holy should acknowledge the validity of the claim. It is to the abbot that they acknowledge it, not to the monk. It is the abbot, not the monk, who is making the claim.

> Nevertheless he must know that he must keep the rule that is given him by the deans and priors. Should he presume to do otherwise he must be considered not as a priest but as a rebel. And if after frequent admonition he do not amend, let even the bishop be brought in as a witness. If even then he do not amend, and his guilt is manifest, let him be cast forth from the monastery; only, however, if his contumacy be such that he will not submit or obey the Rule.

This passage is bristling with problems for the historian and the student of ecclesiastical law. What is this supplementary rule which the deans and priors have laid upon the newly ordained? What is the bishop's official position when he is called in to take part in this strange, but surely quite domestic, trial?

The former point is complicated by the doubt as to whether St. Benedict does not mean the particular rules laid down *for* the deans and not *by* the deans. For this to make sense there has to be the additional supposition that the newly ordained priest ranks now as a dean, and that he must accordingly abide by the regulations to which deans are subject. Since the best texts have *a decanis*, a more reasonable interpretation would be to see in the injunction an assumed code of house rules and local customs which the deans were expected to enforce, and to which the monk who has been promoted must submit.

On the latter point, namely the standing of the bishop in relation to difficult members of the community, the commentators have much to say about the historical and legal aspects of monastic exemption. For our purpose here it is enough to conjecture the intention of St. Benedict without having to sift the evidence.

From the wording of the text, here and still more in earlier chapters, it is clear that contumacious monks are to be judged by the abbot. The bishop is brought in as a witness, *in testimonium*. The bishop may advise, may be asked to pronounce the condemnation, may set his seal to whatever formalities are required. But his intervention is sought primarily for the purpose of bringing the misguided monk to his senses. It is surely St. Benedict's hope that his subject's obstinacy will bow to the experience and dignity of the bishop. Having got himself into this state by reckless vanity, the monk may conclude from the bishop's presence how serious the situation has become; he will think twice before letting matters get any worse.

If even this last remedy fails, and the weight of the bishop's authority united with that of the abbot is not strong enough to elicit the response to grace, then there is nothing for it but expulsion. Inevitably it must mean scandal, but at least if the scandal is open there is the knowledge that outside authority was kept informed of what led up to it. Only twice in the Rule is there mention of the bishop being invited to concern himself with the affairs of monks—here in the present chapter and again in the sixty-fourth where again the bishop acts rather in an advisory than a judicial capacity—and in each case we can see the influences which were at work in St. Benedict's mind as he made the stipulation. Order, reverence, an appeal to an apparently incorrigible disposition. Only, when we next meet it, the occasion for St. Benedict's reference will be higher up the scale.

CHAPTER 63

OF THE ORDER OF COMMUNITY

This chapter comes fittingly where it does in the Rule. We have just been told that for a special reason the order of seniority in the community may be broken. In the chapter which follows the present one we shall be told of another cause which justifies the interruption of the ordinary sequence. Here in the sixty-third chapter St. Benedict delivers what might almost be called a treatise on order. It is a long chapter, giving practical examples to bear out the principle. Having supernaturalized so much in the human relations which exist in a monastery, St. Benedict sets out to supernaturalize the natural, yet often forgotten, virtue of courtesy.

The opening paragraph we have come across before, but it is quoted here because it forms a suitable introduction. It shows us how in every society, however egalitarian, there must be a hierarchy of some sort; and because the monastic society is one of charity, the advancement which must take place in a religious community as well as anywhere else when men live together will be according to charity and not according to the world. Monks move from their clothing to their death by the measured tread of time and spiritual development. For some the tread is more measured than it is for others, but so far as the holy Rule is concerned it is the majority, the rank and file, that are here considered.

Let them so keep their order in the monastery as the time of their conversion and the merit of their lives determine

or as the abbot shall appoint. And let not the abbot disturb
the flock committed to him, nor by the use of arbitrary
power ordain anything unjustly. But let him ever bear in
mind that he will have to give an account to God of all his
judgments and of all his deeds.

The brethren must know, as they stand in their proper places
waiting their turn, that the will of the abbot can override all
questions of rank. But they know too that the abbot is solemnly
enjoined by the Rule not to disturb the flock committed to him.
Nothing will disturb the flock more than an arbitrary display of
power. If the abbot for his part obeys the Rule, the monks for
their part have nothing to fear on the score of unfair advantage.
Any departure of the abbot's from the order established by the
time of entry or profession must be one which is responsible to
God.

Does St. Benedict mean, then, that provided a subject's personal
holiness is judged by his superior to be of a high quality, he can
be taken from his place in the community and placed higher up?
Whatever else it means, it cannot mean this. The fact that a man is
saintly is no qualification for a position on the list to which he has
no right. For the abbot to advance a man on such grounds would
be indeed to "dispose unjustly" and "by the use of arbitrary
power." What our holy Father must mean is that the important
positions in the monastery are better filled by men of God who
are able than by men who are still more able but who are less
men of God.

Commentators observe also, citing the example of a lay brother
being invited to wear the cope and sing as cantor, that natural as
well as supernatural considerations may influence a superior's
appointments. This is perfectly true, but it is still true that the
good singer who is at the time a good monk will both give greater
glory to God, and turn out to be more reliable as a cantor, than
the good singer who is not such a good monk.

Therefore in that order which he shall have appointed,
or which they hold themselves, let the brethren approach
to receive the kiss of peace and to Communion; and in the

same order intone psalms and stand in choir. And in all places whatsoever let not age decide the order or be prejudicial to it. For Samuel and Daniel, when but children, judged the elders.

Even if it were for no more than the smooth running of the place, the necessity for taking one's turn would be apparent. This is not to suggest that the brethren are expected to line up before they move from one room to another, from one field to another, from one side of the house to the other. On formal occasions however, as in choir and in the refectory, the dignity of the act is preserved by the observance of seniority. Always we have to be reminding ourselves that we perform our duties as a community which is giving glory to God. Untidiness of movement alters the direction of the act. If the movement is so confused as to become either a stampede or a traffic block, all idea of recollection, monastic decorum, reserve, is gone.

St. Benedict is not one who canonizes old age. He shows the greatest humanity towards it, and he wants his junior monks to respect it. But he does not allow length of years, as such, to qualify for privilege. Nor on the other hand will he allow old age to be an obstacle to office and responsibility. On its own, neither youth nor antiquity is meritorious. Since each is neutral, objectively neither moral nor unmoral, the use to which each can be put on any given occasion can be judged entirely on the merits of the case. Granted all this, however, St. Benedict seems to come down in favour of the young.

"Because it is often to the young," he has written in the chapter about calling the brethren to council, "that the Lord reveals what is best." But for the very young, the boys who are hoping to become monks, St. Benedict shows less partiality. About these he will have a sentence or two at the close of the present chapter. Our holy Father knows what he wants, but he knows also that it would be a mistake to let young people trade upon his intention. Their personal merit must be the justification—as it was in the cases of Samuel and Daniel—of their being listened to. It must not be his, Benedict's, predilection in youth's favour that wins the younger members a hearing in the community. Rather it must be youth's worthiness that brings the community to share his, Benedict's, confidence in the younger members.

Excepting therefore those whom, as we have said, the abbot has promoted or degraded for solid reasons, let all take the order of their conversion. So that for example he that enters the monastery at the second hour of the day must know that he is junior to him that came at the first hour, whatever may be his age and dignity. But children are to be kept under discipline in all matters and by everyone. Let the younger brethren, then, reverence their elders, and the elder love the younger.

Taking the date of his "conversion" to the monastic life as the point of starting, St. Benedict clearly means the day of the man's entry and not the day of his profession. Tradition, marking a monk's seniority from the time of taking vows, has moved away from the mind of St. Benedict in this matter. But in practice the divergence is found to be more on paper than in fact: applicants are clothed in the order of their arrival, and are consequently professed in the order of their arrival. Where the difference between St. Benedict's usage and that of later times declares itself is in cases where either clothing or profession has been delayed.

Commenting on St. Benedict's phrase "whatever may be his age and dignity," Delatte applies the principle of strict regard for place to child oblates as well as to grown monks. Not only among themselves, Dom Delatte insists, but in relation to the other professed are the children ranked: the years in the habit, whether the monk was three or thirty when he first put it on, are the qualifications according to which the order in the community is established. If this view is correct, we can see why St. Benedict immediately goes on to say that children "are to be kept under discipline in all matters and by everyone." The problem of rank would not arise while the young *oblati* are together in their own quarters—they would then simply follow their order—but whenever they happened to be following the community exercises, this question of seniority must have presented considerable drawbacks. In later monastic history, the *oblati* came to mix less and less with the others. This may not have been what St. Benedict originally intended, but at least it spared embarrassment all round.

The final exhortation quoted above makes a plea for mutual forbearance. It is not the man in the middle who is likely to cause friction, but the man at one or other extreme. Unless the young make allowances for the eccentricities of the old, for their some-times overbearing manner, for even such disagreeable physical habits as their age and infirmities may make them liable to, there will develop in the community the feeling that the old are not wanted and had better be sent away to a home. Nothing could be more contrary to the mind of St. Benedict.

Humanity in the same way must be shown by the elders towards the young. If the seniors hold aloof, complain incessantly about the poor spirit existing among the juniors as compared with the zeal and efficiency which were evident in their day, sneer at their ideals and devotions, make much of their mistakes in choir and in the refectory, and in general display a cynical, censorious, attitude towards them, there can never grow in the community the kind of confidence between old and young which perpetuates a tradi-tion. For the good qualities of the brethren to be handed from generation to generation, there must be the willingness to give and the eagerness—not merely willingness but eagerness—to receive. If an example, even an affectionate example according to St. Benedict, is not forthcoming from the elders, the juniors will pick up what good standards they can from outside sources and will have only disillusioned memories about their seniors in community to carry with them into later life.

> In calling each other by name, let no one address another by his simple name; but let the elders call the younger brethren *fratres*, and the younger call their elders *nonni*, by which is conveyed the reverence due to a father. But let the abbot, since he is considered to represent Christ, be called Lord and Abbot; not that he has taken it upon him-self, but for the honour and love of Christ. Let him reflect and so act as to be worthy of such an honour.

In this imperfect world superiors are always trying to suppress the use of *puro nomine*. The brethren often excuse themselves for their lapses from the perfect observance of the Rule in this matter by saying that to call a brother by his name in religion without any prefix, or even by a nickname, is to show friendliness. But signs of friendliness are not always signs of charity. Marks of fraternal affection as applied to one may connote a want of affection in regard to others. Safer and more regular, says St. Benedict, to employ the correct prefix in every case. And if nicknames die hard, they must be exterminated without misgiving.

But it is not for the sake of orderliness alone that St. Benedict imposes these strictures. There is a spiritual significance in the religious name, used fully with the prefix, which no other mode of address may be allowed to cheapen. The value of taking a new name in the first place lies in retaining both the symbolism and the significance. To call a fellow monk by any other name is to put your relationship with him on an unreligious footing; it is to suggest that you have abstracted from his "conversion" and are now treating him as one man of the world treats another. You have abstracted from your own conversion as well. If everyone in the community adopts the same practice, the relationship between the brethren takes on a natural colour. It may look more friendly, sociable, informal; it is nevertheless against the true spirit of monastic charity because it is less supernatural.

In some communities it is the custom to have the names of saints inscribed over the doors of the cells. This is again a detail which, though there is nothing about it in the Rule, acts as a witness to the supernatural character of the life. The monastic setting is full of such reminders, and it would be a pity if, on grounds of superficiality, they were dropped. The superficial can sometimes be the only available evidence of the profound. Certainly it should not be despised until the profound which it symbolizes is discovered to be absent.

The term *frater* calls for little elaboration here. From the earliest days of monasticism, indeed of Christianity, the word "brother" has denoted unity in the family, in charity. *Nonnus* as an appellation has never been so widely used. Probably of Egyptian origin, it was current in the desert during the times of the early Fathers—when a nun was called *nonna* and a spiritual master *abba*. Somehow in Benedictine usage the term *nonnus* has never really caught on.

If we were faithful to the letter of St. Benedict's Rule, we would call none but the abbot by the title "father." But in this again there has been a deviation from St. Benedict's wish. The title "Dom," an abridgement of *domnus* which is a reflection of the *Dominus* which Christian custom associates primarily with our Lord, was in use before St. Benedict's time. It did not relate specifically to monks, but was a prefix variously given to men of religious standing, known spirituality, clerical rank. The *Jube, domne, benedicere* is a survival of this usage—the petition taking the form of *Jube, Domine, benedicere* when not made in choir. Unlike the word *abbas* which is of Syriac origin, but was used in Western as well as Eastern monastic terminology, the word *domnus* seems to have been proper to the West. It was a recognized title when St. Jerome was writing, and Sulpicius gives it in one of his letters where he is referring to a monk who had recently died.

With us in the English Congregation the title "Dom" is used only after profession. In America it does not appear to be used at all. The French Congregation gives the title only to those professed who are priests. Whether in St. Benedict's day the oblate monks were addressed in the same way as the rest we do not know, but if they ranked according to their date of oblation they presumably enjoyed the same rights. Certainly the system which developed out of the child-oblate idea, and which is observed today, does not entitle the modern adult oblate to the prefix "Dom."

Since we have already dwelt upon the abbot's office as implying fatherhood, we need add nothing here about the designation given in the text. Throughout the Rule the abbot is being constantly faced with the identifications which his abbacy involves. He is a father, a shepherd, a judge, a lord; he is another Christ. *Sic se exhibeat ut dignus sit tale honore.*

> Whenever the brethren meet one another, let the younger ask a blessing of the elder. And when the elder passes by, let the younger rise and give place to him. Nor let the

younger presume to sit unless his senior bid him, so that it may be as was written: "In honour anticipating one another." Let young children take their order in the oratory or at table with discipline. In other places also, wherever they may be, let them be under custody and discipline until they come to the age of understanding.

In the instruments of good works St. Benedict gives the general injunction *seniores venerari, juniores diligere*. Here the admonition takes shape, and we are told of the marks of deference which should be given in a monastery. The idea of giving blessings was better understood in earlier centuries than in our own. The holy Rule contains many references to the kind of salutation which monks either exchange with one another or else bestow upon externs. The porter whom we shall meet in a later chapter is to hail his visitors with a blessing, the monk who has not obtained leave to speak with a guest is to ask the other's blessing and pass on. Of the excommunicated it is particularly noted that they are *not* blessed by their brethren. In the *Dialogues* mention is so frequently made of blessings given by St. Benedict that it would be tedious to give instances here.

Today a wide, though not universal, custom obtains in Benedictine monasteries of opening a conversation with the word *Benedicite*. The monk addressed answers *Deus* or *Dominus*, or simply repeats the other's *Benedicite*. (We shall draw attention to a variation of this when another alternative is suggested in the ordinance laid down for the porter.) Though the custom of starting an interview with the *Benedicite* and a response is of great antiquity—Bernard of Monte Cassino mentions it and it is enjoined in the Rule of the Master—it seems for a time to have lapsed in the very places where it would be expected to prevail, namely Monte Cassino and Subiaco. Warnefrid is against the use of it in times and places of silence, so it may have been this aspect of the observance, since most of the time and almost all places would come under the restriction, that suspended it. Certainly it was in full use again in tenth-century Cluny.

What has been said about the use of the religious name applies here also: the recommendation goes further than the words recommended. It is the spiritual relationship that is brought to the fore by these customs, and nothing which either expresses or furthers fraternal charity is to be despised.

To get up when a senior comes along is only good manners, but monks can grow scornful of good manners; so St. Benedict insists. Hildemar, who is punctilious on questions of decorum, makes an exception in the case of a junior in front of whom the same senior is repeatedly passing by. According to the same authority, and for the same reason of respect to age, boys were required to stand at the common meal when placed at a table of seniors.[1] In fairness to Hildemar, and to the generation he represented, it must be added that seniors were told not to keep juniors for ever on their feet in front of them; any senior who exacted an exaggerated show of deference from the young was to be publicly reproved in chapter.

St. Benedict says nothing here about the deference due to the abbot, and how it is to be expressed. The inference is that if honour is due to one's brethren in the community because they represent Christ, it is all the more due to those who represent Him more closely. Each monastery will have its own customs as to the external acts of reverence given to the abbot, and so long as their inwardness is appreciated it cannot much matter that these customs differ from monastery to monastery.

The inwardness of the final admonition—the somewhat repressive admonition which repeats the need to keep children under custody wherever they are—has also to be appreciated. Until they come to the age of understanding, when they will instinctively recognize the reasonableness of order, boys must have their minds disciplined. Without this discipline, physical and mental, there is a danger that there will be no direction. And direction, rather than discipline, is the purpose proposed.

[1] See Schroll, *op. cit.*, pp. 129, 130.

CHAPTER 64

OF THE APPOINTMENT OF THE ABBOT

This chapter is at once constitutional and exhortatory. In the early part it treats of the abbatial election, and in the latter part of the principles which must guide the exercise of abbatial power. The reason why it is placed here, and not at the beginning of the Rule where the same subject is dealt with, is that it rounds off what has been lately discussed. Questions of internal order, of rank in the community, are to be seen in terms of government from the top. So once again the abbot's authority is surveyed.

In the appointment of the abbot let this principle always be observed, that he be made abbot who is chosen by the whole community unanimously in the fear of God, or even by a part, however small, with the sounder counsel. Let him who is to be appointed be chosen for the merit of his life and the learning of his wisdom, even though he should be the last in the community.

This puzzling, and apparently contradictory, passage can be clarified if we take Dom John Chapman's translation of the word *eligere*. According to this authority[1] there is no question here of a formal election by vote. *Eligere* in St. Benedict's sense meant that the monks chose out one of their number, presented him for canonical appointment. When it comes to the further question

[1] *Downside Review*, 1919.

of actual appointment the word used is either *ordinare* or *constituere*, and in the case of an abbatial appointment an outside authority, whether that of another abbot or of a council of abbots or even of a locally convened synod, is invoked.

In the light of the above conclusion there is no inconsistency, and the minority with the sounder counsel can be found to prevail with the appointing body. But it does mean that the generally received idea of a free election by the votes of the community must be abandoned. Abbot Butler, accepting Abbot Chapman's interpretation and admitting that the provisions of this and the next chapter have been commonly misunderstood, makes the following point. "But as St. Gregory instructed the bishops to appoint as abbot none other than the one chosen by the monks, election in practice came in from the beginning."[2] The same writer goes on to show how a trace of the original method still survives in the confirmation from Rome which has to be obtained before the nomination can be declared canonical.

History shows, however, that St. Gregory's intention was not everywhere fulfilled. Royal appointment and investiture, nomination by right of foundation or even of benefaction, the bestowing of monastic benefices upon lay patrons, the system of *commendam* abbots: these were some of the factors which interfered with the simple, and somewhat democratic, method outlined by St. Benedict and approved by St. Gregory. We can count ourselves fortunate at the present time in enjoying a freedom of election more closely reflecting our holy Father's intention than has been possible at certain periods in our tradition.

Though history can again show many instances of it, the designation of an abbot to succeed the one in office is surely against the mind of St. Benedict. Right of succession, whether following co-adjutorship or simply designated by a retiring or dying abbot, has no place in a Rule which lays down that *illa semper consideretur ratio ut hic constituatur quem sibi omnis concors congregatio . . . elegerit*. In this enactment St. Benedict shows a greater freedom than was allowed by the legislators of his time

[2] *Op. cit.*, p. 408.

and before.[3] And later, in the tenth and eleventh centuries, even the finest houses of the Benedictine tradition admitted the nomination by an abbot of a suitable man to succeed. Though the system produced a line of saints in the case of Cluny, the danger of establishing an abbatial dynasty is a real one: the parallel between the natural and supernatural family breaks down at the concept of hereditary succession.

> But even if all the community with one accord (which God forbid) should elect a person who condones their evil ways, and these come to the knowledge of the bishop to whose diocese the place belongs, or of the abbots or neighbouring Christians, let them prevent the agreement of these wicked men prevailing, and appoint a worthy steward over the house of God, knowing that for this they shall receive a just reward if they do it with a pure intention and for the love of God, as, on the other hand, they will sin if they neglect it.

In the unhappy situation envisaged above, externs must look upon it as their duty in conscience to intervene. But how? We can only suppose that St. Benedict expected the bishop, who would probably learn from his clergy, even if he did not hear from the less unscrupulous among the monks themselves, about what was going on, to take the matter to Rome. Abbots of neighbouring monasteries might bring further pressure to bear, and the witness of influential families having connections with the community would also help, but it is difficult to see what could be done without resorting to the final court. Perhaps it was cases of this sort which brought about the system of ruling monasteries by "canonical" instead of by "regular" abbots. If the Rule (hence the term "regular" in this context) had been tried and found fraught with difficulty on this point, why not let monasteries be

---

[3] See Delatte, *op. cit.*, p. 442, who says that the superiors of Pachomian monasteries were nominated by a superior-general of the congregation who himself designated a successor. The Rule of the Master makes provision for the same procedure though it does not demand it. Cassian alludes to the appointment of a successor in the *Institutes* (4;28).

governed by a bishop or by an ecclesiastic delegated by him?
"The favourable attitude of the commentators [which here means
Warnefrid and Hildemar] toward this state of things is quite
surprising," says Schroll, "and perhaps one of the most significant
departures from the Rule which meets with their approval. They
explain that though monasteries so ruled have no regular abbot,
they do have a provost, deans, and other regular ranking ministers,
and that many canonical abbots are no less solicitous about the
observance of the Rule than regular abbots would have been."[4]

Possible advantages notwithstanding, the institution of canonical
abbots was opposed at Aachen. One of St. Benedict of Aniane's
many reforms was to secure for each monastery the right of
election. In this the great reformer was not entirely successful,
but he did obtain the imperial guarantee that in those relatively
few cases where abbacies remained canonical there should be a
division of monastic property which would ensure the livelihood
of the monks. But though the distinction thus introduced between
abbatial and community revenues provided a certain security for
the monastery, it came later on to be a source of division and
greed. From canonical abbacies the system spread to regular
abbacies, and as late as the fifteenth century the *mensa abbatialis*,
as the abbot's income was called, was still in many abbeys kept
separate from the *mensa communis*. Again we are fortunate in
belonging to a monastic generation which would see in this practice of keeping two accounts in the monastery an abuse of both
religious poverty and the common life.

> Let him that has been appointed abbot always bear in
> mind what a burden he has undertaken . . . and let him know
> that it is for him to profit his brethren rather than to pre-
> side over them. He must therefore be learned in the law of
> God that he may know whence to bring forth new things
> and old. He must be chaste, sober, merciful, and always
> exalt mercy above judgment that he himself may obtain the
> same.

The phrase *prodesse magis quam praeesse* is a neat summing up
of the attitude which St. Benedict wants to see in the abbot. The

[4] *Op. cit.*, p. 58.

abbatial state exists so that the spiritual needs of the community may be served; it does not exist in order to provide the abbot with a position. It is not as a public figure that the abbot rules his monks, but as a person. He should know how to preside, but presidency is not his first consideration. The list of qualities which an abbot is expected to possess would be enough to show that humanity is required before the ability to carry off with dignity the rights of prelacy. Upright men have been corrupted by honours. Vain men, on the other hand, have found their vanity curbed in the exercise of sobriety, understanding, and mercy. The abbot is a monk, and the servant of monks; if he shows himself to be happier and more in his element when pontificating, receiving homage, asserting privilege and making a display than when following the common life, he is showing himself both as less of a monk and less of a servant of monks.

For the benefit of his subjects, if not for the benefit of his own soul, the abbot is exhorted to be learned in the law of God and in the Scriptures. He must be able to draw from the sources of inspiration when he preaches. If he is to instruct men in truth he must know the word of truth, and learn how to expound it. If he is to see to it that his monks are faithful to their *lectio* and get the best out of it, he must be faithful to it himself. An abbot has more and better excuses than most for evading the duty of *lectio*, but if he allows the excuses to weigh with him he will find that his doctrine lacks impulse and that his own interior life is slowing down.

"In his hands he had always a book for the contemplation of the divine," we are told of St. Odilo in the *Acta Sanctorum*, "so that the habitual theme of his talk was the Scriptures. He went to sleep nodding over the pages of the Bible, and took up the reading again to refresh his mind when he awoke. Nothing in his life was more pleasant to him, nothing more to be desired." Another great Benedictine abbot, John Tritheim, has written in a homily delivered to his monks that "we know Christ not by sight, not by hearing, not by touch; but we know Him by the Scriptures." Abbots more than any have need of the support of the Scriptures. Antony and Hilarion, both saints and directors of monks, knew the entire Bible by heart. St. Pachomius does not make the same claim, but he was able to repeat the Book of Psalms and the New Testament word for word; he insisted that his disciples should study to do the same. Perhaps the minds of men in those times, lacking the distractions of our day, were better able to retain what they studied. Perhaps in the East men's memories are in any case more reliable. Learning the word of God, meditating upon it, applying it to His creation and to the immediate personal problem: they were better at this in the East than in the West. To Origen the idea of "conversion" meant nothing else than the decision "to meditate upon the law of God . . . to devote the whole of ourselves, our minds with solicitude, to the word of God." For St. Benedict, frankly Western in training and outlook, there was much to be quarried from Eastern spirituality. Certainly he was anxious to impart to his monks, and above all to his abbots, an appetite for the solid fare of the Scriptures.

> In his correction let him act prudently and not go to excess, lest seeking too eagerly to scrape off the rust he break the vessel. Let him keep his own frailty ever before his eyes . . . by this we do not mean that he should suffer vices to grow up but that he should cut them off prudently and with charity . . . and let him study rather to be loved than feared. Let him not be violent and anxious, nor exacting and headstrong, nor jealous and too prone to suspicion, for he will never be at rest . . . let him be discreet in the tasks which he imposes, bearing in mind the discretion of Jacob who said: "If I cause my flocks to be overridden, they will all die in one day." Taking this example of discretion, the mother of virtue, let him so temper all things that the strong may have something to strive after, and the weak may not be dismayed.

Though the above represents only a selection of passages from the complete text, there is much which we have had before. Clearly St. Benedict, as he gets nearer the end of his Rule, is preoccupied with the fear of straining weak spirits beyond their strength. He is afraid that the high standards which he demands of his abbot may have the effect of imposing upon a community of very ordinary individuals a superman who will try to bend all to his will. St. Benedict is trying to guard against that cowed attitude among the brethren which makes for suspicions, escapes, furtive infidelities, and an observance which lacks enterprise, imagination, zest. If I dare not meet my superior's eye, how shall I have the nerve to do anything?

With the best will in the world, an abbot may have a smothering influence on those whom he is meant to inspire. By insisting that they do everything down to the last detail in his way, he stifles the desire in them to do anything at all. The domination may be indirect, may be unconsciously applied, and even by the monks unconsciously assimilated, but in so far as it reduces the spontaneity of the soul's response to grace it is malign. We are familiar with the superior who says in effect: "Now I don't want you to do it in my way simply because I *tell* you to do it in my way: I want you to do it in my way because I want you to *think* of it in my way." This principle, based on an acknowledged truth, can be carried so far as ultimately to sap the individual's liberty and replace it with a recording tape.

But if the abbot is to exercise discretion, holding his hand when he feels roused to lay it down too forcibly, so also are his monks to be discreet. There are almost as many implications in this chapter for the brethren to ponder as there are explicit recommendations for the abbot to follow. For example if the abbot, obedient to the Rule, restrains his natural eagerness and delays the correction of a fault, it is not for the community to charge him with weakness. Should it come to such a point that his subordinates feel in conscience bound to stir their abbot to action, it is again for the subordinates to show the qualities which he has been trying to show to them. None of us is exempt from practising discretion, tolerance, patience, mercy and the rest. It is simply a question of who, in this combination of circumstances, has more frequent occasion to exercise them.

A monastic house is meant to be a place of peace, and there is no peace where there is either a domineering abbot or a critical community. The two elements grow together and develop one another. If from the top new ventures are always being laid upon the brethren so that they get no time to accustom themselves to a normal routine, or if from below there come complaints and requests for change so that the abbot finds it impossible to preach a doctrine that will be listened to for any length of time, a breakdown of confidence is inevitable. Nor is this simply a question of the good relations which should exist between an abbot and his monks; it is more fundamental even than this. In such a situation the basic principles of Benedictine life are at stake: it is a question here of stability and conversion as well as, more obviously and immediately, obedience.

> And especially let him observe this present Rule in all things, so that having ministered well he may hear of the Lord what the good servant heard who gave wheat to his fellow servants in due season: "Amen, I say unto you, he shall place him over all his goods."

This concluding paragraph cannot be dismissed as yet another bid for good example. The word *conservet* goes beyond keeping the Rule in personal observance; it means preserving it intact for others to observe. The final injunction to the abbot is thus one of immense significance, telling him that whatever freedom he may have been given in deciding *ad hoc* issues, the Rule is still for him the fixed charter of Benedictine perfection, and it is not for him to modify it at pleasure. The abbot is a steward only, a distributor of the fruits of order, and not either a proprietor or a legislator. Only if he "ministers well as a good servant"—nothing here about presiding impressively as a strong lawgiver—shall he merit to be placed over the Lord's goods.

CHAPTER 65

OF THE PRIOR OF THE MONASTERY

Since the subject of government is being considered (this is the impression given by St. Benedict's treatment of the prior's office) we might as well have a chapter on the man who comes second in the monastery after the abbot. Taking into account the possibility of large communities, the abbot must be assisted in the work of government. If the abbot neither went away nor got ill at any time, there would be no need for a prior. It is St. Benedict's expressed opinion that peace is more likely to be preserved when the place is under a number of deans, all on an equal footing of authority, than when a single deputy rules in the abbot's name. Where the power is evenly distributed there is no competition and no one monk will be proud. The abbot's deputy, on the other hand, is tempted to use his authority either arrogantly or subversively. A man who is a substitute will often want to go beyond the one for whom he is doing service, and if this is not his temptation he may want to undermine the influence of the man whom he is meant to represent. Not without reason does St. Benedict prefer to see delegated authority vested in the deans.

It happens very often that by the appointment of the prior grave scandals arise in monasteries; since there are some who, puffed up by the evil spirit of pride, and deeming themselves to be second abbots, take upon themselves a usurped power, and so foster dissensions in the community, and especially in those places where the prior is appointed by the same bishop or the same abbots by whom the abbot himself is appointed.

As an opening, the words could not well be more discouraging. But the warnings about scandals arising in monasteries on account of the unwise appointment of a prior are not over-played. Grave scandal would indeed be occasioned by the formation of an anti-abbot party in the community, and unless the prior is the abbot's own nominee the possibility of rivalry is ever present. Has St. Benedict suffered at the hand of an intriguing prior? There is no evidence to show for it, though the tone of much of this chapter seems to hint at personal experience.

In speaking of the abbot's appointment, and also of the removal of an abbot who had proved unsatisfactory, St. Benedict has mentioned the force from outside which could be invoked. It is probable that the same external authority had the power of appointing a monk to the office of prior. The whole procedure is at this distance obscure, but if St. Benedict's words are allowed to stand, there must have been something more than the right of extraordinary intervention attaching to this outside body. In certain monasteries or under certain circumstances the rights must have extended to the nomination of both abbot and prior to their positions. St. Benedict's disdain for such an arrangement can be seen in what he says next.

> How foolish this custom is can easily be noted; for from his first entering upon office . . . the thought suggests itself that he is freed from the authority of the abbot since he has been appointed by the very same persons. Hence are stirred up envy, quarrels, backbiting, dissensions, jealousy, and disorders. While the abbot and prior are at variance with one another, it must need be that their souls are endangered . . . and those who are their subjects, while favouring one side or the other, run to destruction. The evil of this peril falls chiefly on those who by their appointment have originated such disorders.

So whatever the prevailing custom before the Rule was written, the appointment of prior is to rest with the abbot. The position of

prior as next in rank after the abbot, and with the abbot's
authority when the head of the monastery is away, is mentioned
in some of the earlier Rules, but nowhere apparently is there
mention of the way in which the position came to be filled. Certainly where a federation of monasteries existed under one head
it would have been easy for the arrangement which St. Benedict
so much dislikes to flourish. In later centuries, when congregations
were established, it would again have been easy for the abbot
general to appoint his own man. Indeed if the central authority
had doubts about a local abbot, it would have been highly convenient to introduce its own nominee into the community who
would keep an eye on the superior. But this is all so foreign
to the spirit of St. Benedict that only in one congregation, that
of St. Vanne which did not long survive, was it practised. In the
other centralized congregations of the seventeenth century the
choice of prior was left to the local abbot.

We foresee therefore that it is expedient for the preservation of peace and charity that the ordering of the monastery
depend upon the will of the abbot. If possible let all the
affairs of the monastery be attended to by the deans, as the
abbot shall appoint . . . but if the needs of the place require
it, and the community ask for it, and the abbot judge it
expedient, let the abbot himself appoint a prior, whomso-
ever he shall choose with the counsel of the brethren who
fear God.

To the highest authority in the monastery, then, falls the lot
of seeing to the good order of the monks. This has been mentioned
before, but it has to be insisted on because some would see in the
prior's office the responsibility of attending to almost everything
that goes on in the house. Such commentators would leave to the
abbot questions of general policy and external relations; to the
cellarer they would leave the finances, the care of the buildings,
the management of the farm or other works; to the prior they
allot the discipline, the horarium, the duty of giving permissions
and allocating occupations. The abbot, on this showing, becomes
a remote figure, hardly more than a figurehead; and the prior
becomes the superior. Two recent commentators, again restricting

the abbot's province of authority, give quite different views of what in fact was the usage in the early Benedictine centuries.[1] Since there is no certainty about the historical aspect of the abbot-prior spheres of influence, we can confine our interest to what St. Benedict says that the relationship between the two should be. If both authorities work in agreement, the areas of immediate governance are of secondary importance.

Rather against his better judgment, then, St. Benedict lets the abbot have an assistant. But this is allowed him only if the needs of the place make it necessary, if it is what the community want, and if he himself is personally in favour of the proposal. Even now he must fulfil a further condition by having his choice approved by his advisers. The choice is his, the abbot's, and not either the community's or his advisers'. In no other way can St. Benedict safeguard the abbot's freedom than by laying down provision after provision.

> Let the prior reverently do whatever is enjoined him by his abbot, and nothing against his will or command. For the more he is raised up above the rest, so much the more carefully ought he to observe the precepts of the Rule. And if the prior be found culpable or deceived by pride, or be proved a contemner of the holy Rule, let him be admonished by words until the fourth time. And then if he do not amend, let the correction of regular discipline be applied to him. But if then he do not amend, let him be deposed from the office of prior and another, more worthy, be substituted in his place. If afterwards he be not quiet and obedient in the community, let him be expelled from the monastery.

[1] "Quite unlike this disciplinary service, the duty of the monastic provost [prior] in the early ninth century, according to a recent study, was the direction of external and secular affairs, leaving the **inner guidance of the monastery to the abbot.**" Schroll, p. 62, citing Naberhaus, *Benedict von Aniane: Werk und Personlichkeit*, p. 55. "Another work asserts that though the abbot was nominally the administrator of the abbey's patrimony, the actual work was carried out largely by the provost; that the latter, being in charge of the raw materials, was supervisor of the gardener and similar ministers . . . whereas the cellarer supervised the immediate supplies for the kitchen and refectory." Schroll, p. 62, citing Volpe, *Studi storici*, 14.

The prior, if the abbot decides to have him at all, is to be more than merely the first of the deans. He is *praelatus* (advanced above) *ceteris;* which means that he has a higher authority, not merely a higher place. Clearly if, as sometimes happens, the office of prior is bestowed in recognition of past services to the community, or as a consolation prize to one who had expected something else, nothing can be expected of the appointment. A prior can benefit the community only if he looks upon his office as a work and a responsibility, and not simply as a promotion and a reward. We shall speak about titular priors below; but whatever else it is, the function of claustral prior is not titular.

St. Benedict, having accustomed himself to the necessity of having a prior, makes sure that the man who will be at the abbot's right hand is of truly monastic calibre. His obedience must be beyond question, he must fulfil his duty *cum reverentia*, he must be a sedulous observer of the Rule.

St. Benedict does not say so, but tradition would supply the lack of further direction by requiring of the prior that he be a man of understanding and infinite patience. He must be a good listener, capable of calming down the more violent, and stimulating those who are not violent enough. He must be able to impart zeal without showing criticism of the existing order. He must urge others to better things without getting in front of them and playing the part of leader. He will need great tact, great sympathy, a great sense of loyalty to the abbot. It is never easy to be the shadow of someone more important.

The words which St. Benedict uses with reference to a prior who turns out to be a disturbance in the community can supply us with a text on which to rest what follows in connection with conventual and simple priors. *Alius qui dignus est in loco ejus subrogetur.* If the Rule puts it in the power of the abbot to appoint the prior of his monastery, it puts it also in the power of the abbot to depose him. But this supposes the prior to be his own second in command, his "claustral" prior.[2] A complication

---

[2] The *prior claustralis* is mentioned in the *Statuta*, where Lanfranc accounts for the term by giving to this official the care of all that relates to the cloister.

arises when a foundation is made from the mother house and a prior is placed over the new community. On the principle that no superior is independent of the authority which put him in office, the new prior is subject to the abbot of the mother house. The abbot who has nominated such a prior can remove him at will. The abbot gives to such priors a temporary authority only, and though they rule a community they are not strictly "conventual" but "simple" priors.

Thus modern Benedictine usage takes into account quite different functions attaching to the title of prior. There is the claustral prior, whose duties we have been considering in the present chapter. There is the simple prior, who is an acting superior of a dependent priory. There is the conventual prior, who, though he may have taken office originally as a simple prior, rules a community which has become independent of the mother house. Conventual priors enjoy the jurisdiction of any independent religious superiors, and are abbots in all but name and privileges.

There exists in some congregations the rank of "titular" prior, the title being bestowed as a mark of honour. Such priorates are not intended to convey any idea of authority. St. Benedict's wish that all should be treated equally in the monastery is not seriously infringed by these nominations so long as it is recognized by all that the office is fictional.

The position of subprior came into being during the Middle Ages, when abbots tended to withdraw from the life of the cloister and when the work of the prior was consequently increased. The title "second prior" is mentioned in the constitutions of various later congregations. It is probable that he was simply the senior among the deans, automatically taking the prior's place when this official should happen to be away.

Given so many factors in the problem of government, it is not surprising to find that St. Benedict is driven to the formation of an authority superior to that of the deans. The prior was as unavoidable in St. Benedict's time as the subprior became unavoidable in subsequent centuries. "It is possible that a large amorphous community given up to agriculture," writes Abbot Butler, "could be worked under the abbot by co-ordinate deans. But as soon as such conditions changed, and the life of the monastery became in any degree complex, the practical need for a second in command made itself felt, and this became the universal practice so early that I do not know of any record of a Benedictine monastery with St. Benedict's deans. This second in command has usually borne the title of claustral prior, or in every-day life simply the prior. In accordance with St. Benedict's prescription, he is nominated by the abbot and removable at discretion."[3] The abbot moreover, and not the prior, is responsible for the appointment of the subprior. It is not the claustral prior alone who has need to take the principles of this sixty-fifth chapter to heart. Subpriors and *priores simplices* are every bit as much involved.

[3] *Benedictine Monachism*, p. 217.

CHAPTER 66

OF THE PORTER OF THE MONASTERY

Though it is not a long one, this chapter touches on a number
of points which appear at first sight to be not very closely
connected. In addition to the post mentioned in the title, it treats
of enclosure, the requirements of a self-contained monastery,
and the frequent reading of the Rule. The reason for its inclusion
at this late stage is that having arranged for harmonious co-
operation inside the monastery—the six preceding chapters have
had this as their main concern—St. Benedict wants now to secure
a smooth-working arrangement which will govern external relations. Questions of stability, recollection, charity and organization
are involved. It is a more important chapter than it looks.

> At the gate of the monastery let there be placed a wise
> old man, who knows how to give and receive an answer,
> and whose ripeness of years suffers him not to wander.

The opening strikes a personal note, almost an audible one.
But at once it must be said that St. Benedict has no intention of
giving us romantic notions of a white-haired brother pottering
about the gate-house with an edifying axiom ready upon his lips.
The office of doorkeeper is as practical as that of the accountant,
and the chapter about his duties is as prosaic as that about how
Lauds is to be said on weekdays.

The first point that strikes us is that the functions of this member of the community are not allotted casually to anyone who

happens to be getting old and who can not be relied upon in the regular work of the monastery. The right man has to be found; not everyone can do the job. It would be no good putting a man in the porch who was too old, or the guests would be irritated by his slowness. He has to be of a mature age, and wise. Nor would it be any good entrusting the duty to one who was *too* wise—in the sense of possessing the ready wisdom which gives the sharp answer—or again the guests may be discouraged by his superior wit.

Experience of people, then, and sobriety: these are the qualities required. Unless there is a certain shrewdness of judgment in the monk who has to deal with strangers, the confidence-trickster will have it all his own way. It is not only retreatants and would-be postulants who come to the monastery gate: among the well-intentioned and deserving there will be a smattering of tramps, tourists, hangers-on of one kind or another who will need to be sized up by the man at the door. Not that there should be an air of suspicion in the reception of those who present themselves for monastic hospitality—on the contrary there must, as we shall see, be a warmth of charity—but inevitably there will be occasions when an applicant has to be turned away. The rogue need not be exposed as a rogue, but if he is genuinely judged to be one he can hardly be admitted to the enclosure or guest-house. Only a wise man, and one old enough to command respect, can handle the disagreeable task of dismissing rogues in such a way that feelings are not injured and that the good name of religion does not suffer.

From this alone it must appear that the office of doorkeeper is not one which is handed over at the end of every week to the next *senex sapiens* available on the list. If it were meant to be an hebdomadal work, it would have been mentioned earlier in the Rule when weekly servers and the weekly reader came under review. Placed here, just after the abbot, the prior, and the priests of the monastery have been discussed, the implication is that the work ranks in importance with that done by the higher officials of the monastery.

This would be borne out by pre-Benedictine monastic tradition, which gives unexpected prominence to the post of door-keeper. In the *Lausiac History of Palladius* we read that at Abbot Isidore's monastery of a thousand monks only the doorkeeper and two other monks were priests.[1] St. Pachomius would have none but the most experienced to attend the gate. Cassian seems to identify the office with that of the guestmaster.[2] Sometimes the superior of the monastery used himself to take over the porter's lodge for a little while, receiving saints in disguise as well as sinners on the make.

In Benedictine history the porter figures more as a subject of controversy than as an official of the monastery. In spite of the Council of Aix-la-Chapelle which laid down that monks, and those well-instructed, should replace laymen wherever St. Benedict's regulation had been disregarded, the porter's work was often given to servants. Cluny stoutly defended, on the grounds that it was the waste of a good monk to keep him pinned down to the gate-house when he might be doing more useful work, the introduction of laymen. The Cistercians attacked it. The early commentaries so often referred to in this work speak of compromises such as we have described as being against the Rule's intention. "In regard to the doorkeeper of the monastery," writes Schroll, our authority for this period, "the commentators tell of a development in the ministry due to the increased numbers of guests as compared with earlier times: the two brothers who served the abbot's kitchen formerly were the doorkeepers as well. But now since so many guests come, there should be two porters who do nothing else but announce the guests to the abbot or prior. Two are required so that when one goes to recite the Office, to meals, or is detained with a guest, the other may remain to answer the call of arriving guests."[3]

When St. Benedict says that the porter's responsible age should restrain the desire to wander, he shows considerable psychological insight. To a restless man, and perhaps it is only age that brings a man to the stage when he no longer wants to roam abroad, the

[1] Ch. 71.
[2] *Institutes*, Bk. 4.
[3] *Op. cit.*, p. 65.

temptations occasioned by the work are legion. For a large part of the day the porter has time hanging on his hands; he is tied to the porch and may not come to choir or join in the regular community recreations; he is tempted to take his recreation where he finds it, among seculars and in those boundary rooms which are neither within the full enclosure nor altogether outside it. Easy enough for such a one to feel unsettled in his vocation. He sees the world at closer quarters than his brethren see it, and he has the excuse of his work, given to him under holy obedience, to mix with it. Like the elixir of Frère Gaucher, which again meant work done under obedience, it can go to his head. To guard against this wandering spirit, a danger not confined to the porter, St. Benedict comes back later in the chapter to the principles of enclosure which lead on to the still more important principles of stability.

> This porter ought to have his cell near the gate, so that they who arrive may always find someone at hand to give them a welcome. As soon as anyone shall knock, or a poor man call to him, let him answer *Deo gratias*, or bid God bless him, and then with all gentleness and the fear of God, let him open quickly in the warmth of charity. If the porter need solace, let him have with him one of the younger brethren.

Salutations have been alluded to before. This *Deo gratias* is new. It is better suited in the salutation of laymen, because unlike *Benedicite* it does not expect an answer. From the reference to a blessing it has been conjectured that St. Benedict's porter was an ordained monk and not a choir-brother. But a man may ask God to bless another without having been ordained, and, as we have already seen, it is in keeping with monastic usage to invoke blessings on all occasions. Seeing the representative of Christ in the man who knocks, the representative on this side of the door calls out in blessing.

In order to answer the door in the right spirit, St. Benedict would have the porter be "prompt," "gentle," "warm" in his welcome. It is not often that we today, anyway those of us who are

priests, are called upon to answer the door, but on those occasions
when the opportunity comes our way we might remember these
three elements in the response which we give to those who are
waiting outside. Delatte questions, as being too strict, the statement by Calmet that to leave the work of answering doors to
laymen is a sign of waning monastic sense. It is not for us to say.
It does seem unfortunate, however, that so many meritorious and
grace-bringing services are lightly relinquished by those to whom
they were designed to be of spiritual value. *Cum omni mansue-
tudine* we can still, and in an appropriate medium of our age,
answer the telephone *festinanter cum fervore caritatis.* As helpers
to the guestmaster we can still, at least in spirit, open the door to
those who apply.

The Rule makes mention, once again, of the fear of God which
should animate the monk who has dealings with others. The abbot,
the cellarer, the guestmaster, the infirmarian: all these are expected to have a lively awareness of God's watchful presence. No
office in the community may be performed frivolously. Monks
have no business to be carefree. Adjectives such as "diligent,"
"prudent," "solicitous," "prompt," and "careful," cluster round
every official from the caller upwards. Certainly the doorkeeper
who has no particular interest in the fear of God, who is not
especially serious about the spiritual side of his work, who is happy
to leave efficiency to his young assistant, will do no great work
for God nor much advance his own development.

> The monastery ought if possible to be so constructed that
> all things necessary, such as water, a mill, a garden, a bakery
> and the various crafts may be contained within it; so that
> there may be no need for the monks to go abroad, for this
> is altogether inexpedient for their souls.

In this passage St. Benedict has shown clearly the lines upon
which he would have the monastery constructed. He is not writing specifically of his own monastery at Monte Cassino, because
here there was no well within the enclosure, nor would there
have been the space for a garden, but of the requirements normally attaching to his kind of monastery. He has not by any

means exhausted the list, but he has given enough to define the character of the cenobium, the self-contained and self-supporting household. If he were writing for the monastery of today, he would include a laundry, a power-house for electricity, an engineering shop, and perhaps even a shelter against modern weapons of destruction.

The West inherited from Eastern monasticism the autonomous character of the life, each monastery a separate unit responsible to itself and as far as possible independent of supply from the outside world. Certain necessities would always have to be fetched from neighbouring trade centres, but it was the idea to reduce these needs to the minimum. In the main this tradition was handed on, through St. Benedict's Rule, down the centuries of monasticism, so that even in its less flourishing periods the principle of subsistence within a certain area survived. When everything else about monasticism was running slow—when the observance was down-at-heel, the life of study unproductive, the manual labour nonexistent—there still remained enough of the authentic inheritance to secure the continuity. When the lean centuries were over, the monasteries found themselves again as academies of art, as centres for the apprenticeship of craftsmen to one or other trade, as places of learning, as schools of illuminating and printing. The new growth was from the same soil, spreading out from the old idea of enclosure.

So St. Benedict's words in this chapter have a carrying power far beyond their bricks-and-mortar connotation. The concern is not the architectural but the monastic plan. Nor are his words applicable only to generations other than our own. The concern is just as much for us as for any. This chapter, helped out immediately by the next, bears upon such fundamental monastic issues as sequestration from contact with the world, interest in current events, the effects of travel upon the spiritual life, and the meaning of monastic seclusion.

To pave the way for an opinion, let Abbot Butler be quoted at some length. "In chapter sixty-six St. Benedict lays down that all that is necessary for the life of the community should be within the monastery precincts, 'that there may not be necessity for the monks roaming abroad, because it is very bad for their souls.' And in the next chapter he forbids those that have been out to relate on their return what they had seen or heard outside, 'because it is utter destruction.' All modern Benedictines go out of the monastery freely, with due permission, whenever occasion arises,[4] such strict inclusion not seeming to be one of the points of later-day 'primitive observance'; and not only are things seen outside spoken of on return, but in the most observant and even reformed Benedictine monasteries the daily papers are taken and read freely. What troubles me is not the fact that monks go out, for we know that St. Benedict's monks did so on occasion, nor the fact that they read the newspapers. It does not meet the case to say that they do not, as a matter of fact, feel any the worse for it. Indeed this is precisely the disquieting phenomenon. It would be affectation for the modern monk to say that his spiritual life has been impaired or his soul made any the worse for his having been on a journey or having read the paper; on the contrary we often think we feel the better for a few days' change out of the monastery, and return invigorated and braced up for our monastic life again. But according to St. Benedict we ought to feel worse: *omnino non expedit animabus eorum; plurima destructio est.* How is this? Is it that we have lost all touch with St. Benedict's monachism? Is it a sign that all that has been said here is but specious special pleading, and that, except for the nuns and the Trappists, there is no true Benedictinism left in the world? . . . It seems to me that the answer lies in these considerations: the upbringing of monks, as of everyone else, is in modern times utterly different from that of St. Benedict's monks . . . this has brought it about that contact with the world has not the same effect on them as it had on the simple men who lived at Monte Cassino under St. Benedict. A railway journey, a visit to London, a newspaper, a novel is not, as a matter of fact, a cause of excitement or distraction or seduction. Their mind has been inured to such things from infancy."[5]

[4] The author qualifies this statement in the supplementary notes printed at the end of the later editions of the book. Here, on p. 411, Abbot Butler generously admits as an exception to his comprehensive statement the practice of the French Congregation.

[5] *Benedictine Monachism*, pp. 308-9.

The above is a not unfair statement of the case, and is probably representative of the current opinion. It has been quoted not so that it may now be criticized, but, as already suggested, merely that it may serve as ground for further comment. Might it not be argued, for instance, that the writer is drawing from his own rather than from the common experience when he says that monks feel spiritually none the worse for journeys to London, for reading novels and newspapers? Himself a man of deep recollection, Abbot Butler may not have sensed the least "excitement, distraction, or seduction." But would this be the considered and sincere claim of all—or even of the majority? Monks who have been brought up in conditions of modern society may be less subject to disturbance by the stimuli of the world than monks of St. Benedict's day, but it is not so much a question of education as of psychology. The response of certain emotions to given conditions is, we are told, a fairly constant factor. And who is to say that the stimuli provided by our own civilization are not proportionately intensified? Admittedly it is possible, as Abbot Butler (again drawing from his own experience) points out, that "we feel the better for a few days' change out of the monastery, and return reinvigorated and braced up for our monastic life," but so we would if we took a drug or drank champagne. How do we know that "feeling better and returning reinvigorated" is not a purely superficial and therefore a misleading improvement? How do we know that we may not in the long run be suffering harm from our little indulgence, and that we shall come to need further reinvigorations? Accordingly it is questionable as to whether it would in fact be "affectation for the modern monk to say that his spiritual life has been impaired" by journeys and light reading. Abbot Butler's "real difficulty" remains a difficulty for just so long as it is assumed that monks of today are different from St. Benedict's monks, and that they are differently conditioned from the start. The argument about environment can be pressed too far. Indeed beyond a certain point—the point at which compensating weaknesses and reserves are introduced—it can serve the opposite camp. Abbot Butler's question "is it that we have lost all touch with St. Benedict's monachism?" might therefore be answered firmly in the negative. Only where the original conception *has* been lost touch with do the superficial differences between century and century appear. The differences are then exaggerated, allowances are too generously made, and the structure falls to pieces.

Whatever the self-deceptions that exist on either side in this matter, the fact remains that we have before us the words of the Rule which claim to state a truth: *ut non sit necessitas monachis vagandi foras, quia omnino non expedit animabus eorum.* The ideal is that there should be no need to go out into the world, and the principle is that the monastic spirit is endangered if one does. There is just this to be said in conclusion of the subject, that there are occasions when the ideal cannot in effect be maintained. On such occasions, when obedience and charity take precedence of enclosure, does the second clause of St. Benedict's thesis apply? Is it still a principle even though a higher principle overrides it? In order to answer this satisfactorily we must make the distinction between direct and indirect influence. Neither obedience nor charity prevents exposure to dangerous influences when the monk moves out of his monastery: there is here a direct relationship between the man and his surroundings. But against this has to be put the indirect influence of charity and obedience, bringing to the soul whatever graces are needed not only to counter the dangers of being away from the monastery but on the positive side to develop spiritually. The whole question, then, turns on the word *necessitas*. If it is a *real* need that sends a monk out, and of this the abbot must be the judge, he has nothing to fear. But if he goes out because "he thinks he will feel the better for a few days' change," he does not walk by the light of St. Benedict's ideal; he is also ignoring the second clause in the statement, namely the clause which gives the principle.

> We wish this Rule to be frequently read in the community, that none of the brethren may excuse himself on the ground of ignorance.

It is a theory that the Rule originally ended here, and that the remaining six chapters as we have them were either a postscript or belonged to the second drafting of the text. Certainly, after the discussion of some basic articles of monastic belief, it would be a fitting place to finish. But since there is much important material still to come, the issue is academic.

In all monasteries the Rule is read, in sections of varying length, once a day. On certain days it is read in the refectory, but ordinarily the choir or chapter-house is chosen for the reading. In the English Congregation the reading of the Rule takes place immediately before Compline, and not, as in most congregations and in accordance with the Council of Aix-la-Chapelle, at Prime.

CHAPTER 67

OF BRETHREN WHO ARE SENT
ON A JOURNEY

What St. Benedict has to say here is not a repetition of what he has said about the brethren who are working at a distance from the monastery. The present purpose is to ensure safeguards to the man who goes out on an errand which will keep him away for some days or even weeks. The subject emerges naturally after what has lately been under review. If indeed these last six chapters were an afterthought, the first of them could not have followed more logically.

Let the brethren who are about to be sent on a journey commend themselves to the prayers of all the brethren and of the abbot. And always at the last prayer of the *opus Dei*, let a commemoration be made of all the absent. Let the brethren that return from a journey, on the day that they come back, prostrate themselves in the oratory at the ending of the *opus Dei*, and beg the prayers of all on account of their transgressions, if they happen to have seen or heard anything evil on their journey or have fallen into idle talk.

The provisions made here at least prove that occasions existed when journeys had to be made. If St. Benedict recognized *necessitates vagandi foras*, the distance is lessened between ourselves and him. But far from diminishing the responsibility which we owe today to this section of the Rule, it increases it: we who travel more must pay more attention to what the Rule says about travel.

The regulation about prayers in public for those about to undertake a journey has a twofold object. Immediately it is to secure God's protection for the absent brethren, but it is also a means of demonstrating to all, to those who remain as much as to those who are setting off, the need for taking into the outside world the spiritual element which is generated in the monastery. By the act of assembling together in prayer before the departure, a stress is given to the alien character of the world into which the traveller is about to move. The common prayer of those inside is not meant to suggest that those outside are to be spurned by the monk on his journey—it may be that he is making the journey precisely in order to help them—but is meant rather to suggest that he takes the charity of the brethren with him which he will communicate to those in the world.

It should be the same in the communication of the grace of recollection: the man of prayer takes out into the world what he has been storing up in the cloister, and others come to benefit by it. One of the fathers of the desert expresses this idea where he says that "the man who has learned by experience the quietness of his cell does not avoid meeting his neighbour as though despising him; he avoids meeting him for fear of losing the quietness of his cell."[1] It is only those who have stored up in the cloister who should be allowed to leave it for the world. It is only those who would avoid meeting men and women of the world—not as though despising them but from fear of the effect which they may have upon the interior life—who can safely mix with them and do them spiritual good.

A number of early monastic rules (notably those of St. Pachomius, St. Macarius, St. Basil) insist that a monk who is on a journey must have a companion. The Monastic Capitulary (817) took over this ordinance and applied it to Benedictines, making the unexpected exception in the case of canonically appointed abbots that they travel unaccompanied by any of their community.[2]

St. Benedict's regulations about what is to be done on arrival when the journey is at an end need no comment. The ceremony

[1] *Paradise of the Fathers*, Vol. 2; 34.
[2] Schroll, *op. cit.*, p. 59.

has nothing to do with the chapter of faults, but is designed to restore the traveller to his rightful element. By plunging the soul back at once where it belongs, St. Benedict hopes to rub from the mind of the man who has been away the memories and impressions which might linger and be harmful later on.

> And let no one presume to tell others what he may have seen or heard outside the monastery, for thence comes manifold destruction. If anyone shall so presume, let him be subjected to the punishment of the Rule. He shall undergo a like penalty who presumes to leave the enclosure of the monastery without permission of the abbot.

"Those who return from a journey," says Abbot Delatte, "shall spare their brethren what the Rule endeavours to deliver them from for themselves."[3] The commentator goes on to say that since the Rule does not want to deliver the returning traveller from the edifying or perfectly harmless impressions which he may have gathered while he was away, the presumption is that such impressions may be handed on. Manifold destruction, which means scandal, could hardly be said to threaten when a brother relates at recreation the amusing situations in which he has been involved while on his travels. Certainly this is what is expected of him, and no thought about a transgression of the Rule would cross either the narrator's mind or the minds of those who are listening. What St. Benedict wishes to suppress is any sort of account which might unsettle or distract, any introduction of worldliness.

But if news from outside is to be restricted to what is either edifying or morally neutral, how can listening to news bulletins, political and other broadcasts, be justified? How, if a monk may not repeat worldly information which he has heard abroad, can it be right for monasteries to pay money regularly to have worldly information delivered daily in the form of newspapers? The truth is that according to the letter of St. Benedict's Rule these things cannot be justified. They can be explained; exceptions can be made; there has to be a certain contact with the

[3] *Op. cit.,* p. 470.

world of affairs or some new piece of legislation might come into force without anyone in the monastery knowing anything about it. But if we are talking of what St. Benedict actually wrote for monks, we are forced to conclude that his words must ban the use of newspapers, the radio, and television. For those not in authority the difficulty presented is not great: subjects may use or not use the amenities provided by superiors. If I object on principle to newspapers, I am not bound to read them. If the question is left to my decision as an abbot or a cellarer, or even if as a subject I am expected to express my opinion either by vote or in a private interview, I can follow what light I have in the matter and not worry for an instant about running contrary to the general opinion. I have the words and the spirit of the Rule to guide me.

The final obedience about not leaving the enclosure without permission comes as a seal to what has been said earlier. Men, if they are so minded, can get round permissions as they can get round obedience itself. But having to get permission at least acts as a check, and gives to the superior his cue if he feels that there are limitations to be imposed. It is not the permissions, however, that define the principle of enclosure. Nor is it the boundaries of enclosure that define stability. Yet the three are interlocked: obedience, separation from the world, stability. We are back once again to the Benedictine vows.

CHAPTER 68

IF A BROTHER BE COMMANDED TO DO IMPOSSIBILITIES

If it is true that the Rule, in its first draft, went no further than the chapter which deals with the porter, then it is easy to conjecture the sequence of thought which prompted these supplementary pages. The dominant themes of the Rule are given new emphasis, shown in new lights, raised to new levels. While obedience and charity are the subjects immediately returned to by St. Benedict, the underlying motif throughout is the life of faith. The monastic vocation is the call to live among temporal things in terms of eternal truth. Seen in this perspective the "impossibilities" of religious service, the unfairnesses of community life, the dreariness of waiting for the fulfilment of one's hope—indeed the whole business of being a monk—can be fitted into the harmony of God's love.

> If on any brother there be laid commands which are hard and impossible, let him receive the order of his superior with all meekness and obedience. But if he sees that the burden altogether exceeds his strength, let him lay before his superior the reasons of his incapacity. Let him do this patiently and in due season, showing neither pride, resistance, nor a spirit of contradiction.

The brother who finds the burden of a particular obedience almost insupportable will find if he turns back to the Prologue

441

that this is what he should expect. The religious life is a yoke, and when the yoke presses hardest it is all the more religious. Even if the cross of Christ did not teach us this, we should know it from the fact that religion is faith and faith is religion. We need much faith if we are to receive "with all meekness and obedience" commands which we do not feel we can possibly fulfil.

But even if we cannot fulfil them, we can still obey the superior who commands them: we can tell him of our inability and ask for further orders. Now there can be greater self-deception about this aspect of obedience than about almost any other. St. Benedict is not talking about occasions when we think we cannot *face* what is commanded, but when we think we cannot *do* what is commanded.

Where it is a case of emotional shrinking there will be every danger of showing a willingness to contradict and resist. But St. Benedict says that there must be none of this. The reasons for the supposed incapacity are to be stated—and stated as objectively as possible with no display of histrionics—and the superior's decision is to be patiently waited for in faith. No excuses, no hysteria, no appeals to personal affection.

Monks who have entrenched themselves in certain works are apt to burrow deeper when the signal is given for an uprooting. They get stricken with panic at the thought of a new responsibility, and the panic leads to a sort of paralysis which renders them useless for the work proposed. Without being actually feigned, such incapacity is often induced. *Si omnino virium suarum viderit pondus excedere*: he, the monk, sees it in this way, but perhaps he is quite wrong. It is for the superior to judge whether the subject is capable or not; the subject is often too personally involved; judgments of this sort can be made only where there is calm, where the mind is capable of distinguishing between self-interest and truth. Humility can be a good disguise, and nothing could be easier for self-interest than to hide behind the mask of inefficiency, uselessness, stupidity.[1]

[1] "Bien que l'orgueil se transforme en mille manières, il n'est jamais mieux déguisé et plus capable de tromper que lors qu'il se cache sous la figure de l'humilité." (*Maximes Morales*, no. 204) If La

If, however, after these representations the superior still persist in his command, let the subject know that this is expedient for him, and let him obey out of love, trusting in the help of God.

This final paragraph reminds the subject that perhaps the difficulty which he has experienced in accepting the command has come from his preoccupation with the thing commanded. He has forgotten about grace. He has thought of himself struggling with the work and collapsing under it; he has not thought of God. His mistake has been to make a picture of himself as a dismal failure; he would have done better to leave the imagination out of it altogether. Dismay is never a reason for resisting obedience, and what is dreaded as failure can be approached wide-eyed where there is trust. If the Passion is more to the monk than a devotional study, it is now that the Passion comes to the rescue in practical form.

Remembering that we have in us always a great longing for that state in which we can do what we like, we must train ourselves to see greater spiritual safety in doing things which we do not like. The command which is disagreeable to us should light a beacon on our horizon. But it will be a beacon which shines darkly to the mind as well as to the desires. "He that refuses to go forth in the night to seek his beloved," says St. John of the Cross, "and to be stripped of his own will and to be mortified, but seeks him only upon his own bed and at his own convenience, will not succeed in finding him."[2] We find Him most surely when ordered to do the apparently impossible, because it is then that we can no longer trust to any strength of our own. We find Him because He discovers Himself within us, and it is on His strength that we do what we are told to do.

Rochefoucauld was thinking here of the pride which parades humility rather than the laziness which cites incapacity, the words nevertheless apply. It is pride in the form of self-love that seeks to escape a new duty on the grounds that the old one is being better done.

[2] *Dark Night*, ch. 2.

CHAPTER 69

THAT MONKS PRESUME NOT TO
DEFEND ONE ANOTHER

If the preceding chapter exposed false humility, the present one exposes false charity. Mistaken diffidence can offend against obedience; mistaken friendship can offend against the common life, obedience, detachment and good order. Self-love is lurking behind every virtue, and it seems as though St. Benedict is anxious before the end to drag into the open some of the more shy and subtle deceptions to which good monks are liable. We have noted the temptation to dramatize unworthiness; we note now the temptation to dramatize fraternal charity. It is no function of the monk to play the champion of the oppressed in the community.

> The greatest care must be taken that no one in the community presume for any reason to defend another or to take his part, even though they be joined by some near tie of kinship. Let not the monks presume to do this in any way whatsoever, because the most grievous occasions of scandal may arise of it. If anyone transgresses this rule let him be very severely punished.

To defend another is virtually to claim some sort of proprietary right; it is to take into protective custody and ultimately to suggest ownership. A man may not think of this when he throws the sheltering cloak round the shoulders of an injured brother, but it is nevertheless the first stage in a process which may lead to the possession, first, of a disciple, then of a following, finally of a party within the community. St. Benedict's farsightedness causes him to be what seems to us over-particular about unimportant matters. If the near-at-hand matter is unimportant as we see it, it is so only because we do not see as clearly as he does the lengths to which it can carry the man who judges superficially.

For one member of a community to appoint himself an unofficial guardian of another, or of a group of others, is to draw away from the principle of community. Such a monk becomes sensitive to what is done to his own as though it were done to him. At once he is on his feet, stretching forth his hand for shield and spear. "But it is not as though *I* have anything to gain," he protests, "I am not trying to defend *myself*." He may not be defending himself, but he is asserting himself. In a sense he *is* defending himself, since he has projected something of himself into the one whose cause he has taken up. It is not another's cause so much as his own.

Once we speak of a cause as being our own we are admitting that the common cause of the community is not our own. We are offending against the common spirit by our singularity as much as we would offend against the principle of common property by holding to a material thing and calling it our own. In either case it is the spirit of *proprietas* which gives us away. A monk has no more right to a cause of his own than he has to a disciple of his own, or to a car, house, income of his own. *Omnia omnibus in congregatione sunt communia*, and to defend another is to put a fence round him, labelling the little enclosure "private."

Are there no occasions, then, when one member of a community may take another's part? Must not such a system, by keeping the brethren so detached from each other's concerns, defeat the very purpose which it is presumably meant to serve? Is it St. Benedict's intention to conduct his supernatural family along lines which bear no relation to the natural family—where the sons of the household instinctively take up arms in one another's defence?

In the twenty-seventh chapter, which deals with the treatment of the excommunicate, we get an answer to the above objections. It is true that no reference is to be found here which softens the strictures as to mutual aid, but there is enough in the chapter to show that St. Benedict is not open to the charge of indifference to the human need of giving, and receiving, sympathy. He makes provision for the selection of certain among the brethren to act as go-betweens. He takes the Good Shepherd as the model to put before his abbot. He gives the brother under punishment every chance both of defending himself and of securing the protection of those who are sent to him as *sympaectae*. There are occasions, then, when a brother may come to the aid of a brother, but the manner of bringing it must be in order. The defence must be regulated from above; there may be no free-lance volunteer work. It is when monks who are not *sympaectae* "presume" to act as shepherds to flocks which are not entrusted to them that there is trouble. The abbot is the shepherd, and unless we are invited to act on his behalf it is not for us to pick up the sheep and examine them for wounds. Should we do this we are more their enemies than the wolves from whom we think ourselves to be defending them.

CHAPTER 70

THAT NO ONE PRESUME RASHLY TO STRIKE OR EXCOMMUNICATE ANOTHER

Having just dealt with a misuse of charity, St. Benedict deals now with a misuse of justice. The selfishness concealed in unauthorized sympathy is matched here by the selfishness concealed in unauthorized correction. Where the fault in the first case is due to affection, the fault in the second is due to the lack of it. St. Benedict's purpose is so to raise the level of human relations within the monastery as to reduce the interplay of emotions to the minimum. Questions of justice between man and man must be settled by rule and not by passion. When monks let either their affections or their antipathies get the upper hand they are no longer "converted in manners" but are turned back again towards the world.

In order that in the monastery every occasion of presumption may be avoided, we ordain and decree that it be lawful to no one, unless he be given power to do so by the abbot, to excommunicate or strike any of his brethren. Those that sin before all shall be reproved that the rest may have fear.

Just as in the previous case of unwarranted defending, so here in the case of unwarranted punishing, it is an assumption of the superior's authority that makes the act a sin of pride. It may be a sin of anger, of revenge, of jealousy, and certainly it is a sin of

447

uncharity, but as a sin of pride it offends against all the virtues at once. The mark of Adam has to be overlaid by the mark of Christ, and as Christ "humbled Himself becoming obedient unto death," so the monk, Christlike in direction, must reflect the same humility and obedience.

In our day it is rare, conventions being what they are, for men in the world to fight. In religion it is unheard of. But even if the violence which is never altogether subdued may not express itself as it used to in a rougher age, there are expressions of it which the man of the twentieth century must eliminate if he would serve God as a monk. If words can now do the work which fists once did, then in condemning the use of fists in monasteries St. Benedict banishes from monasteries the kind of words which do duty for fists.

Nor is it only explosive disagreement and undeputed censure that the Rule forbids; it forbids one monk to "excommunicate" another. By excluding a member of my community from my charity I am cutting myself off from something of the free circulation of grace which flows through the monastic body. I do this by deliberately fostering a misunderstanding, by dismissing as far as possible the thought of the other man, by refusing to communicate whatever there is in me which seeks to go out to others, by refusing to accept from him whatever he has to communicate to me. The channel is cut, and we are strangers one to another.

It should be noted that those whose offence is public should be publicly reproved. But again, let no private individual appoint himself administrator of reprimands. We do not have to go back to the sixth century to find men who fail in this respect, to find self-designated reformers and inquisitors. Perhaps because the irascible emotion has fewer physical outlets today, the tendency to denounce and put everybody right is greater. The business of fraternal correction is far more delicate than the correction meted out by father to son. As sons and brothers we should be content to leave the work of correction to the father.

Children shall be kept by all under diligent and watchful care until their fifteenth year; yet this too with all measure and discretion. If anyone presume without leave of the abbot to chastise such as are above that age, or show undue severity even to children, let him be subjected to the discipline of the Rule.

The children had their master to look after them, and the inference is that to him alone was committed the work of punishing either *alumni* or boy oblates. Certainly it is not likely that "leave of the abbot" would be given to anyone else in the community to chastise the young. The point is made by Abbot Delatte here that all correction should fulfil the following three conditions: the corrector should have the authority to correct, the cause should be a just one, and the punishment should be proportionate to the fault.

In dealing with the young, as in dealing with all who are not in a position to retaliate, the force of the correction is to a large extent wasted unless there is restraint in the manner of its application. Anger detracts. Partisan or personal animosity detracts. Exaggeration detracts. In correcting an abuse a man must be careful not to abuse the correction. In redressing an exaggeration it is important not to exaggerate the redress. It is a mistake to stop children fighting by knocking them down; they learn more if, when they are down, they are made to pick one another up.

CHAPTER 71

THAT THE BRETHREN BE OBEDIENT ONE TO THE OTHER

Obedience has to be rendered horizontally as well as vertically. Like the flame of divine charity and wisdom which came down from the Father at Pentecost and ran along the heads of the apostles, spreading its warmth and light from them to men outside, the virtue of obedience comes to us sanctified by the Son of God and is given out to men. The obedience which we give at our own level to one another in the community is referred back again to God, raised by Christ to His own level of filial submission, and at the same time is made a channel of grace to others outside in the world. The service of our obedience, like the service which we give in the Divine Office, is an apostolate. Those who reject God's summons to subjection are given grace by our subjection; the harmful influence of those who resist the law of God as manifested in authority is countered by the influence of souls who recognize God's authority at every level of the monastic hierarchy and in the right of fellow subjects to their obedience.

Not only is the good of obedience to be shown by all to the abbot, but the brethren, knowing that by this path of obedience they shall go to God, must also obey one another. The commands therefore of the abbot or of the superiors appointed by him (to which no private orders are to be preferred) are to have first place. For the rest let all the younger brethren obey with all charity and solicitude.

It is one thing to take upon oneself the work of denouncing, upbraiding, administering blows in anger or zealous correction, and quite another to require a service or bid a man do something which it is easily in his power to do. Having warned so insistently against arrogance on the part of those who issue orders, St. Benedict now feels safe in allowing his monks the right of conveying the *bonum obedientiae* to one another.

Obedience is a "good" because by "the path of obedience we go to God." *Pro Dei amore, imitans Dominum,* the monk perfects his service and arrives with Christ in the presence of the Father. "One who is truly obedient," says St. Catherine in the *Dialogue,* "retains always the desire of submission; continually and unremittingly, this desire is like an inward refrain of music." The same idea is found in St. Benedict's fifth chapter: *quibus ad vitam aeternam gradiendi amor incumbit.* Souls obedient to the calls of grace *look for* occasions of being obedient to men. They not only accept their obediences in a spirit of faith; they watch out for them as being chances of showing their love.

It is because St. Benedict invites to perfect love that he invites to perfect obedience. Our obedience to superiors may be perfect, but if we are obedient only to superiors we limit the scope of our perfection. For holiness to be complete and not departmental— for holiness to have the unity which we see in Christ, in His mother, in the saints—there must be the same quality about obedience which there is about charity: it must be universal.

In a sermon for the feast of St. Andrew we have St. Bernard comparing religious obedience to a piece of money which has value only if it is free of every flaw, every trace of counterfeit metal. "If we obey one precept and not another, the coin of our obedience is broken and Christ will not accept it, because we have promised obedience simply and without restriction." The same applies if we obey one man and not another: the coin is broken. There is lead in restricted obedience, says St. Bernard, and though the use of false and debased currency does not deceive God, it does defraud Him of the homage which is His due.

St. Benedict speaks of the younger monks obeying their seniors "with all charity and solicitude." The phrase indicates the watchfulness which satisfies the other's wish and anticipates the order. It is a mark of humility as well as of charity and obedience to forestall the occasion of outward obedience. Nor would it be against the spirit of obedience, as defined in the chapter which forbids monks to defend one another, for a monk who sees that a fellow monk is exhausted or sick to mention the fact to a superior. To show solicitude for the brethren's welfare is not the same as to assert an officious interest which is prompted by self. To show no concern whatever for the condition of others would be to stand convicted of an isolationism which is wholly alien to Benedictine monasticism.

Younger monks obey seniors; all obey the officials in their appointed order; each obeys his equal in the community. This is St. Benedict's programme. But he adds that one obedience may not be used in playing off another. Precedence must be given in obeying as in the other services performed in the monastery. And if, as the obedience comes down the line, the practical expression of the ideal is found to wear less well than when the act of submission is given to the authority at the top, St. Benedict has again a plan ready which will meet the case:

> If anyone but faintly perceive that the mind of any superior is moved against him or is angered, however little, let him at once cast himself on the ground at his feet and there remain making satisfaction until that feeling be appeased and a blessing is given. If anyone should disdain to do this let him be subjected to corporal chastisement.

This is no mere recommendation; it is a precept. The ancients were strict about these personal abasements on the slightest suspicion of displeasure, and St. Benedict simply embodied what he had read in Cassian and the Rule of St. Macarius into his own legislation. There is no mention of spoken apologies, so perhaps the silent prostration was felt to be just as, if not more, eloquent. The reconciliation is signified by the blessing.

We in our day will find our own means of fulfilling this ordinance of the Rule. If the ritual outlined by St. Benedict would make for self-consciousness on both sides rather than for an easy restoration of relations, there is always the frank admission of one's fault and the humble request for pardon. There need not be, indeed should not be, long explanations and self-justifications on the one side and either reproaches or enquiries on the other. If a very simple formula can bring us back to God when we have sinned, it should not require an elaborate ceremony to put right the misunderstandings which we occasion with our brethren.

CHAPTER 72

OF THE GOOD ZEAL WHICH MONKS
OUGHT TO HAVE

"In the monastic way of life," says St. Bernard in a letter, "the course is easier the more quickly it is run." We know this to be so when we start out, but as we go on running we come to such a desire for ease that we begin to doubt about whether the best way to find it is to run harder. The necessary zeal can be stirred at the beginning, but how is it to be kept stirred? Repeated efforts seem to bring only disappointment, and with each renewed effort there seems to be less of the virtue of hope to draw upon. If this is the common experience of religious, it is St. Benedict's purpose in the present chapter to encourage the soul to further perseverance in loving trust. With the end of the holy Rule in sight the doctrine of persevering in hope and loving trust is the one above all to be preached.

> As there is an evil zeal of bitterness which separates from
> God and leads to hell, so there is a good zeal which separates
> from vices and leads to God. Let monks therefore practise
> this zeal with the most fervent love.

St. Benedict, like St. Augustine before him and St. Bernard after him, is fond of the device which contrasts two extremes and then follows up the one which is positive. The Jacob's-ladder symbol might be found implicit in the text of other chapters after its explicit mention in the treatise on humility in the seventh.

It is implicit here in the separation of the good from the bad zeal, the one leading upwards to God and the other leading downwards to hell.

Zeal is defined by Dom Marmion as "an ardour that burns and is communicated, that consumes and is spread abroad; it is the flame of love, or of hatred, manifested by action."[1] Following the order given in the Rule, we can briefly examine the bitter zeal and then go on to a fuller investigation of the zeal that leads to God.

The zeal of Jehu was bitter, leading to nothing but destruction. The Lord God of Hosts claimed Jehu's loyalty and Jehu gave it, but he gave it harshly and not according to the nature of Him whom he desired to serve.[2] The Essenes were fired by zeal of a sort, but it was a separatist zeal which led to party spirit and defiance of authority. The Pharisees were zealots, but zealous about their prerogatives and not zealous according to God. The Jewish priesthood, supported by the zeal of the Pharisees, was so zealous that the chief among them can be numbered with those most responsible for our Lord's condemnation. In each case just cited the zeal was for the law, the letter of the law, and nothing but the law. The zeal had no concern with the love which gave the law. This is why the zeal was bitter: it had no regard for the nature of the Lawgiver. When zeal is as blind as this, it must inevitably turn to bitterness; because it is joy and love in reverse.

The monk who is enthusiastic for reform but who forgets the purpose of reform will show signs of bitterness in the measures which he takes to secure his reforms. Where self and not Christ is uppermost, the expression of the reformer's zeal must necessarily be according to nature and not according to grace. It will be savage, severe, unloving, unsympathizing. To love reform for reform's sake is a dead-end love, a love to no supernatural purpose.

Against this we have contrasted the *zelus bonus qui separat a vitiis et ducit ad Deum*. Where the jaundiced reformer sees nothing but yellow in the monastic life as it exists all round him, the

---

[1] *Christ the Ideal of the Monk*, p. 397.
[2] See 4 Kings 9;10.

man of true zeal sees everything in terms of God's will. To the bitter monk all things are reminders of his bitterness, reflections of his bitterness; to the zealous monk all things are a challenge to his generosity, eliciting hope and gratitude and love. When a monk is possessed of true zeal he thinks neither of reform nor of himself—and still less of how unreformed his companions are—but thinks only of how God may be better served.

Where there is no conflict between the zealous monk's judgment and the judgment of his abbot and of his brethren the zeal is according to God. It cannot help being so, since it is proved by humility and charity and obedience. The other kind of zeal may have an appearance of good, showing as it does the hunger for better things, but it is not that which "is according to knowledge." *Zelum Dei habent, sed non secundum scientiam.* Unless the zeal is enlightened by the wisdom of the spirit it is the outcome of a private judgment and it leads to further private judgments all along the line. Following a false light, which in fact is darkness, the monk who trusts to a combination of emotional attraction and personal conviction is in considerable danger. So obstinately does he cling to his conviction that he refuses first advice and then submission. The more his abbot tells him to moderate his zeal, which expresses itself violently and in the wrong directions, the more convinced he is that he is the only zealous man in the monastery and that all the others need to be reformed on the pattern which his way of life proclaims.

In this conflict between the *proprium concilium* and the *concilium commune*, the evidence brought by the majority serves only to harden the attachment to the zeal which is not according to knowledge, not according to wisdom. Thus a proud granite-like spirit opposes the less spectacular spirit in the community, and in the division which results there can be much sadness.

St. Bernard must surely have in mind St. Benedict's contrast between the good and bad zeal where he draws a distinction between the fire that goes before the Lord and the fire that is the Lord Himself. "Moses says of Him that He is 'a consuming fire,' and the psalmist that 'a fire goeth before Him.' But there is a difference between these two. For that fire which precedes the

Lord has ardour but not love; it burns but it does not dissolve; it moves that which it touches but it does not carry wholly away. It is sent before Him by God only to arouse and prepare you, and also to make you aware of what you are in yourself, so that you may know what you shall be hereafter by the grace of God."[3] This passage gives us the lead for which we have been looking: it raises the human zeal, the zeal which has a taste of bitterness and more than a share of self, to a new level. It makes of that way which all too easily leads to death a path which prepares for something better. This is entirely in the Benedictine tradition, turning to a good use that which is prone to evil. Just as St. Benedict built oratories where the temple of Apollo had stood, so St. Bernard builds love where before there was ardour without love.

"But the fire which is God Himself," St. Bernard goes on, "consumes indeed but causes no pain; it burns that which it possesses but with indescribable sweetness; it destroys, and destroying confers the supreme felicity. It is truly a consuming fire. But though as a fire it burns up vices, it acts at the same time as a healing unction in the soul. Recognize, then, the virtue of the Lord which changes your heart and the love which fires it. For the right hand of the Lord worketh virtue. But this change worked by the right hand of the Lord takes place only in fervour of spirit and in charity undisguised."[4]

It is thus a consolation to know that our eagerness to walk before the Lord and be perfect before the time may not be wholly wasted, may not be wholly bitter after all. Even if our zeal for reform is not according to knowledge to begin with, we can come by the wisdom which makes us right before God if we pray for it in fervour and practise charity undisguised. The roughness of our approach can be smoothed by grace until only the one way, the way which leads "to God and life everlasting," remains.

Let monks therefore practise this zeal with most fervent love; that is, in honour preventing one another. Let them most patiently endure one another's infirmities, whether of

[3] *Sermons on the Canticles*, 57.
[4] *Ibid*.

> body or of character . . . let no one follow what he judges
> good for himself but rather what seems good for another.
> Let them tender the charity of brotherhood with chaste love.

The work of accommodating ourselves to one another in the
community will have to go on while there is breath left in the
body. Tolerance is constantly being put to the test in community
life, and the only way to develop the virtue is to develop our life
in Christ. The mood reprobated by the psalmist, *dixi in excessu
meo omnis homo mendax,* is a familiar one, and one which must
be ruthlessly dealt with. If we admit how false we ourselves are,
we at least have made a beginning; but the lesson of positive
compassion can come only from a fuller realization of the mind
of Truth Himself.

The saint is no longer preoccupied by the thought of "what is
good for himself"; his whole interest lies in providing "what is
good for another." St. Benedict's words are an echo of St. Paul's
to the Philippians: "Each one not considering the things that are
his own but those that are other men's."[5] If this is the ideal
of Christian charity in the world, it is all the more an ideal of
fraternal charity in the monastery. If we attend to the best interests
of others we attend to the interests of Christ. If we bear one
another's burdens we bear His. Much of the present chapter
is a patchwork of St. Paul's texts skilfully put together, though
the reference to patient endurance of physical and psychological
weaknesses comes from Cassian.[6]

> Let them fear God and love their abbot with sincere and
> humble affection. Let them prefer nothing whatever to
> Christ. And may he bring us all alike to life everlasting.
> Amen.

Christo omnino nihil praeponant repeats the twenty-first
instrument of good works, which reads *nihil amori Christi
praeponere.* In theory every Christian signifies the preference,
but do even religious souls always bear out the choice of Christ
before all else? We can go on for years genuinely believing that

[5] 2;4.
[6] *Conferences,* 6;3.

St. Benedict's words hold no hint of reproach for us; then something happens which shows us that perhaps after all the first place has not been occupied by Christ but by one or other form of self. It is not in the strict sense of the Latin word that we *put* something else in the place of Christ, but rather that Christ is not always found to be there. Not always present where we vaguely hope Him to be, Christ tends to be overlooked in the times of decision as well as in the ordinary unfolding of life.

Since the primacy of Christ's claim in our regard, to be recognized throughout life and especially to be adverted to when rival claims assert themselves, is the measure and test of the "good zeal" which we have as monks, it is important that we should know all about it. If we cannot know it in its implications, we can know it as something which calls for a self-giving that makes no reservations. This *is* St. Benedict's *zelus bonus qui separat a vitiis et ducit ad Deum*. It is a far more enduring zeal than the mere enthusiasm for observance. It is zeal which resides in the will and not in the emotions; it is a direct response to grace rather than an indirect response through forms set by history and law.

But if our zeal is to be tested by our preference for Christ before all things, how in its turn is our preference for Christ to be tested? How may we know that Christ has been chosen as our all, and that we truly mean to maintain ourselves in this state of constant self-oblation? For answer the six signs given by St. Gregory, and quoted by Father Merton, by which lukewarmness declares itself in the religious life may be repeated here. If they do not altogether assure us that we are choosing nothing before Christ, they certainly condemn us if we have chosen away from Him.

The first sign is negligence in the duties of our state; the second, day-dreaming and dissipation of mind; the third, cowardice in the face of sacrifice; the fourth, disillusionment with life and despair of God's continued help; the fifth, bitterness towards men; the sixth, ridicule of holy things. If Christ means everything to us, not one of these points will strike home. Unless He does, all of them will.

CHAPTER 73

THAT THE WHOLE OBSERVANCE OF JUSTICE IS NOT SET DOWN IN THIS RULE

What this concluding chapter tells us in effect is that we do not need to acquire a knowledge of more and deeper religious matters, but rather to possess more and deeper knowledge of those matters which we have learned and practised since we took on the religious life. If we penetrate to the inwardness of our voca- tion, we cannot but be men of zeal, lovers of Christ. It is because we rest so long on the surface, content with the show of religious fidelity, that our true element is denied us. We are like fish who want to float on the water like gulls, and who accordingly never swim deep enough to know the sense of truly belonging.

We have written this Rule in order that, observing it in monasteries, we may show that in some degree we have goodness of conversation and a beginning of religious life. But for those who hasten to the perfection of the religious state, there are the teachings of the Fathers, the observance of which brings a man to the height of holiness. For what page or what word is there in the divinely inspired books of the Old and New Testaments that is not a most accurate rule for human life? Or what book of the holy Catholic Fathers does not loudly proclaim how we may reach our Creator? Moreover the *Conferences of the Fathers*, their *Institutes* and their *Lives*, and the Rule of our holy Father

Basil, what else are they but examples for monks and instruments of virtue? To us, however, who are slothful and ill-living and negligent they bring the blush of shame.

We are little when compared with others, says St. Benedict, but at least we have made a start: there is an *initium conversationis* for which we must be grateful to God. It is this conversion which must be followed up in monasteries so that souls may feel an increasing attraction for the heights. Those who aspire to use God's ever-present grace to the full, who aim at nothing short of union with Him, will find all the means ready to their hand: there are the Scriptures, the Fathers, the accepted exponents of the monastic tradition. In the light of so much which illumines for us the path to perfection we see ourselves as hesitating starters, shuffling walkers, unenterprising explorers. With the country charted and the journey directed on the map, can we not make something more of the venture? *Rubor confusionis nobis est.*

There is humility in St. Benedict's words, but we must not be misled into thinking that the saint offers no more than a comfortable mediocrity to his disciples. He is never for a moment in doubt as to what he offers; he is only a little in doubt as to how much of what he offers is being taken. The holy Rule has been written for men who are not holy—yet.

In the next paragraph to be quoted St. Benedict will be seen to call his work a "little Rule for beginners." It may be this, but the beginners are not meant to remain beginners: in the little Rule they will find large ideas. Like all codes of behaviour the holy Rule contains minute regulations which will have to be kept with scrupulous fidelity if any benefit is to come from the whole. But in its broad outline the Rule is a masterpiece of simplicity, capable of being understood and observed by beginners while at the same time offering scope to the souls who are advancing in the love of God.

Herein lies the precise beauty of the Rule, that the mystic and the ascetic can derive as much benefit from it as can, in his degree, the newly arrived postulant or the unlettered lay brother. Universality is one of the marks of genius which was not wanting in our holy Father.

It is interesting to note the authorities cited by St. Benedict when he has paid due homage to the Scriptures and the Fathers. In choosing out Cassian and St. Basil, when the field of monastic writers was growing larger every day, St. Benedict states his preference for the accredited masters in the ascetical tradition. Cassian, a man of the West but writing of the Eastern interpretation; Basil, a man of the East but already with a Western following. "St. Benedict in a few words indicates to the soul that is eager to realize the monastic ideal," says Delatte, "the sources from which it may complete its supernatural instruction. Let us note well the role given to the intellect. St. Benedict is concerned with the contemplative life . . . we are not bidden to walk and run in the apostolic and active life, but in the life wherein both night and day we scrutinize God and His works, wherein is revealed by way of illumination, love, and praise the mystery of God and of Christ. Nor would our holy Father have us study the ancients merely in order to collect a variety of ascetical counsels, although he emphasizes on four occasions the practical moral benefit of this study: he is thinking of a profound doctrinal study, of an intellectual relish for divine things, which is all the more effectual in influencing our whole life because it is the fruit of a higher knowledge."[1]

If the holy Rule gives us advice on the subject-matter of our reading, monk-saints in subsequent ages of monastic history have endorsed the choice. St. Gregory, St. Bernard, St. Bede, St. Anselm—all indeed who have clung closest to the Rule itself— have been men of scriptural and patristic interest. "The beams of our houses are of cedar, our rafters of cyprus trees."[2] Architecture may develop new techniques, but the supports of our spiritual buildings are the cedar of the Bible, and the roof is made secure by the cyprus of the Fathers. After fourteen centuries St. Benedict's book-list is not dated; it still directs the main activity of our monastic life.

[1] *Op. cit.*, p. 403.
[2] Cant. 1;16.

Whoever you are who hasten towards your heavenly country, fulfil with the aid of Christ this little Rule for beginners which we have set forth. And then at length you shall arrive, under God's protection, at the lofty summits of doctrine and virtue of which we have spoken above.

In the Prologue we were exhorted to "run in the way of God's commandments"; here we are assumed to be "hastening towards our heavenly country." The idea is the same that there must be no slowing down. In the Prologue we are told to "go forward with hearts enlarged in our life of faith"; here in the concluding paragraph of the Rule we "fulfil with the aid of Christ" what we have begun at St. Benedict's direction. So long as we cling to the two thoughts here expressed, which in fact turn out to be different aspects of the one thought, we are in no danger of slowing down. Helped by Christ we enlarge our hearts by living the life of faith, and the life of faith in turn enables us to go forward in the deeper knowledge and love of Christ.

To remain united to God by faith is to hasten; there can be no pace more sure than this. Here is the zeal which separates the soul from vices and from the world, and which listens only to the voice of God. Trust in the voice of God, as sounded through the pages of the holy Rule, gives power to act in perfect obedience to the Word. The very fact of pursuing sanctity in Christ according to the holy Rule gives power to perform what the Rule enjoins. There results a spiral ascent to God whereby the *conversio* assists towards the *culmina virtutum*, and the progress in holiness assists the renunciation of worldly things and manners.

Listening for what God has to say to us through the words of St. Benedict must eventually come to silence what the world has to say to us through our corrupt inclinations. The effort to train our ears to hear one sort of message must eventually weaken their response to the other sort of message. The sensitivity may remain, but the desire matters more than the sensitivity. *Soli Deo placere desiderans*, says St. Gregory of our holy Father,[3] and the degree to which we can follow him in this will be the degree of our sancti-

---

[3] *Dialogues*, Bk. 2; ch. 1.

fication. All the key texts of the Rule are so many echoes of the *si revera Deum quaerit* which is the first condition of the applicant's acceptance as a monk. Perfection for St. Benedict is nothing else than the single-minded pursuit of union with God within the framework established by obedience and the Rule. Herein is true unselfishness, true charity.

If Dionysius the Areopagite is to be believed, we are called monks, μονος, not because we live alone—or else only the solitaries would deserve the name—but because we have one single purpose. We are "one" and "alone" because our vocation draws us into unity and isolation. Our unity is discovered in Him who is undivided, our isolation is secured in the renunciation of earthly consolation. When we have withdrawn ourselves from multiplicity to find our true selves in the simple unity of Christ, then are we truly monks. *Tunc vere monachi sumus.* Then at last we shall have arrived, as the final sentence in the holy Rule says, "under God's protection at the lofty summits of doctrine and virtue of which we have spoken above." We shall have arrived, *ut in omnibus glorificetur Deus*, at the perfection of charity. "My beloved to me, and I to him,"[4] and nothing else in the world matters.

[4] Cant. 2;16.

BIBLIOGRAPHY

Bernard of Clairvaux, Saint. *Opera omnia*. Edited by Dom Jean Mabillon. Translated by Samuel J. Eales. London. Hodges. 1896. New York. Benziger. 1889.

Berlière, Dom Ursmer. *Ascèse Bénédictine*. Paris. 1927.

Berlière, Dom Ursmer. *Ordre Monastique*. Maredsous. 1912.

Besse, Dom Jean. *Le Moine Bénédictin*. Paris. 1898.

Bouyer, Louis. *The Meaning of the Monastic Life*. London. Burns, Oates and Washbourne. 1955. New York. Kenedy. 1955.

Bruyère, Madame Cecilia de; Abbess of Solesmes. *Spiritual life and prayer according to Holy Scripture and monastic tradition*. Translated by the Benedictines of Stanbrook. London. Art and Book. 1900.

Budge, A. Wallis. *The Paradise of the Holy Fathers*. London. Chatto & Windus. 1907.

Butler, Dom Cuthbert. *Sancti Benedicti Regula Monachorum*. Freiburg. Herder. 1927.

Butler, Dom Cuthbert. *Benedictine Monachism*. London. Longmans, Green. 1919. New York. Longmans, Green. 1924.

Cabrol, Dom Fernand. *Saint Benedict*. London. Burns, Oates and Washbourne. 1934.

Calmet, Dom Augustine. *Commentarius litteralis, historico-moralis in Regulam S.P. Benedicti*. Ilger. 1750.

Cassian, John. *Institutes* and *Conferences; Volume XI in the Library of Nicene and Post-Nicene Fathers*. Oxford. Parker. 1904.

Chapman, Dom John. *Saint Benedict and the sixth century*. London. Sheed and Ward. 1929.

Compendium asceseos Benedictinae. Poson. 1852.

Delatte, Dom Paul. *The Rule of St. Benedict; a commentary*. Translated by Dom Justin McCann. London. Burns, Oates and Washbourne. 1921. New York. Benziger. 1921.

Destrée, Dom Bruno. *The Benedictines.* Translated by a Benedictine of Princethorpe. London. Burns, Oates and Washbourne. 1923. New York. Benziger. 1923.

Doyle, Dom Cuthbert. *The Teaching of St. Benedict.* London. Burns and Oates. 1887.

Dudden, F. Homes. *St. Gregory the Great; his place in history and thought.* London. Longmans, Green. 1905. New York. Longmans, Green. 1905.

Gregory the Great, Saint. *The life of our holy father Saint Benedict, being the second book of the Dialogues.* Rome. 1895.

Guéranger, Dom Prosper. *Religious and Monastic Life explained.* Translated by Dom Jerome Veth. St. Louis. Herder. 1908.

Herwegen, Dom Ildephonsus. *Saint Benedict.* Translated by Dom Peter Nugent. London. Sands. 1924. St. Louis. Herder. 1925.

Hildemar. *Expositio Regulae.* Ratisbon. Pustet. 1880.

Huillier, Dom A. l'. *Explication ascétique et historique de la Règle de Saint Benoit.* Paris. Retaux. 1901.

Huillier, Dom A. l'. *Le Patriarche Saint Benoit.* Paris. Retaux. 1905.

Knowles, Dom David. *The Benedictines.* London. Sheed and Ward. 1929.

Lekai, Louis; S.O.Cist. *The White Monks; a history of the Cistercian Order.* Okauchee. Our Lady of Spring Bank. 1953.

Lindsay, T. F. *Saint Benedict.* London. Burns, Oates and Washbourne. 1949. New York. Macmillan. 1950.

Mabillon, Dom Jean, *Acta Sanctorum Ordinis Sancti Benedicti.* Venice. Bettinelli. 1735.

Mabillon, Dom Jean. *Tractatus de studiis monasticis.* Venice. Poleti. 1732.

Maréchaux, Dom Bernard. *Saint Benoit; sa Vie, sa Règle, sa Doctrine Spirituelle.* Paris. Beauchesne. 1911.

Marmion, Dom Columba. *Christ the Ideal of the monk.* London. Sands. 1926. St. Louis. Herder. 1926.

Martène, Dom Edmund. *Commentarius in Regulam S.P. Benedicti.* Paris. Muguet. 1690.

McCann, Dom Justin. *St. Benedict.* London. Sheed and Ward. 1937.

McCann, Dom Justin. *The Rule of Saint Benedict.* London. Burns, Oates and Washbourne. 1952.

Mège, Dom Joseph. *Commentaire sur la règle de S. Benoit.* Paris. 1687.

Merton, Thomas. *The Last of the Fathers; Saint Bernard of Clairvaux and the encyclical letter, Doctor mellifluus.* New York. Harcourt, Brace. 1954.

Merton, Thomas. *The Silent Life.* New York. Farrar, Straus and Cudahy. 1957.

Merton, Thomas. *The Waters of Silence.* London. Hollis and Carter. 1950.

———. U.S. edition: *The Waters of Siloe.* New York. Harcourt, Brace. 1950.

Monléon, Dom Jean de. *Les degrés de l'humilité.* Paris. Éditions de la Source. 1951.

Monléon, Dom Jean de. *Les instruments de la perfection.* Paris. Éditions de la Source. 1936.

Montalembert, Charles, Comte de. *Monks of the West from St. Benedict to St. Bernard.* London and Edinburgh. Blackwood. 1861-79.

Morin, Dom Germain. *The Ideal of the Monastic Life found in the Apostolic Age.* London. R. and T. Washbourne. 1914.

Renaudin, Dom Paul. *Manuductio ad regulam S. Benedicti.* Paris. Lethielleux. 1929.

Sause, Dom Bernard. *The School of the Lord's Service.* St. Meinrad. Grail Publication. 1948-1951.

Schroll, Sister M. Alfred. *Benedictine Monasticism, as reflected in the Warnefrid-Hildemar commentaries on the Holy Rule.* New York. Columbia University Press. 1941.

Schuster, Cardinal. *Saint Benedict and his times.* St. Louis. Herder. 1951.

Smaragdus. *Expositio regulae B. Benedicti Abbatis Sanctissimi.* 1575.

Tosti, Dom. *Saint Benedict; an historical discourse on his life.* Translated by Dom Romuald Woods. London. Kegan Paul, Trench, Trübner. 1896.

van Houtryve, Dom Idesbald. *Benedictine Peace.* Translated by Leonard J. Doyle. Westminster. Newman. 1950.

Warnefrid, Paul. *In sanctam regulam commentarium.* Monte Cassino. 1880.

Wolter, Dom Maur. *La vie monastique.* Bruges. Desclée. 1901.

INDEX

The Library of Congress has catalogued this book as follows:

Van Zeller, Hubert, 1905–
    The holy rule; notes on St. Benedict's legislation for monks.
New York, Sheed and Ward [1958]
    476 p.   20 cm.
    Includes bibliographies.

    1. Benedictus, Saint, Abbot of Monte Cassino. Regula.   1. Title.

BX3004.Z5V3   271.1   58–10554 ‡

Library of Congress

The Rule of Saint Benedict is, in many respects, one of the most significant documents in the history of mankind. It has been called by some historians "the greatest human reflection of the Gospels themselves," since almost every page breathes the spirit of Our Lord's teaching and example.

Little wonder that from this Holy Rule grew in the ensuing centuries hundreds then thousands of monasteries which became in time not only centers of religious life but of economic and social development as well. One cannot write the history of Western civilization without giving generous attention to the Holy Rule of Saint Benedict.

Dom Hubert van Zeller is, of course, not writing in this present work a history of the Rule, but a commentary on it, designed to help those who live under it both to understand and love it more deeply.

It would be unfortunate, however, if this book were read only by religious. There is a certain sense in which *all* spirituality is monastic, and lay readers will find in this Commentary more helpful spiritual reading than in many a book designed explicitly for them.

What can match, for example, Saint Benedict's treatment of the community of monks as a family, with the abbot as its father? Parents will find much here to reflect upon, as well as upon Benedict's countless gems of practical wisdom; the abbot is warned "not to be too suspicious, or he will never be at rest," and that he is "always to exalt mercy above judgment that he himself may obtain the same."

Everywhere Saint Benedict exhibits an understanding of human weakness, a calm patience in the presence of its failure, a serene confidence that man can be perfected, if he will, in the most ordinary ways of his life. Father van Zeller reflects these qualities of his spiritual Father.

As a result, *The Holy Rule* is a wise and compassionate work, filled with that hard-won peace and virile sweetness which is the heritage, not only of the monk, but of all who heed seriously the invitation of Christ.